Knock 'em Dead helps you find jobs *and* turn the interviews into job offers

"I just wanted to say thank you! After reading your book and following its precepts, I got my dream job within two months! (And I've been searching for almost a year!)"

—J. B. D.

"I landed a job that was over double the salary of my previous job, on the same day as I interviewed, which is very, very rare in a state job. *Knock 'em Dead* really says it all. I was able to negotiate to the absolute top end of the starting pay [because] of my resume, cover letter, and interview and the chapter on salary negotiations. Your book was extremely helpful in presenting the best part of me."

—S. J., Kansas

"The interviews nowadays are much tougher than they were four or five years ago. I am so thankful that I had heard about you! I heard of your book right after I bombed out on three interviews. I read and studied it. The first interview that I went on after doing this ended up in a job being offered to me! The interviewer told me that I was the best interviewee she'd seen! Thanks a million for writing your book."

—K. P., Houston, TX

"Your book changed my life!! It really did. It shaped the way that I went about getting back into the workforce and the way that I see myself and what I bring to a company. Thank you!"

—R., Littleton, CO

"One of my most-admired authors in the career advice space. Martin always challenges me to think about career development issues in new and innovative ways."

—*The Wall Street Journal*'s Alexandra Levitt on her Watercooler Wisdom Blog

Knock 'em Dead helps people from everywhere get great jobs anywhere

"I'm a graduating senior from Johnson & Wales University. I read your book, *Knock 'em Dead*, which has helped me score many offers in just the past weeks."

—D. T., Hong Kong–bound

"I have used the UK version of *Knock 'em Dead* to successfully improve my career prospects. This is the best job-hunting book on the market bar none; keep up the good work."

—Paul Bremner, London UK

"WOOOOOOOOHOOOOOOOOO!!!!!
It worked!! I got the job!!!!!!!!!!!!!!!!!!!!!!!!!!!!!!!!!!!
I luv u Martin!"

—A., Edmonton, Canada

Knock 'em Dead works for career changers

"[After leaving the Army] I brought all three of your books, *Knock 'em Dead Resumes, Cover Letters*, and *The Ultimate Job Search Guide*. I read each book cover to cover. I followed each step in your books and I got an entry-level job of my dreams. I was prepared because of your books, Thanks!"

—K. G.

Knock 'em Dead is inspirational

"I've been a reader of the *KED* books for quite some time. You've made a difference in my life and saying 'Thank you' doesn't begin to express my gratitude."

—T. S.

"You helped me get a job a couple years ago; now I've just accepted a new job. Thank you again for everything you do and all the people you help; I've read your books so many times you feel like a friend. You've been an inspiration to me again and I could not take this job in good conscience without acknowledging your contributions. Take care and God bless."

—T. F., Houston, TX

Knock 'em Dead is motivational

"*Knock 'em Dead: The Ultimate Job Search Guide* inspired me. I have turned my job search into multiple interviews and offers in just a couple of months. The motivation and positive energy will steer you to stay focused on getting the best job offer! Thank you, Martin!"

—E. R., New York, NY

"*KED* has been a rock in turbulent emotional waters. It is amazing to see the changes that have occurred so far, I can't wait to see what comes next."

—R. L.

Knock 'em Dead helps professionals at all ages and stages of their career

"I wanted to let you know that I've just landed a National Account Manager job. I can't thank you enough; your help and support in my job search was invaluable."

—K. S., IN

"I just got a new job and $16K raise using your approaches—at my venerable age: Number of years employed: thirty-four."

—S. S., Little Rock, AR

More praise from *Knock 'em Dead* users

"My husband has been wondering why I'm laughing out loud reading a book on job search. Your book is not only imparting valuable advice it is a very refreshing read, sprinkled with humour."

—M. W., Toronto, Canada

"My recommendation to job seekers everywhere: buy it, read it, and use it. It works. Using the techniques in it has led to three initial interviews within the first week of putting it into action. I just wanted to thank you for your excellent book."

—J. R., San Antonio, TX

KnOCK 'em DEaD

THE ULTIMATE JOB SEARCH GUIDE 2011

MARTIN YATE, CPC

Avon, Massachusetts

Published by
Adams Media, a division of F+W Media, Inc.
57 Littlefield Street, Avon, MA 02322. U.S.A.
www.adamsmedia.com

ISBN 10: 1-4405-0586-1
ISBN 13: 978-1-4405-0586-7
eISBN 10: 1-4405-0880-1
eISBN 13: 978-1-4405-0880-6

Printed in the United States of America.

10 9 8 7 6 5 4 3 2

Library of Congress Cataloging-in-Publication Data
is available from the publisher.

CONTENTS

Why *Knock 'em Dead?*...xiii

Part I The Well-Stocked Briefcase...1

Resume creation and job search tactics, interwoven with smart advice on professional growth and long-term career management.

CHAPTER 1 The Realities of a Job Search...5

Get a grip on the essentials for personal economic survival and success in a half-century career. Learn how to develop a personal brand.

CHAPTER 2 The Productive Resume...25

How job search has changed and how your resume must adapt to new screening methods. How to get the right focus on your work history: the magic of Target Job Deconstruction and a great tool to gather the information your resume will need. Three types of resumes for different situations. The rules for creating a powerful resume plus the unique resume layout template.

CHAPTER 3 Networking and the Successful Job Search...51

The most intelligent integrated networking strategies you will find anywhere. Twenty-one networking techniques to help you build cutting-edge social networks for today and tomorrow.

CHAPTER 4 Network Integrated Job Search Tactics...79

In today's competitive job market, you need to leverage the smartest job search strategies and tactics to find and win the best job offers. This is where you will find them, integrated into one practical approach that only a true expert could weave.

Part II Get the Word Out...103

Job search is all about getting into conversation as quickly and as often as you can with the people who can hire you. Tremendous techniques to quadruple your hit ratio on every job posting.

CHAPTER 5 Ace the Telephone Interview...105

Telephone interviews are a common screening device. How to prepare for the scheduled telephone interview and to be ready for the unexpected call. Tactics for turning the telephone interview into a face-to-face meeting.

CHAPTER 6 Dress for Job Interview Success...111
You never get a second chance to make a first impression at a job interview; so unless you dress the part, don't expect an offer. Professional dress guidelines for men and women.

CHAPTER 7 Body Language...125
Learn the seven techniques for body language success during a job interview. Learn to employ positive body language messaging that can help your entire career.

CHAPTER 8 The Curtain Rises on the Job Interview...135
First impressions are the strongest. Here are the many small preparations you can make before you walk into the interviewer's office that will help calm your nerves and psych you up for a successful interview.

Part III Great Answers to Tough Interview Questions...139
Hundreds of tough job interview questions, what's behind them, and how to develop powerful, honest answers. Learn how to ace behavioral interviews every time.

CHAPTER 9 The Five Secrets of the Hire...143
Knowing how an interviewer thinks is a critical element of the job search that is frequently overlooked. Here are the five secrets of the hire—literally how to get inside the hiring authority's head—master them now and they will serve you throughout your career.

CHAPTER 10 How to Knock 'em Dead...153
Discover the transferable skills and learned behaviors common to successful professionals, in all professions, at all levels, in all companies, anywhere in the world, and learn how to weave them into the answers to countless interview questions.

CHAPTER 11 "What Kind of Person Are You Really, Mr. Jones?"...173
Learn the questioning techniques an interviewer uses to find out whether you will fit into the department and the company, whether you are a team player and if you are going to be a management headache.

CHAPTER 12 The Other Side of the Desk...185
Two types of interviewers can spell disaster for your job search: the highly skilled and the unconscious incompetent interviewers. Learning how to handle each of these interviewer types is key to turning job interviews into job offers. Discover how interviews are structured and what to do when interviewers don't ask the questions that allow you to promote your candidacy.

CHAPTER 13 The Stress Interview...195

Your worst nightmare can come true at a stress interview, but once you learn that these questions are just amplified versions of much simpler ones, you'll remain cool and calm. Also: a vital discussion on handling illegal interview questions; what mock-meetings, role-playing, and in-basket tests are looking for; and how to handle them.

CHAPTER 14 Strange Venues for Job Interviews...219

Learn the tips that will help you master job interviews in noisy, distracting hotel lobbies; restaurants; at poolside; and in other unusual settings. Includes an essential review of table manners you'll remember for the rest of your career.

CHAPTER 15 Welcome to the Real World...225

For the entry-level candidate, some special interview questions specifically tailored to discover your business potential when real world experience is lacking.

CHAPTER 16 The Graceful Exit...233

All the critical dos and don'ts to ensure that the lasting impression you leave is the right one.

Part IV Finishing Touches...237

Steps you can take to keep your impression fresh in the interviewer's mind.

CHAPTER 17 Interview Follow-Up...239

The steps that keep you fresh in the interviewer's mind and encourage the continuation of your candidacy.

CHAPTER 18 Snatching Victory from the Jaws of Defeat...245

Rejection? Impossible! Then again, you won't be right for every job. Here are some techniques that help you to create opportunity in the face of rejection.

CHAPTER 19 Negotiating the Job Offer...249

The job offers finally begin to arrive and you're never going to have this much leverage with this employer again. Learn the essentials of salary and benefits negotiations: handling good job offers and poor job offers, negotiating future salary, and how to evaluate the salary and the job offer. Fifty great questions you can ask to make sure the job offer is one you want to accept; and essential information on reference checking, job offer letters, employment agreements, relocation, and stock options.

CHAPTER 20 **Multiple Interviews, Multiple Offers...273**
Relying on one interview at a time can only lead to anxiety, so you must create and foster an ever-growing network of interviews and, consequently, job offers. Implement the *Knock 'em Dead* job search plan and you will be able to both generate multiple job interviews and turn them into job offers. This is not hype: It really happens when you get on-board with the plan.

CHAPTER 21 **How to Ace the Psychological Tests...277**
We are all professional schizophrenics! Approaching psyche tests casually can be hazardous to your professional health. How to prepare for pre-employment tests, and what's behind the questions and techniques for answering correctly in the heat of the moment.

Part V Where the Jobs Are...287
Everyone should pay attention to the changing job market and economic climate.

CHAPTER 22 **Thirty Fast-Growing Occupations...289**
The jobs that are experiencing the strongest job growth and resources to properly examine their suitability for you.

Appendix How to Make Contact and Recognize a Buy Signal...342

Index...361

Acknowledgments

Knock 'em Dead is now in its twenty-fifth year of publication and has become a staple for job searchers around the world. My thanks to the ongoing encouragement of the Adams Media sales team. I would like to thank publishers past and present for their support of the *Knock 'em Dead* books, and for giving me Peter Archer, my current editor; thanks for staying around, Peter ;-). I am also indebted to the many people at Adams Media whose hard work has contributed to the success of the series. It takes a team, and I am grateful to be a part of this one.

WHY *KNOCK 'EM DEAD*?

You didn't come to this book because everything is good in your professional life. You came because these are times of upheaval, crisis, and change. Managing a successful career isn't easy, so I'm not going to waste your time.

You are somewhere in the throes of a half-century-long work life, where, statistically speaking, you are likely to change jobs about every four years (not always by choice), and have three or more distinct careers over the span of your working life.

Add an awareness that recessions causing widespread job loss rear their ugly heads every seven to ten years (I have worked in career management through five of them in the past thirty-five years); and you can see that smart career management strategies integrated with a firm grasp of practical job search tactics are critical to your survival and happiness. *In the context of your whole work life, career management and job search skills are the most important skills you can ever develop, bar none.*

All the advice you've been given about careers—get an education, choose a career, settle down, and do a good a job; patience and loyalty to the company will be rewarded with job security and life success—all the promised rewards of running straight and true have proved themselves a crock.

We live in a global economy where voracious political and corporate greed has turned your life into a disposable commodity to be used and discarded. It is time for a radical shift in your career management strategy. You need to move from hapless employee at the whim of financial currents beyond your control to enlightened professional who puts the pathway to personal success in its proper context.

What's this context? Those job changes coming round every four years or so add up to twelve or more over fifty years, with perhaps three of them involving the greater challenges involved with career change. *This means professional change is constant; professional change is a given.* You need to recognize that your career is not a fixed thing that came as a gift with the purchase of your college diploma. Instead, it's a critical-to-happiness aspect of your life that needs management. Face this and you can begin to change your situation, today and forever.

It's Time for Enlightened Self-Interest

Enlightened self-interest means placing your financial survival front and center in your life. Think of yourself not as a person looking for a job, but as a company, a financial entity that must maintain a steady cash flow over half a century. Start to think of yourself as MeInc., a corporation that must always plan and act in the best interests of its survival and you will perhaps learn to look at this job search and the management of your career in beneficial new ways.

As a corporate-like entity, MeInc. has products and services that are constantly under development. These are the bundle of skills that define the professional you and are positioned and sold to your targeted customer base: those employers who hire people like you.

The success of MeInc. depends on how well you run your company, which means that just like every successful company in the world, you must have ongoing initiatives for:

R&D: Your identification and development of products and services that will appeal to your customers. This translates to skill building in response to market trends; it also relates to your development of job search, interview, and career management skills.

Strategic Planning: The development of effective offensive career management strategies for when you must look for work (sales), and defensive strategies while you pursue success at work (marketing) and branding to position yourself within the company and in the outside professional world.

Marketing and PR: The establishment of personal credibility for the services you deliver, and the positioning of these services so that your professional credibility becomes visible to an ever-widening circle of potential customers.

Sales: A state-of-the-art sales program to sell your products and services, including resume, job search, and interviewing tactics.

Now, this may or may not be your first job search, and it almost certainly won't be your last, but this can be the last one that you enter in confusion.

In these pages you will learn how to achieve your goal of a successful and happy professional life as I show you the best ways to find job openings, effectively turn them into interviews, and transform not one but sometimes many of those interviews into job offers.

This intelligently integrated approach to job search will not only help you land jobs but will also show you how to achieve greater success in each of those jobs. This book has been updated and expanded every year for twenty-five years, always reflecting the changing needs of the job hunter in changing times. People who used this book all those years ago tell me they still use it today. They tell me it is why they are VPs at *Fortune* 50 companies or why they own their own companies and how it changed both their sense of self and their life for the better.

This is not because *Knock 'em Dead* or any of my twelve career books is some motivational quick fix. Instead what this book gives you is an infinitely flexible, completely down-to-earth plan of attack for your job search, which also happens to make sense as a blueprint for a successful professional life. That just happens to be something no one else has really thought through the way I have, but then I've been at it as my chosen mission for more than thirty years.

This is what I think about every day of my life: no hidden religious or political agendas, just me talking to you, using all my insights about work and careers to help you get out of a tough spot in your life and into a better place for the future, so you understand how it works and how to play the game.

No one ever thought to give it to you straight. I will because I understand, and care about your well-being: change and the unexpected are constants in professional life today, and I have an intelligent approach to dealing with these issues. Follow the job search advice in these pages and you will get that next step up the professional ladder. Follow the strategic career management advice in these pages and you will be in far greater control of your destiny.

I update this *Knock 'em Dead* book every year because too much of what I find online and in bookstores lacks real insight into vitally important issues: your financial survival and success.

Twenty-five years and millions of copies later, *Knock 'em Dead* has become a time-tested and proven commodity both here in America and in many countries around the world. If you want to make sense of your career, I think I can help you, too.

Sincerely,
—Martin Yate, CPC

PART I
The Well-Stocked Briefcase

THIS SECTION WILL show you how to discover, define, and package your skills, and to put together a comprehensive plan of attack that uses all the most effective job search techniques.

ONCE UPON A TIME, long ago there lived a man who spent his days watching life go by. He lived in a town ravaged by bears, and one of his dreams was that if he could shoot bears, he could travel the world as a bear slayer. Every day he sat on his porch and waited for a bear to go by. After weeks of watching and waiting, he thought he might go looking for bears.

He didn't know much about them, except that they were out there somewhere. Full of hope, he loaded his single-shot musket, and headed for the edge of the forest, raised his rusty old musket and fired into the trees. Then, disappointed, he went back to sit on the porch.

Because our hero couldn't tell dreams from reality, he went hunting unprepared and earned exactly what he deserved: nothing. The moral is: When you go bear—or job-hunting—get a grip on reality, and don't go off half-cocked.

Out there in the forest of the professional world are countless opportunities. Even in times of severe economic downturn—and remember they are cyclical and likely to come by every seven to ten years throughout your career—there are always jobs out there. Yes, they are harder to find, and yes the competition is tougher, but someone is going to find those jobs and land those job offers. It can be you.

All companies share two things in common: They are in business to make money, but things go wrong, so they hire problem solvers to fix things. This is an important life lesson. Think about your present job. You were hired to cope with certain problems within your area of expertise, to anticipate and prevent them from arising and where they cannot be prevented, to solve them. At some elemental level, everyone, in every profession and at every level, is paid to be a problem solver. There are three lessons you should take away from this:

Lesson 1: Companies are in business to make money; they have loyalty only to the bottom line. They make money by sales and by being efficient and saving time. If they save time, they save money and have more time to make more money; we call this productivity.

Lesson 2: Companies and Me., Inc. are exactly alike. You both want to make as much money as possible in as short a time as possible: Think efficient systems and procedures, time management, and organization. Think of focus and goal, not task and activity.

Lesson 3: There are buyers' markets (advantage: prospective employer) and there are sellers' markets (advantage: prospective employee). Job offers put you in a sellers' market and give you the whip hand.

Lesson One tells you the three things every company is interested in. Lesson Two teaches you to recognize that MeInc. has the same goals as any company. Lesson Three reminds you that anyone with any sense wants to be in a sellers' market.

If you look for jobs one at a time, you put yourself in a buyers' market; if you implement my advice in *Knock 'em Dead*, you can generate multiple job offers (even in a tough economy) and put yourself in a sellers' market. This requires making sure MeInc. is ready with a properly packaged product and integrated sales process. In this first part of the book you will

- Learn to evaluate market needs and package your professional skills for those needs.
- Discover how to identify every company in your target geography that could be in need of your services.
- Get connected to the most influential people in your profession, so that you'll have personal introductions at many prospective companies.
- Implement an integrated job search plan of attack.

While I will cover each of these areas in sequence, I recommend that you mix and match the activities. In other words, when working on your resume starts to drive you nuts, switch to researching your target market, or building your professional networks. An hour of one activity followed by an hour of another will keep your mind fresh and your program balanced.

CHAPTER 1

The Realities of a Job Search

JOB SEARCH ISN'T nanotechnology; you'll find a commonsense logic in everything I show you and wonder why you didn't see it before. In fact you can learn to do it *all* this week, and reap the rewards for the rest of your career. You can do this.

Everyone feels crappy when they are looking for a job—you aren't the only one—but while there used to be a stigma attached, times have changed. Job change is an integral part of modern life. It comes around about every four years, making change and job search a constant factor for everyone.

Because everyone is now starting to recognize the insecurity of the modern workplace, you will find many, many people are ready to give you a helping hand if they can. We live and work at a time of immense change. When you were born, there still existed a world in which hard work, dedication, and sacrifice led to long-term job security and a steady, predictable climb up the ladder of success. The world you now work in is entirely different: Companies still expect hard work, dedication, and sacrifice, but their only loyalty is to the profit imperative. You are expendable.

Different times require different strategies, and technology has caused a revolution in all we do. For today's job search and for your long-term career success, a completely new approach is needed. The job security and professional growth our parents were raised to expect as the norm is a thing of the past. Here are the realities you're facing, expressed in numbers:

50–4–3–7–10
A 50-year work life
Job change about every 4 years
3 or more distinct careers
Economic downturns every 7–10 years

KNOCK 'EM DEAD TIP

Changing a career at the same time you change a job adds another level of complexity to the process because you are leaving behind many of the skills that usually help you land that new job. It is best to plan a career change while you are employed and not after a layoff, when you are under the gun financially. If a career change is part of your job search—for example, if you are changing from a career in finance to another in education—go to Career Management Issues on the Knock 'em Dead website, *www.knockemdead.com/career-success-advice/career-management-lifetime-career-management-issues-and-strategies.html.* Follow the advice you find on those pages first, and once you have got your project in proper perspective, come back to this book to implement the job search.

Integrate the job search advice into the long-term career management plan I outline in these pages and you need never again be caught flat-footed, urgently needing a job to put food on the table. Along the way, we'll discuss many career management initiatives that are *also* essential parts of your job search plan of attack. For example, you'll learn about credibility, visibility, and professional branding. These are all issues that can have great impact on your job search and even greater impact on your long-term career management initiatives.

Not surprisingly, it all starts with your resume. The resume creation process helps you focus on the job you want and package your skills effectively. It's the first step in turning your dreams into realities, and as you'll see the resume techniques you'll learn in the next chapter to help you land a new job can also be leveraged to get you promotions on that job, but first things first.

MeInc. and Branding the Professional You

Long-term career success is much easier to achieve when you are credible and visible within your profession. A believable professional brand created as part of an overall career management strategy will help you achieve this credibility and visibility because an identifiable brand gives you focus and motivation, and others an easy way to differentiate you.

Establishing an accepted professional brand obviously takes time, but you have to start somewhere and you need to start now. The greater effort you put into working toward credibility and visibility in your profession, the quicker you enter the inner circles in your department, your company and ultimately your entire profession; and as you know it is in these inner circles that the plum assignments, raises, and promotions all hide.

Think of your brand as the formal announcement to the professional community of who you are, how you want to be seen in your professional world. It will be reflected

- In your resume as the primary branding tool for disseminating a focused and consistent message about the professional you: your brand.
- In the narrative of your resume that first captures your capabilities and behavioral profile, establishing a clear image of a unique, consummate professional.
- In the approach you bring to your work and to your everyday life: what you say and how you say it, what you do and how you do it.

Components of a Strong Professional Brand

Developing a believable brand involves identifying those skills and behaviors, that combined together, make you different and desirable. Your professional brand captures and consciously positions—in your resume, conversation, and behavior—your best professional qualities. As you might imagine, in order to do this well it helps to understand what employers believe are the most desirable professional qualities.

There exists a selection of transferable skills, values, and behaviors that are admired by employers the world over. Referred to as transferable skills because they can be applied in any job and at any level, they are at the heart of all professional success; these skills are also frequently referred to as learned behaviors.

In fact the predominance of behavioral interviewing techniques used in job interviews are based on their ability to determine your possession of these particular behaviors or skills. This is a topic we will address thoroughly and on which you will become an expert by the end of the book.

Transferable Skills, Learned Behaviors, and Core Values

As you learn about the transferable skills, learned behaviors, and core values that all employers seek in all employees and that identify those people who will become most successful in the professional world, four things will happen:

1. When you identify one of these transferable skills, learned behaviors, and core values as something you possess, it becomes part of your branding signature. It appears in your resume and becomes a conscious part of everything you do in your professional life.
2. When you identify a transferable skill, learned behavior, or core value as a trait you do not possess or one that needs development, it should immediately become part of your professional development program, because these attributes underlie your long-term survival and success.
3. You will become aware of these skills, behaviors, and values and ensure that they are reflected in your attitude to your career. You will work to further develop them. And this is going to set you apart from the vast majority of your peers in this search and in the balance of your career.
4. This awareness is going to positively impact your whole career as you move forward through the years. These skills are the building blocks of success.

The transferable skills/learned behaviors that are most desirable to employers are largely developed as a result of our experiences in the workplace. Remember that first day on your first job, when you eventually got up the courage to go forage for a cup of coffee? You found the coffee machine, and there stuck on the wall was a handwritten sign reading:

YOUR MOTHER DOESN'T WORK HERE
PICK UP AFTER YOURSELF

You thought to yourself, "Pick up after myself? Gee, I gotta learn a whole new way of behaving," and so you started to observe and emulate the more successful professionals around you, and slowly developed a whole slate of learned behaviors/skills that help you succeed in job after job throughout your professional life. There is a recognized sequence of interrelated skills and/or behaviors that are seen as integral to success in every job, at every level, in every profession anywhere in the world. The full list includes:

Communication
Critical thinking
Time management and organization
Teamwork
Creativity
Leadership
Motivation
Determination
Integrity
Productivity
Procedures

You can readily understand that the person seen to be in possession of these skills will be known and respected as a consummate professional; which is another way of saying that she or he has successfully established a valid professional brand.

Transferable skills, behaviors, traits, or values . . . I've heard them called all of these. Which is right? Behavioral psychologists, management, and career management theorists have been thinking and writing about professional success and behavior for many years. They most commonly refer to these "attributes" as transferable skills, learned behaviors, or developed behaviors. They are equally accurately referred to as values: personal values, professional values, etc. You can have communication skills, and when you learn the complexity of subtle skills that make up effective professional communication you will clearly recognize it as a developed behavior. On the other hand integrity is definitely a value, can be a learned behavior, but is unlikely to be referred to as a transferable skill. I'll break them up in a logical way, but don't get hung up on the nomenclature. Nobody else does.

That you have these admirable traits is one thing. That I know you are in possession of excellent Communication, Critical Thinking, Time Management and Organization, Teamwork, Creativity, and Leadership skills, and that you have Integrity and you are Motivated and Determined, well, that's another thing. Developing and applying these skills and reflecting them in your approach to work, your interactions with others in every aspect of your job search should be an obvious step in framing and promoting that brand.

As you read through the breakdown of these skills and values, you'll see, for example, "communication," and think, "Yes, I have good communication skills." When this happens, come up with examples of when your communication skills played an important role in the successful completion of an assignment.

You will read about "time management and organization," and might say, "*Oy vey ist mir*, now there's something I have to work on!" In this instance you have identified a key behavior that needs work, and you can immediately set about a personal development program. You'll find links for skill development in these areas at *www.knockemdead.com*, on the Career Success pages.

The insights you gain about the value of the transferable skills, behaviors, and values you possess and that differentiate you from others is an important component of defining your professional brand. The examples of your application of these skills or the impact of these values on your work product can be used in your resume, in your cover letters, and as illustrative answers to questions in interviews.

Transferable Skills

In the United States, the National Association of Colleges and Employers (NACE is made up of major corporation recruiters and university career services professionals) has defined seven transferable skills that every professional entering the workplace should possess as a necessity for success. This main category includes the seven transferable skills that NACE and everyone in the professional conversation on these matters agree upon.

Technical

The technical skills of your profession are the foundation of all success; without them you won't even land a job, much less succeed in your career. Technical skills speak to your *ability* to do the job, those essentials necessary for success in the day-to-day execution of your duties. It means you know which skills and tools are needed for a particular task and possess the know-how to use them productively and efficiently. These technical skills vary from profession to profession and do not refer to anything technical *per se* or to technology skills.

However, it is a given that one of the technical skills essential to every job is technological adaptivity. You must be proficient in all computer and Internet-based applications relevant to your work. Even when you are not working in a technology field, strong technology skills will enhance stability and help you leverage professional growth.

When people are referred to as "professional," it means they possess the appropriate technical and technology skills necessary for success in their profession and have interwoven them with the other six major transferable skills. Staying current with the essential technical and technology skills of your chosen career path is going to be an integral part of your professional growth and stability. That's why the ongoing education toward the end of your resume can be an important tool in developing your professional brand because it speaks to your technical competence and to your commitment (something we'll address shortly).

You can find useful links for professional development at:

www.knockemdead.com
www.mindtools.com/pages/main/newMN_ISS.htm
www.mindtools.com/page8.html
www.mindtools.com/pages/main/newMN_TED.htm

Communication

Without communication you live in silence and isolation. With communication you make things happen in your life.

As George Bernard Shaw said, "The greatest problem in communication is the illusion that it has been accomplished." Every professional job today requires communication skills; promotions and professional success are impossible without them. Good verbal communication skills enable you to accurately process incoming information, and, considering the interests and sophistication of your audience, present outgoing information persuasively so that it is understood and accepted.

But communication embraces much more than listening and speaking. When the professional world talks about communication skills, it is referring to four primary communication skills and four supportive communication skills.

The primary communication skills are:

- **Verbal skills**—what you say and how you say it.
- **Listening skills**—listening to understand, rather than just waiting your turn to talk.
- **Writing skills**—clear written communication is essential for any professional career. It creates a lasting impression of who you are.
- **Technology communication skills**—the way you communicate and your ability to navigate the new communication media.

The four supportive communication skills are more subtle, but nevertheless impact every interaction you have with others. They are:

- **Grooming and dress**—they tell others who you are and how you feel about yourself.
- **Social graces**—how you behave around others. If your table manners are sketchy, odds are you'll never sit at the chairman's table or represent your organization at the higher levels.
- **Body language**—displays how you're feeling deep inside, a form of communication mankind learned before speech. For truly effective communication, what your mouth says must be in harmony with what your body says.
- **Emotional IQ**—your emotional maturity in dealing with other adults in professional settings.

Develop effective communication skills in all these areas and you'll gain enormous control over what you can achieve, how you are perceived, and what happens in your life.

You can check out resources for developing each of these skills at *www.knockemdead.com.*

Verbal Skills

www.wordsmith.org/awad/index.html
www.mindtools.com/page8.html
www.latrobe.edu.au/careers/students/employable/toolkit-communication.html
www.stress.about.com/od/relationships/ht/healthycomm.htm

Listening Skills

www.mindtools.com/CommSkll/ActiveListening.htm

Writing Skills

www.collegeboard.com/student/plan/boost-your-skills/123.html
www.mindtools.com/CommSkll/WritingSkills.htm
www.smashingmagazine.com/2009/06/28/50-free-resources-that-will-improve-your-writing-skills/
www.essortment.com/all/howtoimprovew_rgka.htm (scroll down on this one)

Body Language

www.helpguide.org/mental/eq6_nonverbal_communication.htm#improving
www.personadev.com/2008/04/07/10-tips-to-boost-your-body-language-skills/
www.positivityblog.com/index.php/2007/09/10/how-to-improve-your-social-skills/

Social Graces

www.menshealth.com/men/style/style-files/the-social-graces-that-say-you-will/article/9d0ad1302eec010VgnVCM10000013281eac

Dress and Grooming

www.tips.learnhub.com/lesson/2800-tips-on-business-dress-etiquette-and-grooming (guys, remember to scroll down)
www.womeninbusiness.about.com/od/businessattireforwomen/a/groomingtips.htmw
www.deed.state.mn.us/cjs/dress.htm
www.jobs.utah.gov/jobseeker/guides/07_33.pdf

Emotional Intelligence

www.psychology.about.com/lr/emotional_intelligence/337325/1/

Teamwork

If you become a successful leader one day, it will be because you were first a great team player; that's the way it works. The professional world revolves around the complex challenges of making money and such complex challenges require teams of people to provide ongoing solutions. This in turn demands that you work efficiently and respectfully with others who have totally different responsibilities, backgrounds, objectives, and areas of expertise.

Teamwork asks that a commitment to the team and its success come first. This means you take on a task because it needs to be done, not because it makes you look good. The payback, of course, is that management always recognizes and appreciates a team player.

As a team player you:

- Always cooperate.
- Always make decisions based on team goals.
- Always keep team members informed.
- Always keep commitments.
- Always share credit, never blame.

Teamwork skills are especially important if you intend to be a leader, because all successful leaders need to first understand the critical dynamics of teamwork. It is only by being a team player that you understand the subtleties of what makes a team pull together and function productively as a unit, and how to recognize and encourage those who display a team spirit; so if you intend to be a leader, learn to be a team player.

Check out these links to learn more about developing your critical thinking and problem solving skills.

www.hku.hk/cepc/taccasu/ref/teamwk.htm

www.latrobe.edu.au/careers/students/employable/toolkit-teamwork.html

Critical Thinking

You know to come in from the rain, right? Then you know critical thinking impacts everything you do in life.

Life and the world of work are full of opportunity, and every one of those opportunities is peppered with problems. With critical thinking skills you can turn those opportunities into achievement, earnings, and fulfillment. This is the professional-world application of all those problem-solving skills you've been developing since grade school: a systematic approach to uncovering all the issues related to a particular challenge that will lead to its solution.

Critical thinking, analytical, or problem-solving skills, allow the successful professional to logically think through and clearly define a challenge and its desired solutions, and then evaluate and implement the best solution for that challenge from all available options.

You examine the problem and ask the critical questions

- What's the problem?
- Who is it a problem for?
- Why is it a problem?
- What is causing this problem?

- What are the options for a solution?
- What problems might a given solution create?
- What is the most suitable solution for the situation?

You look through the factors affecting each possible solution and decide which solutions to keep and which to disregard. You look at the solution as a whole and use your judgment as to whether to use the solution or not. Once you have decided on a course of action, you plan out the steps, the timing, and the resources to make it happen.

- How long will it take to implement this solution?
- How much will it cost?
- What resources will I need?
- Can I get these resources?
- Will the solution really resolve the problem to everyone's benefit?
- Will this solution cause its own problems?

Einstein said that if he had one hour to save the world he would spend fifty-five minutes defining the problem. It's a thought worth remembering because a properly defined problem always leads to a better solution, and 50 percent of the success of any project is in the prep, and critical thinking is an integral part of preparation.

Check out the links on this page to learn more about developing your critical thinking skills.

www.latrobe.edu.au/careers/students/employable/toolkit-ps.html
www.litemind.com/problem-definition/
www.mindtools.com/pages/main/newMN_TED.htm
www.mindtools.com/pages/main/newMN_TMC.htm
www.virtualsalt.com/crebook3.htm

Time Management and Organization

With time management and organization (TM&O) skills you can bring your dreams to life. Without them you will forever spin in underachieving circles.

There are two types of people in the world: the task-oriented who let tasks expand to fill all the time allotted to them; and the goal-oriented who organize and prioritize and strive to get all work completed in an orderly manner and as quickly and efficiently as quality will allow. Sometimes the only difference between these two types is that one group learned how to organize their activities and manage their time. You only get one guess as to who has the most successful and fulfilled lives.

The ability to manage time and organize activities increases productivity. The people who do this, often characterized as high achievers and goal-oriented because they get so much done, are just people who learned how to organize themselves and consequently work with more purpose. The result is that they can multitask and seriously outperform their peers.

If you're effective at managing and organizing your time, you make a *To Do* list, then ABC prioritize:

- The As absolutely must be done today. "A" priority activities always get your full attention; the other activities fill in around them. Just remember, your boss's priority is always your priority!
- It would be good to get the Bs done today. These are the first activities to fill in around your A priorities.
- C items need to get done, but they're not urgent or are someone else's priority, not yours. These fill in odd moments unless approaching deadlines move them to B status.

Having a physical *To Do* list handy means you always have work to do, and referring to it keeps you maximally productive and on track.

Make a habit of this for twenty-one days and you will see *big* changes in your productivity.

Another TM&O technique that encourages productivity without increasing effort is the Daily Plan/Do/Review cycle.

Always set aside time at the end of the day to review what happened:

- What went well and why?
- What went not so well, and what can you do about it?
- What new projects have landed on your desktop?
- What is their A/B/C priority?

Look at each A priority separately and identify exactly where you will jump in on this project tomorrow, what you hope to achieve, and the tools you'll need to do so.

A priorities frequently include large and complex projects, so where will you begin? Break the big task into smaller action steps, things that you can get done tomorrow

This skill is at the very heart of your ability to achieve professional success. Developing TM&O skills enable you to do the things you have to do when they ought to be done in an organized and professional manner.

Check out the other links on the page to learn more about developing this skill, and how it relates to resume, job search, and other career management issues.

www.latrobe.edu.au/careers/students/employable/toolkit-planning.html

www.mindtools.com/pages/main/newMN_HTE.htm

Leadership

"A leader has two important characteristics; first, he is going somewhere; second, he is able to persuade other people to go with him." The guy who said this, Maximilien Robespierre, was a principal figure in the French Revolution and literally changed his world.

As you develop teamwork skills, which is a must if you ever hope to lead, notice how you are willing to follow true leaders, but how you don't fall in line with people who don't respect you and who don't have your best interests at heart.

When you are credible, when people believe in your competence, and believe you have everyone's success as your goal, those people will follow you; you accept responsibility but "we" gets the credit. When your actions inspire others to think more, learn more, do more, and become more, you are on your way to becoming a leader.

Your job as a leader is to make your team function, so your teamwork skills give you the smarts to pull your team together as a cohesive unit.

Your technical expertise, critical thinking, and creativity skills help you correctly define the challenges and their solutions.

Your communication skills enable your team to understand the task and its goals. There's nothing more demoralizing than a leader who can't clearly articulate why we're doing what we're doing.

Your time management and organization skills enable you to create a practical blueprint for success and your team to take ownership of the task and deliver the expected results.

Leadership is the most complex of all the transferable skills that you will develop to make a success of your professional work life. It is a combination and outgrowth of all the seven transferable skills. Leaders aren't born, they are self-made. And just like anything else, it takes hard work. That's the price you pay to achieve this or any other serious goal.

For advice on how to further develop this skill check out the links on this page.

www.mindtools.com/pages/main/newMN_LDR.htm
www.mindtools.com/pages/main/newMN_PPM.htm
www.crfonline.org/orc/ca/ca-2.html
http://top7business.com/?id=2113
www.businessballs.com/leadership.htm
www.career-success-for-newbies.com/developing-leadership-skills.html

Creativity

There's a difference between creativity and just having ideas. Ideas are like headaches: We all get them once in a while, and like headaches they usually disappear as mysteriously as they arrived. Creativity, on the other hand, is the ability to develop those ideas and the strategic and tactical know-how that brings them to life.

Creativity in the professional context is the generation of new ideas as they relate to a specific situation, challenge, or goal. It is a skill that can be learned and applied to anything you do in life. The ability to bring life to your professional creativity comes from

- Your critical thinking skills applied within an area of technical expertise.
- Your time management and organization skills that combine with your critical thinking skills and technical expertise and enable you to break your challenge down into specific steps, with each step broken down into actions that are each small enough that some meaningful progress can be made on them today.
- Your communication skills that allow you to explain your approach and its component building blocks persuasively to your target audience, as well as your teamwork skills whenever others are needed to bring the idea to fruition.
- Your leadership skills come into play as you bring your new ideas forward.

Creative approaches to challenges can take time or can come fully formed in a flash, but the longer you work on developing the supporting skills that bring creativity to life the more often they will come fully formed and in a flash.

Here are five rules for building creativity skills.

1. **Whatever you do in life, engage in it fully.** Commit to developing competence in everything you do, because the wider your frame of reference for the world around you . . . the higher octane fuel you have to propel your ideas to acceptance and reality.
2. **Learn something new every day.** Treat the pursuit of knowledge as a way of life. Absorb as much as you can about everything. Information exercises your brain, and fills your mind with information and the ever-widening frame of reference that allows you to make creative connections where others won't see them.
3. **Catch ideas as they occur.** Note them in your PDA or on scrap of paper. Anything will do so long as you capture the idea.
4. **Welcome restrictions in your world.** They encourage creativity; ask any successful writer, artist, musician, or business leader.
5. **Don't spend your life glued to Facebook or TV.** You need to live life, not watch it go by out of the corner of your eye. If you do watch television, try to learn something or motivate yourself with science, history, or biography programming. If you surf the Internet do it with purpose.

Building creativity skills enables you to bring your dreams to life; and the development of each of these seven interconnected transferable skills will help you do it.

Check out the following link for more insights on creativity.

www.mindtools.com/pages/main/newMN_CT.htm

Professional Values

Motivation and Energy

Employers realize that a motivated professional will do a better job on every assignment. Motivation expresses itself in a commitment to the job and the profession, an eagerness to learn and grow professionally, and a willingness to take the rough with the smooth.

Motivation is invariably expressed by the *energy* you demonstrate in your work. You always give that extra effort to get the job done and to get it done right.

Commitment and Reliability

Commitment to your profession, the role it plays in the larger issues of company success, and the empowerment that comes from knowing how your part contributes to the greater good . . . these are all desirable professional values.

Commitment is also a demonstration of enlightened self-interest. The more you are engaged in your career, the more likely you are to join the inner circles that exist in every department and company, enhancing opportunities for advancement. At the same time, this dedication will repay you with better job security and improved professional horizons.

Your dedication will also express itself in your *reliability*: Showing up is half the battle; the other half is your performance on the job. This requires following up on your actions, not relying on anyone else to ensure the job is done and done well.

Determination

Your determination speaks of a resilient professional who doesn't get worn down or who does not back off when a problem or situation gets tough. It's a value that marks you out as someone who chooses to be part of the solution rather than standing idly by and being part of the problem.

The determined professional has decided to make a difference with his or her presence every day, because it is the *right* thing to do, and because it makes the time go faster.

The determined professional is willing to do whatever it takes to get a job done, even if that includes duties that might not appear in a job description.

Pride and Integrity

Pride in yourself as a professional means always making sure the job is done to the best of your ability; this means paying attention to the details and to the time and cost constraints. Integrity means taking responsibility for your actions, both good and bad, and it also means treating others, within and outside of the company, with respect at all times and in all situations. With pride in yourself as a professional with integrity, your actions will always be in the ethical best interests of the company, and your decisions will never be based on whim or personal preference.

Business Values

Companies have very limited interests: making money, saving money (the same as making money), and saving time (which saves money and makes time to make more money). Actually, you wouldn't want it any other way, as it is this focus that makes your paycheck good come payday. Developing business values that demonstrate sensitivity to the profit imperative of a business endeavor is the mark of a true professional.

Productivity: Always work toward enhanced productivity through efficiencies of time, resources, money, and effort.

Economy: Most problems have two solutions, and the expensive one isn't always the best. Ideas of efficiency and economy engage the creative mind in ways that others would not consider.

Procedures: You recognize the need for procedures and that they are implemented only after careful thought. You understand and always follow the chain of command. You don't implement your own "improved" procedures or organize others to do so.

As you develop this suite of transferable skills, learned behaviors, and professional values your confidence in taking on new challenges will grow. You'll ask questions, look at challenges calmly and at mistakes squarely, and make changes to eradicate those mistakes. In short, you will develop the quiet confidence of the professional that can deliver the goods. And *that's* what employers are looking for.

Identifying Your Competitive Difference

The people who will hire you first need to differentiate you from other candidates. The following questionnaire will help you identify all the differentiators that help make you unique. Each is a component of your professional brand. You won't discover anything earth-shattering, just a continuum of behaviors and values you've always had but the value of which you've perhaps never really understood; it'll be a series of those, "Of course, I knew that" moments. It will then be logical and natural to integrate them into your resume, cover letters, and your performance in job interviews. All of these things will brand the professional you; it will feel right, it will fit.

KNOCK 'EM DEAD TIP
An expandable version of this questionnaire is available in MS Word at *www.knockemdead.com* on the resume advice page under the title: The Competitive Differentiation Questionnaire.

The Competitive Differentiation Questionnaire

Which of the transferable skills, behaviors, and values best captures the essence of the professional you?

____

____

____

Which of the transferable skills, behaviors, and values have you marked for further professional development?

____

____

____

What qualities or characteristics do you share with top performers in your department/profession?

____

____

____

What have you achieved with these qualities?

____

____

____

What makes you different from others with whom you have worked?

____

____

What do you see as your four most important professional traits, and how does each help your performance?

1. ______________________________________
2. ______________________________________

3. ____
4. ____

How does each help your coworkers?

1. ____
2. ____
3. ____
4. ____

How does each help your department and boss?

1. ____
2. ____
3. ____
4. ____

How does each help your company?

1. ____
2. ____
3. ____
4. ____

Why do you stand out in your job/profession? (If you realize you don't stand out and you want to, examine why the people you admire stand out and use them as a model for development, becoming today those things you wish to become tomorrow.)

____

____

How are you better than others holding the same title? Can you quantify this difference?

____

____

What excites you most about your professional responsibilities?

____

____

What are your achievements in these areas?

____

____

What do your peers say about you?

____

____

What does management say about you?

____

____

What do your reports say about you?

____

____

What are your top four professional skills?

Skill 1: ____

Quantifiable achievements with this skill: ______________________________

Skill 2: ____

Quantifiable achievements with this skill: ______________________________

Skill 3: ____

Quantifiable achievements with this skill: ______________________________

Skill 4: ____

Quantifiable achievements with this skill: ______________________________

What are your top four leadership skills?

Skill 1: ____

Quantifiable achievements with this skill: ______________________________

Skill 2: ____

Quantifiable achievements with this skill: ______________________________

Skill 3: ____

Quantifiable achievements with this skill: ______________________________

Skill 4: ____

Quantifiable achievements with this skill: ______________________________

What do you believe are the three key deliverables of your job?

1. ______
2. ______
3. ______

What gives you greatest satisfaction in the work you do?

______

What value does this combination of skills, behaviors, values, and achievements bring to employers in your target market?

______

Benefits of a Defined Professional Brand

All of this may seem like a lot of work, and some of you are probably wondering what it has to do with finding a job. But there are important benefits to developing a personal brand. Your most immediately recognizable advantage is that unlike your competition, you understand the skills and attributes necessary for professional success. That you know who you are, what you offer, and how you want to be perceived will differentiate you from others. And because you understand yourself and can communicate this understanding you will project a unique presence.

Your Professional Brand and the Long Haul

Globalization has made your job less secure than ever. Change is constant in everyone's career. Now that you're developing an initial professional brand identity as part of your job search strategy, you don't want to shelve it once you've landed a new job.

In this new insecure world of work, it makes sense to maintain visibility within your profession. This is nothing more than intelligent market positioning for MeInc. The professional identity/brand built into your new resume is the profile you should keep posted on your professional networking sites on an ongoing basis. This increases your credibility and visibility within your profession and to the recruitment industry, making you more desirable as an employee and increasing your options.

Now let's move on to using some of these life-changing insights as we put your resume together.

CHAPTER 2
The Productive Resume

YOUR CURRENT RESUME doesn't work, and here's how to fix it.

Your resume is the most financially important document you will ever own. When it works, the doors of opportunity open for you. When it doesn't work, you don't either, so this is a job that deserves your full attention. Your resume establishes an achievable goal for your search, opens the doors of opportunity for interviews, prepares you for the questions interviewers will ask, and acts as a powerful ambassador at decision time.

A good resume is not simply a recitation of all the things you have done in your work life. In fact if your resume is just recitation of all the things you happen to think important, it is likely sitting unread in whatever countless resume databases you left it.

The impact of technology on the workplace causes the nature of all jobs to change almost as rapidly as the pages on a calendar. In the not-so-distant past, someone would have reviewed your resume almost as soon as it was received. Today, resumes no longer go straight to a recruiter or manager's desk, they are more likely to go to a resume database. This means that before a human being reviews your resume, it must be chosen from that résumé database as worth reviewing. Since some of those databases contain over 30 million resumes, you can see that your decrepit old resume needs a complete overhaul.

Recruitment and Resume Banks

When recruiters access resume databases, they always do so with a specific Job Description (JD) in mind. This is important to know:

1. Job Postings frequently reflect the exact wording of the Job Descriptions they come from, so these postings contain the words and phrases company personnel used throughout the recruitment and selection cycle.
2. Because these words and phrases have real meaning to the recruiters and hiring managers, they are what the recruiters use when searching resume databases.

Here's how the process works: You and I want to hire an accountant, so, among other resources, we might look in the CareerBuilder database. To access the database, we need to define the job title, by typing "accountant" into the dialogue box, specify where the job will be, and click on the supplied keywords (offered by most resume banks) that we feel best describe that job. We also add words of our own that do not appear in the supplied-keyword choices.

Once programmed to search for a specific set of words, the software scours the database and builds a list of all the resumes that contain *any* of those descriptors or keywords. It then weights the list. Those resumes with the most frequent use *and* greatest number of keywords come to the top of the list.

This is the *first* keyword test your resume *must* pass: Because recruiters very rarely go beyond the top twenty resumes in a database search, not enough relevant keywords in your resume means that no human will review it.

This is the *second* keyword test your resume *must* pass: When your resume gets to human eyes, the process is alarmingly similar. Generally, recruiters will read resumes pulled from the database twice. The first reading is a skim that takes fifteen to forty-five seconds. No relevant keywords/phrases likely means no second read.

The next read is a little more careful. The reviewers are *looking to see if the resume's claims really hang together and tell the story of the job they are trying to fill.* Recruiters and HR typically plow through enough resumes to create a "long list" of up to six candidates.

Here it may land in front of the manager who actually has the authority to hire you, but who hates to read resumes. Managers hate reading resumes—they just want to hire someone and get back to work. You get that? *Managers hate reading resumes—they just want to hire someone and get back to work.*

In fact, no one likes to read resumes; try reading six of them in a row, and feel your brain melting into a gelatinous goop. Bear this in mind, because we will use it to great advantage.

Only those resumes that pass these tests get a more thoughtful reading, one that carefully evaluates the resume against the JD's requirements, and when for the first time your credentials are seen as representing a living, breathing human being.

A resume that tries to cram in everything you have done without any real focus is doomed to fail any and all of these initial hurdles, and failure at any of these points means: no interviews and no job offers. So you can continue doing the same nonproductive activities or you can rethink your approach.

Get Inside the Employer's Head

Fortunately, after much thought I have devised something that I feel is nothing short of a life-changing solution to this huge challenge: Before writing your resume, you are going to get inside the employer's head and examine what he or she looks for when hiring. What I am going to show you will deliver:

- A template for the story your resume must tell to be successful
- An objective tool against which to evaluate your resume's performance
- A complete understanding of where the focus will be at interviews
- A very good idea of the questions that will be heading your way and why
- Relevant examples with which to illustrate your answers
- A behavioral profile for getting hired and for professional success throughout your career
- A behavioral profile for not getting hired and for ongoing professional failure

Start with Simple Common Sense

Your resume will always be more effective if it begins with a clear focus on, and understanding of, a specific target job. When you have this focus you can look backward into your work history for those experiences that best position you for the target job. This will enable you to tailor a killer resume.

The big question is: How do you do this? The answer is what I call the Target Job Deconstruction (TJD) process.

Step 1: Decide on a Specific Target Job

Focus on a specific and realistic target job, one in which you can succeed based on the skills you possess today. Some people think you change jobs to get a promotion, but this is largely incorrect, especially in a tight job market. *People get hired based on their credentials, not their potential.* Most people don't get promotions to the next step up the professional ladder when they change jobs, because that would mean coming onboard as an unknown quantity in a job they've never done.

Typically, most professionals accept a position similar to the one they have now, but one that offers opportunity for growth once they have proved themselves. The most common exception is an employee already doing that higher-level job but without the title recognition. Also, sometimes you can combine experience and credentials from a number of jobs into a new configuration. This is always more likely to happen when the economy is on the upswing. In down economies, there are just too many thoroughly qualified candidates for an employer to warrant the risk, because with every hire made the hiring manager's performance comes under scrutiny.

So of all the jobs you can do—and we can all do more than one—decide on the one that will be the easiest sell for you and the easiest buy for the employer. This will be:

- A job you can do and that you can justify on paper
- A job you can convince skilled interviewers that you can do
- A job in which you can succeed

Let's look at "a job in which you can succeed." The ability to do 70 percent or more of the job will usually get you in the running for the selection cycle in any economy. You'll be able to deliver on the job's requirements and have room for professional growth, making such a target job a good choice. Less than this and you may need to reconsider your target job or anticipate a longer job search to reach your goals.

If you have more than five years of experience, there are probably a couple of jobs you can do. More than fifteen years of experience and there could be half a dozen jobs in which you can succeed. Carefully evaluate and rank these jobs based on their availability, remuneration, fulfillment, and their potential for growth or shrinkage. This way you will target a "primary job" based on practicality and common sense. If you ultimately decide you want to go after that White Water Rafting Guide job because you once owned a canoe . . . well, at least you'll be doing it with your eyes open, knowing that you won't have most of the required skills, and that your search will take considerably longer.

This does not mean you cannot pursue other jobs for which you have the desire and qualifications. However, be sensible, create your primary resume with a single "primary target" job in mind, and make that job one you can nail!

Targeted Resumes for Different Jobs

Once you have tailored a *prime* resume to the most logical focus for your next job, you can quite easily customize it for any of those other jobs you are interested in. Usually there is considerable overlap in the deliverables of the different jobs for which we are qualified, so you can take that primary resume, make a copy, retitle it, and make the necessary changes to give the secondary resume a specific focus. Go through the TJD process for each additional job-targeted resume and you will quickly maximize the impact potential of each one; you won't have to start from scratch, and you'll have customized resumes for each opportunity.

Step 2: Collect Job Postings

Collect a half-dozen job postings for your chosen primary target job and if you want to save some time, try one of these job spiders, each of which will search thousands of job sites for you. Some are free, and some are for a fee, but they all work similarly—the home page has a couple of dialogue boxes: one for a job title and one for a geographic area. If you cannot find half a dozen jobs in your target geography just try another major metro area: For the purpose of TJD it doesn't matter where the jobs are located.

- *www.indeed.com*
- *www.worktree.com*
- *www.jobbankusa.com*
- *www.jobsniper.com*
- *www.jobster.com*

Put them in a folder on your desktop and also print them out.

the collected JDs we will deconstruct the way all employers think about, prioritize, xpress their needs when they think about someone like you. The result will be a template t describes your target job *the way employers themselves think about, prioritize, and describe it.*

Step 3: Look at Your Job from the Other Side of the Desk

This is where you deconstruct your collection of JDs so that you understand exactly how employers *think about, prioritize, and describe the deliverables of your job*:

1. Start a new Word document, and name it "Prime TJD" or something similar.
2. Under the subhead "Target Job Titles," cut and paste all the variations on the job title you are pursuing from your collection of job postings.
3. Under a subhead "Experience/responsibilities/deliverables" write those requirements that are common to all six postings, and highlight them. Choose one, then copy and paste it into your document. (You may want to place a "6" alongside the copy and paste to remind yourself that this requirement is common to all six of your JDs.) Underneath it list any different keywords used in the other five JDs to describe this same requirement.

   For this step you may find it easier to work with the printed copies, since your kitchen counter is bigger than your computer screen ;-).

   Repeat this for all other requirements common to all six JDs, placing the number 6 alongside each one.
4. Repeat this process with requirements that are common to five of the six job postings then four of the six postings . . . and so on down the line.

At the end of this first part of the TJD process you will be able to read the document and say to yourself, *"When employers are looking for _______, these are the job titles they use; this is the order in which these needs are prioritized; these are the skills, experiences, deliverables, and professional behaviors they look for; and these are the words with which they describe the deliverables of the job."*

As you read through such a document, the story your resume needs to tell will be carefully laid out before you.

Step 4: ID What You Bring to the Table for Each Requirement

Add to your TJD the skills and experience you bring to *each one* of these requirements. This is important, because job descriptions, helpful as they are, don't always tell the whole story. In many companies, job descriptions won't go into all the nuts and bolts of a particular job, because all JDs have to be approved by the legal department before they see the light of day. This is part of an overall corporate cost-containment policy designed to protect against the release of job descriptions that might aid individual or class-action lawsuits brought by disgruntled employees. How can I be sure of this? I used to be a director of Human Resources in Silicon Valley. I've overseen this process.

Step 5: Critical Thinking

At their most elemental level, all jobs are the same—all jobs focus on problem identification, avoidance, and solution. This is what we all get paid for, no matter what we do for a living.

Go back to your TJD and start with the first requirement. Think about and note the problems you will typically need to identify, solve, and/or prevent in the course of a normal workday as you deliver on this requirement for the job. Then list specific examples, big and small, of your successful identification, prevention, and/or solution to the problems. Quantify your results when possible.

Repeat this with each of the TJD's other requirements by identifying the problems inherent in that particular responsibility, Some examples may appear in your resume as significant professional achievements, while others will provide you with the ammunition to answer all those interview questions that begin, "Tell me about a time when . . . ."

Step 6: ID Behavioral Profile for Success

Think of the *best* person you have ever seen doing this job and what made him or her stand out. Describe his or her performance, professional behavior, interaction with others, and appearance: "That would be Carole Jenkins; superior communication skills, a fine analytical mind, great professional appearance, and a nice person to work with." You are describing the person all employers want to hire; do this for each and every requirement listed on your TJD. Yes, it will take time and it would be easy to cut corners and skip it, but this is your career and this is your life: Make the choice that is right for your long-term success and happiness.

When you apply what you learn from this to your professional life, it will increase your job security as it opens doors to the inner circles that exist in every department and company—and that leads to the plum assignments, raises, and promotions that over time add up to professional success.

Step 7: ID Behavioral Profile for Failure

Now think of the *worst* person you have ever seen doing this job and what made that individual stand out in such a negative way. Describe the performance, professional behaviors, interaction with others, and appearance of that person: "That would be Jack Dornitz; insecure, critical, passive aggressive, no social graces, and a bully." You are describing the person that all employers want to avoid and, incidentally, a behavioral profile for your own professional suicide.

Once you complete and review your TJD, you will have a clear idea of exactly the way all employers think about, prioritize, and express their needs when they hire someone for the job you want.

KNOCK 'EM DEAD TIP

If you are new to the professional world and cannot bring personal awareness of a job's needs to the Target Job Deconstruction Process, you might want to do a little additional research to ensure that your resume has the proper focus.

For further insight into a specific target job, visit the Occupational Outlook Handbook pages at *www.bls.gov/oco/home.htm*, which give detailed analyses of hundreds of jobs. After that, talk to people who are actually doing the work and have them deconstruct the job for you along the lines discussed. Check the section on networking for ways to identify and reach out to the right people.

Resume Building

Now you know how employers prioritize and express their needs, you are ready to look into your work history to pull out the information that will help you build a resume that reflects your ability to do this job. The following questionnaire will help you assemble all the data you will need for a productive resume.

KNOCK 'EM DEAD TIP

You can find an electronic version of this questionnaire at *www.knockemdead.com* on the resume advice pages. The electronic document on the website is expandable, so if you have had more jobs than are listed on the form here, or need more space for a particular entry, you can expand the document to fit your needs.

Resume Questionnaire

Assuming you use the version available at *www.knockemdead.com*, you should save this questionnaire in a resume development folder (within your career management folder) and back up this data to an external source. Remember, this will not be your last job search, and maintaining all your career information in a digital format will be a great time saver over the years. In answering these questions don't worry about grammar and perfect wording right now (that comes later), but do take the time to think about the issues. Be descriptive—don't just say you were a manager; say that you were a manager with fifty-five direct reports in Decatur and a further fifteen in Mumbai. Be specific whenever possible: Mention full budgetary responsibility (with dollar amount) plus selection, development, discipline, and termination responsibilities. Wherever you can, illustrate with real-world examples, and, wherever you can, quantify those examples in terms of money earned or saved, time saved, and productivity improved. Round these examples down, rather than up. Always identify your role as a team member when appropriate. This makes your claims more believable.

Contact Information

Name
Address
E-mail
Home telephone *(recommend alternate number)*
Cell
Current Job Title
Variations on this Job Title
Operational area *(Sales, Finance, R&D, IT, Supply Chain, etc.)*
Industry/Market sectors *(Technology, Pharma, Financial Services, etc.)*

Education and Skills

Post-secondary education *(you might not use all this but do collect it)*
Degree
Concentration
Graduation date
Major
Minor
GPA
GPA Major
GPA Minor
Ranking
Honors, scholarships
Special accomplishments
International studies
Degree

Concentration
Graduation date
Major
Minor
GPA
GPA Major
GPA Minor
Ranking
Honors, scholarships
Special accomplishments

Professional Education

Ongoing professional education signals commitment to success.

Course name
Completion date
Duration
Certification
Sponsoring organization

Professional Credentials Not Covered Elsewhere

Professional memberships and affiliations (*American Management Association, American Marketing Association, etc.*)
Organization
Leadership role

KNOCK 'EM DEAD TIP

Active membership in a professional association is a key tool for career resilience and success. If you don't know where to start, visit the Association page of the Internet resources area at *www.knockemdead.com.*

Technological Skills

No one gets ahead today without technological competence. Capture your fluency here, and update regularly. That alphabet soup of technology just might help your resume's performance in database searches, so list all that apply.

Corporate Accomplishments

You can also include here your work on projects that resulted in copyright and patents, so long as you make clear your real contribution.

Awards and recognition

Public speaking/presentations

Profession-related publications

Patents and copyrights

Global Experience, Cultural Diversity Awareness

In a global economy, any exposure here is relevant, and it doesn't have to be professional in nature. That you were an army brat and grew up in ten different countries can be a big plus. Just name the countries, not the circumstance.

Foreign languages

Community, Civic Involvement

List all organizations and any special projects/activities/leadership roles.

Other Activities

This should include all the activities with which you fill your out-of-work hours. Your resume may include those activities that can say something positive about the professional you. For example, in sales and marketing just about all group activities show a desirable mindset. Bridge might argue strong analytical skills, and the senior executive who still plays competitive lacrosse and runs marathons is crazy not to let the world know.

Valuable Profession-Related Skills Developed Outside of Your Professional Work

Military

Service

Rank

Discharge

Promotions

Decorations

Honors

Professional Development Courses

Achievements

What professional capabilities/skills do you feel have most contributed to your professional success?

What professional behaviors (analytical or communication skills, for example) do you feel have most contributed to your professional success?

Employment History

(To ensure a proper focus I strongly advise that you complete your target job deconstruction exercises before looking back at your work history.)

Current position

Company

Employment dates

Location

Standing (division, public, private)

Industry/market sector

What does your company do?

EXAMPLE

Squanto Corporation, Inc., Orlando, FL

1997 to Present

$500 million company

One of the largest resort and vacation sales/development companies in the United States.

In rapid growth through international expansion, strategic M&A, industry rollup, and IPO.

What were you hired to do?

EXAMPLE
Worldwide Director of Operations, Entertainment Imaging, 1998–2006

Selected to re-engineer and revitalize this $65 million business unit with accountability for thirty-two direct reports in four cities across the United States. Established strategic vision and developed operational infrastructure. Managed Supply Chain, Logistics/Distribution, Forecasting, System Integration, Project Management, Contracts Administration, and Third-Party Site Operations.

Or, more simply:

EXAMPLE
DryRoc, Inc. Indianapolis, IN, 2004–Present

Production Director

Drove production for world's largest wallboard plant, with 258 employees working in multiple shifts.

Title you report to

Your Title

Department/Unit

Leadership or Membership of Executive Teams, Project Teams, or Committees

Responsibilities/Deliverables

Quotes, Praise, and Endorsements from Management

When described by a professional colleague, how do you hope they would describe your most desirable professional qualities?

Having taken a first pass at the responsibility/deliverables area, take a few moments to review your Target Job Deconstruction. Identify the ways in which your department or unit is expected to contribute to the bottom line (making or saving money, improving productivity, and so on).

EXAMPLE
Internal auditor: to contain costs by audits to ensure adherence to company policies and financial reporting procedures.

Problem (and Opportunity) Identification and Solution

All jobs revolve around problem identification and solution.

At some level every job exists for four major reasons:

1. To identify potential problems and avoid them.
2. To identify and solve the typical problems that arise daily as an integral part of the job.
3. To identify and avoid or solve the major headaches that occur in every business on a regular basis.
4. To identify opportunities for contributing to the bottom line.

Develop examples of problem identification and opportunity initiatives, both small and large, for every job title you have held. The more you come up with the better, because they will add weight and reality to your resume and show that you think with employers' needs in mind, which will boost your resume's punch. All examples are valuable; those most relevant to your target job are most valuable. To help you bring out the information that will be most useful to you in your resume and in interview situations you can apply the PSRV process (you might know this as STAR—same process, different acronym).

- Identify a Problem.
- Envision your Solution, including strategy and tactics.
- Take note of the Result of your actions.
- Understand the Value of this to the company (usually in earnings or productivity enhancements).

Now describe four typical or notable problems with which you have been involved on your last (or current) job. Analyze each in terms of PSRV and include the following information:

Company
Employment dates
Location
Standing (division, public, private)
Industry sector
What does the company do?
What were you hired to do?
Title you report to
Your title
Department/unit
Leadership or membership of executive teams, project teams, or committees

Responsibilities/deliverables
Quotes, praise, and endorsements from management

Now you need to take what you have gathered and package it in a new resume that focuses on your target job. There are three standard types of resumes:

Chronological: The most frequently used format. Use it when your work history is stable and your professional growth is consistent within a profession. The chronological format is exactly what it sounds like: It follows your work history backward from the current job, listing companies, dates, and responsibilities.

Functional: A functional resume concentrates on the skills and responsibilities that you bring to the target job, and it de-emphasizes when, where, and how you got that experience. It is useful when changing careers, returning to the workplace or the profession after an absence, or when current responsibilities don't relate to the job you want. It is written with the most relevant experience to the job you're seeking placed first and de-emphasizes jobs, employment dates, and job titles by placing them toward the end.

Combination: A combination of chronological and functional resumes. Use this format if you have a steady work history with demonstrated growth and if you are continuing your progression within an industry or profession. It often starts with a brief performance profile, then lists job-specific skills relevant to the objective, and segues into a chronological format that lists how, where, and when these skills were acquired.

Check your resume against these six resume rules:

Rule One: *Always Have a Target Job Title.* Place a target job title at the top of your resume, right after your contact information. This will help your visibility in database searches and will give human eyes an immediate focus. Use the most common job title for your target job title because different employers use different titles for the same job, and you want to use a title specific enough to put you in the running. One way you can make a job title "specifically vague" is to add the term "specialist," (Computer Specialist, Administration Specialist) or the term "management" (Operations Management, Financial Management).

John-Taylor Thomas 5389 South Park Street Arlington, Virginia 22205
646.675.6785 *Marcompro@gmail.com*
Corporate Communications Management
Performance Profile
Strategic communications professional with . . .

Rule Two: *Always Have a Performance Profile or Career Summary.* Following your Target Job Title give a summary of your capabilities as they relate to the demands of the target job. You can title this section "Career Summary" or "Performance Profile."

I suggest you stay away from "Job Objective" or "Career Objective" for two very good reasons:

1. Your needs will not help your ranking in the database searches.
2. At this stage no recruiter has the slightest interest in what you want.

If you do need to state a specific Job Objective—for example if you are at the start of your career and have absolutely no experience—follow the advice in the following paragraphs for what you should put here.

I like the new term "Performance Profile" for this important section of your resume because it captures the essence of the professional you as it relates to your TJD. And until everyone and their dog starts using the phrase it subtly positions you as a "performer," and separates you from other applicants.

This should comprise no more than five lines of unbroken text, which can be followed by a second similar paragraph or short list of bullets. Your intent is to capture your ability to do the target job. For what to put in this section, refer back to your TJD exercise and rewrite the major priorities as your performance profile. This will help your resume's database visibility and will create immediate resonance when read by the recruiter. Always note any bilingual skills here since we live in a global economy.

CORPORATE COMMUNICATIONS MANAGEMENT

Performance Profile

Strategic communications professional with nine years' experience developing effective, high-impact, and cost-efficient media outreach plans for consumer, business, and policy audiences in media, entertainment, and technology practice areas. Experienced in managing corporate and crisis communications. Goal and deadline oriented with five years' experience managing internal and external communications team members. Adept at working with multiple teams and stakeholders.

If you are starting your career and have no relevant experience, that's okay—your chief competitors will be in the same boat. You can tilt the game in your favor by starting your objective with "The opportunity to" and then, referring back to your TJD exercise, rewrite the target job's major priorities as your job objective. This will make a big difference in your resume's productivity.

Rule Three: *Always Have a Core Competencies Section* if the list of your core skills creates a block of type longer than five lines (hard for tired eyes to penetrate). Depending on your skills, you may even consider a separate Technology Competencies section. This helps database visibility because it guarantees you are using the words employers use. You can repeat many of them again in the body of your resume in the context of each job for which you used them, further increasing your visibility. For the human eyes that see your resume, each word or phrase acts as the headline for a topic to be addressed at the interview and increases the odds of that interview happening.

You can also use keywords in these sections that won't fit in the body of your resume; this will result in better performance with the database spiders and bots. Here's an example of a Core Competencies section followed by a Technology Competencies section.

—Core Competencies—
Strategic Planning – Full-Cycle Project Management – Technical & Application Standards – IT Governance Process – Technical Vision & Leadership – Architecture Roadmaps – Technical Specifications & Project Design Best Practices – Teambuilding & Leadership – Standards & Process Development

TECHNOLOGY COMPETENCIES	
Hardware	Sun Servers; HP-UX; AIX; p-Series; Windows Server
Operating Systems	Sun Solaris; AIX; HP-UX; Linux; z/OS; OS/400
Languages	C / C++; COBOL; Visual Basic; Java; Unix; Korn Shell Scripting; Perl; Assembler; SQL*Plus; RPG
Databases	Oracle; DB2; SQL Server; Microsoft Access; Informix Visio; HP Service
Applications	MQSeries; Tuxedo; CICS; Microsoft Project, Word, Excel, Outlook, PowerPoint, Sharepoint, and Visio; HP Service Desk; Provision; Telelogic Doors; Change Synergy; Rational System Architect; Rational System Developer; Visual Studio; CA Clarity; LiveLink
Other	Cobit 4.1

Rule Four: *Never Put Salary on a Resume.* It does not belong there. If salary information is requested for a specific opening, put it in your cover letter and don't tie yourself to a specific figure; give a range. If you are earning too little or too much, you could rule yourself out before getting your foot in the door. For the same reason, do not mention your desired salary. For details on developing a realistic salary range, see Chapter 19, "Negotiating the Job Offer."

Rule Five: *Keep Your Resume Focused.* The standard for resume length used to be one page for every ten years of experience, and never more than two pages. However, as jobs have gotten more complex, they require more explanation. The length of your resume is less important than its relevance to the target job. If the first page of your resume is tightly focused and contains a target job title, performance profile, core competencies, and perhaps a career highlight section, you will have the reader's attention. If the first page makes the right argument, the rest of your resume will be read carefully. A longer resume also means that much more space for selling your skills with relevant keywords and more opportunities to establish your brand. You should still make every effort to maintain focus and an "if in doubt, cut it out" editing approach.

Rule Six: *Emphasize Your Achievements.* Make your achievements, problem-solving skills, and professional behavioral profile the focus of your resume.

Following you will see a resume content template. This is to show you all the component parts an ideal resume might contain. Use it to make sure your resume contains all the information necessary to maximize its effectiveness.

RESUME CONTENT TEMPLATE

Name

Mailing address (if appropriate) • Telephone & cell phone • E-mail address

---

Professional Target Job Title

This helps database visibility and gives focus to human eyes about what they will be reading.

Performance Profile / Career Summary

No more than five lines of unbroken text can be followed by a second similar paragraph or short list of bullets. Your intent is to capture your ability to do the target job. What goes in here? Take the most common requirements from your TJD exercise Step 3 and rewrite as your performance profile. This will help your resume's database visibility and will create immediate resonance with the recruiter. Always note bilingual skills, since we live in a global economy.

Core Competencies

Specific and detailed. This is a bulleted list of keywords that you identified in Step 3 of the TJD. It can be as long as you like. This list gives the reader an immediate focus ("Oh, she can talk about this and this") and each word can be repeated in the context of the job where it applied.

Technical Competencies

An optional category, depending on your needs.

Professional Experience

Company name and location

Job title and employment dates

(Repeat this format as many times as necessary.)

Education

This may come at the front of the resume If these credentials are critical, especially relevant to the Target Job Description, or highlight your greatest strength.

Licenses / Professional Accreditations

This may come at the front of the resume if these credentials are critical, especially relevant to the Target Job Description, or highlight your greatest strength.

Ongoing Professional Education

Professional Organization / Affiliations

Publications / Patents / Speaking Languages

Military Service

Extracurricular Interests

If they relate to the job

References Available on Request

Employers *assume* that your references are available. Only end your resume with this if there is no better use of the space. Never list references on your resume.

An excellent final test for your revamped resume is to first reread your TJD and then read your resume from front to back. If it clearly echoes your TJD, then you are likely to have a productive resume. If it doesn't, you'll readily be able to tell where your content needs fine-tuning.

KNOCK 'EM DEAD TIP

Once you are on that new job, keep a low profile for three to six months while you learn the culture of the company, get up to speed with all your job's deliverables, and determine who is in the inner and outer circles of your department and why. Acquire allies by your commitment to doing a good job and by your behavior with the group that will most support your career goals. Quietly identify the next step up the promotional ladder for you at this or any other company, and then start working toward it. Promotions don't come in reward for loyalty and tenure; they come as a result of capabilities.

Identify that next job, collect six to twelve job postings for it, and complete a TJD on the position. Once this is done, do a GAP analysis, identifying the gaps between what you can do and what the job requires. These gaps become your professional development program.

You might need more help with creating your resume, but we are restricted with page count and have to maintain focus. Resume writing is a major topic all on its own, so you can find more help:

- On the resume advice pages at *www.knockemdead.com*
- In the latest edition of *Knock 'em Dead Resumes*
- With a professionally written resume from the credentialed resume writers at *www.knockemdead.com*

Integrating a Professional Brand Into Your Resume

Your professional brand should be communicated throughout your resume, but especially with opening and closing brand statements. The first place you begin to establish a professional brand is with your Target Job Title (TJT), where you consciously decide on the job that best allows you to package your skill-sets and create a professional brand.

Target Job Title and Branding Statement

Your Target Job Title (TJT) and following brand statement gives the reader a focus for what this resume is about and what to expect. The brand statement is a short phrase following the TJT that defines what you will bring to this job. It says, in effect, "These are the benefits my presence on your payroll will bring to your team and your company." Put this statement after your TJT and you have a succinct brand statement or, if you prefer, value proposition.

Notice the following brand statements focus on the benefits brought to the job, but do not take up space identifying the specifics of how this was done.

Professional brand statements often start with an action verb: "Poised to," "Delivering," "Dedicated to," "Bringing," "Positioned to," "Constructing"

Pharmaceutical Sales Management Professional

Poised to outperform in pharmaceutical software sales repeating records of achievement with major pharmaceutical companies

Senior Operations / Plant Management Professional

Dedicated to continuous improvement ~ Lean Six Sigma ~ Start-up & turnaround operations ~ Mergers & change management ~ Process & productivity optimization ~ Logistics & supply chain

Bank Collections Management

Equipped to continue excellence in loss mitigation / collections / recovery management

Mechanical / Design / Structural Engineer

Delivering high volume of complex structural and design projects for global companies in Manufacturing / Construction / Power Generation

Account Management / Client Communications Manager

Reliably achieving performance improvement and compliance within Financial Services Industry

Marketing Communications

Consistently delivering successful strategic marketing, media relations, & special events

Administrative / Office Support Professional

Ready, willing, and competent: detail-oriented problem-solver, consistently forges effective working relationships with all publics

Senior Engineering Executive

Bringing sound technical skills, strong business acumen, and real management skill to technical projects and personnel in a fast-paced environment.

Edit for Consistent Brand Messaging

Review the body copy of your resume to see that the messaging supports the professional brand you have defined. Add action verbs to statements and further empower the clarity of your brand. Pay special attention that your branding is front and center in the following sections of your resume:

- Performance Profile
- Performance/Career Highlights
- Professional Experience

Closing Brand Statement

You will occasionally see a resume closed with a third party endorsement:

> *"I've never worked with a more ethical and conscientious auditor." Petra Tompkins, Controller.*

This endorsement can act as a closing brand statement: a bold statement clarifying the value proposition of the product (that's you, that's the brand). It's a great way to end a resume. If you have just the right kind of supportable quote use it, but suitable quotes aren't always as readily available as we would like.

However, you can achieve an equally powerful effect with a final comment of your own, a comment that relates to your professional brand and is written in the first person to make it conversational and different from the voice of the rest of your resume. Most resumes are written in the third person, allowing you to talk about yourself with the semblance of objectivity. Moving into the first person for a final comment at the resume's end acts both as an exclamation point and a matching "bookend" for the brand statement at the beginning. For example,

> *"I believe that leadership by example and conscientious performance management underlies my department's consistent customer satisfaction ratings."*

You Must Have a True and Truthful Brand

You have to be able to deliver on the brand you create. It must be based on your possession of the technical skills of your profession, plus those transferable skills and learned behaviors that you take with you from job to job and the core values that imprint your approach to professional life.

It is all too easy to over-promise, and while the employer might be initially attracted by the pizzazz of your resume, whether or not you live up to the value proposition decides the length and quality of the relationship.

If a box of cereal doesn't live up to the brand's hype you simply don't buy it again. But sell yourself into the wrong job with exaggerations or outright lies and it is likely to cost you that job, plus the possibility of collateral career damage that can follow you for years.

Your Cover Letter

Even when the majority of resumes end up in resume banks, there is still a need for cover letters.

1. When you identify hiring managers by name (advice on how to do this coming up) you can avoid the resume banks altogether and at these times a cover letter is a very effective marketing tool
2. Many resume banks and corporate websites have a place where you can upload or paste a cover letter along with your resume, and employers look more favorably on candidates who take the extra step.

In a professional world where communication skills are a must for any job, your cover letter introduces you, puts your resume in context, and demonstrates your writing skills. In fact from your first contact with an employer to the day you start that new job there are a number of opportunities to use letters/e-mails to advance your candidacy. There are different types of cover letters for different situations—follow-up letters after telephone and face-to-face interviews, and resurrection, negotiation, acceptance, rejection, and resignation letters to name a few. Again, it's a bigger topic than can be handled here, and for proper coverage you should get the latest edition of *Knock 'em Dead Cover Letters* with over 190 examples covering all these categories and more. Meanwhile here is a very effective form of cover letter.

The Executive Briefing

This is a type of cover letter I developed many years ago, which continues to get rave reviews from users year in and year out. You can use its striking format to clearly link skills to employer needs or to quickly customize an application when your resume doesn't tell the complete story.

An executive briefing enables you to customize your resume quickly to any specific job and is especially helpful on the other side of the desk—for overworked recruiters, hiring managers, HR professionals, or administrative assistants, who may not understand all the requirements of a specific job function. It is a powerful focusing tool for any harried resume reader. Furthermore, the executive briefing allows you to update and customize a more general resume with lightning speed without derailing the rest of your day's mission or missing out on an opportunity.

Like many great ideas, the executive briefing is beautiful in its simplicity. It is a cover letter on your standard letterhead/e-mail with the company's requirements for the job opening listed on the left side and your skills—matching point-by-point the company's needs—on the right. It looks like the example on the facing page.

An executive briefing sent with a resume provides a comprehensive picture of a thorough professional, plus a personalized, fast, and easy-to-read synopsis that details exactly how you can help with current needs. Using the executive briefing as a cover letter for your resume will greatly increase the chance that your query will be picked out of the pile in the Human Resources Department and hand-carried to the appropriate manager.

The use of an executive briefing is obviously not appropriate when the requirements of a specific job are unavailable.

KNOCK 'EM DEAD TIP

As you build a new resume, simultaneously organize a plan of attack for your job search. The change of pace will keep you alert and out of the psychiatric ward.

EXECUTIVE BRIEFING SAMPLE

Executive Briefing
From: A1coordpro@earthlink.net
Subject: Assessment Coordinator
Date: February 28, 2010 11:18:39 PM EST
To: jobs@pepsi.com

Dear HR Staff,
Your advertisement on the *New York Times* website on February 27, 2010, for an **Assessment Coordinator**, seems to perfectly match my background and experience. As the International Brand Coordinator for Kahlúa, I coordinated meetings, prepared presentations and materials, organized a major off-site conference, and supervised an assistant. I believe that I am an excellent candidate for this position, as I have illustrated below:

YOUR REQUIREMENTS	MY QUALIFICATIONS
Highly motivated, diplomatic	Successfully managed project teams involving different flexible, quality-driven professional business units. The defined end results were achieved on every project.
Exceptional organizational skills and attention to detail	Planned the development and launch of the Kahlúa Heritage Edition bottle series. My former manager enjoyed leaving the details and follow-through to me. Coverdale project management training.
College degree and six years of experience	B.A. from Vassar College (1998). 6+ years relevant business experience in productive, professional environments.
Computer literacy	Extensive knowledge of Windows and Macintosh applications.

I'm interested in this position because it fits well with my new career focus in the human resources field. Currently, I am enrolled in NYU's adult career planning and development certificate program and working at Lee Hecht Harrison.

My resume, pasted below and attached in MS Word, will provide more information on my strengths and career achievements. If after reviewing my material you believe that there is a match, please call me. Thank you for your consideration.

Sincere regards,

Jane Swift

CHAPTER 3

Networking and the Successful Job Search

THE MOST EFFECTIVE job search plan of attack reflects corporate recruitment practices and integrates networking into every aspect of the search.

Understand how employers approach recruitment and then build your job search plan of attack to leverage your awareness.

orporate recruitment planning is a complex and lengthy procedure, so the interviews you n this year were mostly planned and budgeted toward the end of last year. Hiring budgets ally open at the start of the new calendar year with hires staggered throughout the year. The rly part of every year usually has plenty of opportunity—so if you read this in November, ou should be diligent about working on your job search right through the holiday season! However, we live in a huge economy, so there are always jobs available if you know how to find them, at any time of year and in any economy. Even in the depths of the current recession there wasn't a month where we didn't see at least 4 million jobs posted on the Internet.

The costs of hiring and training a new employee runs into thousands and often tens of thousands of dollars, so the entire recruitment process is cost/productivity conscious (okay, so tell me something in business that isn't;-)). Consequently, the people involved in a specific search—the hiring manager and the assigned HR and recruitment professionals—all want the same thing: good hires, fast hires, and hires made as cheaply as possible. Understanding how and why things are done, and in what sequence they are done, will help you focus your efforts on the most effective job-finding techniques.

Put yourself on the other side of the desk for a few moments, with a job to fill. Naturally, you would start the recruitment process by asking yourself, your peers, and your staff who within the company could do this job; you want to hire from within because it's cheap, you are dealing with known quantities, and internal promotions are motivational. A promotion usually means another opening created by that promotion/transfer. Because not all positions can be filled with internal promotions, wherever you hear about a job being filled internally, it means another job has opened up somewhere within that company.

This is reinforced by the next step taken in the recruitment process. When a hiring manager can't make an internal hire, he or she will logically ask, "Whom do we know, and whom do my people know?" (Okay, I don't actually know anyone who says, "whom" like that, but it keeps the editors happy.;-))

This goes beyond the casual inquiry. The recruitment team will review all the resumes in the company's database and any promising candidates who have been interviewed in the past for similar position, one of the many reasons why follow-up is important. The manager will also create an internal job posting (often tied to cash incentives for employee referrals) and will actively consider people known to the recruitment team through their involvement in the professional community. This will include professional and alumni associations and related activities.

These are the first steps of any recruitment campaign because they are fast, cheap, and because employees who come to the company as referrals "known by us" in some way, are seen to be better hires, thought to get up to speed more quickly and stay with the company longer.

These approaches account for fully a third of all hires that are made externally. This is why networking is such an effective job search tactic and why you have to ask yourself three questions:

1. How do I get better connected to my local profession?
2. How do I get to know, and be known by, my peers?
3. How do I become more visible in my professional community?

The next step taken in the recruitment process—slightly more expensive and time-consuming—is to search outside the company for candidates who are unknown to the company. The first choice is usually the Internet, and as recruitment costs now become a serious consideration, it won't surprise you to learn that the company website is seen as a valuable recruiting tool.

The explanation for this should impact your job search plan: We don't pay fees when people come to our door on their own, so we naturally look first and more favorably on applicants coming to us through the company website. This is also especially important in depressed economic times, when companies will often decide that they don't need to advertise with the big job banks because plenty of well-qualified and smart people will find their way to them.

A recruiter's preference for specialty job sites also makes sense: she or he can expect more consistently suitable resumes, and fewer time wasters.

KNOCK 'EM DEAD TIP

The newspaper as a source for jobs is largely, but not completely, a thing of the past. Most newspapers post recruitment advertising on their websites. CareerBuilder, the biggest job site in the United States, counts 140 newspapers among its affiliates. But you can probably use the newspapers best when you look for news of promotions and significant new hires, many local papers have a column of news of the movers and shakers in the local business community, citing names, titles, and companies. Information you can use to approach potential hiring managers directly, and with a nice bridge-builder—you saw them in the paper.

The balance of hires—about 30 percent—come mainly from on-campus recruitment, job fairs (both virtual and local), temp-to-perm hires, and headhunters.

So, the breakdown of effective recruitment strategies is very roughly split into thirds: One-third of hires come from personal/professional networks and prior contacts, one-third from the company website and job boards, and one-third from the remaining sources. It is smart to organize your job search plan of attack along lines that reflect corporate recruitment practices.

The Jobs Are There. You Just Have to Find Them

Once on a radio talk show a caller said, "I've been unemployed for two years, and I don't know what to do." I asked her how many employers she had contacted. She said about 200, so I asked her how many possible employers there were for her, and she said about 3,000. I thought of Goofy, the clueless cartoon character, strolling along singing "Oh, the wurld owes me a living." The world doesn't owe Goofy or anyone else a living, you have to go out and make your life happen.

Around the same time I heard from the producer of a national talk show on which I had recently appeared. She told me she used the techniques we are about to discuss and got thirty interviews in three weeks! I can't promise you those kinds of results, but many people do get multiple job offers using these strategies and tactics.

The more things change the more they stay the same: Anyone stumbling through a job search ten years ago was probably relying exclusively on the Sunday help-wanted ads; that same person stumbling through a job search today is probably relying on the modern-day equivalent, the big Internet job sites. No job in the newspaper then meant no job anywhere; no job on the job board today means the same thing. Wrong. It is nothing short of arrogant to imagine that the only companies looking to hire are those who have posted jobs where you happen to be looking this week. Job hunters who search the longest are people who just use the easiest approaches: noodling around on the job sites and posting resumes on resume banks.

Your goal is to land the best possible job for your professional needs as quickly and efficiently as possible. The problem is you won't have a chance to land the best job unless you know about all of them.

If you go beyond cruising on the big three job sites for job postings and uploading your resume to a resume bank, your next step will be applications to the well-known companies—the Googles and Microsofts of the world. But 90 percent of the growth in American commerce is with small companies with fewer than 500 employees. Not only that, the majority of the growth from small companies comes from small companies who are also young companies, 3-10 years in existence being a period of often strong employee growth.

You need to organize a comprehensive job search strategy that will give you maximum penetration in your target area of search and allow you to track all the opportunities and potential employers you discover. I'm going to help you do this in three steps to create a strategy that reflects the employers' approach to recruitment.

Step 1

A third of hires come from employers' personal networks and prior contacts. In the coming pages you'll learn how to build and leverage the professional and personal networks that can give you the inside track on job openings.

Step 2

Another third of hires tend to come from Internet resources and cross-media advertising. Here I'll show you how to get the most out of job sites, resume banks, and how to find and approach companies directly. And in each instance *I'll show you how to double, triple, and even quadruple your chances of getting an interview.*

Step 3

The final third of hires come from job fairs; third-party employment suppliers such as temporary help companies, employment agencies, and headhunters; and what is quaintly referred to as "smoke-tacking"—that is, keeping an eye out for potential employers as you go about your business around town every day.

Social Networking

A typical career spans half a century, and in that time you can reasonably expect the good, the bad, and the downright ugly to occur in your professional life. It's during the rough times that you need people, and networking, with its focus on talking to friends and colleagues, offers a great job search technique that also eases the feelings of rejection everyone suffers at these times.

Job hunters generally like the idea of networking—it's a "warm" activity with diminished chance of rejection. But for most of us it doesn't work as effectively as it should because our networks lack depth and relevance. It is a tremendously valuable career survival tool, and not one to be treated with disrespect. An approach along the lines of, "Hey Harry, how are you? We haven't spoken in ten years but you know where I can get a job?" is likely to fail. Networking is a process of building relationships over time, and your networks' effectiveness will reflect the effort you put into their development.

Networking is also the most time-consuming job search strategy to implement, so we'll handle the ways to build and leverage broad and relevant networks first so you can change the pace by integrating your network development activities with other job search strategies.

Getting personal referrals to job openings with employers demands that you get connected to both your professional community and to the other networks available in your target geography.

KNOCK 'EM DEAD TIP

Effective networking practices can help you land that next job; becoming part of your professional community will increase your visibility and credibility, develop your skills, and forever enhance your employability and promotability. Through networking you will find mentors and become a mentor yourself, further enhancing your abilities and your connectivity. Networking can be so valuable that your career progresses up the ladder of success, you may want to become connected to your professional communities on a national level.

When you connect with your professional community, beyond the people you work with, you get to know all the most dedicated and best-connected professionals in your area, and in turn you become known by them. We all have a number of networks available to us, any of which may produce that all-important job offer. You should think in terms of *networks*, rather than a single *network*. When you connect with your professional community, beyond the people you work with, you get to know all the most dedicated and best-connected professionals in your area, and in turn you become known by them.

Professional Networks

- Other professionals in your field, including online social networking and professional associations.
- College alumni associations. A valuable and overlooked job search resource.
- Company alumni associations. Companies increasingly see the value in maintaining contact with ex-employees.
- Other job hunters. Professionals seeking a position in the same profession or industry can be valuable resources; they don't have to be looking for the same type of job as you.
- Managers, past and present, can be useful to you throughout your job search.
- Coworkers. This includes professional colleagues, past and present.

Community Networks

- Family and relatives. This includes your spouse's family and relatives.
- Friends. This includes neighbors and casual acquaintances and those you know through your personal interests.
- Service industry acquaintances. This includes your banker, lawyer, insurance agent, realtor, doctor, dentist, hairdresser, and the like.
- Social, civic, and spiritual associations. This would include churches and temples, business groups, Little League, and so on.
- Hobbies. This includes everything from chess club to dance class. It's any activity you enjoy, which can involve a loosely knit group of people with the shared enthusiasm.

Smart Networking: Strategies and Tactics

There are more network options than you can cultivate, so you'll need to put all these networks through your personal filters to judge which are most relevant to you. Your goal should be to integrate networking into your life so it is less of a chore and more a part of the joy of living.

While networking can and does bear fruit right away, your harvest will get richer as time passes and you tend your networking contacts. Because change is constant in a career, becoming connected to your profession should be an ongoing career management initiative, not just a job search tactic.

Professional Associations

One of the best things you can do for this job search and your long-term career success is to become an active member of a professional association or two. You'll get job leads and an awesome network immediately, and going forward they provide great vehicles for increasing your credibility and visibility in the profession. In fact, if you have heard disgruntled job hunters mutter, "It's not what you know, it's who you know," it probably means they don't understand networking and are not members of a professional association.

Associations have monthly meetings in most major metro areas, plus regional and national get-togethers every year. The local meetings are of immediate interest, and, unless you work on a national level, membership in the local or state chapters of a national association will be quite adequate for your needs—and cheaper, too. When you join a local chapter of a recognized national association and attend the local meetings, you get to know and be known by the most committed and best-connected people in your profession in your target marketplace. Your membership will help you stay attuned to what is going on in your profession, as associations offer ongoing training that make you a more knowledgeable and therefore a more desirable employee. Of course almost everything that is happening locally is also happening in the association's online groups.

The professional association is a new "old boy/old girl" network for the modern world. Your membership becomes a link to millions of colleagues, most of whom will gladly talk to you, based on your mutual connectivity through the association.

All industries and professions have multiple associations, any of which could be valuable depending on your needs. For example, if you are in retail, you could join any of some thirty national associations and fifty state associations. Together these associations represent employees of over 1.5 million retail organizations, which in turn provide employment for over 14 million people. All professions offer similarly impressive networking potential.

If you fit the profile of a special interest or minority group you will find professional associations that cater to another dimension of the professional you. These include—but are by no means restricted to—associations for African Americans, Latinos, Asian Americans, professionals with disabilities, and women. If you can find a niche association that's a fit, join it as well: It represents an even more finely tuned network that offers all the benefits already mentioned for a professional association, plus companies actively recruit identifiable minorities and advertise on association sites.

A good place to start online is the Wikipedia professional associations page. In your local library check out the *Encyclopedia of Associations* (published by Bowker). Alternatively, you can try a Google search for relevant keywords. For example, a search for "legal association" will generate listings of associations for the legal profession. If you belong to any identifiable minority, use that in your searches as well. For example, "Asian legal association" will generate a listing of local associations specifically for Asian professionals working in the legal field.

The Value of Local Involvement

It is easier to get to know people than you might think. All professional association members are there, at least in part, to advance their careers through networking. Once you have the lay of the land, volunteer for one of the many committees that keep associations running. It's the best way to meet people and expand your sphere of influence, as you can reach out to others while you engage in your volunteer association activities. Committee involvement doesn't take much time because they invariably employ the "many hands make light work" approach, and are structured to function with the help of full-time professionals like you who have mortgages to pay and families to support.

When you join an association, you'll benefit greatly from attending the meetings, because this is where you will meet other professionals in your field. But don't just attend the meetings;

get involved. Associations are largely volunteer organizations and always need someone to set out chairs or hand out paperwork and nametags. The task itself doesn't matter, but your visible willingness to be an active participant most certainly does and will get you on first-name terms with people you would probably never otherwise meet. *These connections can impact success for beyond this job search.*

Given the nature of association membership, you don't have to go straight from introductions to asking for leads on jobs. In fact, it can be productive to have initial conversations where you do not ask for leads or help in your job search, but where you make a contribution to the group; this is always preferable because others are more likely to help you when they see you making an effort toward the common good.

There is a good argument that, from a networking point of view, the bigger the committee the better. Membership and program committees are among the best to join. However, involvement in any committee will serve your needs, because being on one will enable you to reach out to those on other committees. If you join the membership committee, you can initiate contact with just about anyone in your professional world: "Hi, Bill Parsons? I'm Becky Lemon with the conference committee of the local association. I'd like to invite you to a meeting we are having next week on . . . ."

Don't join committees for which you lack the experience to be a productive member, unless you make it clear that the reason you want to become a part of that team is for professional development—if this is the case, expect to become the designated water carrier, at least initially. If you become active in an association, the people with whom you come in contact will identify you as a team player. This perception can be instrumental in landing that new job and surging ahead in your career.

Databases and Directories

Access to the association database/directory provides you with a superb networking resource for telephone and e-mail networking campaigns. You can feel comfortable calling any other member on the phone and introducing yourself: "Hi, Brenda Massie? My name is Martin Yate. We haven't spoken before, but we are both members of the Teachers Federation. I need some advice. Can you spare a minute?"

Your mutual membership, and the commitment to your profession that it demonstrates, will guarantee you a few moments of anyone's time, a courtesy you should always return.

You can also use the database to generate personal introductions for jobs you have heard about elsewhere. For example, you might have found an interesting job posting on a company website, with the request that you upload your resume. This is where your networking can pay big dividends. Upload your resume as requested, then return to your membership directory and find people who work for that company. A judicious call or two will frequently get you a personal referral and some inside information on the opening, and you have just *doubled your chances of landing that interview.* Typically the titles most likely to be responsible for hiring someone like you will be those titles one to three levels above yours, so finding the names that go with these titles enables you to make direct approaches.

Once you have an interview scheduled, these and other contacts can help you prepare for the interview with insider knowledge about the company, the department, and the hiring manager.

Newsletters

Professional associations all have online newsletters, and many have a jobs section that appears on their website and is linked to the newsletter. Companies post job openings with associations because they know the responses will be qualified. For this reason, you will often see job postings that don't appear anywhere else. In down economic times a savvy recruiter will use an association website to skim the cream of available talent, screening out the less committed.

You will also notice that association members write all the articles in the newsletters. As everyone likes to have their literary efforts appreciated, telling a member you have read an article that he or she has written gives you a great introduction to a networking call or letter.

Active association membership puts you on the radar of all the best-qualified and connected professionals in your area. You can also list it at the end of your resume under a "Professional Affiliations" heading. This is guaranteed to get a second glance, as it signifies professional commitment. Employers and headhunters will sometimes use words like "association," "club," and "society" in their keyword searches, so association membership will also help get your resume pulled up from the databases for investigation by human eyes.

Social Networking

Social networking revolves around social and/or professionally oriented online networks that help you reach out to people you know, once knew, or would like to know. You can leverage your professional reach through connecting with others in your field, as well as through people with whom you share common experiences or interests. When you search for contacts by keyword, try job titles, company name, industries, and geographic location, for starters.

Here's an example: A soldier who was cycling out of the military sought my help in her search for a new civilian career. First, to find other individuals with a similar background, I plugged in the word "army" at *www.linkedin.com*, perhaps the premier professional online networking site. I got more than 4,000 profiles of people (today, three years later you get 269,000) who shared her military experience. We then tried a search using the phrase "information technology" (for her desired career change) and got 39,000 profiles (today it is well over one million). Both these potential networks would have relevance to her job search, but it got even better when we combined both the keywords: "information technology and army." This pulled up 908 profiles (today over 26,000) of people who shared her life experience and who had, in about half the hits, already made the transition into her desired profession. Such a degree of initial connectivity ensured she could hold helpful conversations with an enormous number of people, each of whom is relevant to her job search.

Social networking sites have become catnip for corporate recruiters and headhunters, and this should shape the information you make available about yourself. For the professional in a job search this will start with your resume and possibly end the same way, simply cutting and pasting your resume into your official profile. You make yourself visible but because this is a social networking site and not a resume bank you do it without an "I'm for sale" sign, which is useful when you are employed and looking for a new position.

If you don't use your resume word for word as your profile take care that the same keywords appear. Just as you will search for others on the site using keywords, members who are hiring managers, HR pros, or headhunters will be searching for you through the site's search engine using keywords.

KNOCK 'EM DEAD TIP

There are just too many social networks to list, and the more these sites proliferate, the more specialized they become. It is probably a good idea to have a presence on two of the biggest, linkedin.com and facebook.com. Beyond this, go to *www.wikipedia.org* and search for "social networks" for a complete listing. You'll find networking sites by special interests, countries, sex, race, and more.

Many sites allow you to identify topics that you would like to receive feedback on and discuss with others. For example: advice and information on hiring people, looking for job or business opportunities, and partnering opportunities in your area of expertise. The more areas of interest you check, the more options other people will have to contact you. You also have a choice of whether or not to allow direct contact.

Check for Digital Dirt

For those who grew up through their less responsible years with social networking, you need to go back and clean up your digital dirt. As I write this 2011 edition of *Knock 'em Dead*, I have just returned from an appearance at a major convention for college career services and corporate campus recruiters. It was noted at the conference that upwards of 40 percent of recruiters are using publicly available online data about short-list candidates as a screening tool. Twenty-five percent said they would reject a candidate based on this information. This means we all have to police the image we have online, so those once-amusing pictures of you projectile vomiting, or worse, at a frat party need to be deleted.

Online networking can get you useful introductions to people throughout the country and the world—people who might know of jobs at their own companies or who can introduce you to people at companies that have openings. This new application of technology enables you to reach out into an endless horizon of relevant networking contacts.

It works quite simply: You join a social networking site and network without the benefit of personal contacts, but if you in turn invite a selection of your own trusted contacts to connect with you, your resulting connectivity to others grows exponentially. You also expand your network by joining the countless discussion groups that exist on all social networking sites and then linking up with other members of those groups.

For employers and recruiters, networking sites constitute a reliable pathway to recruit qualified candidates, while for a job hunter they constitute a reliable pathway to jobs through the people connected to them. You can search a site's database by zip code, job title, company, or any keywords of your choice. The database will pull up the profiles of people who match your requirements and allow you to initiate contact directly, through your common membership in groups, or through the chain of people who connect you.

Social Networks are Local and Global

The Internet is global, so all sites have a worldwide reach. Facebook, for example, stretches around the Earth and consequently is a major destination for recruiters; in fact, Facebook has overtaken Google as the #1 site.

KNOCK 'EM DEAD TIP

You will find social networking sites especially important when you are involved with or are planning a career transition. If you know you are cycling out of one profession and into another, you can use social networking sites to build a network of people who do the target job in your chosen profession and, whenever possible, people who have made a similar transition. If you are involved in a job search that involves career change, go to *www.knockemdead.com* and read the "Stepping Stones" article.

Professionally focused sites such as Ryze claim members in hundreds of countries. Spoke attracts people in sales worldwide, and *www.linkedin.com* has half its members in the United States and the other half scattered around the globe. In a global economy, people with language skills have a special edge, so sites that encourage bilingual professionals can help you leverage those language skills with any global company searching for multicultural awareness in its employees.

Most social networking sites also offer an array of tools for your professional networking activities:

- Job postings from employers and headhunters
- Reminders of when to follow up with a call or e-mail to nurture your relationships
- Message boards and forums for common-interest groups, such as women in business and profession-specific groups for job hunters
- Links to job boards
- Offline social events to meet and mingle in person

A Very Smart Networking Idea

Intelligent networking means you look to form relationships with people in your profession and industry at many levels. Almost anyone in your industry or geography can be useful regardless of title or experience, but the people of most interest you find will likely fall into these categories:

1. Those who are one to three title levels above you, who might hire you, now or in the future. With this group you can initiate contact by sending an e-mail to introduce yourself, and ask him/her to look at your profile. If this proceeds to a conversation and interviews, fine; if not, you can ask your contact to connect you to others.
2. Those at or below your level but who have common experience or interests.
3. Those who work in the same profession or industry but in other areas. You can interact with these last two groups in the same way: It's best to build a relationship by finding common ground. You can initiate relationships by asking for advice, and many people will give you a few minutes of their time. You will develop the best relationships by reaching out to others with help and advice, because when you do good things, forging a relationship with you becomes important to the other person. It is easy to do this by taking an active part in the special interest groups and also searching the social sites for people in your profession who are actively looking for jobs.

The challenge then becomes how to make a gesture that will encourage a relationship that shares introductions and job leads. The answer is logical and painless: Use the job leads you hear about that are inappropriate for your own use.

It's a not-always-so-funny thing about job search: When you are fresh out of school no one is hiring entry-level workers; they all want you to call back in five years. Five years later when you are once again looking for a job, they now only want someone fresh out of school or with ten years' experience.

In your job search activities you are constantly coming across positions that aren't right for you but that could be just what someone else is aching to hear about. Offer these leads to others as part of your introduction. Here's how it can work: Sometimes you have to send an e-mail stating why you want to make contact, and sometimes you can communicate immediately—it depends on a number of variables. In the first instance you send an e-mail simply stating you have a job lead that he or she might find interesting. This is a nice gesture and will get you lots of introductions.

In the second instance, where you are actually in direct e-mail communication, state your business: "I am involved in a strategic career move right now, and I have come across a job that isn't right for me but that could be perfect for you. If you'd like to talk, let's exchange telephone numbers. I'll be happy to pass the lead on, and perhaps you have heard about something that would suit me . . . I am cycling out of the army and into the private sector and have been looking for jobs in IT in the Southeast. . . ."

KNOCK 'EM DEAD TIP

When networking, never talk about what you want in that ideal next job. It reduces the odds of someone telling you about an opening. Instead, talk about what you can do.

Now you have a use for all those positions that aren't quite right for you. Build your own database of the jobs that are not suitable for you and pass them on to all those people above and below you in your profession who will make perfectly symbiotic networking partners. This is obviously a good tactic for your job search support group.

How Social Networks Expand Your Approach Options

With the job opportunities that do seem appropriate for you, you are usually faced with uploading your resume into a corporate or headhunter database; but now, along with your professional association memberships, your social networks give you additional approaches. Somewhere on one of your social networking sites there are people who work at that company now or did in the past. Search for them, using the company name in your keyword search, then look for job titles one, two, and three levels above your own (these are the people most likely to be able to hire you).

For people you find at or below your level in the corporate hierarchy, explain that you have heard about an opening at the company and hope to get some inside information before you apply. If you make time to visit the company website before any conversation, you will be well informed and make a good impression when you talk.

The more you reach out, the better your reputation becomes and the more others will reach out to you. However, a word of caution: Social networking is a great tool, but a single tool nevertheless; it is most effective when you integrate it, as I am going to show you, into all your other job search strategies.

Alumni Associations

Almost every school, from Acme Welding to Wharton, has an alumni association and being a member of your alma mater's alumni association can have a pivotal role in your professional life. Historically, alumni associations have existed primarily to raise money from alumni for the school, but in these changing times, they increasingly see career outreach as a cost-efficient way to stay in touch with alumni.

If you are an alumni member, you have access to the alumni association membership database, which puts you in touch with the other graduates. People like to extend their help to those with whom they share a college experience.

KNOCK 'EM DEAD TIP

The site *www.alumni.net* will lead you to company, university, high school, and other alumni associations all over the world.

Additionally, volunteer for some activities that will ease you into collegial relationships with people on every rung of the corporate ladder—people who are in a position to boost your career.

Alumni associations all have online newsletters, and many include information about job openings. An increasing number even have semi-formalized job-hunting networks in which alumni are encouraged to pass on their companies' employment needs. As a member of an alumni association, you can also cultivate an informal relationship with the school's career services department. Even when your school days are in the misty past, don't forget these people and the valuable resource they represent.

Build an Alumni Database

Your alumni association is a valuable network waiting for you to become involved and leverage its contacts intelligently. Whenever you have uploaded your resume as a result of a job posting, cross-check your alumni database first for members who hold a job title one to three title levels above your own and second for those at or below your level. Using the same approach we discussed using with professional association contacts you can again double your chances of that job posting turning into an interview by getting an introduction or referral from an alumni.

If you don't know the URL of your alma mater, go to *www.utexas.edu/world/univ/*. For community college URLs you'll find an excellent resource at *www.mcli.dist.maricopa.edu/cc/*. Another site with job search relevance is *www.Classmates.com*.

Company Alumni Associations

In recent years larger, more widely dispersed companies have seen increased value in maintaining contact with ex-employees, since these people provide a source for future hires and leads on future hires. Corporate HR departments are doing this through online corporate alumni associations. Go to *www.job-hunt.org* for over 250 corporate alumni associations.

Your Past Managers and Other References as a Networking Resource

It is a major mistake not to speak to your references at all or only at the end of your search when a job offer is imminent. While as a rule, we are confident that our references will speak well of us, the fact is that some might bear us no good will. It isn't wise to discover this by trial and error, as one potential offer after another bites the dust. If these are people you know well and who you believe will speak well of you, why not confirm it and leverage that goodwill throughout your job search?

KNOCK 'EM DEAD TIP

For a discussion of how to handle your references when you are under serious consideration for a position, or have received and accepted an offer based on successful reference checks, see Chapter 19, "Negotiating the Job Offer."

At the very start of your job search you should identify as many potential references as possible. The more options, the better odds of coming up with excellent references. There are other reasons: References can represent great networking resources, everyone you ask to be a reference for you will be flattered, and they are prime candidates to offer introductions for jobs at their current company.

At the beginning of your job search, excellent references, though important, are simply an added bonus. Your real agenda is to use these contacts as another tactic within your overall networking strategy.

The process is simplicity itself, starting with an introduction: "Bob, this is __________. We worked together at Citibank between 2002 and 2006. How's it going?" It is appropriate here to catch up on gossip and the like. Then broach the subject of your call.

"John, I wanted to ask your advice." (Everyone loves to give their opinion.) "We've had some cutbacks at Fly-By-Night Finance, as you probably heard," or "The last five years at Bank of Crooks and Criminals International have been great, and the __________ project we are just winding down has been a fascinating job. Nevertheless, I have decided that this would be a perfect time for a strategic career move to capitalize on my experience." Then, "John, I realize how important references can be, and I was wondering if you would have any reservations about my using you as one?" It's better to find out now if John doesn't want to be a reference, rather than down the line when it could blow a job offer. The response will usually be positive, so you can then move to the next step.

KNOCK 'EM DEAD TIP

Of course, when employed do not use current managers and coworkers as references. It could cost you a job. If you have never worked anywhere else, you can track down people who have already left your current employer. If you explain your situation, they may act as references for you.

With a little research, you can identify any suitable jobs with the company at which this reference works, putting you in a prime position to ask for a referral or introduction.

"Thanks, John, I hoped you would say that. Let me update you about what I have been doing recently and tell you about the type of job I'm after." Give a capsule description of what you've done since you worked together and specifically what you can do. Remember that talking about what you want in a dream job only reduces your chances of receiving leads. You might also ask John if he would take a look at your resume for you. There are two reasons for this.

1. It gets your resume in his hands so he can pass it on to others.
2. It gives you a reason to follow up with John in two or three weeks, when you can ask for job leads again.

Notice these reasons do not include getting feedback on your resume, although you will often get it. Why don't I cite this as a reason? Opinions about resumes are like headaches: We all have them and if you listen to every suggestion for changing your resume you will just spin in circles. If you did your TJD work (see Chapter 2) and if you followed the resume writing directions here and in *Knock 'em Dead Resumes*, then you've checked the story your resume tells against your TJD and it has all the component parts and the keywords and the prioritization and emphasis that will make it as powerful as your experience will allow. So while you already have objective benchmarks against which to judge it, this doesn't mean you shouldn't listen to suggestions and thank the person who gives them—just that every breeze shouldn't sway you in a new direction.

Show courtesy by following your call with a "thank you" e-mail.

With the scene set in this manner, you can network with each of these potential references every month or two, either for input on a particular opportunity or to ask for other intelligence relevant to your search. This might be leads or information about a specific company; for example, "Tina, do you know anyone who went to work at __________?"

Personal Networks

Personal networking should mean more than just annoying the heck out of your friends until they stop taking your calls. If you are like most people, your friends and acquaintances would like to help, but as these personal networks are rarely that large, they are easily exhausted. Here's a new way to think about personal networks.

First, let's reiterate what we said above about their range:

- **Family, relatives, and friends.** This includes your spouse's family and relatives and their networks.
- **Service industry acquaintances.** Electricians, plumbers, carpenters, accountants, lawyers, hairdressers—anyone whose services you employ is a potential networking resource.
- **Hobby and special interest networks.** This includes anyone with whom you share a common interest: fellow sports-team members, parents involved in Little League, the girls at the knitting shop, or the gang at the gym.
- **Religious and community groups.** This includes all the networks that become available to you when you reach out to help others.

We meet these people at conventions; association meetings; class reunions; fundraisers; continuing-education classes; and at community, religious, fraternal, and sporting events. We are also likely to meet their friends and the friends of their friends.

While networking should become an integral part of your life, it will always move into higher gear when strategic career moves are on your front burner. There are a wide variety of personal and community-based networks available to you, depending on your interests and your willingness to become an active member of your local community.

Some are personal: family, friends, and service industry acquaintances. These tend to be the people you see on a regular basis.

Others are more formal and socially oriented: such as religious, community, local business, and volunteer groups. Some of these are professional in nature but not restricted to a specific profession (Kiwanis, et al.), while others are community-based groups that focus on a common interest (Big Brother, Big Sister). You don't necessarily know the people in these groups, but you do have a potential common bond based on community involvement.

You can find out about these groups in your local newspapers, at the library, through a local school or church, or by conducting an Internet search.

Family and Friends, Good News/Bad News

The good news is that the people who know you best, your family and friends, will really try to help you. The bad news is that since most of them may have known you since you were a snot-nosed brat, you have been categorized, stereotyped, and pigeonholed. They might not really know—or might incorrectly guess—the nature of your career. Odds are they don't know what you are capable of doing or what you want to do. Case in point: After twelve books and millions of copies sold, my immediate family is still genuinely surprised that I know to come in from the rain.

It is easy to squander this potentially valuable resource by tapping into it too soon, too often, and before you have thought through how you can best help your extended family help you.

These people aren't stupid, but unlike the contacts you make in your professional networks, they probably don't have a full grasp of what you do for a living. On the other hand, they are highly motivated to help you. Many job hunters make the mistake of confusing the members of this network by giving too much information about their professional life. With the right guidance, your immediate circle will cast a wide net and come up with leads for you, even if they have nothing to do with the professional world.

Here are the steps to help your loved ones help you:

1. Think carefully about what you do for a living and put it in a one- or two-sentence description that even Aunt Aggie can grasp: "I am a computer programmer; I write the instructions that help computers run."
2. Think carefully about the job you want, the kind of company you will work for, and the kind of people you need to talk to. Condense it into a one- or two-sentence explanation: "I'm looking for a job with another computer company. It would be great if you or your friends know anyone I could talk to who works with computers." Keep it real simple.

3. Give them the information you need to get in touch with these people: "I am looking for the names, e-mail addresses, and telephone numbers of anyone in these areas" (but don't confuse Aunty Aggie with e-mail talk). "I'm not looking for someone to hire me; I'm looking for people in my field with whom I can network."

This process of breaking your networking needs into *just three* simple statements gives your immediate circle something they can really work with. You can do this with them one on one, or you can get everyone together for a barbecue and get the new program moving in one fell swoop.

Civic, Social, Volunteer, Religious, and Special-Interest Networking Groups

It's good to be involved in your local community, both for your own emotional health and for the health of your community. Your involvement will provide you with a richer personal life, as well as a wide array of networking opportunities. You will find that effective networking with these groups is a little more time-consuming than with professional groups; after all, you have no prior professional relationships, and they don't have a familial obligation to help you out.

At the same time, you can't possibly join all the groups your community has to offer, so you will have to make some decisions about what is practical and which activities are going to be valuable to you in and of themselves; if the activity is personally fulfilling, you are more likely to stick with it over time and reap the personal fulfillment and networking rewards that come from your involvement. Most people have time for much more than three ongoing social activities. These might comprise:

Religious/community/volunteer groups. They get you involved with people who wish to make a difference in their lives by reaching out to others. Participation in spiritual and volunteer communities helps us achieve a sense of meaning and balance in our lives, and such groups are especially helpful in the emotionally troubled times of job and career change.

A hobby or special interest group. This could be a book club, a women's/men's group, a dance class, a jogging group, or any of the vast number of community-based special-interest groups. It doesn't matter, so long as the activity is one that energizes the inner you by taking you away from the worries of your professional world. The people you meet will all have professional careers and a common bond based on your shared interests.

A business, professional, or civic group. All communities have networks of professionals joined together in formal groups: Rotarians, Chamber of Commerce, Kiwanis, and many more. These community-based associations, societies, and clubs are professionally oriented in membership, but they aren't focused on one profession; they straddle the line between your professional and community-based networking activities. These groups were conceived as networking tools, and they give you another angle of attack for your job search and perhaps improve your social life.

In your local community networking your need for job leads should take a back seat to being involved as a productive member. Soon enough you'll learn what people do for a living, while they learn about you both as a professional and as a human being. As opportunities arise you can talk about your job search needs.

Your Job Search Network

You will sometimes feel that companies are looking for everyone but you. This can get depressing at times, so you need to be aware of the emotion and manage it. One way is to join or create a support group and job search network with people in the same situation, whether these are online or local community-based networks.

A number of national organizations and many communities support job search networks through religious or other social organizations. Members meet, usually on a weekly basis, to exchange ideas and job leads and, just as important, to share and laugh with others in transition.

You can find groups in your area online at *www.careerjournal.com*, *www.jobbankinfo.org*, or *www.rileyguide.com*. Your local state employment office also maintains lists of job search support groups.

Gathering Leads and Referrals from Networking Conversations

You never know who you are going to meet at the grocery store, coffee shop, hairdresser, or gym. For networking in any of these situations to be maximally effective, you need a "networking mindset" that you can apply as readily in person as you can over the telephone when you have copious notes in front of you and all the time in the world to prepare.

A "networking mindset" means you are always prepared to show an interest in others and speak to them in a friendly way, so that you won't let casual opportunities for expanding your networks slip by. With a networking mindset, you will be surprised at the range of useful people you will meet. Even if they know nothing about your profession, they might know someone involved in the same field as you. Everyone you meet has the potential to know someone who can be useful to your job search.

You can network with people you meet at conventions, association meetings, class reunions, fundraisers, the gym, the coffee shop, continuing-education classes, or at community, social, spiritual, and sporting events. You can talk to them over the telephone, by letter, or via e-mail, online chat, or message posting. While the information-gathering aspects of these conversations will remain fairly constant regardless of the communication medium, there are one or two unique considerations about networking in person.

In-Person Networking

As you never know when you are going to make useful contacts, always maintain a well-put-together appearance in your local community. That doesn't mean that you always have to be dressed for a job interview, just that you should give consideration to your appearance.

And always pick up business cards before leaving the house. Go to Google and type in "create business cards," and you will find suppliers and software for less than $20. When you attend social and professional events, keep those business cards handy. However, for networking in your community, leave your resume at home: Thrusting one at every new acquaintance will come across as overanxious.

You have to make the effort to reach out to others, and that means working out how you will introduce yourself: At the tennis class, "Hello, I'd like to introduce myself. My name is Mark Germino. I just started playing tennis. How about you?" Always try to end with a question that encourages your contact to introduce and talk about himself; it doesn't really matter what the question is. Once there has been a conversational exchange, you can begin to move forward with your networking agenda perhaps by saying what you do. Say, "I'm in accounting, how about you?" rather than plunging into a detailed description of your situation.

Keep It Short

Even though gatherings of associations, clubs, and societies provide excellent networking opportunities, they are not scheduled specifically for that activity. Try to keep your initial in-person networking conversations to less than five minutes. You have an obligation not to be known as needy or a bore. You can end a conversation gracefully with an offer of your business card and should recognize that a request for your card is a signal for you both to move on. If someone you meet isn't carrying a card, have him or her write a name and contact information on the back of one of yours, and always try to get a telephone number and an e-mail address.

Whenever you meet someone in person, send an e-mail to thank him or her for any helpful information you may have gathered from the conversation. It also serves to keep you on that person's radar.

The Secrets of Successful Networking Conversations

Your networks grow in proportion to the energy you put into them, expressed by the number of networking opportunities you create and how intelligently your networking conversations are structured. Networking opportunities can be created on the phone or through e-mail, and for professional networking these communication mediums are far more productive for all concerned, but with local networking, face time will always generate the best results.

Whatever your communication medium, your agenda remains the same. Following are ideas for the content of your networking conversations. Obviously you will have to add the conversational context and take the essence of my words and make them your own. Show interest in your contacts first and then move on with your agenda.

The conversation happens in four stages, none of which should be rushed:

Introduction

Recall the last memorable interaction you had with your contact or mention someone you both know. Ask what is happening in your contact's personal and professional life. Listen to what is said and respond appropriately.

Information Gathering

Prepare a statement that allows you to encapsulate your situation succinctly: "Malcolm, I just got laid off because of the downturn" or "We have a baby on the way, and XYZ is a company where there just isn't room for me to grow professionally" or "My job just got sent to Mumbai, India, so I guess it's time for me to make a move."

Statement of Your Situation

When common professional ground exists through an association or other social network, you can assume that your listener will be well disposed toward you. You can repay this goodwill by showing respect for that person's time and politely cutting to the chase. You could begin, "Brenda, I have been an accountant with Anderson for the last four years. I work in the small business area, and I'm looking to make a change." Rather than rambling, in less than ten seconds you have courteously provided a focus.

Incidentally, it is at this point in the conversation that you have to be careful to avoid a common gaffe. Don't say something like, "My ideal job would be . . ." or "The next step I'd like to take is . . . ."

By describing an ideal job or your desired next step up the professional ladder, you make things more difficult for the listener, who thinks, "This gal/guy is looking for something very specific, and any introductions I can make will probably be a waste of everyone's time." It is more productive to talk in terms of what you do day-to-day, or even just tell the contact in general terms the profession in which you work ("I'm an accountant") and that you are looking for a new opportunity. If you handle yourself in a pleasant and professional manner, most people will try to be helpful.

Note that I'm assuming you are talking to professional colleagues and seeking leads on job openings, rather than talking to the managers, directors, vice presidents, and presidents who can make those hiring decisions. The conversations with anyone who has the potential to hire you are different because you are then making a marketing presentation, which we'll handle in a few pages.

Tell your contacts in general terms what you do, *not* what you want, because this just reduces your chances of getting leads.

Ask for Assistance

You can ask for general guidance about your tactics: "If you were in my situation, Charlie, what would you do?" You can ask if he or she has heard about local companies hiring. These are good questions, and they typically comprise the content of 99 percent of all networking questions, *but you can achieve much more with the right sequence of questions.*

Great Networking Questions

We are now going to work through a sequence of networking questions that will lead you to jobs you would otherwise never hear about; these are the same question sequences asked everyday by headhunters the world over, retooled to fulfill your needs.

These questions follow a logical sequence, but that order might not suit your needs, so as you examine them, figure out what you would ask if you had time for only one question, then if you had time for only two, and so on. The result will be a comfortably prioritized set of questions.

Each question you ask should be specific, so avoid time-wasting questions like "How's business these days?" When you're satisfied with your list of questions, have a copy on your desktop, another by your phone (never at work), and a third that will go in your wallet or purse.

General Questions

You can ask if there are openings in the department or at the company and with whom you should speak about them. *Don't* ask, "Can you or your company hire me?" *Do* ask:

- "What needs does your company have at present?"
- "Who in the company is most likely to need someone with my background?"
- "Who else in the company might need someone with my background?"
- "Is the company/department planning any expansion or new projects that might create an opening?"
- "When do you anticipate a change in company manpower needs?"
- "Does your company have any other divisions or subsidiaries? Where are they?"
- "I'd appreciate any e-mail addresses or telephone numbers of headhunters you hear from."

Profession-Specific Questions

You might wish to add some profession-specific questions. For instance, people in Information Technology might find questions about operating systems, communication protocols, programs, and languages useful. In this instance, after receiving an answer, add a similarly focused follow-up question: "Thanks, Gail. Who else do you know who uses these configurations?" This would lead you to other companies likely to have similar needs. Be sure any professional-specific question you ask is geared toward identifying names, titles, and companies in your target job career.

Leads at Other Companies

When you are sure that no job openings exist within a particular department or company, move on to gathering leads in other companies.

KNOCK 'EM DEAD TIP

Even when an offer of introduction is made—"Let me speak to Charlene Howarth for you," don't rely on your contact to get you into that company. If the door hasn't opened in a few days, it might not. You should execute your own plan of attack, seeking other personal introductions within the company from your networking resources and making direct application by telephone, e-mail, and snail-mail resume submissions.

You can ask, "Do you know of anyone at other banks in town I might speak to?" but you will get a better response if your question is more focused: "Who do you know at . . . ?"

If your contact can't think of a person, ask about other companies: "What companies have you heard about that are hiring now?" or "If you were going to make a move, what companies would you look at?" or "Which are the most rapidly growing companies in the area?"

Whenever you are offered a lead, even if it is an obvious one, say, "Hey, that's a great idea. I never thought of Google as hiring people." Your encouragement is positive reinforcement. Then, after a suitable pause, ask for another company name, as in, "I really appreciate your help, Sam. I never thought of __________. Who else comes to mind?" When people see that their advice is appreciated, they will often come up with more helpful information. When you have gathered two or three company names, you can backtrack with a request for contact names at each of the companies: "Do you know of anyone I could speak to at __________?"

You can also ask for leads at companies you plan to call, or even at those you have already called: "Jack, I was planning to contact __________, Inc. Would you happen to know anyone there who could give me a heads-up?"

When a conversation is going well, and if you are talking to someone in your profession, tacking on a last question that gives you job leads to trade with others can be a good idea: "John, I'm a member of a job search network. If you don't have a need for someone with my background right now, perhaps one of my colleagues could be just what you are looking for. What titles is your company looking for right now?"

If you are changing careers or considering a career change, your priorities might be different. In this case you can explain that you are considering a particular profession for a new career direction and ask what it is like working in the profession; what your contact likes least and most about the work; what education, experience, and professional behaviors help people succeed in the profession; who fails and why; and how one gets into and moves ahead in the profession.

The extent of your questioning depends on the willingness of your contact to continue the conversation; I've known these conversations to run for fifty minutes.

What to Do When You Get a Referral

When you get leads on companies and specific individuals to talk to, be sure to thank your benefactor and ask to use his or her name as an introduction: "Thank you, Bill. I didn't know Wal-Mart was building a facility in town (duh!), and I appreciate getting Holly Barnes's name. May I use your name as an introduction?"

Every time you get a referral be sure to ask whether you can use your contact's name as an introduction. The answer will invariably be yes, but asking demonstrates professionalism and will encourage your contact to come up with more names and leads. For example you can say, "That's very helpful, Bill. Does anyone else come to mind?"

When you get permission to use your contact's name, use it in an introduction: "Holly Barnes? My name is __________. I'm an (accounting) friend of Bill Smith, who suggested I call, so before I go any further, Bill asked me to say hello." This is a bridge-building phrase and usually leads to a brief exchange about your mutual contact before you go into your information-gathering agenda.

When you do get help, say thank you. If you do it verbally, it's a nice touch to follow it up with a note (see the latest edition of *Knock 'em Dead Cover Letters* for networking letter examples). The positive impression you make might get you another lead, and it never hurts to include a copy of your resume with the thank-you letter.

Wrapping It Up

When your networking call or face-to-face conversation comes to its natural conclusion, offer your thanks and willingness to return the favor, and leave the door open for future calls: "Jack, thanks so much for your help. I do appreciate it. At times like this you realize how important your colleagues are, so I'd like to give you my telephone number and e-mail so that one day I might return the favor. Let's stay in touch. Might I call you again sometime?"

Other statements that you might use at the end of your conversation include "I'll let you know how it works out with Holly Barnes," or "Might I get in touch in a couple of months to see if the situation at __________ Inc. has changed?" When talking to a management contact in your profession, you might suggest, "Would it be worth my e-mailing a copy of my resume for your personal talent database?"

All smart managers keep such a database. After all, their job is to get work done through others and being able to locate good talent is essential.

You are going to get some pleasant surprises when you network, but also a few disappointments. You will be surprised at how someone you always regarded as a real pal won't give you the time of day and how someone you never thought of as a friend will go above and beyond the call of duty for you. Networking is a numbers game, so keep calling and e-mailing and start every communication with an open mind. Stay in touch with your networking contacts, whether they were able to help you or not. Let them know when you get a job, and try to stay in contact at least once a year. A career lasts a long time, and next week or a decade from now when a group of managers (including one from your personal network) will talk about filling a new position and they will ask, "Who do we know?" That someone is more likely to be you when you are connected to networks in your profession and your local community.

CHAPTER 4

Network Integrated Job Search Tactics

IN A COMPETITIVE job market, you cannot rely exclusively on networking, or any other single job-search approach. You need to use a number of different job search strategies and integrate networking into each of them.

Go fishing and put one hook in the water and you have only one chance of catching any of the millions of fish in the sea, and one fish is the best you can ever do. Put two hooks in the water and more than double your chances.

The more hooks you have in the water, the better your chances of action. All the job search tools and approaches that we discuss in this section of the book—job banks, resume banks, headhunters, direct research and approach—have proven effective. No single one is a guaranteed silver bullet, and any of them could deliver the ideal opportunity for you. Your plan of attack should embrace as many of these approaches as is practical to your situation. Intelligently pursuing all useful approaches will generate job leads. Then leverage your networks for leads on and introductions to the hiring managers.

It's a Digital World

Corporate recruitment has moved online, so your job search must respond to these recruitment preferences.

With tens of thousands of job sites and resume banks out there, you could spend eternity trolling from one to the next. The danger is that this feels like productive work, and because it involves zero rejection it can be highly addictive. An Internet-based job search can seem magical because the media tells you it is magical, but *Job banks and resume banks are not magical.* The Internet increases your ability to gather and disseminate information, but you need to understand, control, and leverage this power, not be controlled by it.

First, Get Organized

If you've been through a job search before, you are groaning at starting all over again, but if you follow this plan of attack, apart from having a successful job search, you will be prepared for future job searches. You will have the mechanisms in place to track interesting opportunities; you will have a database of relevant employers and a wide range of networking contacts; plus you'll have a database of relevant job banks, resume banks, and headhunters. You will be more proactive in the management of your career and therefore more successful over the long haul.

If you don't organize properly, you will get buried in an avalanche of information and leads, but it doesn't have to be this way. Organization begins with setting up a career management base of operations for your professional life. This job search will be its first use, but the long-term success of your personal brand, MeInc., demands an organized place for your ongoing professional development and career management activities.

Security and Confidentiality

Online privacy is an issue for everyone today and is especially important during a job search.

Professional E-mail Address

I recommend you set up a separate e-mail account devoted exclusively to job search and career management affairs. You need an e-mail address that reflects the professional you, and it's a good time to retire those addresses like *binkypoo@yahoo.com* or *bigboy@hotmail.com* that seemed such a good idea when your professional reputation wasn't an issue. If you have a family, a separate account can also prevent a rugrat destroying critical data.

KNOCK 'EM DEAD TIP

While you know better than to use your office e-mail for a job search, you should also never download your secure e-mail to your office e-mail box. Why? Companies can and do check Internet usage on your computer. Inappropriate activities can cost you a job.

It is easy to set up an additional e-mail account, as your ISP almost certainly allows multiple addresses. Create an account name that reveals something about your professional profile, such as *systemanalyst@hotmail.com* or *topaccountant@yahoo.com*. Addresses such as these help recipients focus on your communication from the start, because they act as headlines for the reader. Many names like *topaccountant@yahoo.com* are long gone, and you will be encouraged to accept *topaccountant1367@yahoo.com*. Before you accept this, try variations such as *top10accountant@*, *greataccountant@*, *smartfinanceguy@*, *moneycounts@*, *PandL@*, etc.

Separate Telephone

Most telephone companies now allow you two or three alternate numbers at no extra charge with your basic service, and usually these come with a distinctive ringtone. This means you can have a dedicated and confidential number for all your job search and career management activities.

A Sanitized Resume

When you are employed—or if you want to create that impression—and involved in a job search, discretion is paramount. Consider sanitizing your resume by removing all "traceable-to-you" contact information (name, address, phone, fax), and replacing them with your career management e-mail.

By removing a current employer's name (all recruiters and employers understand the need for this), you can further protect your identity, replacing it with a generalized description of the company and location. For example, if you work for Pepsi-Cola in Chicago, Illinois, you could describe this as a "Midwestern Beverage Company."

It usually isn't necessary to sanitize prior employer names. However, if you have a senior title associated with a particularly visible company, it could be a clue as to who you are. In this case replace it with a more generic but recognizable job title.

How to Organize and Track Your Job Search

It is important to track the results of your activities, because information you gather can always be used again in some way. Create folders for target companies and your contacts within them, and the same for your contacts within recruitment firms. You might choose to add a Job Leads folder; into this you can put all the job postings you develop. You can add folders to contain contact info for both your on- and offline networking activities

Additions to these groups can be made at any time; when you see recruiters who work in your industry, put them in the appropriate folder. You're creating a reference tool for this and future job searches, and now you've read the networking chapter you know there are uses even for the people and jobs that are not relevant to your search. Organize yourself to capture information today that you can use throughout your work life.

We typically dump job postings or help-wanted ads that don't turn into anything or for other reasons aren't suitable. I don't want you to do this for two reasons:

1. You can offer them to others in the course of your networking activities.
2. A company that hires accountants today is just as likely to be hiring them three years from today. Knowing about the company and its contact information gives you a head start next time. This job search and career management database is a tool you create for the benefit of your entire career. It is part of gaining control of your professional destiny.

Whenever you respond to a job posting, do exactly as requested, but also copy the job posting and all contact information for the company to a folder. You will need this if an interview occurs. Plus, you can cross-reference the job posting with people in your different networks and perhaps come up with a name and a title to whom you can send the resume directly, thus doubling your chances of getting an interview.

On any job site it is a good idea to make your requirements broad to begin with; if a particular site drowns you with inappropriate jobs, gradually redefine your needs more narrowly.

Alternatively, you might not be getting enough responses from a particular site and might want to recast your needs in broader terms.

Job Sites and Resume Banks

There are so many thousands of job sites, you could never hope to visit them all, so you have to integrate the job site/resume bank aspect of your search intelligently. Start by identifying what sites are relevant to your search. At *www.knockemdead.com* you can find a fairly extensive listing of job sites for many different professions, plus you'll find a selection of my favorite job site spiders that crawl thousands of websites for you, so this might be a useful place to start.

KNOCK 'EM DEAD TIP

Everything *Knock 'em Dead* teaches you about job search can be applied at work and for your long-term career management success. A little more on winning promotions:

Assuming you are settled in that new job, you've planned the next step up your professional ladder, performing a TJD and GAP analysis on the next target job (as described in Chapter 2). As well, you have diligently developed the skills needed to warrant promotion. The work you do now in organizing this job search can help you again. Consciously targeting a promotion, identifying the professional development program to achieve that promotion, and then developing those skills are big steps toward that goal. But just in case your current employer won't give you that job in a reasonable time frame, you have a database of area employers who also hire people like this, as well as a network of contacts for introduction.

So we'll assume you have chosen sites to visit from the online resources, and get right into what you do when visiting job sites and resume banks.

1. Does the site have job postings that are suitable for you? If it doesn't, you can move on to the next site. If it does, you will want to keep an eye on the site for relevant job postings as they come in. This means you will want to register with the site and receive a job alert e-mail when new jobs matching your criteria get posted to the site.
2. When you are asked to define the jobs that interest you, set your sights wide. You may get too many responses initially, but you can gradually narrow the parameters. It is better to plow through a little junk than miss a great opportunity.

3. If this is a good site for you, other sites it is linked to might also be useful; check the partners/links pages. These aren't always obvious, so if not look for a site map and in those little links that always crowd the very bottom of the page.
4. Because companies hire more people from smaller niche sites, you must check the specialty sites. You will find a good selection among the Internet resources listed at *www.knockemdead.com*.
5. You will collect two types of job postings: those that are good for you and those that are suitable to offer to your network. Before you file any of these, go through them carefully looking for keywords that describe skill sets you have that are not captured as such in your existing resume. Capture these on a desktop document. You'll use this document to update your resume and to refresh it in the resume banks; more on this in the next section.
6. Make a folder for each relevant site you visit, and as postings come in store them in the appropriate folder. You'll quickly see which sites are most productive.
7. When you are asked to create a profile—and this is usually part of setting up your account on a site—you essentially copy and paste your resume as this represents your most carefully considered packaging of the professional you. But this requires a little more explanation.

KNOCK 'EM DEAD TIP

Remember that those jobs you hear about from the job site that aren't quite right for you are not a waste of your time. They are worth saving in a trading file to share with network contacts, for whom any one of those jobs might be a perfect fit.

Most job sites are free for you to use. It's the employers who are paying to post their job openings and search the resume bank. The job sites work with employers to develop ever more efficient screening tools. Setting up your account and filling out a profile is part of this process: Everything you do online is being tracked by someone for some reason. Whenever you are filling out a profile or questionnaire on a job site keep these things in mind.

Multiple Resumes/Profiles

Job sites recognize that many people can do more than one job and so frequently allow you to register as many as five separate resumes and/or profiles. It is also a tacit acknowledgment that one "general" resume won't cut the mustard. And yes, it is yet another benefit of the TJD exercises from Chapter 2 that allow you to create relevant, intelligent, and deep profiles for each option.

Most job sites break up the registration/profile building/resume uploading process into a number of steps, and there are often twelve or more specific dialogue boxes you have to work your way through. They typically include topics like: Target Job, Career Objective, Competencies, Relocation, Salary, Ideal job, Education, and so on.

The sites often offer examples to help you fill in the dialogue boxes—but remember that behind all this is the screening process.

Target Job Title

Copy and paste in all the different job titles you collected in the first part of the TJD exercise. Putting in more than one title only serves to increase your visibility.

KNOCK 'EM DEAD TIP

You are not always limited to one answer—even in the case of check boxes. Always test and verify to see if you can select more than one answer. Never assume you are limited—not even if the directions on the screen indicate that you are. Similarly, you might not want to answer a supposedly mandatory question. Try leaving it blank; you'll find out if it really was mandatory when you click "submit."

Career/Job Objective/Summary

No one wants to hear about your objectives and putting them out there is only wasting space. Paste in here your Performance Profile as you created it based on your prioritization of employer needs as you determined in the TJD process.

This dialogue box often has lots of space, so you can end it by inserting a header that says, "The opportunity to use these skills." Then paste in the entire collection of Core Competencies you identified in Chapter 2.

Salary Requirements

It is always better to give a range rather than a single figure. I show you how to decide on this salary range in Chapter 19 where we discuss salary negotiation. Even though this box is always marked as mandatory, that isn't always the case. Sometimes you can leave it blank if you feel this will be helpful to your cause.

Ideal Job

No one is interested in your ideal job. The recruiter is searching a database and retrieving possible candidates from a list of keywords that they have put into the system. Copy and paste your performance profile and follow it with your Core Competencies. Test to see if there is more space by pasting in your core competencies again. No person will actually read the repetition (and if they did, they would regard it as a glitch) but the software will catch and reward you for it by increasing your ranking in the search results.

Core Competencies

If they have a separate section for this, paste your Core Competencies in . . . as often as space will allow.

Education

Education is the most questioned area of any candidacy. Much prone to exaggeration and outright lies, educational claims *do get checked*. Untruths can cause offers to be withdrawn and jobs to be terminated. Don't fake it.

If you are involved in the pursuit of any post-secondary education, but haven't yet achieved it, you can use it if you can state the school and the degree and if you can also state a projected graduation date . . . *because* you are enrolled in at least one course toward that degree. That you are pursuing education while you work is a plus in employers' eyes, and you have a right to show it to them.

Relocation

When completing questions about relocation, don't jump to make a selection. Make sure you have to answer the question at all. If you do, select the broadest option possible. Even if you have the ability to list many preferred locations, don't. Choose no preference, and you will get the same responses. Plus:

1. You can always say "no," but you can't say "yes" unless you've been asked.
2. For the right job, opportunity, and money, we would all move to Possum Trot, Kentucky.
3. Any job you interview for but reject will only improve your interviewing skills, which are probably your very weakest professional skill.
4. It gives you leads to trade in your networking initiatives.

Name-Dropping

Recruiters often look for candidates who either are working for or have worked for certain companies or competitors. If you work for name companies and products that is great. You can also drop corporate names and brand names if you have been a vendor or a client.

Resume Banks

If suitable jobs are posted to the job site, it probably means that recruiters are also visiting its resume bank. In that case you may well want to upload your resume. Some considerations to bear in mind:

1. Use the same considerations and values for filling out dialogue boxes as you would on any job site registration
2. Some resume banks require you to upload your resume in something called ASCII format. This is not difficult to do but it is a pain in the neck; you can find step-by-step directions in the latest edition of *Knock 'em Dead Resumes.*
3. Resume banks have purge dates, mostly so that the recruiters who pay for access can be assured that they are not looking at stale resumes. The purge usually happens every ninety days, and you will want to bear the dates in mind so that you can refresh your resume before then.
4. Of course, recruiters also have the ability to restrict their searches by the date a resume was uploaded, so for example they might be able to restrict a search to resumes uploaded in the last ten days. This is important when a particular site has job postings suitable for you, because it also means that recruiters will be cruising its resume bank for candidates.
5. To maintain the highest visibility on a site like this, go in once a week and update your resume with new keywords you have identified in other job postings. Make any change to your resume and the database search engine will recognize it as a new document.
6. When there are no new words you can achieve the same effect quite simply: Log into your account, open up your resume, replace a couple of words with a string of x's, and log out. Take a couple of deep breaths, log in again, and replace the x's with the original words and log out again; to all intents and purposes you now have a brand-new document.

Finding More Hidden Jobs

In addition to what we've talked about above, you can use job sites in other ways. Go to any job site and search their posted openings by putting in minimal keywords and restrictions. For example, if a medical insurance sales manager goes to *www.6figurejobs.com* and does a simple keyword search for "insurance," she may get hundreds of results, and the vast majority will be for jobs that do not interest her. At the same time, those results will reveal recruiters and companies in her profession and target geography.

Visit these sites and see if there are suitable job openings posted. Companies all use their sites as recruitment vehicles and usually have their open job requisitions posted there. Even if they do not appear to have an opening for someone like you, upload your resume anyway. You don't really know what is going on at that company, and at the very least you will be in their database and therefore on their radar when a need arises.

If a company is looking for anyone at all remotely connected with your area of professional expertise, they could also be looking for someone like you. Upload your resume and research the company to approach the appropriate hiring managers directly.

KNOCK 'EM DEAD TIP

This list of companies will also help your social networking activities. You can use the company names in database searches on the social networking sites to find contacts for leads and introductions at these target companies. Everything in a successful job search is geared toward getting into conversation with people who could make the decision to hire you, as we have noted, typically someone three title levels above your own. Always strive to identify and get into a conversation with anyone who holds any of these target titles at any and every company in your geography.

After visiting a company website, add the link to the appropriate folder in your career management database. Identify all the profession-specific employers at all the job sites you visit, then visit each of those employer websites and add them to a potential employers folder; your hit list of potential employers will grow exponentially.

Finding Names of Hiring Authorities for Direct Approach

Responding to job postings is a big part of most job searches, but you can double, triple, and quadruple your chances of getting interviews from job postings by making direct approaches to the people in a position to hire you.

Whenever you see a suitable job, respond to the posting in the requested way. Also flag all contact information for the company, website, and mailing address. As you discover the names and titles of managers one to three title levels above yours you can approach them directly in three different ways, each one much more likely to produce an interview:

- E-mail your resume directly to that manager with a personalized cover letter, at least doubling your chances of a hit.
- Send a resume and personalized cover letter to that manager, at least tripling your chances of a hit.

- Make a follow-up telephone call to that manager first thing in the morning, at lunchtime or at 5 P.M., at least quadrupling your chances of a hit.

A successful job search is all about getting into conversation with people in a position to hire you as often as possible.

The more frequently you get into conversation with managers whose job titles signify that they have the authority to hire you, the faster you will land that new position because you have skipped right over needing to be pulled from the resume database, you have sidestepped the recruiter's evaluation process, and you have the attention of the actual decision maker to make a direct and personal pitch.

Your target for direct approach is always someone who can hire you although any management title offers opportunity for referral. For example, while HR people won't have the authority to hire you, the pivotal nature of their work makes them aware of all areas within a company that could use your skills. I'm not suggesting you target HR management but they are not the monsters usually portrayed.

Getting a resume to someone by name with a personalized pitch gives you a distinct advantage, never more important than when the economy is down or in recovery. At such times your competition is fierce and employers recognize initiative and motivation as a differentiating factors in your candidacy.

Who to Target in Your Job Search

The hiring titles to target during your job search are those titles most likely to be in a position to hire you. As indicated earlier, these people are usually one to three management titles above you.

Other titles likely to be involved in the selection process include management titles (again, one to three levels above you) in departments that have ongoing interaction with your department and peers holding similar titles to that which you're applying for. Titles of those most likely to know people involved in the selection process and be able to refer you include management titles one to three levels above you in any department, and internal recruiters and HR professionals.

In fact any name is better than no name, and with the Internet at your fingertips there is endless opportunity to identify the names of people who carry the appropriate hiring titles for your needs.

Sometimes sending a letter and resume to the levels of titles we see above can mean upward of half a dozen pitches to a desirable target company, just to assure that all the right people know you are available. To illustrate, let's say you are a young engineer crazy for a job with Last Chance Electronics. It is well within the bounds of reason that you would submit a cover letter and resume to any or all of the following people, with each letter and/or e-mail addressed by name to minimize its chances of going straight into the trash.

- Company President
- Vice President of Engineering
- Chief Engineer
- Engineering Design Manager
- Vice President of Human Resources
- Technical Engineering Recruitment Manager
- Technical Recruiter

You might also call each of these people to increase your chances of a referral. Think through all the titles likely to be of use to you, based on the above criteria, and keep all these titles in mind when you go looking for names to attach to them. The more options you have, the more results you will get.

Internet Research Tactics for Finding Names

Apart from cross-referencing target companies with the members of your expanded networks to get referrals and introductions, you can also use online search tactics and tools to locate the names of the people you need to reach.

Start with keyword searches on Google, Bing, Ask, and so forth. They are all likely to deliver names, and they'll all get different results. For example: A professional in pharmaceutical sales looking to make direct contact with hiring authorities for a job at a specific company in the Pittsburgh area could try all the following keyword searches and gather new usable information on each search. Do each of these searches first as a standard Google search then as a Google News search (which looks for mentions of those keywords in media coverage).

Pharmaceutical sales (company name)
Pharmaceutical sales (company name) Pennsylvania
Pharmaceutical sales (company name) Pittsburgh
Pharmaceutical Mgr sales (company name) Pennsylvania
Pharmaceutical Mgr sales (company name) Pittsburgh
Pharmaceutical Director sales (company name) Pennsylvania
Pharmaceutical Director sales (company name) Pittsburgh
Pharmaceutical VP sales (company name) Pennsylvania

Now:

- Repeat all without "pharmaceutical."
- Repeat all without company name.

- Repeat with just the job title.
- Repeat with separate searches for target title plus: "hired," "resigned," "deceased."

Try these and other keyword phrases, and you will come up with job openings and job sites, of course. Drilling down beyond those first couple of pages, you will come up with names to go with your target hiring titles and other target companies in your geography. This can be a very rewarding activity for name and title gathering, and reaching out to hiring managers directly is the fastest route from where you stand to where you want to stand.

KNOCK 'EM DEAD TIP

When you find news information relevant to the subject of your search, use it as an opener for your letter or e-mail. In an e-mail, paste the article and attach it. With a traditional letter, enclose a copy of the article. You can use this sort of relevant coverage with follow-up letters as well.

You can also:

1. Check out the company website. On the "About Us" pages you can sometimes find names and titles of management.
2. Call the company and ask for name of the title-holder. This may sound old-fashioned but it's very effective.

Online Research for Direct Approach

Online resources are a valuable supplement to the information you get from your personal and professional networks. Apart from reaching out to people who work or once worked at the target company through your networks, sites such as *www.vault.com* will tell you what past and current employees think about their employer. Other online resources such as *www.wetfeet.com* will give you great info about your target companies.

As you develop dossiers of information on potential employers, some companies will rise to the top as particularly desirable. This will provide useful background information for interviews and show that you have done your homework. It is also flattering to the interviewer, who sees you've paid attention to detail and shown effort and enthusiasm, each of which can end up being deciding factors in a tight job race.

This effort also has long-term value because you are building a personalized reference file on your industry/specialty/profession that will help you throughout your career.

Here are some other online resources for company research and identification of management title-holders.

www.virtualpet.com/industry/howto/search.htm
www.standardandpoors.com
www.leadershipdirectories.com/products/cor.html
www.idexec.com
www.zapdata.com/lp/ppc.jsp?h=Trying+to+research+companies%3F
www.hoovers.com
www.quintcareers.com
www.vault.com
www.infousa.com
www.thomasnet.com/
www.superpages.com
www.jigsaw.com
www.zoominfo.com
www.corporateinformation.com
www.ceoexpress.com/
www.infospace.com
www.search-it-all.com/
www.searchbug.com

Even More Resources for Finding Names of Hiring Authorities

The resources available reach to the horizon. Standard & Poor's has a database of executives by name and title with contact information called the "Biographical Directory/Database." Higher-level target hiring titles will be identifiable here or through one of these options.

www.onesource.com/providers/list_3.asp
www.knowx.com
www.jigsaw.com
www.lead411.com/about.html
www.privateeye.com/?from=p31702&vw=background&Input=Name&piid=44
www.web.info.com/infocom.us2/search/web/Contact%20List?CMP=2776&itkw=Contact%20List
www.econtentmag.com/Articles/ArticleReader.aspx?ArticleID=4089
www.lambresearch.com/CorpsExecs.htm
www.business.com/directory/advertising_and_marketing/sales/selling_techniques/lead_generation/

Employment Agencies and Headhunters

There are few clear-cut lines of demarcation in this area.

State employment agencies are staffed by government employees. Their job is to help you find a job; they are almost the only people whose focus is entirely on helping you. They are funded by the state labor department and typically carry names like State Division of Employment Security, State Job Service, or Manpower Services. The names vary but the services remain the same. They will make efforts to line you up with appropriate jobs and otherwise help you as best they can. It is not mandatory for employers to list jobs with state agencies, but more and more companies are taking advantage of these free services. These public agencies now list positions that often exceed $100,000 a year, so they're a resource not to be ignored.

KNOCK 'EM DEAD TIP

As you build these dossiers of information about individual companies, one of those folders will likely be for your dream company. Beware of applying for jobs at these "super desirable" employers right away. When you hear about the latest Broadway hit musicals, I am not sure you realize that shows rarely open on Broadway; they go through months of rehearsals, previews with selected audiences, and even road trips to try out the show. They do this because they don't want to screw up when they hit the big time.

The same applies to you. Most likely your resume and interviewing skills (your script and performance skills) are not up to speed at the beginning of your search. The last thing you need to do is fumble an opportunity to join the company of your dreams. It is better to hold off until you know that your resume is top-notch, you won't swallow your tongue in the first few minutes of an interview, and you've made a couple of inside contacts through your professional networks.

If you are moving across the state or across the country, your local employment office can plug you into the national job bank, or you can connect yourself online at *www.nationjob.com*, which claims to be the largest job bank in the world.

Private employment agencies are for profit, and their source of income derives from the company. They will search on behalf of employers, but typically only in their own databases, and they will market someone to employers only if that person is seen to be in high demand and can be used as a tool to develop other fee-paying assignments.

When working with an employment agency, choose your agent with the same care and attention with which you would choose a spouse or a lawyer. The caliber of the individual and company you choose could well affect the kind of the company you ultimately join. Further, if you choose prudently, he or she can become a lifetime counselor who can guide you step by step up the ladder of success.

Career counselors and job search counselors. Their money comes from you, but while there are charlatans in the business, there are also exemplary, talented, and dedicated professionals in this group. Typically, these people work alone or in very small companies, and they can help you with career choice, resume preparation, job search, and interview preparation.

How do you choose whom to work with? Find out how many years they've been in business, what professional degrees they hold, their affiliations with professional associations, and their professional accreditations. Ideally, they should also have a background as contingency or retained recruiters.

Contingency recruiters gain their income from employers and are largely involved with finding employed professionals for hard-to-fill positions. They do this on a contingency basis, the contingency being that they only collect a fee when they fill the position. Typically contingency recruiters will search their databases and actively recruit for a percentage of the openings they have to fill. Most contingency recruiters and some contingency firms will market an "in-demand" professional to target companies for a day or two and as a tool to develop other fee-paying assignments. Contingency recruiters are a hybrid; more professionally sophisticated than employment agency people but not working on a retainer basis.

Executive search firms are also employer-paid. They are the only group entirely focused on the employer's needs and have no interest in you unless you fit an existing requirement. This is because they receive cash up front, more when a candidate/recruit is hired, and the final payment when that person starts work. They are almost exclusively interested in people currently successful in their jobs because an employed person is less of a risk (the firms often guarantee their finds to the employer for up to a year) and is a more desirable commodity.

These people rarely deal with salary levels under $100,000 per year. They are more interested in obtaining your resume for their database than seeing you unless you match a specific job they are trying to fill for a client.

You may have heard the term "headhunter." It is now applied to anyone who provides employment services, but in reality it only fits executive search consultants and a few contingency recruiters.

Who to Work With, and How to Work With Them

What type of employment services company is best for you? Well, the answer is simple: the one that will get you the right job offer. The problem is, there are thousands of companies in each of these broad categories. How do you choose between the good, the bad, and the ugly?

Fortunately this is not as difficult as it sounds. A retained executive search firm is not necessarily better or more professional than a contingency search firm, which in turn is not necessarily better or more professional than a regular employment agency. Each has its exemplary practitioners and its charlatans. Your goal is to avoid the charlatans and get representation by a company with experience placing professionals like you.

Involvement in professional associations is always a good sign, demonstrating commitment and an enhanced level of competence. In the employment services industry, the high-end employment agencies and contingency search firms—as well as some retained search firms—belong to the National Association of Personnel Services (NAPS), the premier professional organization with state associations in all fifty states. The Association for Executive Search Consultants (AESC) is the premier organization for the retained executive search firms. Career Management Institute (CMI) is the leading association for job search and career management counselors, and NATSS (National Association of Temporary and Staffing Services) is the leading association for temp firms.

Involvement in independent or franchise networks of firms can also be a powerful plus for a job search. For example, an independent headhunter network like NPA (*www.npaworldwide.com*) has hundreds of member firms around the world. Membership in one of the leading franchise groups, such as Management Recruiters, Robert Half, or Dunhill likewise gives you access to a coordinated network of employment services professionals. These networks also have extensive training programs that ensure a high-caliber consultant. Franchise networks can be especially helpful if relocation is in your future, as they tend to have powerful symbiotic relationships with other franchise members around the country and the world.

It is prudent to ask whether your contact has professional accreditations. Most of the national professional associations have training programs that offer accreditation, so these can be another sign that the recruiter is a committed and connected member of his or her profession. The most widely recognized of all these is the CPC designation. CPC (or its international equivalent, CIPC) stands for Certified Personnel Consultant. The CPC and CIPC designations are recognized as a standard of excellence and commitment only achieved after rigorous training and study. CIPC designation requires that the holder has already achieved CPC designation, and it requires adherence to an international code of ethics as designated by the International Personnel Association (IPA). Although certification can be applied for after two years of experience in business, even the newest holders of a CPC usually have five years of experience. The average CPC probably has seven to ten years of experience, and with it comes excellent contacts on the corporate side.

Qualified CPCs (like holders of the other accreditations) can also be relied upon to have superior knowledge of the legalities and ethics of the recruitment and hiring process, along with the expertise and tricks of the trade that only come from years of hands-on experience. (I should note that while I hold a CPC accreditation, mine is an honorary one, in recognition of my contributions to the discussion of career management.)

Finally, when dealing with an agency or personnel professional, don't get intimidated. You are not obligated to sign anything, nor are you obligated to guarantee anyone that you will remain in any employment for any specific length of time.

It Finally Comes Down to the Individual

You can develop mutually beneficial relationships with employment professionals in all these categories. Their livelihood depends on the people they know in the professional world. Look at how many years of experience they have in employment services and how well they understand your profession. Look for involvement with their professional community and professional accreditations.

KNOCK 'EM DEAD TIP

For a full list of the accreditations relevant to resume, recruitment, and career management professionals, go to *www.knockemdead.com.*

If a recruiter is interested in representing you, expect a detailed analysis of your background and prepare to be honest. Do not overstate your job duties, accomplishments, or education. If there are employment gaps, explain them. Be circumspect, because an unethical headhunter can create further competition for you when you share information about companies you are talking to. The details of your communications with a company are nobody's business but your own. If the recruiter asks who you are talking with, say your job search is confidential and you'd like to know whom he plans to speak with. Explain that you will happily tell them if you are already in communication with that company.

Find out what the recruiter expects of you in the relationship, and explain what you expect. Reach commitments you both can live with, and stick with them. If you break those commitments, expect the representation to cease. Keep the recruiter informed about all changes in your status: salary increases, promotions, layoffs, or other offers of employment.

Don't consider yourself an employment expert. You get a job for yourself every three or four years. These people do it for a living. Ask for their objective input and seek their advice in developing interviewing strategies with their clients.

Temporary Services Companies

Such companies fill temporary assignments for employers and provide employment services to companies in all industries and at most professional levels, from unskilled and semiskilled labor (referred to as "light industrial") to administration, finance, technical, sales, and marketing professionals, as well as doctors, lawyers, and management up to the CEO and COO levels.

Always useful for quickly getting skills up to speed and re-establishing credentials after an absence from the workforce, temp or interim management work can offer a valuable stopgap in a drawn-out job search.

If you are unemployed and need the cash flow for bills, working with a temp company can supply that and expose you to employers in the community who, if you really shine, could ask you to join the staff full-time. This "temp-to-perm" approach is increasingly popular with companies hiring at all levels, as it allows employers to try before they buy.

KNOCK 'EM DEAD TIP

This latter part of the business is usually referred to as "interim management." To find companies and associations for the interim management sector, simply key "interim management jobs" into your browser.

Here's some advice when considering interim and temp job agencies and services:

- Define the titles and the employment levels they represent, along with geographical areas they cover.
- Determine whether they are members of the National Association of Temporary and Staffing Services (NATSS).
- Select a handful of firms that work in your field; this will increase the odds of suitable assignments appearing quickly.
- Do not overstate your job duties, accomplishments, or education.
- Find out first what the temporary help professional expects of you in the relationship, then explain what you expect. Reach commitments you both can live with, and stick with them.
- Judge the assignments not solely on the paycheck (although that can be important), but also by the long-term benefits to your job search and career. For example, if you have been out of the world of work raising a family, temp work can help you get acclimated and also acquire some current experience.
- Keep the temporary help counselor informed about any and all changes in your status, such as offers of employment or acquisition of new skills.
- Resolve key issues ahead of time. Should an employer want to take you on full-time, will that employer have to pay a set amount, or will you just stay on as a temporary for a specific period and then go on the employer's payroll?

College Career Services

Career services can help recently graduated students, as well as those about to finish school, and an increasing number of these services also try to help alumni. These dedicated professionals are horrendously overworked. So take the time to stand out by having thought through your issues. Stress your willingness to listen to good advice. If you are then seen to act on that advice, when you come back for more you will have earned the department's respect and will garner yourself more personal attention and guidance.

For students, the best way into corporate America is through internships and on-campus recruiters, who can recommend interns and entry-level hires to the company. Career Services is the best way to learn about these recruiters. Treat your entire interaction with Career Services the same way you intend to treat the interview process. Make a real effort with your appearance and professional demeanor.

Campus recruiters go to society and association meetings on campus all year long to see who is engaged, enthusiastic, and professional in their approach to life and career. Most campus recruiters have already chosen the best before they officially arrive on campus for the job fairs. When you take an active part in campus affairs, you will get to know many of these recruiters. Career Services will usually know which recruiters are involved with which campus activities.

You will also start to build a powerful network of peers for your whole career, because these are likely to be the most successful people in the professional world, as they are already engaged and committed.

Job Fairs

Job fairs (occasionally called career days) are occasions where actively hiring companies get together, usually under the auspices of a job fair promoter, to attract large numbers of potential employees to a one-day-only event. They aren't of much value to senior-level professionals.

Job fairs aren't regular events, except in times of high employment, so they won't take much of your time, but you should become an active participant when they do occur.

They often charge a small entrance fee, in return for which you get direct access to all the employers and formal presentations by company representatives and local employment experts. When you organize yourself properly, take the right attitude, and work all the opportunities, job fairs make for a great job search opportunity.

When you attend job fairs, go prepared with:

- Proper business attire. You may be meeting your new boss, and you don't want the first impression to be less than professional.
- Business cards. If you are currently employed, remember to request discretion and confidentiality.
- Resumes. You should take as many copies of your resume as there are exhibitors, times two. You'll need one to leave at the exhibit booth and an additional copy for anyone you

have a meaningful conversation with. If you have resumes targeted to different jobs, take copies of all of them.

- Laptop or notepad and pen, preferably in a folder.

Job fairs are an opportunity for networking with other job hunters as well. If you know other people going to a job fair (perhaps you are a member of a job search support group), you should go with a collaborative effort in mind. You may be in different professions, but if you all make the effort to speak to other attendees and to collect business cards from other attendees regardless of their profession, you can help one another find more leads.

If you are attending solo, still make the effort to network with other attendees. Ask them to meet you later in the day to exchange leads that might be mutually beneficial. I have witnessed this in action at job fairs and seen a group of twenty who were total strangers in the morning happily exchanging handfuls of business cards at the end of the day.

It's easy to walk into a job fair and be drawn like a moth to the biggest and most attractive booths, sponsored by the largest and most established companies, and ignore the lesser ones. Remember that *the majority of the jobs in America are generated by companies with less than 500 employees.* You should visit every booth, not just the ones with the flashing lights and all the moths fluttering around.

Attend with specific objectives in mind.

Talk to someone at every booth. You can walk up and ask questions about the company activities, and who they are looking for, before you talk about yourself. This allows you to present yourself in the most relevant light.

Collect business cards from everyone you speak to so you can follow up with an e-mail and a call when they are not so harried. Very few people actually get hired at job fairs; for most companies the exercise is one of collecting resumes so that meaningful meetings can take place in the ensuing days and weeks. Nevertheless, you should be "on" at all times, because serious interviews do sometimes occur on the spot.

If you have a background and resume that matches you for a specific opportunity, make your pitch. If, on the other hand, there's a job you can do but your resume needs some adaptation to better position your candidacy, take a different approach. By all means pitch the company representative, but don't hand over a resume that will detract from your candidacy (you can come up with a harmless pretext, such as having run out of copies). Instead, get the contact's business card and promise to follow up with a resume, which you can then custom-fit to the opportunity (see TJD process in Chapter 2).

Collect company brochures and collateral materials.

Arrange times and dates to follow up with as many employers as possible: "Ms. Jones, I realize you are very busy today, and I would like to speak to you further. Your opportunities in ________ sounds exactly suited to my skills and interests. I would like to set up a time when we could talk."

In addition to the exhibit hall, there are probably formal group presentations by employers. As all speakers love feedback, move in when the crush of presenter groupies has died down. You will have more knowledge of the company and the time to customize your pitch to the needs and interests of the employer, plus you'll get more time and closer attention.

Job fairs provide the best opportunities for administrative, professional, and technical people. However, this doesn't mean middle management and executive staff can't gather information, collect cards, and generate leads.

On leaving each booth, and at the end of the day, go through your notes while everything is still fresh in your mind. Review each company and what possibilities it may hold for you. Also review what you have learned about industry trends, new skill requirements, marketplace shifts, and long-term staffing needs. Plan to send e-mails and make follow-up calls within the week to everyone with whom you spoke

Newspapers and Magazines

Almost all recruitment has now moved to the Internet, as have newspapers, so their role in your job search is not as it was in years gone by. However, there are still uses for a local or national newspaper in your job search campaign.

1. Companies that rely on the local community for both customers and employees still use the newspaper as a major recruitment vehicle.
2. The business news stories can tell you about company success stories, contracts signed, products and services introduced, and companies coming to town. They keep you informed and mention movers and shakers by name.

   Reminding that person of the article ("I saw you quoted in the *Argus* last week . . .") is flattering and will get you a few minutes of that person's time to make a pitch, get an interview, or get some leads. (If you want to learn how to get yourself quoted in the press, examine the PR chapters in the e-book *Knock 'em Dead Professional Communication* available at *www.knockemdead.com.*
3. Industry overviews and market development pieces can tip you off to subtle shifts in your local professional marketplace.

There are still some great job leads in newspapers and magazines, and the fact that most people aren't using them as a job search resource is a good enough reason to at least check them out. A good place to start online is *www.onlinenewspapers.com*, which helps you identify and link to newspapers all over the world.

Passive Marketing with a Web Portfolio or Web-Based Resume

Almost all job search activities take time and effort, so use passive marketing tactics whenever you can to increase your professional visibility and credibility.

For some time now, artists and designers have been creating online portfolios for their work as a cost-effective marketing device. If audio/video/graphics/multimedia can help promote the professional you, it might be worth considering an e-Resume or e-portfolio for yourself, or have it built for you. This can cost anywhere from $40 up to $3,000.

Think of your web resume as a miniature website (you'll need to update it to reflect current professional activities); it gives you a constant marketing presence and extends your professional visibility and credibility in a couple of other ways. Increased visibility increases your credibility, for example; recruiters are doing Google searches on people before meeting them as part of the selection screening process. A well-put-together web resume will enhance others' perception of you before those initial meetings.

For professionals in the creative arts a web-based resume/e-portfolio allows you to provide a multimedia proof of your achievements and strengths. With a web-based resume on its own site, you have the opportunity to expand beyond the immediate page, offering access to examples and supporting documents in other media.

It will not replace your main resume, which can offer a link to your multimedia site.

But it's a great opportunity to prove you have strong presentation skills, supported with a video or audio clip of a presentation. Including articles, a list of awards, graphics, audio and video clips, blogs, and photos on your site are just some of the options you have to make your multimedia case. Prospective employers, headhunters, clients, and colleagues will get a far more comprehensive picture of the professional you, and because a properly delivered e-portfolio is more engaging, when the content is good, it speaks of a technologically adapted professional.

PART II
GET THE WORD OUT

YOU HAVE TO get the word out and make contact with employers to land job interviews, and you make the most contacts in the shortest time when you make them simultaneously with e-mail, mail, and the telephone.

CHAPTER 5

Ace the Telephone Interview

INTERVIEWERS USE THE telephone to weed out applicants. Your goal is a face-to-face meeting, and these are the methods you must use to get it.

Some aspects of a job search are not clear-cut. For instance, a telephone interview for a job might be scheduled for a certain date and time, so you have plenty of time to prepare for it. Then again, a networking call can turn into a marketing presentation in a flash when you realize that the person on the other end of the phone line is in a position to hire you. Likewise, when that marketing presentation progresses past the initial "buy signs" and objections (as I discuss in the Appendix), it can suddenly become a telephone interview. Telephone interviews can be scheduled in advance, but they are just as likely to occur on the fly.

Employers use the telephone as a time-management tool. It is easier to cut out candidates via the telephone than in person. Your goal is a face-to-face meeting, so all you must do is convince the employer she will not be wasting time if she meets with you in person. Here are the techniques you should use to turn the phone conversation into a face-to-face meeting.

Organization for Marketing Calls and Telephone Interviews

Your first substantive contact with a potential employer will usually be by telephone; for entry-level professionals this first meeting will quite often take place at job fairs. We'll talk about job fairs in the Appendix. For right now, let's concentrate on the telephone interview.

The phone interview happens in one of three ways:

- You are making a marketing or networking call, and the company representative goes into a screening process because you have aroused her interest.
- An employer calls unexpectedly as the result of a resume you have mailed or e-mailed.
- You have arranged a specific time for a telephone interview.

Odds are good that you will experience plenty of telephone interviews during your job search. Whichever activities generate a telephone interview, you must think and act clearly to turn the opportunity into the real thing—a face-to-face meeting. The way you perform will determine whether you move ahead or bite the dust.

A few words about telephone services: Call waiting might be nice to have for social use, but responding to its demands during a job search will only annoy the person you have on the line at the time. If you have call waiting, disconnect it or ignore it. More and more telephone companies are also offering additional lines with distinctive rings for your basic service and at no extra charge. With this, you can have a permanent job search/career management line, and keep a constant eye on the job market without compromising day-to-day home life.

Perhaps the most important consideration about telephone interviews is that the employer has only his ears with which to judge you. If the call comes unexpectedly, and screaming kids or barking dogs surround you, stay calm, sound positive, friendly, and collected: "Thank you for calling, Mr. Wooster. Would you wait a moment while I close the door?" You can then easily take a minute to calm yourself, call up the company website, and get your paperwork organized without causing offense. If you need to move to another phone, say so. Otherwise, put the caller on hold, take a few controlled, deep breaths to slow down your pounding heart, put a smile on your face (it improves the timbre of your voice), and pick up the phone again. Now you are in control of yourself and the situation.

If you are heading out the door for an interview, or if some other emergency makes this a bad time for an unexpected incoming call, say so straight away and reschedule: "I'm heading out the door for an appointment, Ms. Bassett. Can we schedule a time when I will call you back?" Beware of overfamiliarity: You should always refer to the interviewer by his or her surname until invited to do otherwise.

Allow the company representative to guide the conversation and to ask most of the questions, but keep up your end of the conversation. This is especially important when the interviewer does not give you the openings you need to sell yourself. Always have a few intelligent questions prepared to save the situation. These questions will give you an excellent idea of why the position is open and exactly the kind of skilled professional the company will eventually hire:

- "Why is the job open?"
- "Why was it added? Why did they leave/you have to terminate them?"
- "What are the most important deliverables in this job?"
- "What will be the first project(s) I tackle?"
- "What are the biggest challenges the department faces this year and what will be my role as a team member in tackling them?"
- "Which projects will I be most involved with during the first six months?"
- "Who succeeds in this job and why?"
- "Who fails in this job and why?"

When you get a clear understanding of an employer's needs with questions like these, you can seize the opportunity to sell yourself appropriately: "Would it be of value if I described my experience in the area of office management?" or "Then my experience in word processing should be a great help to you," or "I recently completed an accounting project just like that. Would it be relevant to discuss it?"

When you identify an employer's imminent challenges and demonstrate how your skills can lessen the load, you portray yourself as properly focused with a problem-solving mentality and immediately move closer to a face-to-face interview. Everyone hires a problem solver.

You can also keep up your end of the conversation by giving verbal signals that you are engaged in it; you do this with occasional short interjections that don't interrupt the employer's flow but let him know you are paying attention. Comments like "uh-huh," "that's interesting," "okay," "great," and "yes, yes" are verbal equivalents of the body language techniques you'll use to show interest during a face-to-face meeting.

Always speak directly into the telephone, with the mouthpiece about one inch from your mouth. Numbered among the mystical properties of telephone technology is its excellence at picking up and amplifying background noise. This is excelled only by its power to transmit the sounds of food and gum being chewed, or smoke being inhaled and exhaled. Smokers take note: Nonsmokers instinctively discriminate, and they will assume that even if you don't actually light up at the interview, you'll have been chain-smoking beforehand and will carry the smell with you as long as you are around. Taking no chances, they probably won't even give you a chance to get through the door once they hear you puffing away over the phone.

You should take notes when possible; they will be invaluable if the employer is interrupted. You can jot down the topic under discussion, then when he or she gets back on the line, helpfully recap: "We were just discussing . . . ." This will be appreciated and show that you are organized and paying attention. Your notes will also help you prepare for the face-to-face meeting.

The company representative may talk about the corporation, and from your research or the website on your screen, you may also know something about the outfit. A little flattery goes a long way: Admire a company's achievements when you can, and by inference you admire the interviewer. Likewise, if any areas of common interest arise, comment on them, and agree with the interviewer when reasonably possible—people usually hire people like themselves.

On the 200 telephone interviews a year that I average (they are radio interviews, not job interviews, but I'm sure you can appreciate the similar level of nervous tension), I've found that standing for the interview calms the adrenaline a little, helps my breathing, and allows me to sound confident and relaxed. It might work for you, so give it a try.

Answering Questions

Beware of giving yes-or-no answers, as they give no real information about your abilities and do nothing to forward your agenda. At the same time, don't waffle; your answers need to be concise. Understanding someone over the telephone can sometimes be a challenge, so if you didn't hear or didn't understand a question, ask the speaker to repeat it. If you need time to think about your answer, and that is quite acceptable, say so: "Let me think about that for a moment."

Whenever possible, you should give real-world examples to illustrate your points: "That's interesting. I was involved in an audit like that a couple months back and it presented some interesting challenges."

Interviews often start with, "Tell me a little about yourself." Your interviewer is mainly interested in your fit for this job. Cover the big picture first: degree, years in the field, a couple of achievements. Then, having referred to the TJD and Performance Profile of your resume, recap your professional skills as they relate to the universal demands of this job. Do this, and you will make a powerful first impression.

There are some 200 questions you are likely to be asked during an interview, which we'll cover in detail in the coming pages. Meanwhile, there are a handful of questions often asked during telephone interviews in addition to the ones that will come right after you make a marketing presentation. Let's look at them in light of your probable lack of information about the company and the job.

"What are you looking for?" With so little real knowledge about the company at this point, you need to be careful about specificity. Don't say, "I want to move into marketing," unless you know such opportunity exists. Otherwise keep your answer general.

"What are your strengths?" If you know about specific skill requirements, emphasize them; if not, stick to a brief outline of your professional behavioral profile (discussed in Chapter 9).

"What is your greatest weakness?" Don't throw the opportunity away before you even get in the door and have a real understanding of the job. Mention a brand-new technology/skill you have just developed, and say you have been working on it and try to keep abreast of the latest approaches in all aspects of your profession.

"I don't think you'll be suitable because you lack _______ skill." If the statement is true, acknowledge it, then follow with an example of a similar skill you picked up quickly and apply with consummate skill: "Yes, I understand. When I joined my current company I knew nothing about _______, but I studied on my own and with the help of a mentor within the department I was up to speed in a matter of weeks. Given my proven ability to learn quickly and my willingness to invest my own time, would you consider talking to me in more detail about this topic when we meet face-to-face?" With this type of response you are putting a positive spin on your shortcoming, which gives you a good shot at overcoming the objection. If you are successful in arranging a face-to-face interview, you'll now have time to bone up on the subject and identify a sensible self-development program before you meet with the employer.

Under no circumstances, though, should you ask about salary or benefits and vacation time; that comes much later. Your single objective at this point is to meet face-to-face; money is not an issue. If the interviewer brings up a direct question about how much you are earning, you can't get around it, so be honest. On the other hand, if you are asked how much you want, answer truthfully that at this point you don't know enough about the company or the job to answer that question. Chapter 19, "Negotiating the Job Offer," covers the money issue in some detail.

The telephone interview has come to an end when you are asked whether you have any questions—perhaps, "What would you like to know about us?" This is a wind-down question, so it is a good opening to get some specific questions of your own answered that can advance your candidacy:

- "What are the most immediate challenges of the job?"
- "What are the most important projects of the first six months?"
- "What skills and behaviors are most important to success on the job?"
- "Why do some people succeed and others fail doing this work?"

By discovering answers to these questions now, you will have time before the face-to-face meeting to package your skills according to the needs at hand and to create an appropriate executive briefing for distribution with your resume to the different interviewers you meet.

If you have not already asked or been invited to meet the interviewer, now is the time to take the initiative. "It sounds like a very interesting opportunity, Ms. Bassett, and a situation where I could definitely make a contribution. The most pressing question I have now is when can we get together?" (*Note:* Even though the emphasis throughout has been on putting things in your own words, phrases like "make a contribution" show pride in your work—a key professional behavior—and work as shorthand for "I'm a team player.")

When an invitation for an interview is extended, there are practical matters that you need to clarify with a handful of simple questions that address the when (date and time), and where (don't assume the interview will take place at a facility that you associate with the company). You will also want to inquire about the interview procedure:

- "How many interviews typically occur before a decision is made?"
- "Who else will be part of the selection process, and what are their roles within the department or company?"
- "What is the time frame for filling this position and how many other people are in consideration at this time?"

Follow with a casual inquiry as to what direction the meeting will take. You might ask, "Would you tell me some of the critical areas you will discuss on Thursday?" The knowledge gained will help you to package and present yourself, and it will allow you time to bone up on any weak or rusty areas. This is also a good time to establish how long the meeting is expected to last, which will give you some idea of how to pace yourself.

Once the details are confirmed, finish with this request: "If I need any additional information before the interview, I would like to feel free to get back to you." The company representative will naturally agree. No matter how many questions you get answered in the initial conversation, there will always be something you forgot. This allows you to call again to satisfy any curiosity—it will also enable you to increase rapport. Don't take too much advantage of it, though: One well-placed phone call that contains two or three considered questions will be appreciated; four or five phone calls will not.

In closing your conversation, take care to ascertain the correct spelling and pronunciation of the interviewer's name. This shows your concern for the small but important things in life—and it will be noticed, particularly when the interviewer receives your follow-up thank-you note. (See the latest edition of *Knock 'em Dead Cover Letters* for a comprehensive selection of samples.)

It is difficult to evaluate an opportunity properly over the telephone, so even if the job doesn't sound right, go to the interview; it will give you practice, and the job may look better when you have more facts. You might even discover a more suitable opening elsewhere within the company when you go to the face-to-face interview.

CHAPTER 6

Dress for Job Interview Success

WHEN YOU DRESS like a professional, you are likely to be treated as one, and that's a good head start before saying a word.

The moment you set eyes on someone, your mind makes evaluations and judgments with lightning speed. Potential employers also make the same lightning-speed evaluations when you first meet at the beginning of a job interview. It's a fair estimate that nine out of ten of today's employers will reject an unsuitably dressed applicant without a second thought.

"What You See Is What You Get!"

The initial respect you receive at the interview will be in direct proportion to the image you project. The correct professional appearance won't get you the job offer—but it will lend everything you say that much more credence and weight. Wearing a standard business uniform instantly communicates that you understand one of the paramount unwritten rules of professional life and that you have a confident self-image.

Employers rarely make overt statements about acceptable dress codes to their employees, much less to interviewees. Instead, there is a generally accepted but unspoken dictum that those who wish to succeed will dress appropriately and those who don't, won't.

There are a few professions where on-the-job dress (as opposed to interview dress) is somewhat less conservative than in the mainstream: fashion, entertainment, and advertising are three examples. In these and a few other fields, there is a good deal of leeway with regard to personal expression in workplace attire. But for 95 percent of us, jobs and employers require a certain level of traditional professionalism in our wardrobes. While you need not dress like the chairman of the board (although that probably wouldn't hurt), adopting "casual Friday" attire on the day of your interview is not in your best professional interests. For a job interview, it is generally accepted that you should dress one or two levels up from the job you are applying for, while remaining consistent with the type of occupation it is within. To maximize your career options over the long haul of a career you must aim to consistently meet or exceed these standards.

Your Interview Advantage

Your appearance tells people how you feel about yourself as an applicant, as well as how you feel about the interviewer, the company, and the interview process itself. By dressing professionally, you tell people that you understand the niceties of corporate life, and you send a subtle "reinforcing" message that you can, for example, be relied on to deal one-on-one with members of a company's prized client base.

How you dress sends signals about:

- How seriously you take the occasion, and, by extension, how much respect you feel for your interviewers and all others whom you meet at the interviews.
- How well you understand the confidence a look of traditional professionalism gives clients, customers, peers, and superiors.

Yet no matter how important these concerns might be, they pale in comparison to the impact a sharp appearance can have on your own sense of self. When you know you have taken care of your appearance and that you look the best you can, you feel pride and confidence, your posture is better, you smile more, and you feel more "in control" of your destiny. In turn, others will respond positively to the image of professionalism and self-confidence that you present. Portraying the correct image at an interview will give you a real edge over your competition. You can expect what you say to be strongly influenced in the mind of your interviewer by the way you present yourself: Appearances count.

The Look

The safest look for both men and women at interviews is traditional and conservative. Look at investing in a good-fitting, well-made suit as your first step to a successful strategic career move. With your business clothes, quality matters far more than quantity; it's better to have one good outfit than two mediocre ones. Your professional wardrobe is a long-term career asset, so add quality items, and over time the quantity will come.

Up until recent years, this was fairly easy for men, as their professional fashions tended to remain constant. These days, men's fashions are experiencing a metamorphosis, with designers of high fashion offering affordable lines of updated, professionally acceptable looks. However, a man can always interview with confidence and poise in his six-year-old Brooks Brothers suit, provided it isn't worn to a shine.

For women, things are more complicated. Appropriate female attire for the interview should reflect current professional fashions if the applicant is to be taken seriously. Moreover, in selecting a current professional look, a woman must walk a fine line, combining elements of both conformity (to show she belongs) and panache (to show a measure of individuality and style).

The key for both sexes is to dress for the position you want, not the one you have. This means the upwardly mobile professional might need to invest in the clothes that project the desired image.

The correct appearance alone probably won't by itself get you a job offer, but it does go a long way toward winning the attention and respect you need to land the offer. When you know you look right, you can stop worrying about the impression your clothes are making and concentrate on communicating your message.

Every interview and every interviewer is different, so it isn't possible to set down rigid guidelines for exactly what to wear in any given situation. However, there are a handful of commonsense guidelines that will ensure you are perceived as someone savvy, practical, competent, reliable, and professional.

General Guidelines

The right look varies from industry to industry. A college professor can sport tweed jackets with elbow patches on the job, and an advertising executive may don the latest designer dress or wear wild ties as a badge of creativity (that is what they are being paid for). Nevertheless, that same college professor is likely to wear a suit to an important interview, and even professional men and women in advertising and the media are likely to dress more conservatively for a job interview.

Most of us are far more adept at recognizing the dress mistakes of others than at spotting our own image failings. When you look for a second opinion, you often make the mistake of asking only a loved one. Better candidates for evaluation of your interview attire are trusted professional friends who have proven their objectivity in such matters.

Whenever possible, find out the dress code of the company you are visiting. For example, if you are an engineer applying for a job at a high-tech company, a blue three-piece suit might be overpowering. It is perfectly acceptable to ask someone in Human Resources about the dress code (written or informal) of the company. You may even want to make an anonymous visit to get a sense of the corporate style of the company; if that isn't practical, you can always visit the website to see how the company likes to be perceived by its public.

I have been asked, "If everyone wears sweaters at the company where I am interviewing, shouldn't I wear the same if I want to be seen to fit in?" In fact, very few companies allow a very relaxed dress code for all their employees all the time. An increasing percentage allow a somewhat relaxed dress code on a particular day (often Friday), when "casual professional" attire is allowed, if not always encouraged. Sometimes, some younger professionals mistake this to mean they can dress for the beach at all times. Even if the company is casual all the time for all its employees, do not dress casually for a job interview. There are two big reasons to avoid casual interview attire:

1. The company is considering an investment that will probably run into hundreds of thousands of dollars if the hire works out, and potentially as much as tens of thousands of dollars if it doesn't—hardly a casual event.
2. Companies sometimes allow casual dress at times and in circumstances that will not jeopardize business. They are comfortable doing this because they already know everyone on the payroll knows how to dress appropriately. The interview is where the company needs to know you appreciate the niceties of business dress; they already have a fair idea that you own a sweater and a pair of khakis.

Tattoos and Piercings

If you are contemplating a professional career, recognize that visible body piercings and tattoos will forever close many doors to your entry, and most of the rest to your ascent. While tattoos and piercings are an individual expression and your right, corporations also have a right not to hire people who they feel are unable to represent company interests in the best light. Like it or not, any and all body decoration is *frowned upon by the vast majority of employers.*

In other words if you sport tats or piercings, conceal them during the interview and at all times during your professional endeavors. If you are considering body decoration, ask yourself if in the history of humankind there has ever been one item in any man or woman's wardrobe she or he has willingly worn every day for the rest of his or her life. Soberly weigh your personal interests against your professional success.

Men

Following are the best current dress guidelines for men preparing for a professional interview.

Men's Suits

A *Wall Street Journal* survey of CEOs showed a 53 percent preference for navy blue and dark blue, while 39 percent favored gray or charcoal gray. Brown can be acceptable for subsequent interviews at some companies. In summer months, a lightweight beige suit is fine at second or third interviews; you would never wear a light-colored suit except during the warmer months. Ideally, wear a 100 percent wool suit, as wool looks and wears better than any other material. The darker the suit, the more authority it carries. (Beware: A man should not wear a black suit to an interview unless applying for an undertaker's job.) Pinstripes and solids, in dark gray, navy, or medium blue, are equally acceptable, although many feel a dark solid suit is the best option because it gives authority to the wearer and is seen as less stuffy than a pinstripe suit. Somewhat less common but also acceptable are gray-colored glen plaid (also called "Prince of Wales") or houndstooth suits.

A well-cut two-piece suit is preferable (with the standard two-button suit jacket, although the older three-button, single-breasted jacket is quite acceptable) to a three-piece suit that includes a vest or waistcoat. The three-piece is seen as ultraconservative, which might be a useful tool in some situations, but the extra layer of clothing brings in the heat and sweat factor, which argues against it for more practical reasons. Double-breasted jackets are seen as more edgy and you are more likely to wear them to an interview at an advertising agency than at the local bank.

Above all, it's the quality and fit of your suit that matters. Current fashions favor a slimmer cut, particularly in the trousers. However, the fit and cut must complement your own build. The leaner, tapered look elongates your appearance; the looser cuts add bulk. There should be no pull at the jacket shoulders and no gape at the back, and the jacket cuffs should break at your wrists. Your trousers should fit comfortably at the waist. A flat front is most flattering (unless you are enviably scrawny), and there should be only a slight break where the trouser hits the shoe. If your ankles are visible in the mirror, the pants are too damn short! Cuffed trousers add a very sophisticated and conservative look, but an important consideration might be that uncuffed trousers are seen to enhance your height.

Men's Shirts

The principles here are simple:

Rule One: Always wear a long-sleeved shirt.

Rule Two: Always wear a white, cream, or pale blue shirt.

Rule Three: Never wear a short-sleeved shirt.

By white, I do not mean to exclude, for instance, shirts with very thin red or blue pinstripes. Nevertheless there is a presence about a solid white shirt that seems to convey honesty, intelligence, and stability; it should be your first choice. It is true that artists, writers, software engineers, and other creative types are sometimes known to object to white shirts because they feel that it makes it look like "the suit is wearing them." If this is you and you can't get over it, pale blue may be the best option. Remember—the paler and more subtle the shade, the better the impression you will make. Pale colors draw attention, and your collar is right next to your face, which is where you want the interviewer to stay focused.

While monograms are common enough, those who don't wear them may feel strongly about the implied ostentation of stylized initials on clothing. If you can avoid it, don't take the chance of giving your interviewer a reason to find fault in this area.

Cotton shirts look better and hold up under perspiration more impressively than their synthetic counterparts. If at all possible, opt for a cotton shirt that's been professionally cleaned and starched. A cotton and polyester blend can be an acceptable alternative, but keep in mind that the higher the cotton content, the better the shirt will look. While these blend shirts wrinkle less easily, you are advised to ignore the "wash-and-wear" and "no need to iron" claims you'll read on the front of the package when you purchase them.

Make sure your shirt fits the neck properly; the sleeve cuff should end at the wrist. Details such as frayed fabric and loose buttons will not go unnoticed when you are under professional scrutiny. It's best to choose your interview clothes well in advance, make any minor repairs, have them cleaned, and keep them ready.

Ties

While a cheap-looking tie can ruin the look of an expensive suit, the right tie can do a lot to pull the less-than-perfect suit together for a professional look. When you can't afford a new suit for the interview, you can upgrade your whole look with the right tie.

A pure silk tie makes the most powerful professional impact, has the best finish and feel, and is easiest to tie well. A pure silk tie or a 50 percent wool/50 percent silk blend (which is almost wrinkle-proof) should be your choice for the interview. Linen ties are too informal, can only be tied once or twice between cleanings because they wrinkle easily, and only look right during warmer weather anyway. A wool tie is casual in appearance and has knot problems. Most manmade fibers are too shiny, with harsh colors that may undercut your professional image.

The tie should complement your suit. This means that there should be a physical balance: The rule of thumb is that the width of your tie should approximate the width of your lapels. The prevailing standard, which has held for over a decade now, is that ties can range in width between 2 and 3½ inches. Wearing anything wider may mark you as someone still trapped in the disco era. Currently, ties are being worn narrower in the pages of the fashion magazines, but that really doesn't have to concern you.

While the tie should complement the suit, it should not match it. You would never, for instance, wear a navy blue tie with a navy blue suit. Choose an appropriate tie that neither vanishes into nor battles with your suit pattern. The most popular and safest styles are solids, foulards, stripes, and paisleys.

Do not wear ties with large polka dots, pictures of animals such as leaping trout or soaring mallards, or sporting symbols such as golf clubs or (God forbid) little men on polo ponies. Avoid wearing any piece of apparel that has a manufacturer's symbol emblazoned on the front as part of the decoration.

Other considerations include the length of the tie (it should, when tied, extend to your trouser belt), the size of the knot (smaller is better), and whether you should wear a bow tie to an interview (you shouldn't).

Men's Shoes

Shoes should be either black leather or brown leather. Stay away from all other materials and colors. Lace-up wingtips are the most universally acceptable. Slightly less conservative, but equally appropriate, are slip-on dress shoes—not to be confused with boating shoes. The slip-on, with its low, plain vamp or tassel is versatile enough to be used for both day and evening business wear. Those who are hyperconscious of fashion will say that a lace-up wingtip can look a bit cloddish at dinner. This may be true if you have a dinner interview with the senior law partner of a firm in Chicago, Los Angeles, or New York, but otherwise don't lose sleep over it.

In certain areas of the South, Southwest, and West, heeled cowboy boots are not at all unusual for business wear, and neither are those Grand Ole Opry versions of the business suit. But beware: Outside of Dallas, Nashville, Muskogee, and similar municipalities, you will attract only puzzled stares—so try to be aware of the regional variations in professional dress.

Men's Socks

Socks should complement the suit. Accordingly, they should be blue, black, gray, or brown. When they match the suit color, they extend the length of your leg, giving more height and authority. They should also be long enough for you to cross your legs without showing off bare skin, and should not fall in a bunch toward the ankle as you move. Elastic-reinforced, over-the-calf socks are your best bet.

Men's Accessories

The right accessories can enhance the professional image of any applicant, male or female, just as the wrong accessories can destroy it. The guiding principle here is to include nothing that could be misconstrued or leave a bad impression. For instance, you should not wear obvious religious or political insignias in the form of rings, ties, or pins, as they draw attention to matters that employers are forbidden to address by federal law. This does not necessarily apply when you are aware that a particular spiritual association will establish connectivity, such as wearing a cross when you interview with the local archdiocese.

The watch you wear should be simple and preferably plain, which means that funky Mickey Mouse is out. Sports and Swatch-style watches, or digital monsters, are acceptable nowadays but aren't the best choice. Don't be afraid to wear a simple, slim analog watch with a leather strap; you will notice it is what the most successful and sophisticated business professionals wear.

A briefcase is always perceived as a symbol of authority and can make a strong professional statement. Leather makes the best impression, with brown and burgundy being the colors of choice. The case is best unadorned—embellishments can only detract from the effect of quiet confidence and authority.

It's a good idea to take a cotton or linen handkerchief on all interviews. Plain white is best because it looks crisp, but the color isn't really that important. You aren't taking a handkerchief to put in a breast pocket but for far more practical reasons. That handkerchief can be used to relieve the clammy-hands syndrome so common before an interview—anything to avoid the infamous "wet fish" handshake. Keep it in an inside pocket, avoiding the matching tie-and-pocket-square look of a dyed-in-the-wool doofus at all costs.

Belts should match or complement the shoes you select. Accordingly, a blue or gray suit will require a black belt and black shoes, while brown, tan, or beige suits call for brown. Wear a good-quality leather belt if you can. The most common mistake made with belts is the buckle; an interview is not the place for your favorite Harley Davidson, Grateful Dead, or Bart Simpson buckle. Select a small, simple buckle that doesn't overwhelm the rest of your look or make personal statements that you cannot be certain will resonate with an interviewer.

Men's Jewelry

Men may wear a wedding band, and cuff links are acceptable with French cuffs. Anything more in the way of jewelry can be dangerous. Necklaces, bracelets, neck chains, and earrings can send the wrong message, and tie tacks and clips are passé in most areas of the country.

Men's Raincoats

The safest and most utilitarian colors for raincoats are beige and blue; stick to these two exclusively. If you can avoid wearing a raincoat, do so (it's an encumbrance and adds to clutter), but it is better to have a raincoat than to have your suit drenched.

Women

Following are the best current dress guidelines for women preparing for a professional interview.

Women's Suits

You have more room for creativity in this area than men do, but also more room for mistakes. Until recent years, your professional fashion creativity had to remain within certain accepted guidelines dictated not by the fashion industry, but by the consensus of the business world—which trails far behind the pages of fashion magazines. And while there are still the limits of good taste and necessary conservatism for the interviewer, the fashion designers have worked hard to create workable professional alternatives for the ever-growing female workforce.

A woman's business wardrobe need no longer be simply a pseudo-male selection of drab gray skirts and blouses. With the right cuts, pinstripes and even ties can look both stylish and professional.

Wool and linen are both accepted as the right look for professional women's suits, but linen can present a problem. Linen wrinkles so quickly that you may feel as though you leave the house dressed for success and arrive at your destination looking like a bag lady. Cotton-polyester blends are great for warm climates; they look like linen but lack the "wrinkle factor." Combinations of synthetics and natural fabrics have their advantages: Suits made of such material will certainly retain their shape better. The eye trained to pay attention to detail, however (read: the interviewer's), may detect the type of fabric—say, a cheap polyester blend—and draw unwarranted conclusions about your personality and taste. The choice is up to you. If you do opt for natural fabrics, you will probably want to stay with wool. It provides the smartest look of all and is most versatile and rugged. There are wonderful, ultralight wool gabardines available now that will take you through the toughest interview on the hottest summer day.

Like her male counterpart, the professional woman should stick to solids or pinstripes in gray, navy, and medium blues. The ubiquitous Prince of Wales plaid (glen plaid) or houndstooth check can both look very distinguished on a woman as well. At the same time, a much wider palette of colors is open for consideration by the professional woman, from lilac to fire engine red. While there are situations where you will want to choose one of the more powerful colors, it might be best at one of the subsequent interviews, rather than the first.

A solid skirt with a coordinating subtle plaid jacket is also acceptable, but make sure there is not too much contrast or it will detract from the focus of your meeting: the interview. Colors most suitable for interview suits include charcoal, medium gray, steel gray, black (whereas a man is advised against black, the color is open and acceptable for the professional woman), and navy blue. Of all these looks, the cleanest and most professional is the simple solid navy or gray suit with a white blouse.

Jackets should be simple, well tailored, and stylish, but not stylized. This is probably not the time to wear a peplum-style jacket—a standard length that falls just at the hips is preferable. The cut and style should flatter your build and reflect your personal style, without detracting from what you have to say. Attention to details such as smooth seams, even hemlines, correctly hanging linings, and well-sewn buttons are essential.

How long a skirt should you wear? Any hard-and-fast rule I could offer here would be in danger of being outdated almost immediately, as the fashion industry demands dramatically different looks every season in order to fuel sales. (After all, keeping the same hemlines would mean that last season's clothes could last another season or two.) It should go without saying that you don't want to sport something that soars to the upper thigh if you want to be taken seriously as an applicant. Your best bet is to dress somewhat more conservatively than you would if you were simply showing up for work at the organization in question. Hemlines come and go, and while there is some leeway as to what is appropriate for everyday wear on the job, the safest bet is usually to select something that falls at or no more than two inches above the knee.

Increasingly popular is the one-piece business dress with a matching jacket. This outfit is particularly useful for the "business day into evening" crowd, but can be perfectly suitable for interviews if it is properly styled and fitted. It is particularly important to stick with subtle solid colors for this look.

Blouses

Blouses with long sleeves will project a responsible and professional look. Three-quarter-length sleeves are less desirable, followed in turn by short sleeves. Never wear a sleeveless blouse to an interview; you may be confident that there is absolutely no chance that you will be required to remove your jacket, but why take the risk of offending someone with unexpected glimpses of undergarments?

Solid colors and natural fabrics, particularly cotton and silk, are the best selections for blouses—although silk is warm and therefore raises perspiration concerns for a nervous interviewee. Combinations of natural and synthetic fabrics are wrinkle-resistant but do not absorb moisture well, so with these choices you will need to take perspiration countermeasures into account.

The acceptable color spectrum is wider for blouses than for men's shirts, but it is not limitless. The most prudent choices are still white or cream or gray; these offer a universal professional appeal. Pale pink or light blue can also work, but should be worn only if it fully blends into your overall look. Light colors are "friendly" and draw attention to your face, yet will not distract the interviewer from what you have to say. The blouse with a front-tie bow has become dated; a classic softened shirt collar works best with a suit. The button-down collar always looks great, particularly if you are interviewing with a conservative company or industry.

Women's Neckwear

While a woman might choose to wear a string of pearls instead of a scarf to an interview, the scarf can still serve as a powerful status symbol. Opting to wear a scarf says something dramatic about you; make sure it's something positive. A pure silk scarf will offer a conservative look, a good finish, and ease in tying. Some of the better synthetic blends achieve an overall effect that is almost as good. While some books on women's clothing will recommend buying blouses that have matching scarves attached to the collar, there is an increasingly vocal lobby of stylish businesswomen who feel this is the equivalent of mandating that a man wear a clip-on bow tie. As with men's ties, the objective is to complement the outfit, not match it. Avoid overly flamboyant styles, and stick with solids or basic prints (foulards, small polka dots, or paisleys) in subtle colors that will complement—not compete with—your outfit or your conversation.

Women's Shoes

The professional woman has a greater color selection in footwear than does her male counterpart. The shoes should preferably be leather, but in addition to brown and black, a woman is safe in wearing navy, burgundy, forest green, or even, if circumstances warrant and it is not a first interview, red. The color of your shoes should always be the same or a darker tone than your skirt.

It is safest to stay away from faddish or multicolored shoes (even such classics as two-toned oxfords). First, all fashion is transitory, and even if you are up-to-date, you cannot assume that your interviewer is. Second, a good proportion of your interviewers might be men, who are less likely to appreciate vivid color combinations. As with the rest of your wardrobe, stay away from radical choices and opt for the easily comprehensible professional look.

Heel height is important, as well. Flats are fine; a shoe with a heel of up to about 2½ inches is perfectly acceptable. Stay away from high heels; at best you will wobble slightly, and at worst you will walk at an angle. The pump, or court shoe, with its closed toe and heel, is perhaps the safest and most conservative look. A closed heel with a slightly open toe is acceptable, too, as is the slingback shoe with a closed toe. The toe on any style should not be overly pointed. Just think moderation in all things; the goal is to get hired, not dated.

Pantyhose

These should not make their own statement. Neutral skin tones are the safest, most conservative choice, though you are perfectly within the realm of professional etiquette when wearing a sheer white or cream if it complements your blouse or dress. You may make an exception if you are interviewing for a job in the fashion industry, in which case you might coordinate colors with your outfit, but be very sure of the company dress code that is already in place. Even in such an instance, avoid loud or glitzy looks. As you well know, pantyhose and stockings are prone to developing runs at the worst possible moment, so keep an extra pair in your purse or briefcase.

Women's Accessories

Because a briefcase is a symbol of authority, it is an excellent choice for the professional woman. Do not, however, bring both your purse and a briefcase to the interview. (You'll look awkward juggling them.) Instead, transfer essential items to a small clutch bag you can store in the case. In addition to brown and burgundy (recommended colors for the men), you may include navy and black as possible colors for your case, which should always be free of personal, expensive, or distracting embellishments.

Belts should match or complement the shoes you select. A black or gray suit will require a black belt and black shoes; brown, tan, or beige suits will call for brown; and navy looks best with navy or burgundy accessories. In addition, women may wear snakeskin, lizard, and the like (though beware of offending animal rights activists). Remember that the belt is a functional item; if it is instantly noticeable, it is wrong.

Women's Jewelry

As far as jewelry goes, less is more. A woman should restrict rings to engagement or wedding bands if these are applicable, but she can wear a necklace and earrings, as long as these are subdued and professional looking. I should note that some men are put off by earrings of any description in the workplace, so if you wear them keep them small, discreet, and in good taste. Avoid fake or strangely colored pearls, anything with your name or initials on it, and earrings that dangle or jangle. A single bracelet on a woman's wrist is acceptable; anything around the ankle is not. Remember, too much of the wrong kind of jewelry could cost you a job offer or inhibit your promotional opportunities once on the team.

Makeup

Take care never to appear overly made-up; "natural" is the key word. Eye makeup should be subtle, so as not to overwhelm the rest of the face. As a general rule, I advise very little lipstick at an interview because it can cause negative reactions in some interviewers, and because it can smudge and wear off as the hours wear on. (Who can say, going in, how long the meeting will last?) However, women tell me that as they advance into their thirties and beyond, the natural pinkness of the lips can fade; you might feel you look pale and washed out without lipstick. So if you feel "undressed" without your lipstick, use some but apply it sparingly and carefully, choose a neutral or subdued color, and, of course, never apply it in public.

For Men and Women: A Note on Personal Hygiene

Bad breath, dandruff, body odor, and dirty, un-manicured nails have the potential to undo all your efforts at putting across a good first impression. These and related problems all speak to an underlying professional slovenliness, which an interviewer may feel will manifest itself in your work. You want to present yourself as an appealing, self-respecting, and enjoyable professional to be around. You can't achieve this if the people you meet have to call on their powers of self-control in order to stay in the same room with you.

What was that old TV body odor commercial tag line: "What even your best friend won't tell you"? So don't ask yourself whether any friend or colleague has actually come out and suggested that you pay more attention to personal hygiene; it is such a touchy issue that most people will avoid you rather than discuss it. Ask yourself how you felt the last time you had to conduct business of any sort with someone who had a hygiene problem. Then resolve never to leave that kind of impression.

Personal grooming of hair, skin, teeth, and nails is easy and straightforward, but body odor is a different challenge. When it comes to body odor you are literally what you eat; onions, garlic, cilantro, and junk food can all give your bodily odors a distinctly unpleasant pungency. Because it takes time for your body to rid itself of such smells, the best advice is to start paying attention to diet as you begin to put your wardrobe together.

CHAPTER 7

Body Language

LEARN TO CONTROL negative body movements and encourage positive ones. Discover the seven guidelines for good body language during your interview.

Given the awful choice of going either blind or deaf, which would you choose? If you're like most people, you would choose to go deaf. As human beings, we rely to a remarkable degree on our ability to gather information visually. This really is not all that surprising, because while speech is a comparatively recent development, humans have been sending and receiving nonverbal signals since the dawn of the species.

In fact, the language of the body is the first means of communication we develop after birth. We master the spoken word later in life, and in so doing we forget the importance of nonverbal cues—but the signals are still sent and received (usually at a subconscious level).

It is common to hear people say of the body language they use, "Take me or leave me as I am." This is all very well if you have no concern for what others think of you. For those seeking professional employment, however, it is important to recognize that your body is constantly sending messages and to make every effort to understand and control the information stream. If your mouth says, "Hire me," but your body says, "I'm not being truthful," you are likely to leave the interviewer confused. "Well," he or she will think, "the right answers all came out, but there was something about that candidate that just rubbed me the wrong way." Such misgivings are generally sufficient to keep a candidate from making the short list. The interviewer may or may not be aware of what causes the concern, but the messages will be sent, and your cause will suffer.

Of course, interviewers can be expected to listen carefully to what you say, too. When your body language doesn't contradict your statements, you will generally be given credence. When your body language complements your verbal statements, your message will gain a great deal of impact, but when your body language *contradicts* what you say, the interviewer will be skeptical. In short, learning to use positive body signals and control negative ones during an interview can have a significant impact on your job search and on the new job.

Under the Microscope

The challenge for the interviewer is to determine, using every means at his or her disposal, what kind of an employee you would make. Your task as a candidate is to provide the clues most likely to prompt a decision to hire.

Let's begin at the beginning. When you are invited in for an interview, you are probably safe in assuming that your interviewer believes you meet certain minimum standards and could conceivably be hired.

In this context, the adage that actions speak louder than words appears to be something you should take quite literally. Studies done at the University of Chicago found that over 50 percent of all effective communication relies on body language. Since you can expect interviewers to respond to the body language you employ at the interview, it is up to you to decide what messages you want them to receive.

There are also studies that suggest the impression you create in the first few minutes of the interview is the most lasting. Since the first few minutes after you meet the interviewer is a time when he or she is doing the vast majority of the talking, you have very little control over the impression you create with your words—you can't say much of anything! It is up to your body to do the job for you.

The Greeting

For a good handshake:

1. Your hands should be clean and adequately manicured.
2. Your hands should be free of perspiration.

It is best to allow the interviewer to initiate the handshake. If, through nerves, you find yourself initiating the handshake, don't pull back, as you will appear indecisive. Instead, make the best of it, smile confidently, and make good eye contact.

Your handshake should signal cooperation and friendliness. Match the pressure extended by the interviewer—never exceed it. A typical professional handshake lasts for between two and five seconds, just two or three reasonably firm up and down pumps accompanied by a smile. The parting handshake may last a little longer; smile and lean forward very slightly as you shake hands before departing.

Certain professional and cultural differences should also be considered as well. Many doctors, artists, and others who do delicate work with their hands can and do give less enthusiastic handshakes than other people. If you work in media you'll notice that quite frequently on-air personalities don't want to shake hands at all; it's the easiest way to catch a cold and they depend on their voices and appearance more than most. Similarly, the English handshake is considerably less firm than the American, while the German variety is typically firm.

Use only one hand and always shake vertically. Do not extend your hand parallel to the floor with the palm up, as this conveys submissiveness. By the same token, you may be seen as too aggressive if you extend your hand outward with the palm facing down.

While a confident and positive handshake helps break the ice and gets the interview moving in the right direction, proper use of the hands throughout the rest of the interview will help convey an above-board, "nothing-to-hide" message.

Watch out for hands and fingers that take on a life of their own, fidgeting with themselves or other objects such as pens, paper, your tie, or your hair. Pen tapping is interpreted as the action of an impatient person; this is an example of an otherwise trivial habit that can take on immense significance in an interview situation. Rarely will an interviewer ask you to stop doing something annoying. Instead, he'll simply make a mental note that you are an annoying person and congratulate himself for picking this up before making the mistake of hiring you.

Other negative hand messages include:

- Clasping your hands behind your head: You'll expose perspiration marks, and you run the risk of appearing smug, superior, bored, and possibly withdrawn.
- Showing insecurity by constantly adjusting your tie: When interviewing with a woman, this gesture might be interpreted as displaying something beyond a businesslike interest in the interviewer.
- Slouching in your chair, with hands in pockets or thumbs in belt: This posture can brand you as insolent and aggressive (just recall any teenage boy). When this error is made in the presence of an interviewer of the opposite sex, it can carry sexually aggressive overtones as well.
- Pulling your collar away from your neck: This may seem like an innocent enough reaction to the heat of the day, but the interviewer might assume that you are tense or masking an untruth. The same goes for scratching your neck during, before, or after your response to a question.
- Moving your hands toward a personal feature that you perceive as deficient: This is a common unconscious reaction to stress. A man with thinning hair, for example, may thoughtlessly put his hand to his forehead when pondering how to respond to the query, "Why aren't you earning more at your age?" This habit may be extremely difficult for you to detect in the first place, much less reverse, but make the effort. Such protective movements are likely to be perceived—if only on a subliminal level—as acknowledgments of low self-esteem.
- Picking at invisible bits of fluff on one's suit: This gesture looks exactly like what it is, a nervous tic. Keep your focus on the interviewer. If you do have some bit of lint somewhere on your clothing, the best advice is usually to ignore it until you can remove it discreetly.

By contrast, employing the hands in a positive way can further your candidacy:

- Subtly exposing your palms now and then as you speak can help demonstrate that you are open, friendly, and have nothing to hide. You can see this technique used to great effect by politicians and television talk show hosts.
- It can, very occasionally, be beneficial to "steeple" your fingers for a few seconds as you consider a question or when you first start to talk. Unless you hold the gesture for long periods of time, it will be perceived as a neutral demonstration of your thoughtfulness. Of course, if you overuse this or hold the position for too long, you may be taken as condescending. Steepling also gives you something constructive to do with your hands; it offers a change from holding your pad and pen.

Taking Your Seat

Some thirty inches from my nose
The frontier of my person goes.
Beware of rudely crossing it,
I have no gun, but I can spit.
—W. H. Auden

Encroaching on another's "personal zone" is a bad idea in any business situation, but it is particularly dangerous in an interview. The thirty-inch standard is a good one to follow: It is the distance that allows you to extend your hand comfortably for a handshake. Maintain this distance throughout the interview, and be particularly watchful of personal-space intrusions when you first meet, greet, and take a seat.

A person's office is an extension of his or her personal zone; this is why it is not only polite but also sound business sense to wait until the interviewer offers you a seat.

It is not uncommon to meet with an interviewer in a conference room or another supposedly "neutral" site. Again, wait for the interviewer to motion you to a spot, or, if you feel uncomfortable doing this, tactfully ask the interviewer to take the initiative: "Where would you like me to sit?"

The type of chair you sit in can affect the signals your body sends during an interview. If you have a choice, go with an upright chair with arms. Deep armchairs can restrict your ability to send certain positive signals, and encourage the likelihood of slumping. They're best suited for watching television, not for projecting the image of a competent professional.

Always sit with your bottom well back in the chair and your back straight. Slouching, of course, is out, but a slight forward-leaning posture will show interest and friendliness toward the interviewer. Keep your hands on the sides of the chair; if there are no arms on the chair, keep your hands in your lap or on your pad of paper.

Crossed legs, in all their many forms, send a mixture of signals; most of them are negative:

- Crossing one ankle over the other knee can show a certain stubborn and recalcitrant outlook (as well as the bottom of your shoe, which is not always a pretty sight). The negative signal is intensified when you grasp the horizontally crossed leg or—worst of all—cross your arms across your chest.
- Some body language experts feel crossed ankles indicate that the person doing the crossing is withholding information. Of course, since the majority of interviews take place across a desk, crossed ankles will often be virtually unnoticeable. For women, some dress fashions encourage decorous ankle crossing. This posture is probably the most permissible body language faux pas, so if you must allow yourself one body language vice, this is the one to choose.

- When sitting in armchairs or on sofas, crossing the legs may be necessary to create some stability amid all the plush upholstery. In this instance, the signals you send by crossing your legs will be neutral, as long as your crossed legs point toward, rather than away from, the interviewer.

Facial Signals

Once you take your seats, most often across a desk, and the conversation begins, the interviewer's attention will be focused on your face.

Our language is full of expressions testifying to the powerful influence of facial mannerisms. When you say that someone is shifty-eyed, tight-lipped, has a furrowed brow, flashes bedroom eyes, stares into space, or grins like a Cheshire cat, you are speaking in a kind of shorthand and using a set of stereotypes that enables us to make judgments—consciously or unconsciously—about that person.

Tight smiles and tension in the facial muscles often bespeak an inability to handle stress; little eye contact can communicate a desire to hide something; pursed lips are often associated with a secretive nature; and frowning, looking sideways, or peering over one's glasses can send signals of haughtiness and arrogance. Hardly the stuff of which winning interviews are made!

The Eyes

Looking at someone means showing interest in that person, and showing interest is a giant step forward in making the right impression. Remember: We are all our own favorite subjects!

Looking away from the interviewer for long periods while he is talking, closing your eyes while being addressed, and repeatedly shifting focus from the subject to some other point are all likely to leave the wrong impression.

Of course, there is a big difference between looking and staring at someone! Rather than looking at the speaker straight on at all times, create a mental triangle incorporating both of the eyes and the mouth; your eyes will follow a natural, continuous path along the three points. Maintain this approach for roughly three-quarters of the time; you can break your gaze to look at the interviewer's hands as points are emphasized or to refer to your notepad. This is the way we maintain eye contact in nonstressful situations, and it will allow you to appear attentive, sincere, and committed.

Be wary of breaking eye contact too abruptly and of shifting your focus in ways that will disrupt the atmosphere of professionalism. Examining the interviewer below the head and shoulders, for instance, is a sign of overfamiliarity. This is especially important when being interviewed by someone of the opposite sex.

The eyebrows send messages as well. Under stress, one's brows may wrinkle; this sends a negative signal about your ability to handle challenges in the business world. The best thing to do is take a deep breath and collect yourself. Most of the tension that people feel at interviews has to do with anxiety about how to respond to what the interviewer will ask.

The Head

Nodding your head slowly shows interest, validates the comments of your interviewer, and subtly encourages her to continue. Tilting the head slightly, when combined with eye contact and a natural smile, demonstrates friendliness and approachability. The tilt should be momentary and not exaggerated, almost like a bob of the head to one side. (Do not overuse this technique unless you are applying for a job in a parrot shop!) Rapidly nodding your head can leave the impression that you are impatient and eager to add something to the conversation—if only the interviewer would let you.

The Mouth

One guiding principle of good body language is to turn your mouth upward rather than downward. Look at two boxers after a fight: The victor's arms are raised high, his back is straight, and his shoulders are square. His smiling face is thrust upward and outward, and you see happiness, openness, warmth, and confidence. The loser, on the other hand, is slumped forward, brows knit and eyes downcast, and the signals you receive are those of anger, frustration, belligerence, and defeat.

Your smile is one of the most powerful positive body signals in your arsenal, and it exemplifies the up-is-best principle. Offer an unforced, confident smile as frequently as opportunity and circumstances dictate; avoid grinning idiotically, as this indicates that you may not be quite right in the head.

You should be aware that the mouth also provides a seemingly limitless supply of opportunities to convey weakness. This may be done by touching the mouth frequently, faking a cough when confronted with a difficult question, or gnawing on one's lips absentmindedly. Employing any of these "insincerity signs" when you are asked about, say, why you lost your last job, might instill or confirm suspicions about your honesty or openness.

Glasses

People who wear glasses sometimes leave them off when going on an interview in an attempt to project a more favorable image. There are difficulties with this approach. Farsighted people who don't wear their glasses will (unwittingly) seem to stare long and hard at the people they converse with, and this is a negative signal. Also, pulling out glasses for reading and peering over the top of your glasses—even if you have been handed something to read and subsequently asked a question—carries professorial connotations that can be interpreted as critical. If you wear glasses for reading, you should remove them when conversing, replacing them only when appropriate.

Wearing dark glasses to an interview will paint you as secretive, cold, and devious. Even if your prescription glasses are tinted, the effect will be the same. You might consider un-tinted glasses for your interview, or contacts. At the same time, glasses on a younger-looking person can add an air of seriousness and might be considered a plus.

Body Signal Barricades

Folding or crossing your arms, or holding things in front of the body, sends negative messages to the interviewer: "I know you're there, but you can't come in. I'm nervous and closed for business."

It is bad enough to feel this way, but worse to express it with blatant signals. Don't fold your arms or "protect" your chest with hands, clipboard, briefcase, or anything else during the interview. You can, however, keep a pad and pen on your lap. It makes you look organized and gives you something to do with your hands.

Feet

Some foot signals can have negative connotations. Women and men wearing slip-on shoes should beware of dangling the loose shoe from the toes; this can be distracting, and, as it is a gesture often used to signal physical attraction, it has no place in a job interview. Likewise, avoid compulsive jabbing of floor, desk, or chair with your foot; this can be perceived as a hostile and angry motion, and is likely to annoy the interviewer.

Some people (your author is included in the front ranks on this one) have an annoying habit of jiggling one leg up and down on the ball of the foot. Those of us who do this know it is a tic that says we are totally engaged and excited about some topic (and sometimes even the one under discussion), but those forced to endure it find it distracting and can interpret it as impatience. If you are a dreaded jiggler, you must get this under control for your job interviews!

Walking

Many interviews will require that you walk from one place to the next—on a guided tour of facilities, from one office to another, or to and from the table in a restaurant. (Of course, if you are interviewing in a restaurant, you will have to walk with your interviewer to and from the dining facility.) How long these walks last is not as important as how you use them to reinforce positive professional behaviors and impressions.

Posture is your main concern: Keep your shoulders back and maintain an erect posture. Smile and make eye contact as appropriate. Avoid fidgeting with your feet as you move, rubbing one shoe against the other, or kicking absentmindedly at the ground if you stand to talk; these signals will lead others to believe that you are anxious or insecure. Crossing your arms or legs while standing carries the same negative connotations as it does when you are sitting. Hands-in-pockets, hands-on-hips, or thumbs-in-belt postures are all to be avoided. These send messages that you are aggressive and dominating. It is better to hold a pad and pen or keep your arms on the arms of the chair, which will also help you avoid slouching. Remember to show one or both of your palms occasionally as you make points, but do not overuse this gesture.

Putting It All Together

Now you have the big picture, and you can begin to be more aware of the signals your body can unwittingly send. Let's reduce all this information into a handful of simple recommendations. Positive signals reinforce one another; employing them in combination yields an overwhelming positive message that is truly greater than the sum of its parts.

So far we have focused primarily on the pitfalls to avoid—but what messages *should* be sent, and how? Here are seven general suggestions on good body language for the interview:

1. Walk slowly and stand tall upon entering the room.
2. On greeting your interviewer, give a smile, make eye contact, and respond warmly to the interviewer's greeting and handshake.
3. As you sit, get your butt well back in the chair; this allows the chair back to help you sit upright. Increase the impression of openness ("I have nothing to hide!") by unbuttoning your jacket as you sit down. Keep your head up. Maintain eye contact a good portion of the time, especially when the interviewer begins to speak and when you reply. Smile naturally whenever the opportunity arises.
4. Use mirroring techniques to reproduce the positive signals your interviewer sends. Say the interviewer leans forward to make a point; a few moments later, you too lean forward slightly, demonstrating that you don't want to miss a word. Perhaps the interviewer leans back and laughs; you "laugh beneath" the interviewer's laughter, taking care not to overwhelm your partner by using an inappropriate volume level. This can seem contrived at first, but through observing those in your own social circle, you'll notice that this is natural behavior for good communicators.
5. Keep your head up and your eyes front at all times—and don't slouch in your seat.

6. Try to remain calm and do not hurry your movements; you'll look harried and are more likely to knock things over. Most people are more klutzy when they are nervous, and consciously slowing your body movements will lessen the chances of disaster and give you a more controlled persona.
7. Remember to breathe. When we are nervous we can forget to do this, which leads to oxygen deprivation and obviously screws up cognitive processes.

Open for Business

The more open your body movements during the interview, the more you will be perceived as open yourself. Understanding and directing your body language will give you added power to turn interviews into cooperative exchanges between two professionals.

Just as you interpret the body language of others, both positive and negative, your body language makes an indelible impression on those you meet. It tells them whether you like and have confidence in yourself, whether or not you are pleasant to be around, and whether you are more likely to be honest or deceitful. Like it or not, your body carries these messages for the world to see.

Job interviews are reliable in one way: They bring out insecurities. All the more reason to consciously manage the impressions your body sends. You will absorb the lessons in this chapter quite quickly if you take the time to observe and interpret the body signals of friends and family. When you see and can understand body language in others, you'll be more aware of your own, and more capable of controlling it.

CHAPTER 8
The Curtain Rises on the Job Interview

FIRST IMPRESSIONS ARE the strongest. Here are the preparations to make before heading out to the interview.

Backstage in the theater, the announcement "Places, please" is made five minutes before the curtain rises. It's the performers' signal to psych themselves up, complete final costume adjustments, and make time to reach the stage. They are getting ready to go onstage and *Knock 'em Dead*. You should go through a similar process to get thoroughly prepared for your time in the spotlight.

Winning a job offer depends not only on the things you do well but also on the mistakes you avoid. As the interview approaches, settle down with your resume and the exercises you performed in building it. Immerse yourself in your past successes and the professional behaviors that made them possible. Interview nerves are to be expected; the trick is to use them to your benefit by harnessing that nervous energy for your physical and mental preparation.

The company dossier: Always take copies of the resume you customized for this job and an executive briefing that clearly defines how you match the job's requirements: one for you and one for each of the interviewers you might meet. Your main interviewer will invariably have a copy of your resume, but you can't be certain of that with other people you meet. It is perfectly acceptable to have your resume in front of you at the interview; it shows you are organized, and it makes a great cheat sheet. It is not unusual to hear, "Mr. Jones wasn't hired because he didn't pay attention to detail and couldn't even remember his employment dates"—just the kind of thing you are likely to forget in the nervousness of the moment.

A decent folder with pad of paper and writing instruments: These demonstrate your preparedness, and they give you something constructive to do with your hands during the interview; you can keep your resume in the folder.

Reference letters: If you have reference letters from past employers, take them along. Some employers don't put much stock in written references and prefer a one-on-one conversation with past employers. Nevertheless, having them with you and getting them placed in your candidate file can't do any harm.

A list of job-related questions: The details of the job you already know are likely to be general in nature. Asking questions that give you the practical details of the activities you will be involved with in the first few months will make you think about your experience with a focus that is complementary to that of your interviewers. You might ask:

- "What are the most immediate challenges of the job?"
- "What are the most important projects of the first six months?"
- "What skills and behaviors are most important to success on the job?"
- "Why do some people succeed and others fail doing this work?"
- "Why is the job open?"
- "What is the job's relationship to other departments?"
- "How do the job and the department relate to the corporate mission?"

You can find more questions to ask at the end of Chapter 10. (*Note*: In the early rounds of interviewing, stay away from questions about where the job can lead and what the pay and benefits are. It's not that these questions aren't important to you, just that the timing is wrong. It won't do you any good to know what a job pays when you aren't going to get a job offer. Instead, ask the questions that will lead to a job offer being extended, and then ask the questions you need to evaluate that offer. For questions to ask during the negotiation phase, see Chapter 19, "Negotiating the Job Offer.")

Any additional information you have about the company or the job: If time permits, visit the company website, review any company literature and research you might have, and do a Google search for news articles mentioning the company by name and for articles that relate to your profession.

Directions to the interview: Decide on your form of transportation and finalize your time of departure, leaving enough time to accommodate travel delays. Check the route, distance, and travel time. If you forget to verify date, time, and place (including floor and suite number), you might not even arrive at the right place, or on the right day, for your interview. Write it all down legibly and put it with the rest of your interview kit.

To arrive at an interview too early indicates overanxiousness and to arrive late is inconsiderate, so arrive at the interview on time, but at the location early. This allows you time to visit the restroom (usually your only private sanctuary at an interview) and make the necessary adjustments to your appearance, review any notes, and put on your "game face." Remember to add contact telephone numbers to your interview kit, so if you are delayed on the way to the interview, you can call and let the interviewer know.

Your dress should be clean-cut and conservative. As you could be asked to appear for an interview at a scant couple of hours' notice, keep your best outfit freshly cleaned, shirts or blouses wrinkle-free, shoes polished, and all readied for interviews at a moment's notice.

Visit the hairdresser once a month so that you always look groomed, and keep your nails clean and trimmed at all times (even if you work with your hands). While you will naturally shower or bathe prior to an interview, and the use of an unscented deodorant is advisable, you should avoid wearing after-shave or perfume; you are trying to get a job, not a date. Never drink alcohol the day before an interview. It affects eyes, skin tone, and your wits.

When you get to the interview site, visit the restroom to check your appearance and take a couple of minutes to do the following:

- Review the company dossier.
- Recall your commitment to the profession and the team, and the professional behaviors that help you succeed.
- Breathe deeply and slowly for a minute to dispel your natural physical tension.
- Review the questions you will need to identify first projects and initial needs.
- Smile and head for the interview—you are as ready as you are ever going to be. Afterward you will review your performance to make sure the next one goes even better.

Under no circumstances should you back out because you do not like the receptionist or the look of the office—that would be allowing personal insecurities to triumph. You are here to improve one of your most critical professional skills—turning interviews into job offers. Whatever happens, you can and must learn from this experience.

KNOCK 'EM DEAD TIP

Turn off your cell phone. It is inappropriate and distracting for you and for the interviewer to have a phone ring during an interview. If for any reason you forget and it does ring, just apologize and turn it off. Never answer a personal call at a job interview.

As you are shown into the office, you are on!

This potential new employer wants an aggressive and dynamic employee, but someone who is less aggressive and dynamic than he or she is, so take your lead from the interviewer.

Do:

- Give a firm handshake—respond to the interviewer's grip and duration.
- Make eye contact and smile. Say, "Hello, Ms. Larsen. I am John Jones. I have been looking forward to meeting you."

Do not:

- Use first names (unless asked).
- Smoke (even if invited).
- Sit down (until invited).
- Show anxiety or boredom.
- Look at your watch.
- Discuss equal rights, sex, race, national origin, religion, or age.
- Show samples of your work (unless requested).
- Ask about benefits, salary, or vacation.

Now you are ready for anything—except for the tough questions that are going to be thrown at you next. We'll handle those in the following pages.

PART III
Great Answers to Tough Interview Questions

IN THIS PART of the book you will learn why interviewers do the things they do. You'll also learn the formulas for answering tough interview questions without sounding like a snake oil salesman.

"LIKE BEING ON TRIAL FOR YOUR LIFE" is how many people look at a job interview. With the interviewer as judge and jury, you are at least on trial for your livelihood, so you must have winning strategies. F. Lee Bailey, one of America's most celebrated defense attorneys, attributes his success in the courtroom to preparation. He likens himself to a magician going into court with fifty rabbits in his hat, not knowing which one he'll really need, but ready to pull out any single one. Bailey is successful because he is ready for any eventuality and because he takes the time to analyze every situation and every possible option. He never underestimates his opposition, he is always prepared, and he usually wins.

Another famous attorney, Louis Nizer, successfully defended all of his fifty-plus capital offense clients. When lauded as the greatest courtroom performer of his day, Nizer denied the accolade. He claimed for himself only the distinction of being the ***best prepared.***

You won't win your day in court just based on your skills. As competition for the best jobs increases, employers are comparing more candidates for every opening and becoming more skilled in the art of selection. To consistently win against stiff competition, like Bailey and Nizer, you have to be prepared for the questions that can be thrown at you, and that requires understanding what is behind them.

During an interview, employers ask you dozens of searching questions—questions that test your knowledge, skills, confidence, poise, and professional behaviors (we'll address this in some detail in a few pages). There are questions that can trick you into contradicting yourself and questions that probe your analytical skills and integrity. They are all designed so the interviewer can make decisions in these critical areas:

- Can you do the job?
- Are you motivated to take the extra step?
- Are you manageable and a team player?
- Are you professional in all your behaviors?
- Are you a problem solver?

Being able to do the job is only a small part of getting an offer. Questions of whether you are motivated to make an extra effort, whether you are manageable and a team player, and whether you think of yourself as a problem-identifier and problem-solver, are just as important to the interviewer. In this era of high unemployment and deep specialization, companies look more actively at the way you behave in the workplace and your professional behavioral profile. Specific desirable professional behaviors cannot be ascertained by a single question or answer, so the interviewer will seek a pattern in your replies that shows your possession of such behaviors—I discuss them in detail in Chapter 10.

You not only have to make a case for yourself in these five areas, you need to avoid these deadly traps that can damage your candidacy:

- Failing to listen to the question.
- Answering a question that was not asked.
- Providing superfluous, inappropriate, or irrelevant information.
- Being unprepared for the interview.

The effect of these blunders is cumulative, and each reduces your chance of receiving a job offer.

The number of offers you win in your search for the ideal job depends on your ability to answer a staggering array of questions in terms that have value and relevance to the employer: "Why do you want to work here?" "What are your biggest accomplishments?" "How long will it take you to make a contribution?" "Why should I hire you?" "What can you do for us that someone else cannot do?" "What is your greatest weakness?" "Why aren't you earning more?" and "What interests you about this job?"

The questions and answers in the following chapters come from across the job spectrum. Though a particular sample answer might come from the mouth of an administrator (while you are a scientist or perhaps an executive in one of the service industries), we all have a common ground in the ways we contribute to our respective bottom lines; this overlap guarantees their relevance to your concerns. I'll give you the question, then explain its motivation and the types of information the employer will be looking for in your answers.

Notice that many of the sample answers teach a small lesson in professional survival—something you can use both to get the job and to help you climb the ladder of success.

The answers provided in the following chapters should *not* be repeated word for word, exactly as they come off the page. You have to tailor them to your profession, illustrate them with examples from your own real-world experience, and, since you have your own style of speech, put the answers into your own words.

CHAPTER 9
The Five Secrets of the Hire

KNOWING HOW AN interviewer thinks is a critical element of the job search too frequently overlooked.

Every hire in every profession and every company, at every level, all over the world, was made based on the five criteria that unfold in this chapter, so you might want to read it twice—it's that important. Understanding these five secrets of the hire will revolutionize the way you perform at job interviews; they will also propel your climb up the professional ladder.

An employer never wakes up in the morning and says, "It's a wonderful day in the neighborhood; I think I'll go hire us an accountant." Employees never get added to the payroll for the fun of it. Rather, they get added to the payroll to make a difference with their presence, to make a contribution to the bottom line (make money, save money, save time), and to solve and prevent problems in their area of expertise. You get hired to prevent problems and, when prevention isn't an option, to solve them as they arise in the daily discharge of your duties. In the process, you are also expected to make a contribution to the bottom line by contributing either to revenue generation or productivity. The following five criteria that employers apply to each and every hire they make all relate to this overriding "problem identification and solution" concern that gave rise to the job opening in the first place.

The First Secret: Ability and Suitability

Saying, "Hey, I can do this job—give me a shot and I'll prove it to you" is not enough. You have to prove it by demonstrating a combination of all the skills that define your ability to do the job in question and your suitability for the position. How well you program that computer, service that client, or sew up that appendix is part of the picture; but knowing the steps involved well enough to be able to explain them clearly and simply to others is equally important.

In this chapter we are going to deconstruct jobs and the selection cycle in a number of different ways to give you a complete understanding of how to ace job interviews. The first step we have taken is to recognize that all of our jobs are, at some level, those of problem solvers. Another way of distilling work down to its essence, in a way that will increase your understanding and interview performance, is to recognize that you bring two sets of skills to a job:

1. The professional/technical skills that allow you to be productive in your area of expertise and application.
2. The profession/industry knowledge that helps you understand "the way things get done in banking/agribusiness/pharmaceuticals." Those ways differ from one industry to the next.

For example, a computer programmer working in a bank has technical and professional skills; that is, he can write a program as requested by the employer, and at the same time he also has a knowledge of how to get things done in the industry in which he operates (in this case, understanding why the banking industry operates the way it does). Such professional or industry knowledge speaks to another level of awareness and suitability. Demonstrating both professional/technical and industry skills will help set you apart.

When you can explain the work you do in clear, simple terms and demonstrate how that role fits into the overall efforts of the department (and, in turn, the company), it helps your interview performance. An objective understanding of what employers are actually going to be looking for and asking you questions about during the interview to determine your ability and suitability will also make a significant difference in your performance. Make sure that you go through the steps of Target Job Deconstruction as described in Chapter 2. The information and understanding you gather through that process will really help you ace any job interview.

With this Target Job Deconstruction Process, you learn both what employers will want to talk about and the nuts and bolts that will hold your answers together. In a few chapters we'll talk about handling different types of interviewers, one of which will be the one who doesn't know how to interview, and consequently doesn't ask the questions to allow you to shine. You've probably met these characters along the way and wondered how to deal with them. Now you have the tools: You know what they need to hear about even if they don't ask the right questions, and I'll show you how to get the information across in Chapter 12, "The Other Side of the Desk."

The Second Secret: Motivation

Employers are leery of people who can do the job but who want to do as little of it as possible. Identifying candidates motivated by a professional commitment to take the rough with the smooth, the rotten assignments with the plum ones, is a major consideration for any employer.

Occasionally, you may find an interviewer asking you such questions as "Are you willing to make coffee?" The issue isn't whether you are prepared to do demeaning tasks. It is whether you are the kind of person who is prepared to do whatever it takes to help the team survive and prosper. Can you take the rough with the smooth? Are you prepared to go that extra mile? You are? Great. Think of a time when you did. Figure out how doing so helped your team and helped the company. Now rehearse the story until you can tell it in about ninety seconds. Show enthusiasm for your work and your profession, and show enthusiasm for the opportunity; it just might be the tiebreaker for your ideal job.

When it comes to a tightly run job race between equally qualified candidates, the offer will always go to the most enthusiastic contender. When you know a number of things about the company (and this is often easy to research on the Internet) and are clearly excited about the opportunity to become a member of the team, your visible motivation will tip the scales in your favor; this is because your enthusiasm is interpreted as an indicator of the energy you will put into your work.

The Third Secret: Manageability and Teamwork

There isn't a manager in the world who enjoys the challenges caused by an unmanageable employee. Avoiding such problems is a major concern for managers, who develop a remarkable sixth sense when it comes to spotting and cutting out mavericks.

Manageability is defined in different ways: the ability to work alone; the ability to work with others; the ability to take direction and criticism when it is carefully and considerately given; and, possibly dearest to the manager's heart, the ability to take direction when it isn't carefully and considerately given, perhaps because of a crisis. Equally crucial is a willingness to work with others regardless of their sex, sexual orientation, age, religion, physical appearance, abilities or disabilities, skin color, or national origin.

Such "manageability" considerations make a job interview tricky. Yes, you should certainly state your strongly held convictions—after all, you don't want to appear wishy-washy—but you should do so only as long as they are professional in nature and relate to the job at hand.

Let me give you an example of what I mean. Readers have asked me occasionally about what they perceive as discrimination as a result of their strongly held religious beliefs. Today's managers will usually go well out of their way to avoid even the perception of intolerance toward sincerely held spiritual beliefs. Yet, by the same token, they are deeply suspicious of any strident religious rhetoric that surfaces in a professional setting. (This also holds true of political, ethnic, and other inappropriate issues raised by a candidate during an interview.) The potential employer's caution in these circumstances, far from representing discrimination, is a sign of concern that the candidate might not be tolerant of the views of others—and might thereby become an obstacle to a harmonious work group.

The rules here are simple: Don't bring up religious, political, social, or racial matters during the job interview. If in doubt, ask yourself, "Is this topic relevant to my ability to do the job?" The interview is a potential paycheck—don't mess with it. You're a team player with a genuine liking for your fellow man. You are someone who gets along well with others, and because you have respect for other human beings, you have no problem tolerating the opinions or beliefs of others. Demonstrate this with your every word and action, and you will embody the spirit of decent people the world over.

The Fourth Secret: Professional Behavior

We discussed this topic already in Chapter 1 when we were talking about building your professional brand, MeInc. I emphasize professional behavior throughout this book because, to a large extent, the behaviors that are most desirable to employers are learned and developed as a result of our experiences in the workplace, not the behaviors we developed growing up.

An important component of your interview arsenal is the ability to show employers you are in possession of the full slate of professional behaviors they universally seek. You'll be able to do this as a result of the time and trouble you took at the beginning of your job search process to construct and understand a consistent view of yourself—your brand. The essence of that brand is these learned behaviors that get you hired, get you noticed, land top assignments, and generate promotions and raises—in short, they enable you to succeed in all your professional endeavors.

Showing possession of these universally admired professional behaviors, and exhibiting them in action with illustrative examples you give in answers to tough interview questions, is your passport to success at any interview. They will give your answers substance and a ring of truth. Going through the list of learned professional behaviors, you probably recognize that you apply many of them on a regular basis in your work; if not, they are readily learnable and you'll be able to begin developing these valuable career assets as soon as you recognize their importance. As you read through Chapter 1 with its list of behaviors, you saw, for example, "determination," and thought, "Yes, I'm a determined kind of gal." And you went through an exercise to come up with times when you used determination in the execution of your duties. You came across "time management and organization" and said, "Now there's something I have to work on!" In this instance you have identified a key behavior that needs work, and you can immediately set about an improvement program.

All of this is intended to give you a good answer to the question, "So why are you different?" As a result of your work on your personal brand, not only will *you* understand why you're different from all other candidates, but you'll have a portfolio of illustrations that you provide, which will give that aura of truth to your claims. Absorbing this list of learnable professional behaviors and making them part of the professional you will win you interviews and job offers, as well as provide the backbone of your long-term career success.

We went over these in some detail in Chapter 1, but it's worth reviewing them here, before you go into the interview.

Communication and Listening Skills: The ability to communicate effectively to people at all levels in a company is a key to success. It refers to verbal and written skills along with technological know-how, dress, and body language. This is an especially important consideration when it comes to your cover letter and resume, because these written documents are the first means an employer has of judging your communication skills. It means you must take the time to craft, edit, and re-edit your cover letter until it communicates what you want it to, including the fact that you have adequate communication skills.

I recently counseled an executive vice president in the 400K-a-year range, and he was having problems getting in front of the right people. The first paragraph of his resume stated that he was an executive with "superior communication skills"; unfortunately, the last twelve words of the sentence gave away his lie—they contained two spelling errors! In an age of spell checkers, this sloppiness isn't acceptable at any level.

Communication embraces listening skills: Listening and understanding, as opposed to just waiting your turn to talk. Consciously develop your "listening to understand" skills, and the result will be improved and more persuasive communication abilities.

Goal Orientation: All employers are interested in goal-oriented professionals: those who achieve concrete results with their actions and who constantly strive to get the job done, rather than just fill the time allotted for a particular task. You might be able to include an example or reference regarding this behavior, or others, in your letters and resume.

Willingness to Be a Team Player: The highest achievers (always goal oriented) are invariably *team players*; employers look for employees who work for the common good and always keep the group's goals and responsibilities in mind. Team players take pride in group achievement rather than personal aggrandizement, and they look for solutions rather than someone to blame.

Motivation and Energy: Employers realize that a motivated professional will do a better job on every assignment. Motivation expresses itself in a commitment to the job and the profession, an eagerness to learn and grow professionally, and a willingness to take the rough with the smooth.

Motivation is invariably expressed by the *energy* someone demonstrates in their work, and is demonstrated by always giving that extra effort to get the job done and to get it done right.

Analytical Skills: This includes being able to weigh the short- and long-term benefits of a proposed course of action against all its possible negatives. We see these skills demonstrated in the way a person identifies potential problems and thereby minimizes their occurrence. Successful application of analytical skills at work requires an understanding of how your job and your department fit into the overall goal of profitability. It also means thinking things through and not jumping at the first or easiest solution.

Dedication and Reliability: Dedication to your profession, the role it plays in the larger issues of company success, and the empowerment that comes from knowing how your part contributes to the greater good are all desirable professional characteristics. The more you are engaged in your career, the more likely you are to join the inner circles that exist in every department and company, enhancing opportunities for advancement. At the same time, this dedication will repay you with better job security and improved professional horizons.

Your dedication will also express itself in your *reliability*. This requires following up on your actions, not relying on anyone else to ensure the job is done well, and keeping management informed every step of the way.

Determination: A determined individual is one who does not back off when a problem or situation gets tough. He or she is the one who chooses to be part of the solution rather than standing idly by and being part of the problem. Determined professionals have decided to make a difference with their presence every day and are willing to do whatever it takes to get a job done, even if that includes duties that might not appear in a job description.

Confidence: As you develop desirable professional behaviors, your confidence grows in the skills you have and in your ability to develop new ones, and with this comes confidence in taking on new challenges. You have the confidence to ask questions, the confidence to look at challenges calmly and at mistakes squarely, and the confidence to make changes to eradicate those mistakes. In short, you develop a quiet confidence in the ability of the professional you to deliver the goods.

Pride and Integrity: Pride in yourself as a professional means always making sure the job is done to the best of your ability; this means paying attention to the details and to the time and cost constraints. Integrity means taking responsibility for your actions, both good and bad, and it also means treating others, within and outside of the company, with respect at all times and in all situations. With pride in yourself as a professional with integrity, your actions will always be in the ethical best interests of the company, and your decisions will never be based on whim or personal preference.

When it comes down to it, companies have very limited interests: making money, saving money (the same as making money), and saving time (which saves money and creates time to make more money). Actually, you wouldn't want it any other way, as it is this focus that makes your paycheck good come payday. Developing these professional behaviors and maintaining sensitivity to the profit interests of any business endeavor is the mark of a true professional. To this end, behavior that demonstrates an awareness of the need for procedures, efficiency, and economy rounds out the profile of the consummate professional.

Efficiency: Always keeping an eye open for wasted time, effort, resources, and money.

Economy: Most problems have two solutions, and the expensive one isn't always the best. Ideas of efficiency and economy engage the creative mind in ways that other workers might not consider; they are an integral part of your analytical proficiency.

Ability to Follow Procedures: Procedures exist to keep the company profitable, so don't try to work around them. You follow the chain of command, and don't implement your own "improved" procedures or organize others to do so.

Remember, understanding what the desirable professional behaviors are and seeing that you possess them is only part of the secret. Let's talk about the importance of illustrating these behaviors at work.

Harry works in Shipping and Receiving. He reads the list of learned professional behaviors in the next chapter, comes across the category labeled "Determination," and thinks, "Yeah, that's me. I'm a determined kind of guy."

It's good for Harry to know this and be able to mention it at the interview, but how much better if he could give the interviewer a short movie to watch to illustrate his claim with a real-life work experience. So Harry recalls the time he came in over the weekend to clear the warehouse in time to make room for the twenty-ton press due in Monday morning at seven. When he tells this story to the interviewer, he gets a lot further than he would if he simply said, "Hire me because I'm determined"—a bland, unsubstantial claim that would be forgotten almost the instant it left Harry's mouth. Instead, the interviewer gets a mental image of Harry coming in on the weekend to make room for that press. Actually, the interviewer sees something much more important—namely, Harry applying the same level of determination and extra effort on behalf of the interviewer's company.

Simple statements don't leave any lasting impression on employers; anecdotes that prove a point do.

If you're still in any doubt about this, go back and reread the sections of Chapter 1 dealing with personal branding. Expressing that brand in everything you do, especially in the interview, is key to your success, both in finding a job that's best for you and advancing in all parts of your career.

The Fifth Secret: Everyone Hires for the Same Job

Regardless of profession, at some level we are all problem solvers. This applies to any job, at any level, in any organization, anywhere in the world, and being aware of this is absolutely vital to job search and career success in any field.

Mr. Wanton Grabbit, eighty-year-old senior partner at the revered Washington law firm of Sue, Grabbit, and Runne, was looking for someone with five years of experience as an administrative assistant in a legal environment. He also wanted someone with experience in using his firm's state-of-the-art Bambleweeny 5000 computer network.

Grabbit interviewed seven candidates with exactly the experience his advertisement demanded. Each of them came away from the interview convinced that a job offer was imminent. None of them got the job. The person who did get the job had three years of experience and had never before set foot inside a law office.

Fiona Sneddon, the successful candidate, understood the fifth secret of the hire and asked a few intelligent questions of her own during the interview. Specifically, she asked, "What are the first projects I will be involved with?" This led Mr. Grabbit to launch into a long discourse on his desire to see the law firm rush headlong into the twenty-first century. The first project, he explained, would be to load the firm's entire filing system onto the Bambleweeny.

Although Fiona had never worked in a law firm before, she had handled these kinds of problems before. Having faced the problem before, even though it had not been in a legal environment, she demonstrated an understanding of the immediate problems the position had been created to solve. Furthermore, she could tell the illustrative stories from her last job that enabled Mr. Grabbit to see her, in his mind's eye, tackling and solving these immediate, specific, short-term problems successfully. The ability to handle immediate needs helps overcome problems caused by the absence of other qualifications.

Think of your profession in terms of its problem-identification/avoidance/solution responsibilities. Once you have identified the particular problem-solving business you are in, you've gone a long way toward isolating what the interviewer will want to talk about. Identify and list for yourself the typical problems you tackle for employers on a daily basis. Come up with plenty of specific examples. Then move on to the biggest, dirtiest problems you've faced. Recall specifically how you solved them.

Here's a technique used by corporate outplacement professionals to help people develop examples of their problem-solving skills and the resulting achievements (you went through a similar exercise while developing your resume):

1. **State the problem.** What was the situation? Was it typical of your job, or had something gone wrong? If the latter, be leery of apportioning blame.
2. **Isolate relevant background information.** What special knowledge or education were you armed with to tackle this dilemma?
3. **List your key qualities.** What professional skills and professional behaviors did you bring into play to solve the problem?
4. **Recall the solution.** How did things turn out in the end?
5. **Determine what the solution was worth.** Quantify the solution in terms of money earned, money saved, or time saved. Specify your role as a team member or as a lone gun, as the facts demand.

With a subtle problem-identification/avoidance/solution orientation, you will be focused in a way that will appeal to any employer. If you follow the steps outlined here, you will develop a host of illustrative stories you can use to answer any of the interview questions you will face. Remember, stories help interviewers visualize you solving their problems—as a paid member of the team.

We get two very special benefits when we understand and apply the fifth secret. First, we show that we possess the problem-solving abilities of a first-rate professional in the field. Second, when we ask about the problems, challenges, projects, deadlines, and pressure points that will be tackled in the early months, we show we will be able to hit the ground running on those first critical projects.

Integrate this awareness of why some people get hired over others as you read the following chapters in this section, and you will reap the rewards—while your competitors resign themselves to harvesting sour grapes.

CHAPTER 10
How to Knock 'em Dead

THERE ARE A couple of handfuls of learned professional behaviors that are catnip to all employers. Learn how to apply them during the interview process.

If you are like most people, you are terrified of job interviews, partly because you don't know exactly what questions are going to be asked. Even though there are questions you think the interviewer might ask, you have no idea how best to answer them. Even if you have an arsenal of rehearsed answers to likely questions, you know canned, slick answers are going to make you sound like an aluminum-siding salesman.

Take a look at these scary questions and statements: Do you know how to answer them?

- "Describe a situation where your work or an idea was criticized."
- "Have you done the best work you are capable of doing?"
- "What problems do you have getting along with others?"
- "How long will you stay with the company?"
- "I'm not sure you're suitable for the job."
- "Tell me about something you are not very proud of."
- "What are some of the things your supervisor did that you disliked?"
- "What aspects of your job do you consider most crucial?"

Can you respond to all these off the top of your head? Can you do it in a way that will set your worth above the other job candidates? I doubt it—but after you have read this section you will be thoroughly prepared for these questions and hundreds more like them. You know it isn't enough to have slick, canned answers ready, because each answer you give must help satisfy one of those five secrets of the hire that employers apply to each candidate.

As you learned in the last few pages, an employer is looking for more than just the ability to flip a burger, write code, or balance a departmental budget.

Professional Behaviors

An important part of your interview weaponry is the ability to show employers you are in possession of a full slate of the professional behaviors—such as those described in Chapter 1 and reviewed in Chapter 9—that are universally sought by all employers. These are the very behaviors that get you noticed, land plum assignments, and enable you to succeed in all your professional endeavors.

Showing possession of these universally admired professional behaviors, and showing them in action with the illustrative examples you give in answers to tough interview questions, are your passports to success at any interview. They will give your answers substance and a ring of truth. Going through the list of learned professional behaviors in Chapter 9, you will probably recognize that you apply many of them on a regular basis in your work; if not, they are all readily learnable and you'll be able to begin developing these valuable career assets just as soon as you recognize their importance.

Go back and look at the questionnaire you filled out in Chapter 1. As you read through the list of behaviors, try to come up with times when you used determination in the execution of your duties. The examples you generate can be used in your resume, in your cover letters, and as answers to questions in interviews. Then when you get asked, "So why are you different?"

you will have something meaningful to say, and the stories you provide will give that aura of truth to your claims. Absorbing the list of learnable professional behaviors and making them part of the professional you will win interviews and job offers and provide the backbone of your long-term career success.

The reason these learnable behaviors are so universally admired is that they relate to profit and the ongoing competitiveness of a company. Using examples of them in your answers to interview questions (as well as in your resume and cover letters) will make you stand out as someone worthy of special consideration.

Get Ready for the Tough Questions

We are now going to look at all those sneaky, dirty, mean, lowdown trick questions that can be thrown at you in the course of an interview. I will help you understand what is behind each question, the kind of information an employer is likely to be seeking, and give an example of the kind of points you might want to make in your answers. The examples should be used as a starting point; you'll look within your own experience for the responses to use at an actual interview.

As the requirements of the job unfold for you at the interview, meet them point by point with your qualifications. If your experience is limited, stress the appropriate professional behavior (such as energy, determination, motivation), your relevant interests, and your desire to learn. If you are weak in a particular area, keep your mouth shut—perhaps that dimension will not arise. If the area is probed, stress skills that compensate or demonstrate that you are a fast learner.

Do not show discouragement if the interview appears to be going poorly. You have nothing to gain by showing defeat, and it could merely be an interview tactic to test your self-confidence by putting you under stress (we'll be handling stress techniques in Chapter 13).

If for any reason you need time to think, say, "Let me think about that for a moment. . . ." If you get flustered or lost, gain time to marshal your thoughts by asking, "Could you help me with that?" or "Would you run that by me again?" or "That's a good question; I want to be sure I understand. Could you please explain it again?"

When studying the tough questions that follow, remember to use the information you have gathered about your professional self from exercises earlier in the book to create the examples and explanations that reflect your skills, experiences, and professional behaviors.

"What are the reasons for your success in this profession?"

With this question, the interviewer is not so much interested in examples of your success—he or she wants to know what makes you tick. Keep your answers short, general, and to the point. Using your work experience, personalize and use examples from your professional behavior profile.

In the following suggested answer, and in those for the next few questions, the most important words to include in any answer are italicized (words like *solution*, *problems*, and *contribution*). You might answer the question this way: "I attribute my success to three things: First, I've always received support from coworkers, which encourages me to be *cooperative* and look at my job in terms of what *we* as a department are trying to achieve. That gives me great *pride* in my work and its *contribution to the department's efforts*, which is the second factor. Finally, I find that every job has its *problems*, and while there's always a costly *solution*, there's usually an economical one as well, whether it's in terms of time or money." Give an example from your experience that illustrates those points.

"What is your energy level like? Describe a typical day."

You must demonstrate good use of your *time* and show that you believe in *planning* your day beforehand; you must also show that when your day is over, you *review* your own performance to make sure you are reaching the *desired goals*. No one wants a part-time employee, so you should sell your *energy* level. For example, your answer might end with, "At the end of the day when I'm ready to go home, I make a rule always to type one more letter [make one more call, etc.]. Then I clear my desk, *review* the day's *achievements*, and *plan* for the next day."

In many of the discussions about how to answer questions, you will learn valuable lessons that will help you be a more successful professional. For example, from the previous question you might pick up some useful, and successful, ideas about the "Plan, Do, Review" cycle that successful people apply every day to keep themselves organized and on track.

"Why do you want to work here?"

To answer this question, you must have researched the company and built a dossier. Your research and visits to the company website are now to be rewarded. Reply with the company's attributes as you see them. Cap your answer with reference to your belief that the company can provide you with a stable and happy work environment—the company has that reputation—and that such an atmosphere would encourage your best work: "I have a bachelor's degree in communications, and I've worked in pharmaceutical sales for three years. I am currently ranked fourth in the region. I have long competed against your company, and I know and respect your products *[you'll add plenty of specific details to show you really know the company]*. Your location in Macon will also help me get closer to family."

"What kind of experience do you have for this job?"

This is a golden opportunity to sell yourself, but before you do, be sure you know what is most critical to the interviewer. The interviewer is not just looking for a competent engineer, accountant, or what have you—he or she is looking for someone who can contribute quickly to current projects. When interviewing, companies invariably give everyone a broad picture of the job, but the person they hire will be a *problem solver*, someone who can *contribute* to specific projects in the first six months. Only by asking will you identify the areas of your interviewer's greatest urgency and therefore interest.

If you do not know the projects you will be involved with in the first six months, you must ask. Level-headedness and *analytical* ability are respected, and the information you get will naturally let you answer the question more appropriately. For example, a company experiencing shipping problems might appreciate this answer: "I have worked in the shipping and receiving area all my life in both durables and perishables. I understand *deadlines*, delivery schedules, and the *bottom-line* importance of getting the product shipped, and my awareness of *making money by saving money* has always kept rejects from careless handling to a bare minimum."

"What are the broad responsibilities of your job?"

This is becoming a very popular question with interviewers, and rightly so. There are three layers to it. First, it acknowledges that all employees nowadays are required to be more productivity oriented and need to know how individual responsibilities fit into the big picture. Second, the answer provides some idea of how much you will have to be trained if and when you join the company. Third, it is a very effective knockout question—if you lack a comprehensive understanding of your job, that's it! You'll be knocked out then and there.

To answer effectively you need to understand the small role your job plays in the *bigger picture of departmental responsibilities* (including your responsibilities as a *team player*) and how the department's role in turn helps contribute to the *bottom line*. Whatever your job, you have customers, or end users, of your service; they are always front and center in your considerations. Explain your day-to-day responsibilities, whom you are serving with your presence, and how your function serves the *profit motive of the organization*.

"Describe how your job relates to the overall goals of your department and company."

This can be a standalone question or a follow-up to the last one (when your answer wasn't comprehensive). It examines your understanding of department and corporate missions and obliquely checks your ability to function as a team member. Consequently, whatever the specifics of your answer, include words to this effect: "The quality of my work directly affects the ability of others to do their work properly. As a team member, one has to be aware of the other players and our *common goals*."

"What aspects of your job do you consider most crucial?"

A wrong answer can knock you out of the running. The executive who describes expense reports as the job's most crucial aspect is a case in point. The question is designed to determine time management, prioritization skills, and any inclination for task avoidance. This question demands that you have a clear awareness of the role of your job in contributing to the overall success of the company.

"Are you willing to go where the company sends you?"

Unfortunately with this one, you are, as the saying goes, damned if you do and damned if you don't. What is the real question? Do they want you to relocate or just travel on business? If you simply answer "no," you will not get the job offer, but if you answer "yes," you could end up in Monkey's Eyebrow, Kentucky. So play for time and ask, "Are you talking about business travel, or is the company relocating?" In the final analysis, your answer should be "yes." You don't have to accept the job, but without the offer you have no decision to make. Your single goal at an interview is to sell yourself and win a job offer.

"What did you like/dislike about your last job?"

The interviewer is looking for incompatibilities. If a trial lawyer says he or she dislikes arguing a point with colleagues, the statement will weaken—if not immediately destroy—his or her candidacy.

Most interviews start with a preamble by the interviewer about the company. Pay attention: that information will help you answer the question. In fact, any statement the interviewer makes about the job or corporation can be used to your advantage.

So, in answer, you liked everything about your last job. You might even say your company taught you the importance of certain keys from the business, achievement, or professional profile. Criticizing a prior employer is a warning flag that you could be a problem employee. No one intentionally hires trouble, and that's what's behind the question. Keep your answer short and positive. You are allowed only one negative about past employers, and then only if your interviewer has a "hot button" about his or her department or company; if so, you will have written it down on your notepad. For example, the only thing your past employer could not offer might be something like "the ability to contribute more in different areas, as in the smaller environment you have here." You might continue with, "I really liked everything about the job. The reason I want to leave it is to find a position where I can make a greater contribution. You see, I work for a large company that encourages specialization of skills. The smaller environment you have here will, as I said, allow me to contribute far more in different areas." Tell them what they want to hear—replay the hot button.

Of course, if you interview with a large company, turn it around. "I work for a small company and don't get the time to specialize in one or two major areas." Then replay the hot button.

"What is the least relevant job you have held?"

If your least relevant job is not on your resume, it shouldn't be mentioned. Some people skip over those six months between jobs when they worked as soda jerks just to pay the bills and would rather not talk about it, until they hear a question like this one. But a mention of a job that, according to all chronological records, you never had, will throw your integrity into question and your candidacy out the door.

Apart from that, no job in your profession has been a waste of time if it increases your knowledge about how the business works and makes money. Your answer will include: "Every job I've held has given me new insights into my profession, and the higher one climbs, the more important the understanding of the lower-level, more menial jobs. They all play a role in making the company profitable. And anyway, it's certainly easier to schedule and plan work when you have firsthand knowledge of what others will have to do to complete their tasks."

"What have you learned from jobs you have held?"

Tie your answer to your business and professional profile. The interviewer needs to understand that you seek and accept constructive advice, and that your business decisions are based on the ultimate good of the company, not your personal whim or preference. "More than anything, I have learned that what is good for the company is good for me. So I listen very carefully to directions and always keep my boss informed of my actions."

"How do you feel about your progress to date?"

This question is not geared solely to rate your progress; it also rates your self-esteem (personal profile keys). Be positive, yet do not give the impression you have already done your best work. Make the interviewer believe you see each day as an opportunity to learn and contribute, and that you see the environment at this company as conducive to your best efforts.

"Given the parameters of my job, my progress has been excellent. I know the work, and I am just reaching that point in my career where I can make significant contributions."

"Have you done the best work you are capable of doing?"

Say "yes," and the interviewer will think you're a has-been. As with all these questions, personalize your work history. For this particular question, include the essence of this reply: "I'm proud of my professional achievements to date, especially *[give an example]*. But I believe the best is yet to come. I am always motivated to give my best efforts, and in this job there are always opportunities to contribute when you stay alert."

"How long would you stay with the company?"

The interviewer might be thinking of offering you a job. So you must encourage him or her to sell you on the job. With a tricky question like this, end your answer with a question of your own that really puts the ball back in the interviewer's court. Your reply might be: "I would really like to settle down with this company. I take direction well and love to learn. As long as I am growing professionally, there is no reason for me to make a move. How long do you think I would be challenged here?"

"How long would it take you to make a contribution to our company?"

Again, be sure to qualify the question: In what area does the interviewer need rapid contributions? You are best advised to answer this with a question: "That is an excellent question. To help me answer, what do you anticipate my responsibilities will be for the first six or seven months?" or "What are your greatest areas of need right now?" You give yourself time to think while the interviewer concentrates on images of you working for the company. When your time comes to answer, start with: "Let's say I started on Monday the seventeenth. It will take me a few weeks to settle down and learn the ropes. I'll be earning my keep very quickly, but making a real contribution. . . . *[give a hesitant pause]* Do you have a special project in mind you will want me to get involved with?" That response could lead directly to a job offer, but if not, you already have the interviewer thinking of you as an employee.

"What would you like to be doing five years from now?"

The interviewer wants to know if you think of your career beyond it being a series of jobs. Do you intend to move up in the company heirarchy or do you hope to to be doing the same job in five years without any interest in advancing? The danger here is that you don't know what the company wants or what the interviewer's personal agenda might be so caution is advised or perhaps a little further inquiry on your part first.

"From my research and what you have told me about the growth here, it seems that organizational development is where the heavy emphasis is going to be. It seems that's where you need the effort and where I could best contribute toward the company's goals'. Are there opportunities for advancement within this area or are you looking for someone content with their level and profesional expertise?"

Be guided by the interviewer's response; remember that at this point you don't have a job offer to evaluate so your main goal is to get a job offer on the table. You might continue along the lines of:

"Now five years out is farther than we can realistically see, so let me say this: I have always felt that professional skill development and delivering on current projects opens opportunities for the future. So if I can find a manager who is looking for someone with a desire to earn the respect of a reliable right hand, I'll be confident I can get a shot at some exciting opportunities as needs develop."

"What are your qualifications?"

Be sure you don't answer the wrong question. Does the interviewer want job-related or academic job qualifications? Ask. If the question concerns job-related information, you need to know what problems must be tackled first before you can answer adequately. If you can determine this, you will also know what is causing the manager most concern. If you can show yourself as someone who can contribute to the solution of those projects or problems, you have taken a dramatic step ahead in the race for the job offer. Ask for clarification, then describe your appropriate professional behaviors tied in with relevant skills and achievements. You might say: "I can give you a general answer, but I feel my response might be more valuable if you could tell me about specific work assignments in the early months."

Or: "If the major task right now is to upgrade the filing system, I should tell you that in my last job I was responsible for overhauling the outdated database for the firm."

"What are your biggest accomplishments?"

Keep your answers job-related; from earlier exercises, a number of achievements should spring to mind. If you exaggerate contributions to major projects, you will be accused of suffering from "coffee-machine syndrome," the affliction of a junior clerk who claimed success for an Apollo space mission based on his relationships with certain scientists, established at the coffee machine. You might begin your reply with: "Although I feel my biggest achievements are still ahead of me, I am proud of my involvement with . . . . I made my contribution as part of that team and learned a lot in the process. We did it with hard work, concentration, and an eye for the bottom line."

"How do you organize and plan for major projects?"

Effective planning requires both forward thinking ("Who and what am I going to need to get this job done?") and backward thinking ("If this job must be completed by May 20, what steps must be made, and at what time, to achieve it?"). Effective planning also includes contingencies and budgets for time and cost overruns. Show that you cover all the bases.

"How many hours a week do you find it necessary to work to get your job done?"

No absolutely correct answer here. Some managers pride themselves on working nights and weekends or on never taking their full vacation quota. Others pride themselves on their excellent planning and time management that allows them never to work more than regular office hours. You must pick the best of both worlds: "I try to plan my time effectively and usually can. Our business always has its rushes, though, so I put in whatever effort it takes to get the job finished." It is rare that the interviewer will then come back and ask for a specific number of hours. If that does happen, turn the question around: "It depends on the projects. What is typical in your department?" The answer will give you the right cue, of course.

"Tell me how you moved up through the organization."

A fast-track question, the answer to which says a lot about your personality, your goals, your past, your future, and whether you still have any steam left in you. The answer might be long, but try to avoid rambling. Include a fair sprinkling of your professional behaviors in your stories and illustrations (because this is the perfect time to do it). As well as listing the promotions, demonstrate that they came as a result of dedicated, long-term effort, substantial contributions, and flashes of genius.

"Can you work under pressure?"

You might be tempted to give a simple "yes" or "no" answer, but don't. It reveals nothing, and you lose the opportunity to sell your skills and value profiles. Actually, this common question often comes from an unskilled interviewer, because it is closed-ended. (Ways to handle different types of interviewers are covered in Chapter 12, "The Other Side of the Desk.") As such, the question does not give you the chance to elaborate. Whenever you are asked a closed-ended question, mentally add: "Please give me a brief yet comprehensive answer." Do that, and you will give the information requested and seize an opportunity to sell yourself. For example, you could say: "Yes, I usually find it stimulating. However, I believe in planning and proper management of my time to reduce panic deadlines within my area of responsibility."

"What is your greatest strength?"

This is a chance to make some serious points about your candidacy; you want to make points in two distinct categories.

- First, you should talk about your job-specific skills. For example, an attorney might talk about her research skills, if possible giving an answer that shows that skill being put to good use on the job.
- Second, you will want to talk about some aspect of your behavioral profile. For example, that same attorney might talk about the roles that planning, organization, and time management play when carrying a heavy caseload.

The best answer is a balance between the job-specific skills and the behavioral profile of any serious professional.

"What are your outstanding qualities?"

This is essentially the same as an interviewer asking you what your greatest strengths are. While in the former question you might choose to pay attention to job-specific skills, this question asks you to talk about your personality profile. Now while you are fortunate enough to have a list of the business world's most desirable professional behaviors at the beginning of this chapter, try to do more than just list them. In fact, rather than offering a long "laundry list," you might consider picking out just two or three and giving an illustration of each.

"What interests you most about this job?"

Be straightforward, unless you haven't been given adequate information to determine an answer, in which case you should ask a question of your own to clarify. Perhaps you could say,

"Before answering, could I ask you to tell me a little more about the role this job plays in the departmental goals?" or "Where is the biggest vacuum in your department at the moment?" or "Could you describe a typical day for me?" The additional information you gather with those questions provides the appropriate slant to your answer—that is, what is of greatest benefit to the department and to the company. Career-wise, that is obviously of the greatest benefit to you, too. Your answer then displays the personality traits that support the existing need. Your answer in part might include, "I'm looking for a challenge and an opportunity to make a contribution, so if you feel the biggest challenge in the department is __________, I'm the one for the job." Then include the professional behaviors and experience that support your statements. Perhaps: "I like a challenge, my background demonstrates excellent problem-solving abilities *[give some examples]*, and I always see a project through to the finish."

"What are you looking for in your next job?"

You want a company where your personal profile keys and professional profile keys will allow you to contribute to business value keys: "Ask not what your company can do for you, but what you can do for your company." The key word in the following example is "contribution": "My experience at the XYZ Corporation has shown me I have a talent for motivating people. That is demonstrated by my team's absenteeism dropping 20 percent, turnover steadying at 10 percent, and production increasing 12 percent. I am looking for an opportunity to continue that kind of contribution, and a company and supervisor who will help me develop in a professional manner."

"Why should I hire you?"

Your answer will be short and to the point. It will highlight areas from your background that relate to current needs and problems. Recap the interviewer's description of the job, meeting it point by point with your skills. Finish your answer with: "I have the qualifications you need *[itemize them]*, I'm a team player, I take direction, and I have the desire to make a thorough success."

"What can you do for us that someone else cannot do?"

This question will come only after a full explanation of the job has been given. If not, qualify the question with: "What voids are you trying to fill with this position?" Then recap the interviewer's job description, followed by: "I can bring to this job a determination to see projects through to a proper conclusion. I listen and take direction well. I am analytical and don't jump to conclusions. I understand we are in business to make a profit, so I keep an eye on cost and return." End with: "How do these qualifications fit your needs?" or "What else are you looking for?"

You finish with a question that asks for feedback or a powerful answer. If you haven't covered the interviewer's hot buttons, he or she will cover them now, and you can respond accordingly.

"Describe a difficult problem you've had to deal with."

This is a favorite tough question. It is not so much the difficult problem that's important—it's the approach you take to solving problems in general. It is designed to probe your professional profile; specifically, your analytical skills.

"Well, I always follow a five-step format with a difficult problem. One, I stand back and examine the problem. Two, I recognize the problem as the symptom of other, perhaps hidden, factors. Three, I make a list of possible solutions to the problem. Four, I weigh the consequences and cost of each solution, and decide on the best. And five, I go to my boss, outline the problem, make my recommendation, and ask for my superior's advice and approval."

Then give an example of a problem and your solution. Here is a thorough example: "When I joined my present company, I filled the shoes of a manager who had been fired. Turnover was very high. My job was to reduce turnover and increase performance. Sales of our new copier had slumped for the fourth quarter in a row, partly due to ineffective customer service. The new employer was very concerned, and he even gave me permission to clean house. The cause of the problem? The customer-service team never had any training. All my people needed was some intensive training. My boss gave me permission to join the American Society for Training and Development, which cost $120. With what I learned there, I turned the department around. Sales continued to slump in my first quarter. Then they skyrocketed. Management was pleased with the sales and felt my job in customer service had played a real part in the turnaround. My boss was pleased because the solution was effective and cheap. I only had to replace two customer-service people."

"What would your references say?"

You have nothing to lose by being positive. If you demonstrate how well you and your boss got along, the interviewer does not have to ask, "What do you dislike about your current manager?"

It is a good idea to ask past employers to give you a letter of recommendation. That way, you know what is being said. It reduces the chances of the company representative checking up on you, and if you are asked this question you can pull out a sheaf of rousing accolades and hand them over. If your references are checked by the company, it must by law have your written permission. That permission is usually included in the application form you sign. All that said, never offer references or written recommendations unless they are requested.

"Can we check your references?"

This question is frequently asked as a stress question to catch the too-smooth candidate off guard. It is also one that is occasionally asked in the normal course of events. Comparatively few managers or companies ever check references—this astounds me, yet it's a fact of life. On the other hand, the higher up the corporate ladder you go, the more likely it is that your references will be checked. There is only one answer to this question if you ever expect to get an offer: "Yes."

Your answer may include: "Yes, of course you can check my references. However, at present, I would like to keep matters confidential, until we have established a serious mutual interest [*i.e., an offer*]. At such time I will be pleased to furnish you with whatever references you need from prior employers. I think you'll find they'll say I am professional, committed to making a difference with my presence, easy to be around, and a team player."

You are under no obligation to give references of a current employer until you have a written offer in hand. You are also well within your rights to request that reference checks of current employers wait until you have started your new job.

Most people only ever talk to their references immediately before they are to be checked, if at all. I suggest you contact the people who you think will speak well of you at the beginning of your job search (or as soon as you read this). They might also be able to come up with job leads and introductions.

"What type of decisions did you make on your last job?"

If you have taken the time to deconstruct the target job in the way we discussed in Chapter 9, "The Five Secrets of the Hire," you will have a clear understanding of the job's expected deliverables and the decision-making events that typically accompany that job. You might expect the interviewer to follow with a question about how you reached those decisions. So this will often be a two-part question:

- The level and application of your decision making
- The analytical processes applied

This is an opportunity, however humble your position, to demonstrate your professional profile.

For example: "Being in charge of the mailroom, my job is to make sure people get information in a timely manner. The job is well defined, and my decisions aren't that difficult. I noticed a year or two ago that all activity in the company stopped in the middle of the morning when I took the mail around, because people were taking a break from work to read their mail. I had an idea and gave it to my boss. She got it cleared by the president, and ever since, we take any mail around just before lunch. Mr. Gray, the president, told me my idea improved productivity and saved time, and that he wished everyone was as conscientious."

"What was the last book you read (or movie you saw)? How did it affect you?"

It doesn't really matter what you say about the latest book or movie, just as long as you have read or seen it. Don't be like the interviewee who said the name of the first book that came to mind—*In Search of Excellence*—only to be caught by the follow-up, "To what extent do you agree with Peters's simultaneous loose/tight pronouncements?" Also, by naming such a well-known book, you have managed only to say that you are like millions of others, which doesn't make you stand out in the crowd. Better that you should name something less faddish—that helps to avoid nasty follow-up questions. You needn't mention the most recent book or movie you've seen; your answer should simply make a statement about you as a potential employee. Come up with a response that will set you apart and demonstrate your obvious superiority. Ideally you want to mention a work that in some way has helped you improve yourself; anything that has honed any of the admired professional behaviors will do this. For example there is a book on the *Knock 'em Dead* website that changed my life and could change yours: *How to Get Control of Your Time and Your Life* by Alan Lakein. Give this as an example, cite a time-management tip, then make reference to the importance of time management for everyone.

"How do you handle pressure/tension?"

This question is different from "Can you handle pressure?"—it asks *how* you handle it. You could reply, "Tension is caused when you let things pile up. It is usually caused by letting other areas of responsibility slip by for an extended period. For instance, if you have a difficult presentation coming up, you may procrastinate in your preparations for it. I've seen lots of people do things like that—a task seems so overwhelming they don't know where to begin. I find that if you break those overwhelming tasks into little pieces, they aren't so overwhelming anymore (a useful time-management tip from Lakein). So I suppose I don't so much handle tension as handle the causes of it, by not letting things slip in other areas that can give rise to it."

"How long have you been looking for another position?"

If you are employed, your answer isn't that important—a short or long time is irrelevant to you in any follow-up probes, because you are just looking for the right job, with the right people and outfit that offers you the right opportunities. If, on the other hand, you are unemployed at the time of the question, how you answer becomes more important. If you say, "Well, I've been looking for two years now," it isn't going to score you any points. The interviewer thinks, "Two years, huh? No one else wanted him in that time. I certainly don't." If you must talk of a period of several months or more be careful to add something like, "Well, I've been looking for about a year now. I've had offers in that time, but I have determined that as I spend most of my waking hours at work, the job I take, the company I join, and the people I work with have got to share values I can identify with. I don't want to work with clock-watchers; I want to work in a happy atmosphere where everyone is focused on productivity and really making a difference with their presence."

"Have you ever been fired?"

Say "no" if you can; if not, act on the advice given regarding the next question. Many people confuse getting laid off, being downsized, or having their jobs automated out of existence or exported overseas with getting fired. So if you were laid off as part of general workforce reduction, be straightforward, short, and then shut up. Do not overexplain; it makes you sound guilty.

"Why were you fired?"

If you have been terminated with cause, this can be a tough question to answer. Like it or not, termination with cause is usually justified, because managers loathe taking away someone's livelihood. Virtually no one fires an employee for the heck of it.

Having been fired creates questions in the mind of the interviewer. If you have been fired, the first thing to do is bite the bullet and take responsibility for the behaviors that led to the event, because 99 times out of 100 the fault lies at your door. Remember the three fingers of blame: Whenever we point the finger of blame at others for our problems we forget that three of our own fingers are pointing right back at us. If you cannot take responsibility for your actions you cannot change them, and the problems of that job will repeat themselves ad infinitum and destroy the true potential of your career.

If you can take real responsibility for your actions, you can clean up your act and clean up the past. Call the person who fired you; your aim is to clear the air, so whatever you do, don't be antagonistic. Reintroduce yourself, explain that you are looking (or, if you have been unemployed for a while, say you are "still looking") for a new job. Say that you appreciate that the manager had to do what was done and you learned from the experience. Then address specifically what you learned and ask, "If you were asked as part of a pre- or post-employment reference check, what would you say about me? How would you describe my leaving the company? Would you say that I was fired or that I simply resigned? You see, every time I tell someone about my termination, whoosh, there goes another chance of getting back to work!" Most managers will plump for the latter option (describing your departure as a resignation). Taking responsibility and cleaning up the past really works and is the first step in putting yourself back on a success track.

Back to answering the question. Whatever you do, don't advertise the fact you were fired. If you are asked, be honest, but make sure you have packaged the reason in the best possible light. Perhaps: "I'm sorry to say, I deserved it. I was having some personal problems at the time, and I let them affect my work. I was late to work and lost my motivation. My supervisor (whom, by the way, I still speak to) had directions to trim the workforce anyway, and as I was hired only a couple of years ago, I was one of the first to go."

If you can find out the employee turnover figures, voluntary or otherwise, you might add: "Fifteen other people have left so far this year." A combination answer of this nature minimizes the stigma. You have even managed to demonstrate that you take responsibility for your actions, which shows your analytical and listening skills.

"Have you ever been asked to resign?"

When someone is asked to resign, it is a gesture on the part of the employer: "You can quit, or we will can you, so which do you want it to be?" Because you were given the option, though, that employer cannot later say, "I had to ask him to resign"—that is tantamount to firing and could lead to legal problems. In the final analysis, it is usually safe to answer "no."

"Were you ever dismissed from your job for a reason that seemed unjustified?"

Another sneaky way of asking, "Were you ever fired?" The sympathetic phrasing is geared toward getting you to reveal all the sordid details. The cold hard facts are that hardly anyone is ever fired without cause, and you're kidding yourself if you think otherwise. With that in mind, you can quite honestly say, "No," and move on to the next topic.

"In your last job, what were some of the things you spent most of your time on, and why?"

Employees come in two categories: goal oriented (those who want to get the job done), and task oriented (those who believe in "busy" work). You must demonstrate that you have good time-management skills, and that you are, therefore, goal oriented, as that is what this question probes.

You might reply: "I work on the telephone like a lot of businesspeople; meetings also take up a great deal of time. What is important to me is effective time management and prioritization of activities based on the deliverables of my job. I find more gets achieved in a shorter time if a meeting is scheduled, say, immediately before lunch or at the close of business. I try to block my time in the morning and the afternoon for main thrust activities. At four o'clock, I review what I've achieved, what went right or wrong, and plan adjustments and my main thrust for tomorrow."

"In what ways has your job prepared you to take on greater responsibility?"

This is one of the most important questions you will have to answer. Only the context of the question can tell you if it is focused on your ability to do well in the new, more responsible, job, or whether it is to determine your potential for future growth; this determination will affect the particular slant of your answer. Again, your careful target job deconstruction will help you determine the kinds of specific information the employer is seeking. Regardless of context and other considerations, the interviewer is always hoping in part to see you take personal responsibility for your professional development, so your answer in part needs to demonstrate this. This simple example shows self-awareness, growth, planning and listening skills, and ethical behavior. Parts of it—perhaps the then-and-now aspect of the answer—can be adapted to your personal experience.

"When I started my job, my boss would brief me morning and evening. I made some mistakes, learned a lot, and got the work in on time. As time went by I took on greater responsibilities *[list some of them]*. Now, I meet with her every Friday to discuss the week and proposed directional changes so that she can keep management informed. I think this demonstrates not only my growth but also the confidence management has in my judgment and ability to perform consistently above standard." The exact nature of your answer should reflect your ability to meet the deliverables of the target job.

"In what ways has your job changed since you originally joined the company?"

Very similar to the previous question, and you can use the same structural approach.

"What skills are most critical to this job?"

The question examines your practical understanding of the day-to-day responsibilities of the job and the skills required to execute them (that Target Job Deconstruction coming into play yet again). If your answer fails to demonstrate a clear grasp, you can kiss an offer goodbye. Even if you know your job well, always take a few minutes to deconstruct it into component parts and identify the skill sets necessary to execute each part of the job. As you identify each skill, try to come up with an illustration of your application of that skill and work into it the professional behaviors that enable you to execute that skill. For example:

"With high-end marketing of product launches into new territories I think there are two overwhelming skills needed. First, there are strategic marketing skills: the identifying, prioritizing, and penetration of the new market—something I have done in the Atlanta area in both of my prior jobs. Second, I'd have to say negotiating skills. And here I'm not just talking about negotiation tactics, along with written and verbal communication skills—all of which are ongoing areas of study for me. But I'm also talking about skills in regulatory analysis, which have given me an edge in countless deals."

If, however, you are trying to break into a new profession, you need to do a little research to see if that profession is suitable for you. In the process, you will learn to answer the question in a convincing manner. Here are two sources that can supply the information you'll need:

- Talk to people already doing the job, through your personal contacts and through membership in a professional association.
- Look up the job in the *Dictionary of Occupational Titles* either in your local library or online at *www.bls.com*.

Don't shy away from making this effort. The rewards can include job offers and a better understanding of what it takes to be successful in your chosen profession.

"What skills would you like to develop on this job?"

Behind the question is an interest in your motivation to do the work being offered. The interviewer is looking for a fit between your dreams and his reality. All worthwhile jobs require hard work and a desire to learn—a mindset often notable for its absence.

It is helpful to gather as much information about the job, the department, and their entwined futures as you can. The more information you have, the better you will be able to customize your answers to an employer's specific needs.

As most interviews start with a quick overview of the job and the department, try to turn this overview into an information-gathering conversation by showing an interest in the role of the department within the company and how this might affect the responsibilities of department members. These insights will help ensure the compatibility of your answers with the job's future. If this is not possible, fall back on the further development of core skills and professional behaviors that you know are pivotal to your profession. It's important to stress the "further" here; you don't want to give the impression of inadequacy in the basics.

"Why do you want to work in this industry?" or "Why do you think you will shine in this profession?"

These are both questions most likely to be asked either when you are at the entry level or perhaps an experienced professional in the midst of a strategic career shift. Your answer should speak both to your pragmatism and to your motivation. An answer along the following lines will work in both instances.

"At this point in my career I am looking at the profession/industry because I believe it offers stability and professional growth potential over the years *[explain why]*. Also, I'll be using skills *[itemize strong skill sets that are relevant to the job]* that are areas of personal strength, from which I derive great personal satisfaction. So I think that my carefully considered choice of profession, the skills I can bring to the table, and my interest in __________ all lead to my confidence in being able to make a contribution."

"How resourceful are you?"

This is a question about creativity and initiative; it is also asking you to talk about analytical skills, how you anticipate problems and how you approach them when they do arise. The problem you wrestled with doesn't need to be of planetary proportions to show you in a positive light, because the question is really examining your professional behavior: It's not the problem so much as how you handle it. Talk about your analytical skills in discovering root causes, your resilience in the face of challenges, and your ability to stay with difficult tasks until completion, and you'll be thinking along the right lines.

Your answer can follow a simple sequence: the problem, your approach and solution, the result, and its value to the company . . . the PSRV process we discussed earlier.

As always, having an illustrative story ready enables the interviewer to "watch" you being resourceful. Besides, you never know when an interviewer will ask, "Can you give me an example of that?" as a follow-up question.

"How does this job compare with others you have applied for?"

This is a variation of more direct questions, such as "How many other jobs have you applied for?" and "Who else have you applied to?" but it is a slightly more intelligent question and therefore more dangerous. It asks you to compare. Answer the question and sidestep at the same time.

"No two jobs are the same, and this one is certainly unlike any other I have applied for." If you can highlight some of the interviewer's stated pluses about the job, so much the better. Remember that first and foremost you are there to get a job offer. You have nothing to evaluate until then.

If you are pressed further, say, "Well, to give you a more detailed answer, I would need to ask you a number of questions about the job and the company." Ask about major projects: who succeeds at the job, and who fails, and why; how the company encourages professional growth; and so on. For more on good questions to ask, see Chapter 19, "Negotiating the Job Offer."

"What makes this job different from your current/last one?"

If you don't have enough information to answer the question, say so, and ask some of your own: "Well to help me answer this properly it would help if I knew a little more about . . . ." Such questions might address responsibilities, deliverables of the job, extent of authority, and perceived role of the job within the company structure (see Chapter 19 on negotiation for many good questions to ask). Behind the question is the interviewer's desire to uncover the experience you are lacking. Focus on the positive: "From what I know of the job, I seem to have all the experience required to make a thorough success *[itemize here, as it's a good opportunity to reinforce the match]*. I would say that the major differences seem to be . . ." and here you play back the positive attributes of the department and company as the interviewer gave them to you, either in the course of the interview or in answer to your specific questions.

"Do you have any questions?"

A good question. Almost always, this is a sign that the interview is drawing to a close and that you have one more chance to make an impression. Remember the adage: People respect what you inspect, not what you expect.

Most people ask questions about money and benefits. These are nice-to-know questions that the interviewer is not really interested in discussing at this point. As your goal at the interview is to bring the interviewer to the point of offering you the job, these questions are really irrelevant at this point, and even detrimental. Better that you concentrate on gathering information that will help you further your candidacy.

Create questions from any of the following:

- Find out why the job is open, who had it last, and what happened to him or her. Did he or she get promoted or fired? How many people have held this position in the last couple of years? What happened to them subsequently?
- Why did the interviewer join the company? How long has he or she been there? What is it about the company that keeps him or her there?
- To whom would you report? Will you get the opportunity to meet that person?
- Where is the job located? What are the travel requirements, if any?
- What type of training is required, and how long is it? What type of training is available?
- What would your first assignment be?
- What are the realistic chances for growth in the job? Where are the opportunities for greatest growth within the company?
- What are the skills and attributes most needed to get ahead in the company?
- Who will be the company's major competitor over the next few years? How does the interviewer feel the company stacks up against them?
- What has been the growth pattern of the company over the last five years? Is it profitable? How profitable? Is the company privately or publicly held?
- Is there a written job description? May you see it?

CHAPTER 11

"What Kind of Person Are You Really, Mr. Jones?"

LEARN THE TECHNIQUES an interviewer uses to find out whether you will fit into the company and department, and, most important, whether you are a good person to work with.

If you are offered the job and accept, you will be working together fifty weeks of the year, so the interviewer really wants to know if you are going to reduce his life expectancy. Every employer wants to know whether you will fit in with the rest of the staff, whether you are a team player, and most of all, whether you are manageable.

Here are a number of questions the interviewer might use to examine this area. They will mainly be geared toward your behavior and attitudes in the past, because it is universally believed that your past actions predict your future behavior.

"How do you take direction?"

The interviewer wants to know whether you are open-minded and can be a team player. Can you follow directions or are you a difficult, high-maintenance employee? It is hoped that you are a low-maintenance professional who is motivated to ask clarifying questions about a project before beginning, and who then gets on with the job at hand, coming back with requests for direction as circumstances dictate.

This particular question can also be defined as "How do you accept criticism?" Your answer should cover both points: "I take direction well and recognize that it can come in two varieties, depending on the circumstances. There is carefully explained direction, when my boss has time to lay things out for me in detail; then there are those times when, as a result of deadlines and other pressures, the direction might be brief and to the point. While I have seen some people get upset with that, personally I've always understood that there are probably other considerations I am not aware of. As such, I take the direction and get on with the job without taking offense, so my boss can get on with her job."

"Would you like to have your boss's job?"

It is a rare boss who wants his or her livelihood taken away. On my own very first job interview, my future boss said, "Mr. Yate, it has been a pleasure to meet you. However, until you walked in my door, I wasn't out on the street looking for a new job." You see I had this case of wanting to start at the top rather than actually working my way up.

The interviewer wants to know if you are the type of person who will be confrontational or undermining. He also seeks to determine how goal oriented and motivated you are in your work life—so you may also want to comment on your sense of direction. But while ambition is admired, it is admired most by those far enough above the fray not to be threatened. Be cautiously optimistic; perhaps, "Well, if my boss were promoted over the coming years, I would hope to have made a consistent enough contribution to warrant his consideration. It's not that I am looking to take anyone's job; rather, I am looking for a manager who will help me develop my capabilities.

"What do you think of your current/last boss?"

Be short, sweet, and shut up. People who complain about their employers are recognized as the people who cause the most disruption in a department. This question is the interviewer's way of finding out if you're going to cause trouble. "I liked her as a person, respected her professionally, and appreciated her guidance." The question is often followed by one that tries to validate your answer.

"Describe a situation where your work or an idea of yours was criticized."

This is a doubly dangerous question as you are being asked to describe how you handle criticism and to detail possible faults. If you are asked this question, describe a poor idea that was criticized, not poor work. Poor work can cost money and is a warning sign to the interviewer.

One of the wonderful things about a new job is that you can leave the past entirely behind, so it does not matter how you handled criticism in the past. What does matter is how the interviewer would like you to handle criticism, if and when it becomes his unpleasant duty to dish it out; that's what the question is really about. So relate one of those it-seemed-like-a-good-idea-at-the-time ideas; you will want to put this situation in the past, address how you handled the criticism, and, just as important, what you learned from the experience. You might say something that captures the essence of this example: "*[after describing the situation]* . . . I listened carefully and asked a couple of questions for clarification. Then I fed back what I heard to make sure the facts were straight. I asked for advice, we bounced some ideas around, then I came back later and represented the idea in a more viable format. My supervisor's input was invaluable." Those are steps you go through to become maximally productive in these situations. Listen for understanding (not just waiting for your turn to speak), confirm the understanding, ask guidance for the desired solution, confirm the path/outcome expected, show that a satisfactory resolution was ultimately reached, recognize the positive impact of the manager, then demonstrate what you learned and how your thinking/approach has changed as a result.

"Tell me about yourself."

This is invariably one of the first questions we all face. It helps the interviewer get a picture of you, and it helps you get used to talking; it is not an invitation to ramble.

Your interviewers are meeting with you to see if you are the right person to fill a position that has been carefully defined by a job description. You will recall in Chapter 2 how I took you through that Target Job Deconstruction exercise, and the very clear picture it gave you of the issues an employer is likely to want to discuss. Taking the results of this exercise as your frame of reference, you have a clear idea of what the interviewer wants to hear about: how your professional life experiences have qualified you to be at this meeting, throwing your hat in the ring for this particular job. This question will frequently come up at the beginning of an interview, so it is worthwhile to spend a few minutes preparing a succinct statement that says who you are today and how you got here. For example:

"I'm the area director of marketing for the ________ metroplex area. I oversee all aspects of marketing to acquire and retain basic, digital, and online customers through tactics such as mass media and direct mail, as well as launch new products/services like VOD. I have a team of forty-six employees, which also includes twenty-six door-to-door sales reps.

"I rose to this position year by year, climbing through the ranks based on my performance, achievement, and an ever-growing frame of reference for my profession and our business. As we get into the nuts-and-bolts discussion of the job I hope to show you that I have a real understanding of the challenges faced by my direct reports and a steady hand with the managerial skills required for a motivated and productive department."

This isn't a question that you can answer effectively without thought and preparation. Take some time in advance to think about your career to date and how it has prepared you for the position at hand.

"How do you get along with different kinds of people?"

You don't have to talk about respect for others, the need for diversity, or how it took you ten years to realize Jane was a different sex and Charley a different color, because that is not what this question is about. If you respect others, you will demonstrate this by explaining to your interviewer how you work in a team environment (because this is, in reality, a "team player" question), and how you solicit and accept input, ideas, and viewpoints from a variety of sources. If you can give a quick, honest, illustration of learning from a coworker who is obviously different from you in some way, it won't hurt.

"Rate yourself on a scale of one to ten."

This question is meant to plumb the depths of your self-esteem and self-awareness. If you answer ten, you run the risk of portraying yourself as insufferable. On the other hand, if you say less than seven, you might as well get up and leave. You are probably best claiming to be an eight, saying that you always give of your best, which includes ongoing personal and professional development, so that in doing so you always increase your skills and therefore always see room for improvement. It helps to give an example, "I just read a great book on time management called *How to Get Control of Your Time and Your Life,* and found that a daily plan/do/review cycle is a really useful tool for staying on top of and prioritizing multiple projects."

"What kinds of things do you worry about?"

Some questions, such as this one, can seem so off-the-wall that you might start treating the interviewer as a confessor in no time flat. Your private phobias have nothing to do with your job, and revealing them can get you labeled as unbalanced. It is best to confine your answer to the sensible worries of a conscientious professional. "I worry about deadlines, staff turnover, tardiness, back-up plans for when the computer crashes, or that one of my auditors burns out or defects to the competition—just the normal stuff. It goes with the territory, so I don't let it get me down." Whatever you identify as a worry might then be the subject of a follow-up question, so think through what you identify as worrying and in turn what you do to eradicate the worry.

"What is the most difficult situation you have faced?"

The question looks for information on two fronts: "How do you define difficult?" and "What was your handling of the situation?" You must have a story ready for this one in which the situation was tough and allowed you to show yourself in a good light. Avoid talking about problems with coworkers. As we have talked about the importance of problem solving throughout the book, and steps you can take to identify proper approaches and solutions, you should have numerous examples with which to illustrate your answer. Just remember the sequence: *Problem, Solution, Result, Value.*

"What are some of the things that bother you?" "What are your pet peeves?" "Tell me about the last time you felt anger on the job."

These questions are so similar they can be treated as one. It is tremendously important that you show you can remain calm. Most of us have seen a colleague lose his or her cool on occasion—not a pretty sight and one every sensible employer wants to avoid. This question comes up more and more often the higher up the corporate ladder you climb, and the more frequent your contact with clients and the general public. To answer it, find something that angers conscientious workers: "I enjoy my work and believe in giving value to my employer. Dealing with clock-watchers and people who regularly get sick on Mondays and Fridays really bothers me, but it's not something that gets me angry." An answer of this nature will help you much more than the kind given by a California engineer, who went on for some minutes about how he hated the small-mindedness of people who don't like pet rabbits in the office.

"What have you done that shows initiative?"

The question probes whether you are a doer, someone who will look for ways to increase sales or save time or money—the kind of person who gives a manager a pleasant surprise once in a while, who makes life easier for coworkers. Be sure, however, that your example of initiative does not show a disregard for company policies and procedures.

"My boss has to organize a lot of meetings. That means developing agendas, letting employees around the country know the dates well in advance, getting materials printed, or, as is more often the case nowadays, organizing the webinar and getting the PowerPoint graphics created and rehearsal times scheduled. Most people in my position would wait for the work to be given them. I don't. Every quarter, I sit down with my boss and find out the dates of all his meetings for the next six months. I immediately make the hotel and flight arrangements, and attend to all the web-hosting details. I ask myself questions like, 'If the agenda for the July meeting is to reach the field at least six weeks before the meeting, when must it be finished by?' Then I come up with a deadline. I do that for all the major activities for all the meetings. I put the deadlines in his PDA, and in mine two weeks earlier to ensure everything is done on time. My boss is the best organized, most relaxed manager in the company. None of his colleagues can understand how he does it."

"What are some of the things about which you and your supervisor disagreed?"

It is safest to state that you did not disagree.

"In what areas do you feel your supervisor could have done a better job?"

The same goes for this one. No one admires a Monday-morning quarterback.

You could reply, though: "I have always had the highest respect for my supervisor. I have always been so busy learning from Mr. Jones that I don't think he could have done a better job. He has really brought me to the point where I am ready for greater challenges. That's why I'm here."

"What are some of the things your supervisor did that you disliked?"

If you and the interviewer are both nonsmokers, for example, and your boss isn't, use it. Apart from that: "You know, I've never thought of our relationship in terms of like or dislike. I've always thought our role was to get along together and get the job done."

"How well do you feel your boss rated your job performance?"

This is one very sound reason to ask for written evaluations of your work before leaving a company. Some performance-review procedures include a written evaluation of your performance—perhaps your company employs it. If you work for a company that asks you to sign your formal review, you are quite entitled to request a copy of it. You should also ask for a letter of recommendation whenever you leave a job: You have nothing to lose. If you don't have written references, perhaps say: "My supervisor always rated my job performance well. In fact, I was always rated as being capable of accepting further responsibilities. The problem was there was nothing available in the company—that's why I'm here."

If your research has been done properly you can quote verbal appraisals of your performance from prior jobs: "In fact, my boss recently said that I was the most organized engineer in the work group, because . . . ."

"How did your boss get the best out of you?"

This is a manageability question, probing whether you are going to be a pain in the neck or not. Whatever you say, make it clear you don't appreciate being treated like a dishrag. You can give a short, general answer: "My last boss got superior effort and performance by giving me the same personal respect with which she liked to be treated herself." This book is full of answers that get you out of tight corners and make you shine, but this is one instance in which you really should tell it like it is. You don't want to work for someone who is going to make life miserable for you. Or you might add to it, going on to identify how your manager explained projects and their deliverables clearly to you at the outset along with their deadlines and kept you carefully apprised of any changes.

"How interested are you in sports?"

The interviewer is looking for your involvement in groups, as a signal that you know how to get along with others and pull together as a team.

"I really enjoy most team sports. I don't get a lot of time to indulge myself, but I am a regular member of my company's softball team." A recently completed survey of middle- and upper-management personnel found that the executives who listed group sports/activities among their extracurricular activities made an average of $3,000 per year more than their sedentary colleagues. Don't you just love baseball suddenly?

Apart from team sports, endurance sports are seen as a sign of determination: swimming, running, and cycling are all OK. Games of skill (bridge, chess, and the like) demonstrate analytical skills; given the recent popularity of poker and recognizing it as a game of analytical, math, or communication and negotiation skills I nevertheless feel that mentioning poker should be done carefully; you do not want to leave an image of yourself as a compulsive gambler.

"What personal characteristics are necessary for success in your field?"

You know the answer to this one: It's a brief recital of your learned professional behaviors.

You might say: "To be successful in my field? Drive, motivation, energy, confidence, determination, good communication, and analytical skills. Combined, of course, with the ability to work with others."

"Do you prefer working with others or alone?"

This question is usually used to determine whether you are a team player. Before answering, however, be sure you know whether the job requires you to work alone. Then answer appropriately. Perhaps: "I'm quite happy working alone when necessary. I don't need much constant reassurance. But I prefer to work in a group—so much more gets achieved when people pull together."

"Explain your role as a group/team member."

You are being asked to describe yourself as either a team player or a loner. Think for a moment about why the job exists in the first place: It is there to contribute to the bottom line in some way, and as such it has a specific role in the department to contribute toward that larger goal. Your department, in turn, has a similar, but larger, role in the company's bottom line. Your ability to link your small role to that of the department's larger responsibilities, and then to the overall success of the company, will demonstrate a developed professional awareness. Most departments depend on harmonious teamwork for their success, so describe yourself as a team player: "I perform my job in a way that helps others to do theirs in an efficient manner. Beyond the mechanics, we all have a responsibility to make the workplace a friendly and pleasant one, and that means everyone working for the common good and making the necessary personal sacrifices toward it."

"How would you define a conducive work atmosphere?"

This is a tricky question, especially because you probably have no idea what kind of work atmosphere exists in that particular office. The longer your answer, the greater your chances of saying the wrong thing, so keep it short and sweet: "One where the team has a genuine interest in its work and desire to turn out a good product/deliver a good service."

"Do you make your opinions known when you disagree with the views of your supervisor?"

If you can, state that you come from an environment where input is encouraged when it helps the team's ability to get the job done efficiently. "If opinions are sought in a meeting, I will give mine, although I am careful to be aware of others' feelings. I will never criticize a coworker or a superior in an open forum; besides, it is quite possible to disagree without being disagreeable. However, my past manager made it clear that she valued my opinion by asking for it. So, after a while, if there was something I felt strongly about, I would make an appointment to sit down and discuss it one-on-one."

"What would you say about a supervisor who was unfair or difficult to work with?"

"I would make an appointment to see the supervisor and diplomatically explain that I felt uncomfortable in our relationship, that I felt he or she was not treating me as a professional colleague, and therefore that I might not be performing up to standard in some way—that I wanted to right matters and ask for his or her input as to what I must do to create a professional relationship. I would enter into the discussion taking responsibility for any communication problems that might exist, and acknowledging that this wasn't just the manager's problem."

"Do you consider yourself a natural leader or a born follower?"

Ouch! The way you answer depends a lot on the job offer you are chasing. If you are a recent graduate, you are expected to have high aspirations, so go for it. If you are already on the corporate ladder with some practical experience in the school of hard knocks, you might want to be a little cagier. Assuming you are up for (and want) a leadership position, you might try something like this: "I would be reluctant to regard anyone as a natural leader. Hiring, motivating, and disciplining other adults and at the same time molding them into a cohesive team involves a number of delicately tuned skills that no honest person can say they were born with. Leadership requires first of all the desire; then it is a lifetime learning process. Anyone who reckons they have it all under control and have nothing more to learn isn't doing the employer any favors."

Of course, a little humility is also in order, because just about every leader in every company reports to someone, and there is a good chance that you are talking to such a someone right now. So you might consider including something like, "No matter how well developed any individual's leadership qualities, an integral part of leadership ability is to take direction from your immediate boss, and also to seek the input of the people being supervised. The wise leader will always follow good advice and sound business judgment wherever it comes from. I would say that given the desire to be a leader, the true leader in the modern business world must embrace both." How can anyone disagree with that kind of wisdom?

"Why do you feel you are a better [e.g.,] manager/scientist/assistant than some of your coworkers?"

If you speak disparagingly of your coworkers, you will not put yourself in the best light. That is what the question asks you to do, so it poses some difficulties. The trick is to answer the question but not to accept the invitation to show yourself in anything but a flattering light: "I don't spend my time thinking about how superior I am, because that would be detrimental to our working together as a team. I believe, however, some of the qualities that make me an outstanding secretary are. . . ." From here, go on to illustrate job-related skills and behavioral characteristics that make you a beacon of productivity.

"You have a doctor's appointment arranged for noon. You've waited two weeks to get in. An urgent meeting is scheduled at the last moment, though. What do you do?"

What a crazy question, you mutter. It's not. It is even more than a question—it is what I call a question shell. The question within the shell—in this instance, "Will you sacrifice the appointment or sacrifice your job?"—can be changed at will. This is a situational-interviewing technique, which poses an on-the-job problem to see how the prospective employee will respond. A Chicago company asks this question as part of its initial screening, and if you give the wrong answer, you never even get a face-to-face interview. So what is the right answer to this or any similar shell question?

Fortunately, once you understand the interviewing technique, it is quite easy to handle—all you have to do is turn the question around: "If I were the manager who had to schedule a really important meeting at the last moment, and someone on my staff chose to go to the doctor's instead, how would I feel?"

It is unlikely that you would be an understanding manager unless the visit was for a triple bypass. To answer, you start with an evaluation of the importance of the problem and the responsibility of everyone to make some sacrifices for the organization, and finish with: "The first thing I would do is reschedule the appointment and save the doctor's office inconvenience. Then I would immediately make sure I was properly prepared for the emergency meeting."

"How do you manage to interview while still employed?"

As long as you don't explain that you faked a dentist appointment to make the interview you should be all right. Beware of revealing anything that might make you appear at all underhanded. Best to make the answer short and sweet, and let the interviewer move on to richer areas of inquiry. Just explain that you had some vacation time due, or took a day off in lieu of overtime payments: "I had some vacation time, so I went to my boss and explained that I needed a couple of days off for some personal business and asked her what days would be most suitable. Although I plan to change jobs, I don't in any way want to hurt my current employer in the process by being absent during a crunch."

"How have your career motivations changed over the years?"

This question only crops up when you have enough years under your belt to be regarded as a tenured professional. The interviewer's agenda is to examine your emotional maturity and how realistic you are about future professional growth.

Your answer requires self-awareness. While the desire to rule the world can be seen as motivation in young professionals, it may not be interpreted so positively coming from a tenured corporate soldier from whom more realism is expected.

Your answer should reflect a growing maturity as well as a desire to do a good job for its own reward and to make a contribution as part of the greater whole. Here's an example you can use as a starting point in crafting your own:

"I guess in earlier years I was more ego-driven, with everything focused on becoming a star. Over the years I've come to realize that nothing happens with a team of one—we all have to function as part of a greater whole if we are to make meaningful contributions with our professional presence. Nowadays I take great pleasure in doing a job well, in seeing it come together as it should, and especially in seeing a group of professionals working together in their different roles to make it happen. Maybe the best way to say this is that I've discovered that the best way to stand out is to be a real team player and not worry about standing out."

"How do you regroup when things haven't gone as planned?"

In reality, we can all react to adversity in pretty much the same way we did as kids, but that isn't always productive. Here's a way you can deal with setbacks in your professional life and wow your interviewer in the process:

"I pause for breath and reflection for as long as the situation allows—this can be a couple of minutes or overnight. I do this to analyze what went wrong and why. I'm also careful to look for the things that went right, too. I'll examine alternate approaches and, time allowing, I'll get together with a peer or my boss and review the whole situation and my proposed new approaches to get a second opinion."

You can go on to explain that the next time you face the same kind of problem you'll know what to avoid, what to do more of, and what other new approaches you can try.

You might consider finishing your answer with a statement about the beneficial effects of experiencing problems: "Over the years I've learned just as much from life's problems as from its successes."

"What would your coworkers tell me about your attention to detail?"

Say that you are shoddy and never pay attention to the details, and you'll hear a whoosh as your job offer flies out the window.

Your answer obviously lies in the question. You pay attention to detail, your analytical approach to projects helps you identify all the component parts of a given job, and your time-management and organizational skills ensure that you get the job done in a timely manner without anything falling through the cracks.

"When do you expect a promotion?"

Tread warily, show you believe in yourself, and have both feet firmly planted on the ground: "That depends on a few criteria. Of course, I cannot expect promotions without the performance that marks me as deserving of promotion. I also need to join a company that has the growth necessary to provide the opportunity. I hope that my manager believes in promoting from within and will help me grow so that I will have the skills necessary to be considered for promotion when the opportunity comes along."

If you are the only one doing a particular job in the company, or you are in management, you need to build another factor into your answer. "As a manager, I realize that part of my job is to have done my succession planning and that I must have someone trained and ready to step into my shoes before I can expect to step up. That way I play my part in preserving the chain of command." To avoid being caught off guard with queries about your having achieved that in your present job, you can finish with: "Just as I have done in my present job, where I have a couple of people capable of taking over the reins when I leave."

"Tell me a story."

Wow. What on earth does the interviewer mean by that question? You don't know until you get him or her to elaborate. Ask, "What would you like me to tell you a story about?" To make any other response is to risk making a fool of yourself. Very often the question is asked to see how analytical you are: People who answer the question without qualifying show they do not think things through carefully. The subsequent question will be about either your personal or professional life. If it is about your personal life, tell a story that shows you like people and are determined. Do not discuss your love life. If the subsequent question is about your professional life, tell a story that demonstrates your willingness and manageability.

"What have your other jobs taught you?"

Talk about the professional skills you have learned and the professional behaviors you have polished. Many interviewees have had success finishing their answer with: "There are two general things I have learned from past jobs. First, if you are confused, ask—it's better to ask a dumb question than make a dumb mistake. Second, it's better to promise less and produce more than to make unrealistic forecasts."

"Define cooperation."

The question asks you to explain how to function as a team player in the workplace. Your answer could be: "Cooperation is a person's ability to sacrifice personal wishes and beliefs whenever necessary to assure the department reaches its goals. It is also a person's desire to be part of a team, and by hard work and goodwill make the department greater than the sum of its parts."

"What difficulties do you have tolerating people with different backgrounds and interests from yours?"

Another "team player" question with the awkward implication that you do have problems. Say, "I don't have any." But don't leave it there:

"I don't have any problems working with people with different backgrounds than myself. In fact I find it energizing; different backgrounds mean different life experiences and different ways of coming at problems. The opportunity to work with people different from yourself is a golden opportunity."

"In hindsight, what have you done that was a little harebrained?"

You are never harebrained in your business dealings, and you haven't been harebrained in your personal life since graduation, right? The only safe examples to use are ones from your deep past that ultimately turned out well. One of the best, if it applies to you, is: "Well, I guess the time I bought my house. I had no idea what I was letting myself in for, and at the time, I really couldn't afford it. Still, I managed to make the payments, though I had to work like someone possessed. Yes, my first house—that was a real learning experience." Not only can most people relate to this example, but it also gives you the opportunity to sell one or two of your very positive and endearing professional behaviors.

If you think the interview is only tough for the interviewee, it's time to take a look at the other side of the desk. Knowing what's going on there can really help you shine.

CHAPTER 12

The Other Side of the Desk

TWO TYPES OF interviewers can pose problems for the unprepared: the highly skilled and the unconscious incompetent. Find out how to recognize and respond to each one.

There are two terrible places to be during an interview—in front of the desk wondering what on earth is going to happen next and behind the desk asking the questions. The average interviewer dreads the meeting almost as much as the interviewee, yet for opposite reasons.

Business frequently yields to the mistaken belief that any person, on being promoted to the ranks of management, becomes mystically endowed with all necessary managerial skills. That is a fallacy; perhaps only half of all managers have been taught how to interview. Most just bumble along and pick up a certain proficiency over a period of time.

Two types of interviewers can spell disaster for the unprepared. One is the totally incompetent interviewer, who may even lack the ability to phrase a question adequately. The other is a highly skilled interviewer, who has been trained in systematic techniques for probing your past performance and future potential. Both are equally dangerous when it comes to winning the job offer.

The Skilled Interviewer

Skilled interviewers understand that a manager's first job is to get work done through others, so they recognize that making the right hires is a serious task. They know exactly what they want to discover, having taken the time to learn the strategies that will help them hire only the best for their company. They follow a set format for the interview process to ensure objectivity in the selection process, and a set sequence of questions to ensure the facts are gathered logically and in the right areas; all this in turn ensures productive hires. There are many ways for a manager to build and conduct a structured interview, but all have similar goals.

- To ensure a systematic coverage of your work history and applicable job-related skills.
- To determine ability, motivation, manageability and team orientation, problem-solving skills, and your professional behavior profile.
- To provide a technique for gathering all the relevant facts.
- To provide a uniform strategy that objectively evaluates all job candidates.

An interviewer using structured interview techniques will usually follow a standard format for each interview to help maintain objectivity. The interview will begin with small talk and a brief introduction to relax you. Following close on the heels of that chit-chat comes a statement designed to assure you that baring your faults is the best way to get the job. It's not—but neither is it necessary for you to lie. Your interviewer will then outline the steps in the interview. This will include you walking through a chronological description of your work history, then specific questions about different aspects of your experience. Finally, you will be given an opportunity to ask your own questions.

Sounds pretty simple, huh? Well, watch out! The skilled interviewer knows exactly what questions to ask, why they will be asked, in what order they will be asked, and what the desired responses are. He or she will interview and evaluate every applicant for the job in exactly the same fashion. You are up against a pro.

Like the hunter who learns to think like his or her prey, you will find the best way to win over the interviewer is to think like the interviewer, to understand what he or she is likely to ask and why. To do that, you must learn how the interviewer has prepared for you. By going through the same process, you will beat out your competitors for the job offer.

The dangerous part of this type of structured interview is called "skills evaluation." The interviewer has analyzed all the different skills it takes to do the job, and all the professional behaviors that complement those skills. Armed with this analysis, he or she has developed a series of carefully sequenced questions to draw out your relative merits and weaknesses.

Graphically, it looks like this:

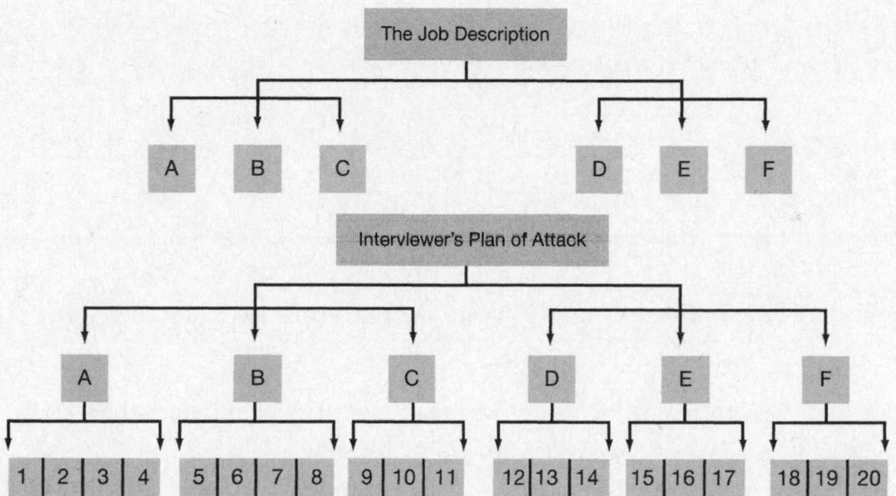

Letters A through F represent the separate skill sets (or deliverables, as they are often called) necessary to do the job; numbers 1 through 20 are questions asked to identify and verify each particular skill. This is where the tough questions will come, and the only way to prepare effectively is to take the interviewer's viewpoint and complete this exercise in its entirety. That effort requires a degree of objectivity but will generate multiple job offers. You have already done a little work in this area, when you were tweaking your resume.

✎**Look at the** position you seek: What role does it play in helping the company achieve its corporate mission and make a profit?

✎**What are the five most important duties of that job?** From a management viewpoint, what are the skills and attributes necessary to perform each of these tasks?

Write it all down. Now, put yourself in the interviewer's shoes. What topics would you examine to find out whether a person can really do the job? If for some reason you get stuck in the process, use your past experience. You have worked with good and bad people, and their work habits and skills will lead you to develop the potential questions and thereby the essence of the correct answers. When you do this exercise, you will not only understand what it will take to get the job, but you will also know what you will have to do, and how you will have to behave to succeed, once in the saddle.

Each skill set or deliverable you identify is fertile ground for the interviewer's questions. Don't forget the intangible skills that are so important to many jobs—like self-confidence and creativity—because the interviewer won't. Develop a number of questions for each skill set you identify.

Looking back at coworkers (and still wearing the manager's hat), what are the professional behaviors that would make life easier for you as a manager? These dimensions are likely to be examined by the interviewer. Once you have identified the questions you would ask in the interviewer's position, you are in a position to build great answers.

KNOCK 'EM DEAD TIP

If you are entering the world of work for the first time, or making a substantial career shift, you might not have the knowledge to analyze the job's deliverables. In this case go back to your networks and call people already in the profession to identify the skill sets and behaviors necessary to succeed in the initial target job of your new career.

This is how managers are trained to develop structured interviews. You now have the inside track; we'll develop answers over the coming pages.

These sharks have some juicy questions with which to probe your abilities, attitude, and professional behavior profile. Now we are going to lay out some of the most challenging questions they can ask, and show what is behind those questions and how you should approach building your answers. Notice these questions tend to present a problem for you to solve but in no way lead you toward the answer. They are often two- and three-part questions as well. The additional question that can be tagged onto them all is, "What did you learn from this experience?" Assume it is included whenever you get one of these questions—you'll be able to sell different aspects of your success profile.

"You have been given a project that requires you to interact with different levels within the company. How do you do this? What levels are you most comfortable with?"

This is a two-part question that probes communication and self-confidence skills. The first part asks how you interact with superiors and motivate those working with and for you on the project. The second part is saying, "Tell me whom you regard as your peer group—help me categorize you." To cover those bases, include the essence of this: "There are two types of people I would interact with on a project of this nature. First, there are those I report to, who bear the ultimate responsibility for its success. With them, I determine deadlines and a method for evaluating the success of the project. I outline my approach, breaking the project down into component parts, getting approval on both the approach and the costs. I would keep my supervisors updated on a regular basis and seek input whenever needed. My supervisors would expect three things from me: the facts, an analysis of potential problems, and that I not be intimidated, as this would jeopardize the project's success. I would comfortably satisfy those expectations.

"The other people to interact with on a project like this are those who work with and for me. With those people, I would outline the project and explain how a successful outcome will benefit the company. I would assign the component parts to those best suited to each, and arrange follow-up times to assure completion by deadline. My role here would be to facilitate, motivate, and bring the different personalities together to form a team.

"As for comfort level, I find this type of approach enables me to interact comfortably with all levels and types of people."

"Tell me about an event that really challenged you. How did you meet the challenge? In what way was your approach different from that of others?"

This is a straightforward, two-part question. The first part probes your problem-solving abilities. The second asks you to set yourself apart from the herd. Outline the problem. The clearer you make the situation, the better. Having done so, explain your solution, its value to your employer, and how it was different from other approaches:

"My company has offices all around the country; I am responsible for seventy of them. My job is to visit each office on a regular basis and build market-penetration strategies with management, and to train and motivate the sales and customer service forces. When the recession hit, the need to service those offices was more important than ever, yet the traveling costs were getting prohibitive.

"Morale was an especially important factor: You can't let outlying offices feel defeated. I reapportioned my budget and did the following: I dramatically increased telephone contact with the offices and instituted a monthly sales-technique letter—how to prospect for new clients, how to negotiate difficult sales, and so forth. I bought and rented sales training and motivational tapes and sent them to my managers with instructions on how to use them in a sales meeting. I stopped visiting all the offices. Instead, I scheduled weekend training meetings in central locations throughout my area: one day of sales training and one day of management training, concentrating on how to run sales meetings, early termination of low producers, and so forth.

"While my colleagues complained about the drop in sales, mine increased, albeit by a modest 6 percent. After two quarters, my approach was officially adopted by the company."

"Give me an example of a method of working you have used. How did you feel about it?"

You have a choice of giving an example of either good or bad work habits. Give a good example, one that demonstrates your understanding of corporate goals, your organizational skills, analytical ability, or time-management skills.

You could say: "Maximum productivity requires focus and demands organization and time management. I do my paperwork at the end of each day, when I review the day's achievements; with this done, I plan for tomorrow. When I come to work in the morning, I'm ready to get going without wasting time. I try to schedule meetings right before lunch; people get to the point more quickly if it's on their time. I feel this is an efficient and organized method of working."

"When you joined your last company and met the group for the first time, how did you feel? How did you get along with them?"

Your answer should include: "I naturally felt a little nervous, but I was excited about the new job. I shared that excitement with my new friends, and told them that I was enthusiastic about learning new skills from them. I was open and friendly, and when given the opportunity to help someone myself, I jumped at it."

"In your last job, how did you plan to interview?"

That's an easy one. Just give a description of how the skilled interviewer prepares.

"How have you benefited from your disappointments?"

Disappointments are different from failures. It is an intelligent—probably trained—interviewer who asks this one. This question is also an opportunity for the astute interviewee to shine. The question itself is positive—it asks you to show how you benefited; also, it doesn't ask you to give specific details of specific disappointments, so you don't have to open your mouth and insert your foot. Instead, be general. Edison once explained his success as an inventor by claiming that he knew more ways not to do something than anyone else living: You can do worse than to quote him. In any event, sum up your answer with, "I treat disappointments as a learning experience: I look at what happened, why it happened, and how I would do things differently at each stage should the same set of circumstances appear again. That way, I put disappointment behind me and am ready with renewed vigor and understanding to face the new day's problems."

A side note: A person with strong religious beliefs may be tempted to answer a question like this in terms of religious values. If you benefit from disappointments in a spiritual way, remember that not everyone feels the same as you do. More important, the interviewer is, by law, prohibited from talking about religion with you, so you can unwittingly put the interviewer in an awkward position of not knowing how to respond. Making an interviewer feel awkward in any way is not the way to win a job offer.

"What would you do if you had a decision to make and no procedure existed?"

This question probes your analytical skills, integrity, and dedication. Most of all, the interviewer is testing your manageability and adherence to procedures—the "company way of doing things." You need to cover that with, "I would act without my manager's direction only if the situation was urgent and my manager was not available. Then, I would take command of the situation, make a decision based on the facts, and implement it. I would update my boss at the earliest opportunity." If possible, tell a story to illustrate.

"That is an excellent answer. Now to give me a balanced view, can you give me an example that didn't work out so well?"

There are two techniques that every skilled interviewer will use, especially if you are giving good answers. In this question, the interviewer looks for negative balance; in the follow-up, the person will look for negative confirmation. Here, you are required to give an example of an inadequacy. The trick is to pull something from the past, not the present, and to finish with what you learned from the experience. For example: "That's easy. When I first joined the workforce, I didn't really understand the importance of systems and procedures. There was one time when I was too anxious to contribute and didn't have the full picture. There was a sales visit report everyone had to fill out after visiting a customer. I always put a lot of effort into it until I realized it was never read; it just went in the files. So I stopped doing it for a few days to see if it made any difference. I thought I was gaining time to make more sales for the company. I was so proud of my extra sales calls, I told the boss at the end of the week. My boss explained that the records were for the long term, so that should my job change, the next salesperson would have the benefit of a full client history. It was a long time ago, but I have never forgotten the lesson: There's always a reason for systems and procedures. I've had the best-kept records in the company ever since."

To look for negative confirmation, the interviewer may then say something like, "Thank you. Now can you give me another example?" He or she is trying to confirm a weakness. If you help, you could cost yourself the job. Here's your reaction: You sit deep in thought for a good ten seconds, then look up and say firmly, "No, that's the only occasion when anything like that happened." Shut up and refuse to be enticed further.

The Unconscious Incompetent

Now you should be ready for almost anything a professional interviewer could throw at you. Your foresight and strategic planning will generate multiple offers of employment for you in all circumstances except one, and that's when you face the unconsciously incompetent interviewer. He or she is probably more dangerous to your job-offer status than everything else combined.

The poor interviewer, consciously or otherwise, bases hiring decisions on "experience" and "knowledge of mankind" and "gut feeling." In any event, he or she is an unconscious incompetent. You have probably been interviewed by one in your time. Remember leaving an interview and, upon reflection, feeling the interviewer knew absolutely nothing about you or your skills? If so, you know how frustrating that can be. In the future, good managers who are poor interviewers will be offering jobs with far greater frequency than ever before. Understand that a poor interviewer can be a wonderful manager; interviewing skills are learned, not inherited or created as a result of a mystical corporate blessing.

The unconscious incompetents abound. Their heinous crime can only be exceeded by your inability to recognize and take advantage of the proffered opportunity. As in handling the skilled interviewer, it is necessary to imagine how the unconscious incompetent thinks and feels. There are many manifestations of the poor interviewer. Each of the next examples is followed by instructions for appropriate handling of the unique problems posed for you.

✎**Example 1:** The interviewer's desk is cluttered, and the resume or application that was handed to him or her a few minutes before cannot be found.

Response: Sit quietly through the bumbling and searching. Check out the surroundings. Breathe deeply and slowly to calm any lingering interview nerves. As you bring your adrenaline under control, you produce a certain calming effect to the interviewer and the interview. (This example, by the way, is the most common sign of the unconscious incompetent.)

✎**Example 2:** The interviewer experiences constant interruptions from the telephone or people walking into the office.

Response: This provides good opportunities for selling yourself. Make a note on your pad of where you were in the conversation and refresh the interviewer on the point when you start talking again. He or she will be impressed with your level head and good memory. The interruptions also give time, perhaps, to find something of common interest in the office, something you can compliment. You will also have time to compose the suitable value key follow-up to the point made in the conversation prior to the interruption.

✎**Example 3:** The interviewer starts with an explanation of why you are both sitting there, and then allows the conversation to degenerate into a lengthy diatribe about the company.

Response: Show interest in the company and the conversation. Sit straight, look attentive, make appreciative murmurs, and nod at the appropriate times until there is a pause. When that occurs, comment that you appreciate the background on the company, because you can now see more clearly how the job fits into the general scheme of things and that you see, for example, how valuable communication skills would be for the job. Could the interviewer please tell you some of the other job requirements? Then, as the job's functions are described, you can interject appropriate information about your background with questions like, "Would it be of value, Mr. Smith, if I described my experience with . . . ?"

✎**Example 4:** The interviewer begins with, or quickly breaks into, the drawbacks of the job. The job may even be described in totally negative terms. That is often done without giving a balanced view of the duties and expectations of the position.

Response: An initial negative description often means that the interviewer has had bad experiences hiring for the position. Your course is to make it known that you recognize the importance of (for example) reliability, especially in this particular type of job. (You will invariably find in these instances that what your interviewer has lacked in the past is someone with a serious understanding of value keys.) Illustrate your proficiency in that particular aspect of your profession with a short example from your work history. Finish your statements by asking the interviewer what some of the biggest problems to be handled in the job are. The questions demonstrate your understanding, and the interviewer's answers outline the areas from your background and skills to which you should draw attention.

✎**Example 5:** The interviewer spends considerable time early in the interview describing "the type of people we are here at XYZ Corporation."

Response: You have always wanted to work for a company with that atmosphere. It creates the type of work environment that is conducive to a person really giving his or her best efforts.

✎**Example 6:** The interviewer asks closed-ended questions, ones that demand no more than a yes-or-no answer (e.g., "Do you pay attention to detail?"). Such questions are hardly adequate to establish your skills, yet you must handle them effectively to secure the job offer.

Response: A yes-or-no answer to a closed-ended question will not get you that offer. The trick is to treat each closed-ended question as if the interviewer has added, "Please give me a brief yet thorough answer." Closed-ended questions also are often mingled with statements followed by pauses. In those instances, agree with the statement in a way that demonstrates both a grasp of your job and the interviewer's statement. For example: "That's an excellent point, Mr. Smith. I couldn't agree more that the attention to detail you describe naturally affects cost containment. My track record in this area is . . . ."

✎**Example 7:** The interviewer asks a stream of negative questions (as described in the next chapter, "The Stress Interview").

Response: Use the techniques and answers described earlier. Give your answers with a smile and do not take the questions as personal insults; they are not intended that way. The more stressful the situations the job is likely to place you in, the greater the likelihood of your having to field negative questions. The interviewer wants to know if you can take the heat.

Example 8: The interviewer has difficulty looking at you while speaking.

Response: The interviewer is someone who finds it uncomfortable being in the spotlight. Try to help him or her by being a good audience. Ask specific questions about the job responsibilities and offer your skills in turn.

A hiring manager will often arrange for you to meet with two or three other people. Frequently, the other interviewers have been neither trained in appropriate interviewing skills nor told the details of the job for which you are interviewing. So you will take additional copies of your executive briefing with you to the interview to aid them in focusing on the appropriate job functions.

When you understand how to recognize and respond to these different types of interviewers, you will leave your interview having made a favorable first impression. No one forgets first impressions.

CHAPTER 13
The Stress Interview

YOUR WORST NIGHTMARE can come true at a stress interview, but once you learn that these questions are just amplified versions of much simpler ones, you'll remain cool and calm. Also included in this chapter is a vital discussion on handling illegal interview questions.

For all intents and purposes, every interview is a stress interview. The interviewer's negative and trick questions can act as the catalyst for your own fear. The only way to combat that fear is to be prepared, to know what the interviewer is trying to do, and to anticipate the various directions he or she will take. Whenever you are ill-prepared for an interview, no one will be able to put more pressure on you than you do on yourself. Remember: A stress interview is just a regular interview with the volume turned all the way up—the music is the same, just louder. Only preparedness will keep you cool and collected.

You've heard the horror stories. An interviewer demands of a hapless applicant, "Sell me this pen," or asks, "How would you improve the design of a teddy bear?" Or the candidate is faced with a battery of interviewers, all demanding rapid-fire answers to questions like, "You're giving a dinner party. Which ten famous people would you invite and why?" When the interviewee offers evidence of foot-in-mouth disease by asking, "Living or dead?" he receives his just desserts: "Ten of each."

Such awful-sounding questions are thrown in to test your poise, to see how you react under pressure, and to plumb the depths of your confidence. Many people ruin their chances by reacting to them as personal insults rather than challenges and opportunities to shine.

Previously restricted to the executive suite for the selection of high-powered executives, stress interviews are now widespread throughout the professional world. They can come with all the intimidating and treacherous tricks your worst nightmare can devise. Yet a good performance at a stress interview can mean the difference between a job in the fast lane and a stalled career. The interviewers in a stress interview are invariably experienced and well organized, and have developed tightly structured procedures and advanced interviewing techniques. The questions and tension they generate have the cumulative effect of throwing you off balance and revealing the "real" you—rather than someone who can respond with last night's rehearsed answers to six or seven stock questions.

Stress questions can be turned to your advantage or merely avoided with nifty footwork. Whichever approach you choose, you will be among a select few who understand this line of questioning. As always, when addressing the questions in this chapter, remember to develop personalized answers that reflect your experience and profession. Practice your responses aloud—by doing that, your responses to these interview gambits will become more natural and will help you feel more confident during an interview. You might even consider making a recording of tough questions, spacing them at intervals of thirty seconds to two minutes. You can then play the tape back and answer the questions in real time.

As we will see in this chapter, reflexive questions can prove especially useful when the heat is on. Stress questions are designed to sort out the clutch players from those who freeze under pressure. Used with discretion, the reflexives (". . . don't you think?") will demonstrate to the interviewer that you are able to function well under pressure. At the same time, of course, you put the ball back in the interviewer's court.

One common stress interview technique is to set you up for a fall: a pleasant conversation, one or a series of seemingly innocuous questions to relax your guard, then a dazzling series of jabs and body blows that can leave you gibbering. For instance, an interviewer might lull you into a false sense of security by asking some relatively stress-free questions: "What was your initial starting salary at your last job?" then, "What is your salary now?" then, "Do you receive bonuses?" etc. To put you on the ropes, he or she might then completely surprise you with, "Tell me what sort of troubles you have living within your means," or "Why aren't you earning more at your age?" Such interviewers are using stress in an intelligent fashion, to simulate the unexpected and sometimes tense events of everyday business life. Seeing how you handle unexpected stress gives a fair indication of how you will react to the real thing.

The sophisticated interviewer talks very little, perhaps only 20 percent of the time, and that time is spent asking questions. Few comments, and no editorializing on your answers, means that you get no hint, verbal or otherwise, about your performance.

The questions are planned, targeted, sequenced, and layered. The interviewer covers one subject thoroughly before moving on. Let's take the simple example of "Can you work under pressure?" As a reader of *Knock 'em Dead*, you know to answer that question with an example and thereby deflect the main thrust of the stress technique. The interviewer will be prepared for a simple yes-or-no answer; what follows will keep the unprepared applicant reeling.

"Can you work under pressure?"

A simple, closed-ended question that requires just a yes-or-no answer, but you won't get off so easy.

"Good, I'd be interested to hear about a time when you experienced pressure on your job."

An open-ended request to tell a story about a pressure situation. After this, you will be subjected to the layering technique—six layers in the following instance.

"Why do you think this situation arose?"

It's best if the situation you describe is not a peer's or manager's fault. Remember, you must be seen as a team player.

"When exactly did it happen?"

Asking when an event happened can often lead to further questions. This is why the process of self-discovery in the earlier part of the book pays dividends throughout the entire interview cycle.

"How do you feel others involved could have acted more responsibly?"

An open invitation to criticize peers and superiors, which you should diplomatically decline.

"Who holds the responsibility for the situation?"

Another invitation to point the finger of blame, which should be avoided.

"Where in the chain of command could steps be taken to avoid that sort of thing happening again?"

This question probes your analytical skills and whether you are the type of person who always goes back to the scene of the crime to learn for the next time.

This is a reporter's technique of asking why, when, who, what, how, and where. The technique can be applied to any question you are asked and is frequently used to probe those success stories that sound too good to be true. You'll find them suddenly tagged on to the simple closed-ended questions as well as to the open-ended ones. Typically, they'll start with something like "Share with me," "Tell me about a time when," or, "I'm interested in finding out about," followed by a request for specific examples from your work history.

After you've survived that barrage, a friendly tone may conceal another zinger: "What did you learn from the experience?" This question is geared to probe your judgment and emotional maturity. Your answer should emphasize whichever of the key professional behaviors your story was illustrating.

When an interviewer feels you were on the edge of revealing something unusual in an answer, you may well encounter "mirror statements." Here, the last key phrase of your answer will be repeated or paraphrased, and followed by a steady gaze and silence. For example, "So, you learned that organization is the key to management." The idea is that the silence and an expectant look will work together to keep you talking. It can be disconcerting to find yourself rambling on without quite knowing why. The trick is knowing when to stop. When the interviewer gives you an expectant look in this context, expand your answer (you have to), but by no more than a couple of sentences. Otherwise, you will get that creepy feeling that you're digging yourself into a hole.

There will be situations where you face more than one interviewer at a time. When these occur, remember the story of a female attorney who had five law partners all asking questions at the same time. As the poor interviewee got halfway through one answer, another question would be shot at her. Pausing for breath, she smiled and said, "Hold on, ladies and gentlemen. These are all excellent questions, and, given time, I'll answer them all. Now who's next?" In so doing, she showed the interviewers exactly what they wanted to see and what is behind every stress interview and every negatively phrased question—a desire to find the presence of poise and calm under fire, combined with a refusal to be intimidated.

You never know when a stress interview will raise its ugly head. Often it can be that rubber-stamp meeting with the senior vice president at the end of a series of grueling meetings. That is not surprising. While other interviewers are concerned with determining whether you are able, willing, and a good fit for the job in question, the senior executive who eventually throws you for a loop may be probing you for potential promotability.

The most intimidating stress interviews are recognizable before the interviewer speaks: no eye contact, no greeting, either silence or a noncommittal grunt, and no small talk. You may also recognize such an interviewer by his general air of boredom, lack of interest, or thinly veiled aggression. ;-)

"What is your greatest weakness?"

This is a direct invitation to put your head in a noose. Decline the invitation.

This is perhaps one instance where the need for ongoing education in the modern world of work can come to your rescue in a sticky situation. The changes in technology give everyone an ongoing challenge getting up to speed with new skills. Your answer can address these very issues, and in the process show yourself as someone capable of staying on top of a rapidly changing workplace.

"With all the legal and technological changes impacting finance these days, staying up to date is a real challenge. Then, of course, there's working out how this affects the job and developing new knowledge or skills the changes demand." You might well finish this with examples of how you are keeping up to speed with the technological changes that affect your competence and productivity.

This is an honest answer to which anyone can relate, and it's all the better if you complete it with a course of action such as: "I'm currently reading about . . ."; "I just attended a weekend workshop where . . ."; or "I'm signed up for classes at . . . ."

With this type of answer you identify your weakness as something that is only of concern to the most dedicated and forward-looking professionals in your field.

You can also consider the following effective alternatives.

If there is a minor part of the job at hand where you lack knowledge—but knowledge you will pick up quickly—use that. For instance: "I haven't worked with this type of spreadsheet program before, but given my experience with six other types, I don't think it should take me more than a couple of days to pick it up." Here you remove the emphasis from weakness and put it onto a developmental problem that is easily overcome. Be careful, however; this very effective ploy must be used with discretion.

Another good option is to give a generalized answer that takes advantage of value keys. Design the answer so that your weakness is ultimately a positive characteristic. For example: "I enjoy my work and always give each project my best shot. So when sometimes I don't feel others are pulling their weight, I find it a little frustrating. I am aware of that weakness, and in those situations I try to overcome it with a positive attitude that I hope will catch on."

Also consider the technique of putting a problem in the past. Here you take a weakness from way back when and show how you overcame it. It answers the question but ends on a positive note. An illustration: "When I first got into this field, I always had problems with my paperwork—leaving an adequate paper trail. To be honest, I let it slip once or twice. My manager sat me down and explained the potential troubles such behavior could cause. I really took it to heart, and I think you will find my records some of the best around today. You only have to tell me something once." With that kind of answer, you also get the added bonus of showing that you accept and act on criticism.

Congratulations! You have just turned a bear of a question into an opportunity to sell yourself. In deciding on the particular answer you will give, remember that the interviewer isn't really concerned about your general weaknesses—no one is a saint outside of the interview room. He or she is simply concerned about any red flags that might signal your inability to perform the job or work well under supervision.

"With hindsight, how could you have improved your progress?"

Here's a question that demands, "Tell me your mistakes and weaknesses." If you can mention ways of improving your performance without damaging your candidacy, do so. The end of your answer should contain something like: "Other than that, I don't know what to add. I have always given it my best shot." Then shut up.

"What kinds of decisions are most difficult for you?"

You are human—admit it, but be careful what you admit. If you have ever had to fire someone, you are in luck, because no one likes to do that. Emphasize that, having reached a logical conclusion, you act. If you are not in management, tie your answer to key profiles: "It's not that I have difficulty making decisions—some just require more consideration than others. A small example might be vacation time. Now, everyone is entitled to it, but I don't believe you should leave your boss in a bind at short notice. I think very carefully at the beginning of the year when I'd like to take my vacation, and then think of alternate dates. I go to my supervisor, tell him what I hope to do, and see whether there is any conflict. I wouldn't want to be out of the office for the two weeks prior to a project deadline, for instance. So by carefully considering things far enough in advance, I don't procrastinate, and I make sure my plans jibe with my boss and the department for the year."

Here you take a trick question and use it to demonstrate your consideration, analytical abilities, and concern for the department—and for the company's bottom line.

"Tell me about the problems you have living within your means."

This is a twister to catch you off guard. Your best defense is first of all to know that it exists, and second to give it short shrift: "I know few people who are satisfied with their current earnings. As a professional, I am continually striving to improve my skills and to improve my living standard. But my problems are no different from that of this company or any other—making sure all the bills get paid on time and recognizing that every month and year there are some things that are prudent to do and others that are best deferred."

"What area of your skills/professional development do you want to improve at this time?"

Another "tell me all your weaknesses" question. You should try to avoid damaging your candidacy by tossing around careless admissions. One effective answer to this is to say, "Well, from what you told me about the job, I seem to have all the necessary skills and background. What I would really find exciting is the opportunity to work on a job where . . . ." At this point, you replay the interviewer's hot buttons about the job. You emphasize that you really have all the job-related skills and also tell the interviewer what you find exciting about the job. It works admirably.

You can reiterate one or two areas that combine personal strengths and the job's most crucial responsibilities, and finish with saying, "These areas are so important that I don't think anyone can be too good or should ever stop trying to polish their skills."

"Your application shows you have been with one company a long time without any appreciable increase in rank or salary. Tell me about this."

Ugh. A toughie. To start with, you should analyze why this state of affairs does exist (assuming the interviewer's assessment is accurate). When you have determined the cause, practice saying it out loud to yourself as you would say it during an actual interview. It may take a few tries. Chances, are no matter how valid your explanation really is, it will come off sounding a little tinny or vindictive without some polishing. Avoid the sour-grapes syndrome at all costs.

Here are some tactics you can use. First of all, try to avoid putting your salary history on application forms. No one is going to deny you an interview for lack of a salary history if your skills match those the job requires. And of course, you should never put such unnecessary information on your resume.

If the interviewer is intent, and asks you outright for this information, you'll find a great response in the section on salary histories in Chapter 19.

Now, we'll address the delicate matter of "Hey, wait a minute; why no promotions?" The interviewer has posed a truly negative inquiry. The more time either of you spend on it, the more time the interviewer gets to devote to concentrating on negative aspects of your candidacy. Make your answer short and sweet, then shut up. For instance, "My current employer is a stable company with a good working environment, but there's minimal growth there in my area—in fact, there hasn't been any promotion in my area since ___________. Your question is the reason I am meeting here with you; I have the skills and ability to take on more responsibility, and I'm looking for a place to do that."

"If you had to stay in your current job, what would you spend more time on, and why?"

Without a little self-control you could easily blurt out what you consider to be your greatest weaknesses. Tricky question, but with a little foreknowledge your answer will shine.

Practically speaking, each of your job changes should occur within the context of an overall career management strategy. While sensible career management blends personal fulfillment with ongoing solvency, an employer is only concerned with the latter. It's your continued employability that determines solvency, which is achieved by a growing competence in the profession-critical skills that make you desirable to employers.

Enlightened self-interest dictates that an ongoing career management concern is to identify and develop the skills demanded in an ever-changing work environment. So your answer might begin, in part: "In the modern world of work, existing skills always need to be improved and new skills learned, to handle the changing nature of our work. For instance, in this job *[now give a job-specific example]*. I think the organizational software now available can have a major impact on personal productivity, so . . . ."

With an answer along these lines you show foresight instead of a weakness.

"How do you stay current?"

The age of technological innovation in which we live means that the nature of every job is changing about as quickly as you turn these pages. Continual changes in the nature of your professional work mean you must look at ongoing professional education as the price of sustained employability. In your answer, talk about your appreciation of this and the importance of keeping abreast of changes in the profession, and then illustrate with the following:

- Courses you have taken and are planning to take
- Books you have read or book clubs you belong to
- Memberships in professional associations
- Subscriptions to professional journals

Such an answer will identify you as an aware, connected, and dedicated professional.

"Are you willing to take calculated risks when necessary?"

First, qualify the question: "How do you define calculated risks? What sort of risks? Give me an example of a risk you have in mind; what are the stakes involved?" That will show you exactly the right analytical approach to take in evaluating a calculated risk, and while the interviewer is rattling on, you have bought time to come up with an answer. Whatever your answer, you will include, "Naturally, I would never take any risk that would in any way jeopardize the safety or reputation of my company or colleagues. In fact, I don't think any employer would appreciate an employee at any level taking risks of any nature without first having a thorough briefing and chance to give input."

"See this pen I'm holding? Sell it to me."

This is not a request, as you might think, that would only be asked of a salesperson. In today's professional workplace, everyone is required to communicate effectively and sell appropriately—sometimes products, but more often ideas, approaches, and concepts. As such, you are being examined about your understanding of the features and benefits of selling, how quickly you think on your feet, and how effectively you use verbal communication. For example, the interviewer holds up a yellow highlighter. First you will want to establish the customer's needs with a few questions like, "What sort of pens do you currently use? Do you use a highlighter? Do you read reports and need to recall important points? Is comfort important to you?" Then you will proceed calmly, "Let me tell you about the special features of this pen and show you how they will satisfy your needs. First of all it is tailor-made for highlighting reports, and that will save you time in recalling the most important points. The case is wide for comfort and the base is flat so it will stand up and be visible on a cluttered work area. It's disposable—and affordable enough to have a handful for desk, briefcase, car, and home. And the bright yellow means you'll never lose it." Then close with a smile and a question of your own that will bring a smile to the interviewer's face: "How many gross shall we deliver?"

"How will you be able to cope with a change in environment after five years [for example] with your current company?"

Another chance to take an implied negative and turn it into a positive: "That's one of the reasons I want to make a change. After five years with my current employer, I felt I was about to get stale. Everyone needs a change of scene once in a while. It's just time for me to make some new friends, face some new challenges, and experience some new approaches. Hopefully, I'll have the chance to contribute from my experience."

"Why aren't you earning more at your age?"

Accept this as a compliment to your skills and accomplishments: "I have always felt that solid experience would stand me in good stead in the long run and that earnings would come in due course. Also, I am not the type of person to change jobs just for the money. At this point, I have a solid background that is worth something to a company." Now, to avoid the interviewer putting you on the spot again, finish with a question: "How much should I be earning now?" The figure could be your offer.

"What is the worst thing you have heard about our company?"

This question can come as something of a shock. As with all stress questions, your poise under stress is vital: If you can carry off a halfway decent answer as well, you are a winner. The best response to this question is simple. Just say with a smile and a laugh: "You're a tough company to get an interview with." It's true, it's flattering, and it shows that you are not intimidated.

"How would you define your profession?"

With questions that solicit your understanding of a topic, no matter how good your answer, you can expect to be interrupted in mid-reply with, "That has nothing to do with it," or "Whoever put that idea into your head?" Ninety-nine times out of a hundred these comments are not serious criticisms. Rather, they are tests to see how well you could defend your position in a no-holds-barred conversation with a client or the chairman of the board, people who usually say what they think. Defend yourself, without taking or showing offense.

First, gain time and get the interviewer talking: "Why do you say that?" you ask, answering a question with a question. Turning the tables on your aggressor displays your poise, calm, and analytical skills better than any other response.

"Why should I hire an outsider when I could fill the job with someone from inside the company?"

The question isn't as stupid as it sounds. Obviously, the interviewer has examined existing employees with an eye toward their promotion or reassignment. Just as obviously, the job cannot be filled from within the company. If it could be, it would be, and for two very good reasons: It is cheaper for the company to promote from within, and it is better for employee morale.

Hiding behind this intimidating question is a pleasant invitation: "Tell me why I should hire you." Your answer should include two steps. The first is a simple recitation of your skills and personality profile strengths, tailored to the specific requirements of the job.

For the second step, realize first that whenever a manager is filling a position, he or she is looking not only for someone who can do the job, but also for someone who can benefit the department in a larger sense. No department is as good as it could be—each has weaknesses that need strengthening. So in the second part of your answer, include a question of your own: "Those are my general attributes. However, if no one is promotable from inside the company, you must be looking to add strength to your team in a special way. How do you hope the final candidate will be able to benefit your department?" The answer to this is your cue to sell your applicable qualities.

"Have you ever had any financial difficulties?"

The potential employer wants to know whether you can control not only your own finances but also finances in general. If you are in the insurance field, for example—in claims, accounting, supervision, or management—you can expect to hear this one. The question, though, is not restricted to insurance: Anyone, especially a person who handles money in day-to-day business, is fair game.

For someone to check your credit history, he or she must have your written consent. This is required under the 1972 Fair Credit and Reporting Act. Invariably, when you fill out a job application form, sign it, and date it, you've also signed a release permitting the employer to check your credit history. If you have already filled out the form, you might not hear this specific question during your interview, but your creditors might. I should note here that the reader who asked me about this question also described how she'd handled it during the interview: by describing her past problems with bankruptcy in every detail. However, in trying to be open and honest, she had actually done herself a disservice.

The interviewer does not want to hear sob stories. If your credit history is spotty, concentrate on the information that will damage your candidacy the least and enhance it the most. You might find it appropriate to bring the matter up yourself if you work in an area where your credit history is likely to be checked. If you choose to wait until the interviewer brings it up, you might say (if you had to file for bankruptcy, for instance), "I should tell you that some years ago, for reasons beyond my control, I was forced into personal bankruptcy. That has been behind me for some time. Today, I have a sound credit rating and no debts. Bankruptcy is not something I'm proud of, but I did learn from the experience, and I feel it has made me a more proficient account supervisor." The answer concentrates on today, not past history.

"How do you handle rejection?"

This question is common if you are applying for a job in sales, including face-to-face sales, telemarketing, public relations, and customer service. If you are after a job in one of these areas and you really don't like the heavy doses of rejection that are any salesperson's lot, consider a new field. The anguish you will experience will not lead to a successful career or a happy life.

With that in mind, let's look behind the question. The interviewer simply wants to know whether you take rejection as rejection of yourself or whether you simply accept it as a temporary rejection of a service or product. Here is a sample answer that you can tailor to your particular needs and background: "I accept rejection as an integral part of the sales process. If everyone said 'yes' to a product, there would be no need for the sales function. As it is, I see every rejection as bringing me closer to the customer who will say 'yes.' Sales is a profession of communication, determination, and resiliency, and rejection is just part of the process; it's nothing personal. I always try to leave the potential customer with a good feeling, as no sale today can well become a sale next month."

"Why were you out of work for so long?"

You must have a sound explanation for all gaps in your employment history. If not, you are unlikely to receive a job offer. Emphasize you were not just looking for another paycheck—you were looking for a company with which to settle and make a long-term contribution:

"I decided that I enjoy my work too much just to accept another paycheck. I determined that the next job I took would be one where I could do my best to make a solid contribution. From everything I have heard about this company, you are a group that expects people to pull their weight, because you've got a real job to do. I like that, and I would like to be part of the team. What do I have to do to get the job?"

You answer the question, compliment the interviewer, and shift the emphasis from your unemployment to how you can get the job offer.

"Why have you changed jobs so frequently?"

If you have jumped around, blame it on youth (even the interviewer was young once). Now you realize what a mistake your job-hopping was, and with your added domestic responsibilities you are now much more settled. Or you may wish to impress on the interviewer that your job-hopping was never as a result of poor performance and that you grew professionally as a result of each job change.

You could reply: "My first job had a long commute. I soon realized that, but I knew it would give me good experience in a very competitive field. Subsequently, I found a job much closer to home where the commute was only half an hour each way. I was very happy at my second job. However, I got an opportunity to really broaden my experience base with a new company that was just starting up. With the wisdom of hindsight, I realize that move was a mistake; it took me six months to realize I couldn't make a contribution there. I've been with my current company a reasonable length of time. So I have broad experience in different environments. I didn't just job-hop; I have been following a path to gain broad experience. So you see, I have more experience than the average person of my years, and a desire to settle down and make it pay off for me and my employer."

Or you can say: "Now I want to settle down and make my diverse background pay off in my contributions to my new employer. I have a strong desire to contribute and I am looking for an employer that will keep me challenged; I think this might be the company to do that. Am I right?"

"Tell me about a time when you put your foot in your mouth."

Answer this question with caution. The interviewer is examining your ability and willingness to interact pleasantly with others. The question is tricky because it asks you to show yourself in a poor light. Downplay the negative impact of your action and end with positive information about your candidacy. The best thing to do is to start with an example outside of the workplace and show how the experience improved your performance at work:

"About five years ago, I let the cat out of the bag about a surprise birthday party for a friend, a terrific faux pas. It was a mortifying experience, and I promised myself not to let anything like that happen again." Then, after this fairly innocuous statement, you can talk about communications in the workplace: "As far as work is concerned, I always regard employer-employee communications on any matter as confidential unless expressly stated otherwise. So, putting my foot in my mouth doesn't happen to me at work."

"Why do you want to leave your current job?" or "Why did you leave your last job?"

This is a common trick question. You should have an acceptable reason for leaving every job you have held, but if you don't, pick one of the six acceptable reasons from the employment industry formula, the acronym for which is CLAMPS:

- **Challenge:** You weren't able to grow professionally in that position.
- **Location:** The commute was unreasonably long.
- **Advancement:** There was nowhere for you to go. You had the talent, but there were too many people ahead of you.
- **Money:** You were underpaid for your skills and contribution.
- **Pride or prestige:** You wanted to be with a better company.
- **Security:** The company was not stable.

For example: "My last company was a family-owned affair. I had gone as far as I was able to go. It just seemed time for me to join a more prestigious company and accept greater challenges."

Under no circumstances should you badmouth a manager—even if she was a direct descendant of Attila the Hun. Doing so will only raise a red flag in the interviewer's mind: "Will he be complaining about me like this in a few months?"

"What interests you least about this job?"

This question is potentially explosive, but easily defused. Regardless of your occupation, there is at least one repetitive, mindless duty that everyone groans about and that goes with the territory. Use that as your example in a statement of this nature: "Filing is probably the least demanding part of the job. However, it is important to the overall success of my department, so I try to do it with a smile." This shows that you understand that it is necessary to take the rough with the smooth in any job.

"What was there about your last company that you didn't particularly like or agree with?"

You are being checked out as a potential fly in the ointment. If you have to answer, you might discuss the way the company policies or directives were sometimes consciously misunderstood by some employees who disregarded the bottom line—the profitability of the corporation.

Another option: "You know how it is sometimes with a big company. People lose awareness of the cost of things. There never seemed to be much concern about economy or efficiency. Everyone wanted his or her year-end bonus, but only worried about it in December. The rest of the year, nobody gave a hoot. I think that's the kind of thing we could be aware of almost every day, don't you agree?"

Or: "I didn't like the way some people gave lip service to 'the customer comes first,' but really didn't go out of their way to keep the customer satisfied. I don't think it was a fault of management, just a general malaise that seemed to affect a lot of people."

"What do you feel is a satisfactory attendance record?"

There are two answers to this question—one if you are in management, and one if you are not. As a manager: "I believe attendance is a matter of management, motivation, and psychology. Letting the employees know you expect their best efforts and won't accept half-baked excuses is one thing. The other is to keep your employees motivated by a congenial work environment and the challenge to stretch themselves. Giving people pride in their work and letting them know you respect them as individuals have a lot to do with it, too."

If you are not in management, the answer is even easier: "I've never really considered it. I work for a living, I enjoy my job, and I'm rarely sick."

"What is your general impression of your last company?"

Always answer positively. Keep your real feelings to yourself, whatever they might be. There is a strong belief among the management fraternity that people who complain about past employers will cause problems for their new ones. Your answer is "Very good" or "Excellent." Then smile and wait for the next question.

"What are some of the problems you encounter in doing your job, and what do you do about them?"

Note well the old saying, "A poor workman blames his tools." Your awareness that careless mistakes cost the company good money means you are always on the lookout for potential problems. Give an example of a problem you recognized and solved.

For example: "My job is fairly repetitive, so it's easy to overlook problems. Lots of people do. However, I always look for them; it helps keep me alert and motivated, so I do a better job. To give you an example, we make computer-memory disks. Each one has to be machined by hand, and, once completed, the slightest abrasion will turn one into a reject. I have a steady staff and little turnover, and everyone wears cotton gloves to handle the disks. Yet about six months ago, the reject rate suddenly went through the roof. Is that the kind of problem you mean? Well, the cause was one that could have gone unnoticed for ages. Jill, the section head who inspects all the disks, had lost a lot of weight and her diamond engagement ring was slipping around her finger, scratching the disks as she passed them and stacked them to be shipped. Our main client was giving us a big problem over it, so my looking for problems and paying attention to detail really paid off."

The interviewer was trying to get you to reveal weak points; you avoided the trap.

"What are some of the things you find difficult to do? Why do you feel that way?"

This is a variation on a couple of earlier questions. Remember, anything that goes against the best interests of your employer is difficult to do. If you are pressed for a job function you find difficult, answer in the past tense. That way, you show that you recognize the difficulty, but that you obviously handle it well:

"That's a tough question. There are so many things that are difficult to learn in our business if you want to do the job right. I used to have forty clients to sell to every month, and I was so busy touching base with all of them that I never got a chance to sell to any of them. So I graded them into three groups. I called on the top 20 percent of my clients every three weeks. The balance of my clients I called on once a month, but with a difference—each month, I marked ten of them to spend time with and really get to know. I still have difficulty reaching all forty of my clients in a month, but my sales have tripled and are still climbing."

"Jobs have pluses and minuses. What were some of the minuses on your last job?"

A variation on the question, "What interests you least about this job?" which was handled earlier. Use the same type of answer. "Like any salesperson, I enjoy selling, not doing the paperwork. But as I cannot expect the customer to get the goods, and me my commission, without following through on this task, I grin and bear it. Besides, if I don't do the paperwork, that holds up other people in the company."

If you are not in sales, use the sales force as a scapegoat: "In accounts receivable, it's my job to get the money in to make payroll and good things like that. Half the time, the goods get shipped before I get the paperwork because sales says, 'It's a rush order.' That's a real minus to me. It was so bad at my last company that we tried a new approach. We met with sales and explained our problem. The result was that incremental commissions were based on cash in, not on bill date. They saw the connection, and things are much better now."

"What kinds of people do you like to work with?"

This is the easy part of a tricky three-part question. Obviously, you like to work with people who have pride, honesty, integrity, and dedication to their work. Now . . .

"What kinds of people do you find it difficult to work with?"

The second part of the same question. You could say: "People who don't follow procedures, or slackers—the occasional rotten apples who don't really care about the quality of their work. They're long on complaints, but short on solutions." Which brings us to the third part of the question . . .

"How have you successfully worked with this difficult type of person?"

This is the most difficult part to answer. You might reply: "I stick to my guns, stay enthusiastic, and hope some of it will rub off. I had a big problem with one guy—all he did was complain, and always in my area. Eventually, I told him how I felt. I said if I were a millionaire, I'd clearly have all the answers and wouldn't have to work, but as it was, I wasn't, and had to work for a living. I told him that I really enjoyed his company ;-) but I didn't want to hear it anymore. Every time I saw him after that, I presented him with a work problem and asked his advice. In other words I challenged him to come up with positives, not negatives."

You can go on to say that sometimes you've noticed that such people simply lack enthusiasm and confidence, and that energetic and cheerful coworkers can often change that. If the interviewer follows up with an inquiry about what you would do if no amount of good effort on your part solved the problem, respond, "I would maintain cordial relations, but not go out of my way to seek more than a businesslike acquaintance. Life is too short to be de-motivated by people who always think their cup is half empty."

"How did you get your last job?"

The interviewer is looking for initiative. If you can, show it. At the least, show determination:

"I was turned down for my last job for having too little experience. I asked the manager to give me a trial before she offered it to anyone else. I went in and asked for a list of companies they'd never sold to, picked up the phone, and in that hour I arranged two appointments. How did I get the job? In a word, determination!"

"How would you evaluate me as an interviewer?"

The question is dangerous, maybe more so than the one asking you to criticize your boss. Whatever you do, of course, don't tell the truth if you think the interviewer is an incompetent. It may be true, but it won't get you a job offer. This is an instance where honesty is not the best policy. It is best to say, "This is one of the toughest interviews I have ever been through, and I don't relish the prospect of going through another. Yet I do realize what you are trying to achieve." Then go on to explain that you understand the interviewer wants to know whether you can think on your feet, that there is pressure on the job, and that he or she is trying to simulate some of that real-life pressure in the interview. You may choose to finish the answer with a question of your own: "How do you think I fit the profile of the person you need?"

"I'm not sure you're suitable for the job."

Don't worry about the tone of the statement—the interviewer's "I'm not sure" really means, "I'd like to hire you, so here's a wide-open opportunity to sell me on yourself." He or she is probing three areas from your personal profile: your confidence, determination, and listening profiles. Remain calm and put the ball straight back into the interviewer's court: "Why do you say that?" You need both the information and time to think up an appropriate reply, but it is important to show that you are not intimidated. Work out a program of action for this question; even if the interviewer's point regarding your skills is valid, come back with value keys and alternate compatible skills. Counter with other skills that show your competence and learning ability, and use them to show that you can pick up the new skills quickly. Tie the two together and demonstrate that with your other attributes you can bring many pluses to the job. Finish your answer with a reflexive question that encourages a "yes" answer:

"I admit my programming skills in that language are a little light. However, all languages have similarities, and my experience demonstrates that with my competence in four other languages, getting up to speed with this one will take only a short while. Plus, I can bring a depth of other experience to the job." Then, after you itemize your experience: "Wouldn't you agree?"

If the reason for the question is not a lack of technical skills, it must be a question about one of your key profile areas. Perhaps the interviewer will say, "You haven't convinced me of your determination." This is an invitation to sell yourself, so tell a story that demonstrates determination.

For example: "It's interesting you should say that. My present boss is convinced of my determination. About a year ago we were having some problems with a union organization in the plant. Management's problem was our 50 percent Spanish monolingual production workforce. Despite the fact that our people had the best working conditions and benefits in the area, they were strongly pro-union. If they were successful, we would be the first unionized division in the company. No one in management spoke Spanish, so I took a crash Berlitz course—two hours at home every night for five weeks. I got one of the maintenance crew to help me with my grammar and diction. Then a number of other production workers started saying simple things to me in Spanish and helping me with the answers. I opened the first meeting with the workforce to discuss the problems. My *'Buenos días. Me llamo Brandon'* got a few cheers. We had demonstrated that we cared enough to try to communicate. Our division never did unionize, and my determination to take the extra step paid off and allowed my superiors to negotiate from a position of caring and strength. That led to English lessons for the Spanish-speaking, and Spanish lessons for the English-speaking. We are now a bilingual company, and I think that shows we care. Wouldn't you agree my work in that instance shows determination?"

"Wouldn't you feel better off in another firm?"

Relax, things aren't as bad as you might assume. This question is usually asked if you are really doing quite well or if the job involves a certain amount of stress. A lawyer, for example, might well be expected to face this one. The trick is not to be intimidated. Your first step is to qualify the question. Relax, take a breath, sit back, smile, and say, "You surprise me. Why do you say that?" The interviewer must then talk, giving you precious time to collect your wits and come back with a rebuttal.

Then answer "no," and explain why. All the interviewer wants to see is how much you know about the company and how determined you are to join its ranks. Your earlier research and knowledge of personal profile keys (determination) will pay off again. Overcome the objection with an example, show how that will help you contribute to the company, and end with a question of your own. In this instance, the question has a twofold purpose: first, to identify a critical area to sell yourself; and second, to encourage the interviewer to consider an image of you working at the company.

You could reply: "Not at all. My whole experience has been with small companies. I am good at my job and in time could become a big fish in a little pond. But that is not what I want. This corporation is a leader in its business. You have a strong reputation for encouraging skills development in your employees. This is the type of environment I want to work in. Coming from a small company, I have done a little bit of everything. That means that no matter what you throw at me, I will learn it quickly. For example, what would the first project I would be involved with be?"

You end with a question of your own that gets the interviewer focusing on those immediate problems. You can then explain how your background and experience can help.

"What would you say if I told you your presentation this afternoon was lousy?"

"If" is the key word here, with the accusation there only for the terminally neurotic. The question is designed to see how you react to criticism and so tests your manageability. No company can afford to employ the thin-skinned applicant today. You will come back and answer the question with a question of your own. An appropriate response would be: "First of all, I would ask which aspects of my presentation were lousy. My next step would be to find out where you felt the problem was. If there was miscommunication, I'd clear it up. If the problem was elsewhere, I would seek your advice and be sure that the problem did not recur." This would show that when it is a manager's duty to criticize performance, you are an employee who will respond in a businesslike and emotionally mature manner.

The Illegal Question

Of course, one of the most stressful—and negative—questions is the illegal one, a question that delves into your private life or personal background. Such a question will make you uncomfortable if it is blatant, and could also make you angry.

Your aim, however, is to overcome your discomfort and to avoid getting angry: You want to get the job offer, and any self-righteousness or defensive reaction on your part will ensure you *don't* get it. You may feel angry enough to get up and walk out, or say things like, "These are unfair practices; you'll hear from my lawyer in the morning." But the result will be that you won't get the offer, and therefore won't have the leverage you need. Remember, no one is saying you can't refuse the job once it's offered to you.

So what is an illegal question? Title VII is a federal law that forbids employers from discriminating against any person on the basis of sex, age, race, national origin, or religion. More recently, the Americans with Disabilities Act was passed to protect this important minority.

✎**An interviewer may not** ask about your religion, church, synagogue, or parish, the religious holidays you observe, or your political beliefs or affiliations. He or she may not ask, for instance, "Does your religion allow you to work on Saturdays?" But he or she may ask something like, "This job requires work on Saturdays. Is that a problem?"

✎**An interviewer may not** ask about your ancestry, national origin, or parentage; in addition, you cannot be asked about the naturalization status of your parents, spouse, or children. The interviewer cannot ask about your birthplace. But he or she may ask (and probably will, considering the current immigration laws) whether you are a U.S. citizen or a resident alien with the right to work in the United States.

✎**An interviewer may not** ask about your native language, the language you speak at home, or how you acquired the ability to read, write, or speak a foreign language. But he or she may ask about the languages in which you are fluent if knowledge of those languages is pertinent to the job.

✎**An interviewer may not** ask about your age, your date of birth, whether you are married or pregnant, or the ages of your children. But he or she may ask you whether you are over eighteen years old.

✎**An interviewer may not** ask about maiden names or whether you have changed your name; your marital status, number of children or dependents, or your spouse's occupation; or whether (if you are a woman) you wish to be addressed as "Miss," "Mrs.," or "Ms." But the interviewer may ask about how you like to be addressed (a common courtesy) and whether you have ever worked for the company before under a different name. (If you have worked for this company or other companies under a different name, you may want to mention that, in light of the fact that this prospective manager may check your references and additional background information.)

As you consider a question that seems to verge on illegality, take into account that the interviewer may be asking it innocently and may be unaware of the laws on the matter. Your best bet is to be polite and straightforward, just as you would be in any other social situation. You also want to move the conversation to an examination of your skills and abilities, not your status. Here are some sample illegal questions—and some possible responses. Remember, your objective is to get job offers; if you later decide that this company is not for you, you are under no obligation to accept the position.

"What religion do you practice?"

If you do practice, you can say, "I attend my church/synagogue/mosque regularly, but I make it my practice not to involve my personal beliefs in my work. My work for the company and my career are too important for that."

If you do not practice a religion, you may want to say something like, "I have a set of personal beliefs that are important to me, but I do not attend any organized services. And I do not mix those beliefs with my work, if that's what you mean."

"Are you married?"

If you are, the company is concerned with the impact your family duties and future plans will have on your tenure there. Your answer could be, "Yes, I am. Of course, I make a separation between my work life and my family life that allows me to give my all to a job. I have no problem with travel or late hours; those things are part of this line of work. I'm sure my references will confirm this for you."

"Do you plan to have children?"

This isn't any of the interviewer's business, but he or she wants to know whether you will leave the company early to raise a family. You can answer "no," of course, since a no answer isn't binding (it's only about your current plans). If you answer "yes," you might add, "but those plans are for the future, and they depend on the success of my career. Certainly, I want to do the best, most complete job for this company I can. I consider that my skills are right for the job and that I can make a long-range contribution. I certainly have no plans to leave the company just as I begin to make meaningful contributions."

If the questions become too pointed, you may want to ask—innocently—"Could you explain the relevance of that issue to the position? I'm trying to get a handle on it." That response, however, can seem confrontational; you should only use it if you are *extremely* uncomfortable, or are quite certain you can get away with it. Sometimes, the interviewer will drop the line of questioning.

Illegal questions tend to arise not out of brazen insensitivity, but rather out of an interest in you. The employer is familiar with your skills and background, feels you can do the job, and wants to get to know you as a person. Outright discrimination these days is really quite rare. With illegal questions, your response must be positive—that's the only way you're going to get the job offer, and getting a job offer allows you to leverage other jobs. You don't have to work for a discriminatory company, but you can certainly use the firm to get to something better.

Mock Meetings, Role-Playing, and In-Basket Tests

Some employers use even more elaborate versions of the stress interview when selecting personnel. Groups of candidates may be put in a room together and asked to stage a mock meeting or be asked to give an impromptu presentation. You may even be asked to demonstrate your organization and time-management skills by sorting out and acting on an in-basket full of an overwhelming amount of supposedly urgent data, all while being interrupted by telephone calls.

Collectively, these approaches are referred to as *assessment center techniques*. They are frequently run—on an employer's behalf—by a third-party operation that specializes in skill and aptitude tests. Some companies use this approach when hiring executives, some when choosing sales and customer service professionals, and others when identifying the best candidates for administrative positions. Unfortunately, assessment center techniques are so common today that anyone in the job market risks facing their myriad tortures. The good news is that I have one or two techniques that can help.

One of the reasons that assessment center techniques are growing in popularity is the corporate world's increasing focus on teamwork. Many employers figure they can hire the best workers for a team environment by using group interviews. (Forget the fact that assessment centers haven't proven themselves better or worse than other selection methods!) Since you may encounter this old-new approach during your job search, I want you to be ready for it.

Racks, Beds of Nails, and Iron Maidens

Assessment centers use a broad variety of techniques, including:

- Mock meetings
- In-basket tests
- Role-playing

With these selection techniques, forewarned is forearmed. With a little bit of time to prepare, and an understanding of how these situations work, you can survive anything they might throw at you. Besides, it's only pretend—so there's no need to break out in a cold sweat.

Mock Meetings: Taking Control, Taking Charge, and Being a Team Player

Some employers will want to see you take charge of, or perhaps take over, the leadership of the group. Others want to see your skills at interacting with people. Some employers will want to see both. Your first step in preparing for a mock meeting is to outline the challenges you would face in the daily routine of the job you've applied for. These challenges are likely to form the basis of the situations you'll be asked to respond to. For example, if your job will involve making sales presentations on big-ticket items to groups of people, you can expect the mock meeting to include all of the difficult questions, problems, and people you would be likely to meet in such a context. There are only two differences: First, the whole range of problems is going to appear in one meeting, and second, it's just pretend. If you are a competent professional and react to the situations you face in a professional manner, you'll do just fine.

Your assessors may set up a leaderless group discussion and watch what happens. These groups may include an assortment of applicants, existing employees, and selection center staff—some of them "planted" there to cause disruption or otherwise throw you off balance. Just knowing who is who and why they're there can be a big help. Now that overwhelmingly belligerent SOB can be treated as what he really is: a test of your assertiveness skills.

Anything you face in one of these situations will mirror the challenges you face in the real work world. If your appraisal of the job is that "taking control" and "demonstrating leadership" are likely to be the goals of the mock meeting, *how* you take control and demonstrate leadership will be crucial to your success. You need to set a standard of democratic leadership; you have to become the parent who sets firm limits but gives support. Be sure to give everyone "air time," while keeping the group on target and on schedule.

Sometimes taking charge can be dangerous, however. If you come across as too tough, bossy, or autocratic, forget it! You can't just say, "OK, this is a test of my decision-making and leadership skills, so move over, rover, and let *me* take over." You should encourage a more team-oriented approach: "Let's take a moment to gather our thoughts, then each, in turn, address the issues from his or her unique perspective." You must keep the meeting moving if someone tries to dominate the discussion or move it away from the agenda. You can then demonstrate your leadership by thanking everyone for his or her contributions.

If someone else beats you to the punch and assumes the leadership role, don't try to show everyone how tough you are by fighting to regain control. Instead, act like the archetypal active team member. Use the time you have while the leader is busy managing the meeting to plan your strategy and develop your contributions to the idea or plan the group is working on. Position yourself as a team player and consensus builder, but show that you can take the initiative, too.

From this position, you can be ready to scoop the opposition at the end of the meeting. While the "leader" is busy making sure that every voice gets heard, you can prepare to help the group summarize its common ground, and establish possible next steps.

In-Basket: A Test of Organized Action

You're staring at a huge stack of reports, memos, and phone messages on your desk. The red light on the phone is flashing to let you know you've got voice mail messages. The computer screen glares at you with a dozen as-yet-unread e-mail messages. Confronting applicants with a virtual day at the office is yet another way companies try to separate the wheat from the chaff. In this example, you're facing an in-basket test of your time-management and organization skills.

The in-basket test confronts the job candidate with overwhelming amounts of information, and often with conflicting priorities. Then the observers sit back, put their feet up, and watch you wither or shine before their eyes. There are many ways to tackle this kind of test, but the main thing is to make sure that you come prepared with a system to prioritize and organize the work.

Alan Lakein, the godfather of time management, introduced me to a wildly effective and widely accepted approach to time management. Take everything out of the in-basket and place it in one of three piles:

- The A pile is urgent, and you will act on it "today"—in other words, during the test.
- The B pile is important and needs attention. You'll start on it when and if you get through your A pile. If not, much of it will move into your A pile, as you plan for "tomorrow" at the end of "today."

- The C pile is to file or just put in a drawer. It is still important work, but not as urgent as your A and B work. If someone makes it urgent for you—via a telephone call or an urgent e-mail message—you'll know where to find it.

Working out these priorities is the first step in acing an in-basket test. Once established, you'll be able to prioritize those pesky interruptions that are always programmed into this particular type of test. When the calls come in, as they inevitably will, you must have a system in place that can help you decide how to respond. For example, you need to find out:

- Who's calling, and that person's title. You want to establish the person's name, department, and reporting relationship. If your "boss" of the day calls, he or she has the power to move something from your C pile directly to your A pile.
- What they're calling about. You can put the person on hold while you find the appropriate paperwork, consider the relative importance of the call, and decide how to handle it with efficiency and professionalism.

It is important, at the end of the test, to make sure that the assessor understands that you have been using an effective and logical system. *How to Get Control of Your Time and Your Life*, by Alan Lakein, can teach you world-class time-management and organization skills.

Role Playing

You may be asked to handle a sticky personnel problem, an employee calling in sick from the golf course, a malfunctioning team, an inventory problem, a broken machine, or cold calls to a series of prospective "clients." The goal of role playing is invariably to see how you handle the people and situations that are likely to crop up in the day-to-day execution of your duties.

Are you a hard-nosed SOB, or do you cave in at the slightest pressure? Do you want the world to love and admire you, or are you out to settle a score? How do you handle a belligerent customer or salvage a tough sale when it turns sour at the last moment?

What's the best way to handle these situations? Consider the role you are playing: Is it to land a job as a customer service representative, sales training specialist, vice president of finance, or union lawyer? You need to be clear about the job you're facing—and the challenges it typically generates. You will then understand exactly what the testers are looking for and the role you should play in their scenarios.

In each of these stressful interviewing situations the key is to determine which professional hat you should be wearing and to demonstrate the behaviors the testers will expect from someone wearing that hat. For more on getting in touch with the professional you, see Chapter 21, "How to Ace the Psychological Tests."

◆◆◆

Interviewers may pull all kinds of tricks on you, but you will come through with flying colors once you realize they're trying to discover something extremely simple—whether or not you can take the heat. After all, those interviewers are only trying to sort out the good corporate warriors from the walking wounded. If you are asked and successfully handle these tricks and negatively phrased questions, the interviewer will look on you favorably. Stay calm, give as good as you get, and take it all in stride. Remember that no one can intimidate you without your permission.

CHAPTER 14
Strange Venues for Job Interviews

LEARN THE TIPS that will help you master interviews in noisy, distracting hotel lobbies, restaurants, at poolside, and in other unusual settings.

Why are some interviews conducted in strange places? Are meetings in noisy, distracting hotel lobbies designed as a form of torture? What are the real reasons that an interviewer invites you to eat at a fancy restaurant?

For the most part, these tough-on-the-nerves situations happen because the interviewer is a busy person, fitting you into a busy schedule. A woman I know had heard stories about tough interview situations but never expected to face one herself. It happened at a retail convention in Arizona, to which she had been asked for a final interview. The interview was conducted by the pool. The interviewer was there, taking a short break between meetings, in his bathing suit. The first thing the interviewer did was suggest that my friend slip into something comfortable.

That scenario may not lurk in your future, but the chances are you will face many tough interview situations in your career. They call for a clear head and a little gamesmanship if you want to stay ahead of the competition. The interviewee at the pool used both. She removed her jacket, folded it over the arm of the chair, and seated herself, saying pleasantly, "That's much better. Where shall we begin?"

It isn't easy to remain calm at such times. On top of interview nerves, you're worried about being overheard in a public place, or (worse) surprised by the appearance of your current boss. That last item isn't too far-fetched. It actually happened to a reader from San Francisco. He was being interviewed in the departure lounge at the airport when his boss walked through the arrivals door. Oops—he had asked for the day off "to go to the doctor."

Could he have avoided the situation? Certainly, if he had asked about privacy when the meeting was arranged. That would have reminded the interviewer of the need for discretion. The point is to do all you can in advance to make such a meeting as private as possible. Once that's done, you can ignore the rest of the world and concentrate on the interviewer's questions.

Hotel Lobbies and Other Strange Places

Strange interview situations provide other wonderful opportunities to embarrass yourself. You come to a hotel lobby in full corporate battle dress: coat, briefcase, perhaps an umbrella. You sit down to wait for the interviewer. "Aha," you think to yourself, opening your briefcase, "I'll show him my excellent work habits by delving into this computer printout."

That's not such a great idea. Have you ever tried rising with your lap covered with business papers, then juggling the briefcase from right hand to left to accommodate the ritual handshake? It's quite difficult. Besides, while you are sitting in nervous anticipation, pre-interview tension has no way of dissipating. Your mouth will become dry, and your "Good morning, I'm pleased to meet you" will come out sounding like a cat being strangled.

To avoid such catastrophes in places like hotel lobbies, first remove your coat on arrival. Instead of sitting, walk around a little while you wait. Even in a small lobby, a few steps back and forth will help you reduce tension to a manageable level. Keep your briefcase in your left hand (unless you are a leftie) at all times—it makes you look purposeful, and you won't trip over it when you meet the interviewer.

If, for any reason, you must sit, breathe deeply and slowly. This will help control the adrenaline that makes you feel jumpy.

A strange setting can actually put you on equal footing with the interviewer. Neither of you is on home turf, so in many cases the interviewer will feel just as awkward as you do. A little gamesmanship can turn the occasion to your advantage.

To gain the upper hand, get to the meeting site early to scout the territory. By knowing your surroundings, you will feel more relaxed. Early arrival also allows you to control the outcome of the meeting in other subtle ways. You will have time to stake out the most private spot in an otherwise public place. Corners are best. They tend to be quieter, and you can choose the seat that puts your back to the wall (in a physical sense, that is). In this position, you have a clear view of your surroundings and will feel more secure. The fear of being overheard will evaporate.

The situation is now somewhat in your favor. You know the locale, and the meeting place is as much yours as the interviewer's. You will have a clear view of your surroundings, and odds are that you will be more relaxed than the interviewer. When he or she arrives, say, "I arrived a little early to make sure we had some privacy. I think over here is the best spot." With that positive demonstration of your organizational abilities, you give yourself a head start over the competition.

The Meal Meeting

Breakfast, lunch, and dinner are the prime choices for interviewers who want to catch the seasoned professional off guard. In fact, the meal is arguably the toughest of all tough interview situations. The setting offers the interviewer the chance to see you in a non-office (and therefore more natural) setting, to observe your social graces, and to consider you as a whole person. Here, topics that would be impossible to address in the traditional office setting will surface, often with virtually no effort on the part of the interviewer. The slightest slip in front of that wily old pirate—thinly disguised in a Brooks Brothers suit—could get your candidacy deep-sixed in a hurry.

Usually you will not be invited to a "meal meeting" until you have already demonstrated that you are capable of doing the job. An invitation to a meal means that you are under strong consideration, and therefore intense scrutiny.

This meeting is often the final hurdle and could lead directly to the job offer—assuming that you properly handle the occasional surprises that arise. The interviewer's concern is not whether you can do the job but whether you have the growth potential that will allow you to fill more senior slots as they become available.

But be careful. Many have fallen at the final hurdle in a close-run race. Being interviewed in front of others is bad enough; eating and drinking in front of them at the same time only makes it worse. If you knock over a glass or dribble spaghetti sauce down your chin, the interviewer will be so busy smirking that he or she won't hear what you have to say.

To be sure that they remain as attentive to the positive points of your candidacy as possible, let's discuss table manners.

Your social graces and general demeanor at the table can tell as much about you as your answer to a question. For instance, over-ordering food or drink can signal poor self-discipline. At the very least, it will call into question your judgment and maturity. Highhanded behavior toward waiters and busboys could reflect negatively on your ability to get along with subordinates and on your leadership skills. Those concerns are amplified when you return food or complain about the service, actions which, at the very least, find fault with the interviewer's choice of restaurant.

By the same token, you will want to observe how your potential employer behaves. After all, you are likely to become an employee, and the interviewer's behavior to servers in a restaurant can tell you a lot about what it will be like on the job.

✎**Alcohol:** Soon after being seated, you will be offered a drink—if not by your host, then by the waiter. There are many reasons to avoid alcohol at interview meals. The most important reason is that alcohol fuzzes your mind, and research proves that stress increases the intoxicating effect of alcohol. So, if you order something to drink, try to stick with something nonalcoholic, such as a club soda, Coke or Pepsi, or simply a glass of water.

If you do have a drink, never have more than one. If there is a bottle of wine on the table, and the waiter offers you another glass, place your hand over the top of your glass. It is a polite way of signifying no.

You may be offered alcohol at the end of the meal. The rule still holds true—turn it down. You need your wits about you even if the interview seems to be drawing to a close. Some interviewers will try to use those moments, when your defenses are at their lowest, to throw in a couple of zingers.

✎**Smoking:** Don't smoke unless encouraged. If both of you are smokers, and you are encouraged to smoke, never smoke between courses, only at the end of a meal. Even most confirmed nicotine addicts, like the rest of the population, hate smoke while they are eating.

✎**Utensils:** Keep all your cups and glasses at the top of your place setting and well away from you. Most glasses are knocked over at a cluttered table when one stretches for the condiments or gesticulates to make a point.

Here are some other helpful hints:

- Never speak with your mouth full.
- To be on the safe side, order something that is easy to eat, as you are there for talking, not eating. Of course, while this rule makes sense in theory, you probably will be asked to order first, so ordering the same thing can become problematic. Solve the problem before you order by complimenting the restaurant during your small talk and then, when the menus arrive, asking, "What do you think you will have today?"
- Do not change your order once it is made, and never send the food back.
- Be polite to your waiters, even when they spill soup in your lap.
- Don't order expensive food. Naturally, in our heart of hearts, we all like to eat well, especially on someone else's tab. But don't be tempted. When you come right down to it, you are there to talk and be seen at your best, not to eat.
- Eat what you know. Stay away from awkward, messy, or exotic foods (e.g., artichokes, long pasta, and escargot, respectively). Ignore finger foods, such as lobster or spare ribs. In fact, you should avoid eating with your fingers altogether, unless you are in a sandwich joint, in which case you should make a point of avoiding the leaky, overstuffed menu items.
- Don't order salad. The dressing can often get messy. If a salad comes with the meal, request that the dressing be on the side. Then, before pouring it on, cut up the lettuce.
- Don't order anything with bones. Stick with fillets; there are few simple, gracious ways to deal with any type of bone.

Checks and Goodbyes: I know an interviewer whose favorite test of composure is to have the waiter, by arrangement, put the bill on the interviewee's side of the table. She then chats on, waiting for something interesting to happen. If you ever find yourself in a similar situation, never pick up the check, however long it is left by your plate. When ready, your host will pick it up, because that's the protocol of the occasion. By the same token, you should never offer to share payment.

When parting company, always thank the host for his or her hospitality and the wonderful meal. Of course, you should be sure to leave on a positive note by asking good-naturedly what you have to do to get the job.

Strange interview situations can arise at any time during the interview cycle, and in any public place. Wherever you are asked to go, keep your guard up. Your table manners, listening skills, and overall social graces are being judged. The question on the interviewer's mind is: Can you be trusted to represent the company gracefully and with professional demeanor?

CHAPTER 15

Welcome to the Real World

FOR THE RECENT graduate, here are some tough questions specifically tailored to discover your business potential.

Of all the steps a recent graduate will take up the ladder of success over the years, none is more important or more difficult than getting a foot on the first rung. The interviewing process designed for recent graduates is particularly rigorous, because management regards the hiring of entry-level professionals as one of its toughest jobs.

When a company hires experienced people, there is a track record to evaluate. With recent graduates, there is little or nothing. Often, the only solid things an interviewer has to go on are SAT scores and high school or college diplomas. That's not much on which to base a hiring decision—grades don't tell the interviewer whether you will fit in or make a reliable employee. Many recruiters liken the gamble of hiring recent graduates to storing wines for the future: They know some will develop into full-bodied, reliable vintages, but others will be disappointments. Recruiters have to find different ways to predict your potential accurately.

After relying, as best they can, on school performance to evaluate your ability, interviewers concentrate on questions that reveal how willing you are to learn and get the job done, and how manageable you are likely to be, both on average days and when the going gets rough.

Your goal is to stand out from all the other entry-level candidates as someone altogether different and better. Don't be like thousands of others who, in answer to questions about their greatest strength, reply lamely, "I'm good with people," or, "I like working with others." Such answers do not separate you from the herd. In fact, they brand you as average. To stand out, a recent graduate must recount a past situation that illustrates *how* he or she is good with people, or one that demonstrates an ability to be a team player.

Fortunately, the key professional behaviors discussed throughout the book are just as helpful for getting your foot on the ladder as they are for aiding your climb to the top. They will guide you in choosing the aspects of your personality and background that you should promote at the interview.

It isn't necessary to have snap answers ready for every question, because you never will. It is more important for you to pause after a question and collect your thoughts before answering; you must show that you think before you speak. That way, you will demonstrate your analytic abilities, which age feels youth has in short supply.

By the same token, occasionally asking for a question to be repeated is useful to gain time and is quite acceptable, as long as you don't do it with every question. And if a question stumps you, as sometimes happens, do not stutter incoherently. It is sometimes best to say, "I don't know" or, "I'd like to come back to that later." Odds are the interviewer will forget to ask again; if he or she doesn't, at least you've had some time to come up with an answer.

Knowing everything about a certain entry-level position is not necessary, because business feels it can teach you most things. But, as a vice president of Merrill Lynch once said, "You must bring to the table the ability to speak clearly." Knowing what is behind the questions that are designed especially for recent graduates will give you the time to build informative and understandable answers.

"How did you get your summer jobs?"

All employers look favorably on recent graduates who have any work experience, no matter what it is. "It is far easier to get a fix on someone who has worked while at school," says Dan O'Brien, head of employment at Grumman. "They manage their time better, are more realistic, and more mature. Any work experience gives us much more in common." So, as you make your answer, add that you learned business is about making a profit, doing things more efficiently, adhering to procedures, and putting out whatever effort it takes to get the job done. In short, treat your summer jobs, no matter how humble, as any other business experience.

In this particular question, the interviewer is looking for something that shows initiative, creativity, and flexibility. Here's an example: "In my town, summer jobs were hard to come by, but I applied to each local restaurant for a position waiting tables, called the manager at each one to arrange an interview, and finally landed a job at one of the most prestigious. I was assigned to the afternoon shift, but with my quick work, accurate billing, and ability to keep customers happy, they soon moved me to the evening shift. I worked there for three summers, and by the time I left, I was responsible for the training and management of the night-shift waiters, the allotment of tips, and the evening's final closing and accounting. All in all, my experience showed me the mechanics of a small business and of business in general."

"Which of the jobs you have held have you liked least?"

The interviewer is trying to trip you up. It is likely that your work experience contained a certain amount of repetition and drudgery, as all early jobs in the business world do. So beware of saying that you hated a particular job "because it was boring." Avoid the negative and say something along these lines: "All of my jobs had their good and bad points, but I've always found that if you want to learn, there's plenty to pick up every day. Each experience was valuable." Then describe a seemingly boring job, but show how it taught you valuable lessons or helped you hone different aspects of your personality profile.

"What are your future vocational plans?"

This is a fancy way of asking, "Where do you want to be five years from now?" The mistake all entry-level professionals make is to say, "In management," because they think that shows drive and ambition. It has become such a trite answer, though, that it immediately generates a string of questions most recent graduates can't answer: What is the definition of management? What is a manager's prime responsibility? A manager in what area? Your safest answer identifies you with the profession you are trying to break into and shows you have your feet on the ground: "I want to get ahead, and to do that I must be able to channel my energies and expertise into those areas that my industry and employer need. So in a couple of years I hope to have become a thorough professional with a clear understanding of the company, the industry, and where the biggest challenges and opportunities lie. By that time, my goals for the future should be sharply defined." An answer like that will set you far apart from your contemporaries.

"What college did you attend, and why did you choose it?"

The college you attended isn't as important as your reasons for choosing it—the question is trying to examine your reasoning processes. Emphasize that it was your choice, and you didn't go there as a result of your parents' desires or because generations of your family have always attended the Acme School of Welding. Focus on the practical: "I went to Greenbriar State—it was a choice based on practicality. I wanted a school that would give me a good education and prepare me for the real world. State has a good record for turning out students fully prepared to take on responsibilities in the real world. It is *[or isn't]* a big school, *[but/and]* it has certainly taught me some big lessons about the value of *[whatever personality values apply]* in the real world of business."

If the interviewer has a follow-up question about the role your parents played in the selection of your school, be wary—he or she is plumbing your maturity. It is best to reply that the choice of the school was yours, though you did seek the advice of your parents once you had made your selection, and they supported your decision.

"Are you looking for a permanent or temporary job?"

The interviewer wants reassurance that you are genuinely interested in the position and won't disappear in a few months to pursue postdoctoral studies in San Tropez. Try to go beyond saying "Permanent." Explain why you want the job. You might say, "Of course, I am looking for a permanent job. I intend to make my career in this field, and I want the opportunity to learn the business, face new challenges, and learn from experienced professionals." You will also want to qualify the question with one of your own: "Is this a permanent or a temporary position you are trying to fill?" Don't be scared to ask. The occasional unscrupulous employer will hire someone fresh out of school for a short period of time—say, for one particular project—then lay him or her off.

"How did you pay for college?"

Avoid saying, "Oh, Daddy handled all of that," as it probably won't create the impression you'd like. Your parents may well have helped you out, but you should explain, if it's appropriate, that you worked part-time and took out loans (as most of us must during college).

"We have tried to hire people from your school/your major before, and they never seem to work out. What makes you different?"

Here's a stress question to test your poise and analytical skills. You can shout that, yes, of course you are different and can prove it. So far, though, all you know is that there was a problem, not what caused the problem. Respond this way: "First, may I ask you exactly what problems you've had with people from this background?" Once you know what the problem is (if one really exists at all—it may just be a curve ball to test your poise), you can illustrate how you are different—but only then. Otherwise, you run the risk of your answer being interrupted with, "Well, that's what everyone else said before I hired them. You haven't shown me you are different."

"I'd be interested to hear about some things you learned in school that could be used on the job."

While specific job-related courses could form part of your answer, they cannot be all of it. The interviewer wants to hear about "real-world" skills, so explain what the experience of college taught you rather than a specific course. In other words, explain how the experience honed your relevant personality profiles: "Within my major and minor I tried to pursue those courses that had most practical relevance, such as . . . . However, the greatest lessons I learned were the importance of . . ." then list your personality profile strengths.

"Do you like routine tasks/regular hours?"

A trick question. The interviewer knows from bitter experience that most recent graduates hate routine and are hopeless as employees until they come to an acceptance of such facts of life. Explain that, yes, you appreciate the need for routine, you expect a fair amount of routine assignments before you are entrusted with the more responsible ones, and that that is why you are prepared to accept it as necessary. As far as regular hours go you could say, "No, there's no problem there. A company expects to make a profit, so the doors have to be open for business on a regular basis."

"What have you done that shows initiative and willingness to work?"

Again, tell a story about how you landed or created a job for yourself, or even got involved in some volunteer work. Your answer should show that you both handled unexpected problems calmly and anticipated others. Your willingness is demonstrated by the ways you overcame obstacles. For example: "I worked for a summer in a small warehouse. I found out that a large shipment was due in a couple of weeks, and I knew that room had to be made. The inventory system was outdated, and the rear of the warehouse was disorganized, so I came in on a Saturday, figured out how much room I needed, cleaned up the mess in the rear, and cataloged it all on the new inventory forms. When the shipment arrived, the truck just backed in. There was even room to spare."

Often after an effort above and beyond the call of duty, a manager might congratulate you, and if it happened to you in this instance, you might conclude your answer with the verbal endorsement: "The divisional manager happened along just when I was finishing the job, and he said he wished he had more people who took such pride in their work."

"Can you take instructions without feeling upset or hurt?"

This is a manageability question. If you take offense easily or bristle when your mistakes are pointed out, you won't last long with any company. Competition is fierce at the entry level, so take this as another chance to set yourself apart: "Yes, I can take instruction—and more important, I can take constructive criticism without feeling hurt. Even with the best intent, I will still make mistakes, and at times someone will have to put me back on the right track. I know that if I'm ever to rise in the company, I must first prove myself to be manageable."

"Have you ever had difficulties getting along with others?"

This is a combination question, probing willingness and manageability. Are you a team player or are you going to disrupt the department and make the interviewer's life miserable? This is a closed-ended question that requires only a yes-or-no answer, so give one and shut up.

"What type of position are you interested in?"

This another of those questions that tempts you to mention management. Tell the interviewer you are interested in an entry-level job, which is what you will be offered anyway: "I am interested in an entry-level position that will enable me to learn this business inside and out and will give me the opportunity to grow when I prove myself, either on a professional or on the managerial ladder."

"What qualifications do you have that will make you successful in this field?"

There is more to answering this question than reeling off your academic qualifications. In addition you will want to stress relevant work experience and illustrate your strong points as they match the key professional behaviors required in the position you seek. It's a wide-open question that says, "Hey, we're looking for an excuse to hire you. Give us some help."

"Why do you think you would like this type of work?"

This is a deceptively simple question because there is no pat answer. It is usually asked to see whether you really understand what the specific job and profession entails on a day-to-day basis. To answer it requires you to have researched the company and job functions as carefully as possible. Call another company in the field and request to speak to someone doing the job you hope to get. Ask what the job is like and what that person does day to day. How does the job fit into the department? What contribution does it make to the overall efforts of the company? Why does he or she like that type of work? Armed with that information, you will show that you understand what you are getting into; most recent graduates do not.

"What's your idea of how industry works?"

The interviewer does not want a dissertation, just the reassurance that you don't think it works along the same lines as a registered charity. Your understanding should be something like this: "The role of any company is to make as much money as possible, as quickly and efficiently as possible, and in a manner that will encourage repeat business from the existing client base and new business from word of mouth and reputation." Finish with the observation that it is every employee's role to play as a team member in order to achieve those goals.

"Why do you think this industry will sustain your interest over the long haul?" or "Why do you think you will shine in this profession?"

Your answer should speak both to your pragmatism and to your motivation. "At this point in my career, I am looking at the industry because I believe it offers stability and professional growth potential over the years *[explain why]*. Also, I'll be using skills *[itemize strong skill sets that are relevant to the job]* that are areas of strength, from which I derive great personal satisfaction."

"What do you know about our company?"

This can be a simple conversation gambit, helping the interviewer know where to start in explaining the company activities, or it can be a more loaded question. In the tight job race we have today, the offer always goes to the person who is most knowledgeable and enthusiastic about the company. It makes sense when you think about it, because that knowledge and enthusiasm are endorsements of both the work and the place that the interviewer is a part of for the majority of his waking hours.

Enthusiasm for your profession and the job is a matter of your attitude. Learning something about the company is as simple as doing a little Internet research and personal networking.

For the Internet research aspect, browse the company website, and enter the company name or their products and services into a couple of search engines and absorb as much as time allows. Print out as much as you can and use it as bedtime reading the night before the interview. It's probably better than Sominex as a sleep aid, and it's good psychological preparation, too. For the networking aspect, talk to acquaintances who have knowledge of the company. Membership in the local chapter of a professional association is the best bet for learning about any company in your town.

You can't answer this question unless you have enough interest to research the company thoroughly. If you don't have that interest, you should expect someone who does will get the job.

"What do you think determines progress in a good company?"

Your answer will include all the positive professional behaviors you have been illustrating throughout the interview. Include allusions to the listening profile, determination, ability to take the rough with the smooth, adherence to systems and procedures, and the good fortune to have a manager who wants you to grow.

"Do you think grades should be considered by first employers?"

If your grades were good, the answer is obviously "yes." If they weren't, your answer needs a little more thought: "Of course, an employer should take everything into consideration. Along with grades will be an evaluation of willingness and manageability, an understanding of how business works, and actual work experience. Combined, such experience and professional skills can be more valuable than grades alone."

◆◆◆

Many virtuous candidates are called for entry-level interviews, but only those who prepare themselves to answer the tough questions will be chosen. Interviews for recent graduates are partly sales presentations. The more you interview, the better you get, so don't leave preparing for them until the last minute. Start now and hone your skills to get a head start on your peers. A professor from a top-notch business school once told me: "You are taking a new product to market. Accordingly, you've got to analyze what it can do, who is likely to be interested, and how you are going to sell it to them." Take some time to get to know yourself and your particular values as they will be perceived in the world of business.

CHAPTER 16
The Graceful Exit

IS PARTING SUCH sweet sorrow? The end of an interview will more likely mean relief, but here are some dos and don'ts to bear in mind as your meeting comes to a close.

To paraphrase Shakespeare, all the working world's a stage. Curtains rise and fall, and your powerful performance must be capped with a professional and memorable exit. To ensure you leave the right impression, this chapter will review the dos and don'ts of leaving an interview.

A signal that the interview is drawing to a close comes when you are asked whether you have any questions. Ask questions, and by doing so, highlight your strengths and show your enthusiasm. Remember, your goal at the interview is to generate a job offer. Make sure your exit is as graceful as your entrance.

Dos

1. Ask appropriate job-related questions. When the opportunity comes to ask any final questions, review your notes. Bring up any relevant strengths that haven't been addressed.
2. Show decisiveness. If you are offered the job, react with enthusiasm. Then sleep on it. If it's possible to do so without making a formal acceptance, lock the job up now and put yourself in control; you can always change your mind later. Before making any commitment with regard to compensation, see Chapter 19, "Negotiating the Job Offer."
3. When more than one person interviews you, be sure you have the correct spellings of their names: "I enjoyed meeting your colleagues, Ms. Smith. Could you give me the correct spellings of their names, please?" This question will give you the names you forgot in the heat of battle and will demonstrate your consideration.
4. Review the job's requirements with the interviewer. Match them point-by-point with your skills and attributes.
5. Find out whether this is the only interview. If so, you must ask for the job in a positive and enthusiastic manner. Find out the time frame for a decision and finish with, "I am very enthusiastic about the job and the contributions I can make. If your decision will be made by the fifteenth, what must I do in the meantime to assure I get the job?"
6. Ask for the next interview. When there are subsequent interviews in the hiring procedure, ask for the next interview in the same honest and forthright manner: "Is now a good time to schedule our next meeting?"
7. Keep yourself in contention. A good leading question to ask is, "Until I hear from you again, what particular aspects of the job and this interview should I be considering?"
8. Always depart in the same polite and assured manner in which you entered. Look the interviewer in the eye, put on a smile (there's no need to grin), give a firm handshake, and say, "This has been an exciting meeting for me. This is a job I can do, and I feel I can contribute to your goals, because the atmosphere here seems conducive to doing my very best work. When will we speak again?"

Don'ts:

1. Don't discuss salary, vacation, or benefits. It is not that the questions are invalid, just that the timing is wrong. Bringing up such topics before you have an offer is asking what the company can do for you—instead, you should be saying what you can do for the company. Those topics are part of the negotiation (handled in Chapter 19, "Negotiating the Job Offer"); remember, without an offer you have nothing to negotiate.
2. Don't press for an early decision. Of course, you should ask, "When will I know your decision?" But don't press it. Don't try to use the "other opportunities I have to consider" gambit as leverage when no such offers exist—that annoys the interviewer, makes you look foolish, and may even force you to negotiate from a position of weakness. Timing is everything; the issue of how to handle other opportunities as leverage is explored in detail later.
3. Don't show discouragement. Sometimes a job offer can occur on the spot. Usually it does not. So don't show discouragement if you are not offered the job at the interview, because discouragement shows a lack of self-esteem and determination. Avoiding a bad impression is the foundation of leaving a good one, and the right image to leave is one of enthusiasm, guts, and openness—just the professional behaviors you have been projecting throughout the interview.
4. Don't ask for an evaluation of your interview performance. That forces the issue and puts the interviewer in an awkward position. You can say that you want the job, and ask what you have to do to get it.

PART IV
Finishing Touches

STATISTICS SHOW THAT the last person to get interviewed usually gets the job. Here are some steps you can take that will keep your impression strong.

THE SUCCESSFUL COMPLETION OF EVERY INTERVIEW is a big stride toward getting job offers, yet it is not the end of your job search.

A company rarely hires the first competent person it sees. A hiring manager will sometimes interview as many as fifteen people for a particular job, but the strain and pace of conducting interviews naturally dim the memory of each applicant. Unless you are the last person to be interviewed, the impression you make will fade with each subsequent interview the interviewer undertakes. And if you are not remembered, you will not be offered the job. You must develop a strategy to keep your name and skills constantly in the forefront of the interviewer's mind. These finishing touches often make all the difference.

Some of the suggestions here may not seem earth-shattering, just simple, sensible demonstrations of your manners, enthusiasm, and determination. But remember that today all employers are looking for people with that extra little something. You can avoid a negative or merely indifferent impression, and be certain of creating a positive one, by following these guidelines.

CHAPTER 17

Interview Follow-Up

OUT OF SIGHT means out of mind and out of mind means out of the job-offer stakes! Following up after your interviews shows an interviewer that you pay attention to detail and are enthusiastic about the job. Competency and enthusiasm are powerful statements to make when you aren't even there.

The first thing you do on leaving the interview is to breathe a sigh of relief. The second is to make sure that "out of sight, out of mind" will not apply to you. You do this by starting a follow-up procedure immediately after the interview: Sitting in your car, or on the bus, train, or plane, do a written recap of the interview while it's still fresh in your mind.

Answer these questions:

- Whom did you meet? (names and titles)
- What does the job entail?
- What are the first projects, the biggest challenges?
- Why can you do the job?
- What aspects of the interview went well? Why?
- What aspects of the interview went poorly? Why?
- What is the agreed-upon next step?
- Where is the employer in the hiring cycle, and when will a decision be made?
- What was said during the last few minutes of the interview?

Your next step is to send follow-up e-mails and/or letters to the interviewer(s). Sending a follow-up letter shows that you are professional and organized, pay attention to detail, and are enthusiastic about the job. In a tightly run job race, when there is little difference between two candidates, the job offer *always* goes to the candidate who is most enthusiastic about the opportunity.

KNOCK 'EM DEAD TIP

Identify aspects of your interview that went poorly. A person does not get offered a job based solely on strengths; those questions will be easy enough for you to answer. On the other hand, you may get that job offer based on your lack of negatives compared to the other candidates. It is important to identify any negatives from your performance so that you can overcome them in your follow-up and during subsequent interviews.

It's common sense when you think about it from the employer's viewpoint: The enthusiastic person is going to put more effort into the job, deliver a better work product and become a more dynamic part of the team; plus, your intelligent enthusiasm for the job is subtly flattering to the hiring manager.

1. Depending on the pacing of the selection cycle, a decision tomorrow morning will require a faster and more determined response than a decision next week or securing the next interview when this round is completed at the end of the month.

   Write a follow-up letter to be sent as an e-mail or as a traditional letter. Whenever your letter is sent it should make these points clear to the interviewer:

   - The date and time you met and the title of the job.
   - You know why you can do the job.

- You paid attention to what was being said.
- You are excited about the job and want it.
- You have the experience to contribute to those first major projects.

2. Here are some ideas and phrases you'll find useful:

 - **Appreciation:** "I enjoyed meeting you to discuss . . . ." Professional etiquette requires you express appreciation for the interview; remember to identify the date and time you met and the job you interviewed for.
 - **Recognition:** "I recognize the importance of . . . ."
 - **Observation:** "Listening to the points you made . . . ."
 - **Motivation:** "I am excited about the job . . . ." Let the interviewer catch your enthusiasm and see that you are motivated by the opportunity. This is very effective, especially as your communication may well arrive while other, less prepared applicants are stumbling their way through the interview.
 - **Enthusiasm:** "I was impressed . . . ." Let the interviewer know you were impressed with the people/product/service/facility/market/position, but do not overdo it: "It was energizing to meet a group of people who really cared about their work."
 - **Confidence:** Draw attention to one of the topics that was of special interest, "I feel confident I can handle the challenge of . . . ." There is a job to be done and a challenge to be met, let the interviewer know you are confident of doing both well.
 - **Interest:** "I want this job, and you can rely on me to do a good job for you." If you want the job (or next interview), say so. At this stage, the company is buying and you are selling. Ask for the job in a positive and enthusiastic manner.

If interview nerves caused you to forget something, you can introduce it with "Upon reflection," or "Having thought about our meeting," "Interview nerves got the better of me," "When we were talking about," or "I should have mentioned my work with."

1. Whenever possible and appropriate, mention the names of the people you met at the interview.
2. Address the follow-up e-mail/letter to the main interviewer. You can send separate e-mails/letters to others in the selection cycle. Each makes a positive impression and shows extra effort and attention to detail.
3. Don't write too much. Keep it short—less than one page—and don't make claims that will not withstand scrutiny.
4. Depending on the time constraints, send an e-mail within forty-eight hours and a letter within twenty-four hours; this gives you time to write, edit, and polish. If the decision is going to be made in the next couple of days, e-mail and/or hand-deliver

a traditional letter. This way your follow-up will refresh your image in the mind of the interviewer just when it would normally be starting to dim.

E-mail is the way almost all business communication is done today; the average executive gets 90 percent less traditional mail than she or he used to ten years ago, but this doesn't mean you should ignore traditional mail. Incoming mail used to provide a pleasant and much missed short break from the affairs of the day. With so little mail arriving, the break it offers is even more appreciated, and a large and neatly hand-addressed envelope will almost always get opened, something you can no longer say about an e-mail. Sending letters by traditional mail is contrarian thinking and more effective because of this.

5. If a hiring decision is imminent, follow up with an e-mail, then a telephone call as the decision timeline dictates. A phone call might begin, "Mr. Massie? Martin Yate. We met for an interview on Wednesday afternoon at 2 P.M. about the __________ position. I know you are making a decision by close of business tomorrow and I wanted to catch up with you personally to say . . . "

   - "Thanks for your time."
   - "I can do the job and this is why."
   - "I am excited about the job and this is why."
   - "I will make a good hire and this is why."

   If you are making a call, it is best not to write everything out in full sentences, you'll sound like one of those telemarketers; instead, write down the bullet point you want to make, you'll sound more natural.

6. If you are in an extended interview cycle, you will need to pace yourself a little differently. If you do not hear anything after five days (which is quite normal), put in a telephone call to the interviewer; it's always a good idea to make sure that the interviewer is reminded of your candidacy right before the weekend begins. Cover the same points as addressed in the last item, asking for either the job or the next interview in the cycle, whichever is appropriate.

Sometimes interview cycles can stretch into weeks and occasionally months, so there are a couple of considerations here. You can't e-mail and call every week, but you can touch base every couple of weeks. Google has a nice feature that allows you to track news on any topic you choose. Taking advantage of this allows you to keep up to speed on your profession and factors affecting it, and this knowledge-gathering can be put to additional good use.

E-mail a quick note with a link and, for special effect and another impact, send it via regular mail, with a neatly handwritten note: "Mr. Massie, I just came across this article about the impact of __________ on productivity in our profession and thought you might like to see it. By the way, I am enthusiastic and determined to be your next *[title]*. Regards, Martin Yate."

KNOCK 'EM DEAD TIP

Check out *Knock 'em Dead Cover Letters* at *www.knockemdead.com*. Here you'll find four different categories of cover letters, plus advice on networking, follow-up (telephone and face-to-face), candidacy resurrection, negotiation, rejection, acceptance, resignation, and after-hire thank-you letters.

During economic downturns a job might stay open for long periods or be put on hold after you have interviewed and then relisted a second time with a different job title. Here's what you do:

1. Match the needs of the new job description with your resume and what was addressed at the interviews. Refocus a customized copy of the resume using as many keywords from the job posting as you reasonably can.
2. If you are out of touch with the decision makers, apply again in the requested manner.
3. If in touch with decision makers, approach them again with the newly customized resume, reiterating your continued interest and qualifications.
4. Make a follow-up call to the recruiter and the hiring manager.
5. After a couple of follow-up letters to decision makers, you need to change the tone and maybe try the article from the professional media approach mentioned earlier; something that is of relevance to your profession and therefore by extension your target decision makers.

Not sure this will work? As I was writing these updates I heard from Michael, who wrote to me at *www.knockemdead.com*; he said, in part, "I have been tracking jobs since last spring that are now reappearing and I'm wondering what to do."

Not long after I sent him the above ideas I heard from him again: "Thanks Martin, I spoke with the recruiter a couple of times, then last Thursday, called the hiring manager directly. We spoke for almost ten minutes, so it was a well-received call. *She admired my guts in calling her directly because she had recently been out of work herself, and hated making those calls.*" My italics. It is this kind of extra effort that pays off in job offers.

Now, while you will follow up enthusiastically on all your interviews, you should recognize a difficult fact of life: The longer an interview cycle drags out, the less likely it is to result in an offer. Consequently, you will not place your professional future on that ever-diminishing chance. Instead, stick to your plan, making new contacts, reaching out by e-mail, mail, and telephone and focusing on the generation of new interviews every day, remember: the job offer that cannot fail invariably will.

This is simply the sensible approach. Just as every job is not right for you, you will not be right for every job. Once in a while though, you might come in second on a job you really want. In the next chapter I'll show you ways to snatch victory from the jaws of defeat.

CHAPTER 18

Snatching Victory from the Jaws of Defeat

REJECTION? IMPOSSIBLE! THEN again, you won't be right for every job. Here are some techniques that help you to create opportunities in the face of rejection.

During the interviewing process, there are bound to be interviewers who come to the erroneous conclusion that you are not the right person for the job they need to fill. When that happens, you will be turned down.

Such an absurd travesty of justice can occur in different ways:

- At the interview
- In a letter of rejection
- During your follow-up telephone call

Whenever the turndown comes, you must be emotionally and intellectually prepared to take advantage of the opportunity being offered to you.

When you get turned down for the only prospect you have going, the rejection can be devastating to your ego. That is why I have stressed the wisdom of having at least a few interviews in process at the same time.

You will get turned down. No one can be right for every job. The right person for a job doesn't always get it; however, the best prepared and most determined often does. While you may be responsible in part for the initial rejection, you still have the power to correct the situation and win the job offer. What you do with the claimed victory is a different matter—you will then be in a seller's market with choice and control of your situation. Almost every job you desire is obtainable once you understand the hiring process from the interviewer's side of the desk. Your initial—and temporary—rejection is attributable to one of these reasons:

- The interviewer does not feel you can do the job.
- The interviewer feels you lack a successful profile.
- The interviewer did not feel your personality would contribute to the smooth functioning of the department—perhaps you didn't portray yourself as either a team player or as someone willing to take the extra step.

With belief in yourself, you can still succeed. Repeat to yourself constantly through the interview cycle: "I will get this job, because no one else can give as much to this company as I can!" Do that and implement the following plan immediately when you hear of rejection, whether in person, via mail, or over the telephone.

Step 1: Thank the interviewer for the time and consideration. Then ask politely: "To help my future job search, why wasn't I chosen for the position?" Assure the interviewer that you would truly appreciate an honest, objective analysis. Listen to the reply and do not interrupt. Use your time constructively and take notes. When the company representative finishes speaking, show that you understood the comments. (Remember, understanding and agreeing are different animals.)

"Thank you, Mr. Smith, now I can understand the way you feel. Because I don't interview that often I'm afraid my nerves got in the way. I'm very interested in working for your company *[use an enthusiastic tone]* and am determined to get the job. Let me meet with you once again. This time, when I'm not so nervous, I am confident you will see I really do have the skills you require" *[then provide an example of a skill you have in the questionable area]*. "You name the time and the place, and I will be there. What's best for you, Mr. Smith?"

End with a question, of course, and note here that you're asking *when* you can meet again, and not *if*. An enthusiastic request like that is very difficult to refuse and will usually get you another interview—an interview, of course, at which you must shine.

✎ **Step 2:** Check your notes and accept the company representative's concerns. Their validity is irrelevant; the important thing is that the negative points represent the problem areas in the interviewer's perception of you. List the negative perceptions, and using the techniques, exercises, and value keys discussed throughout the book, develop different ways to overcome or compensate for every negative perception.

✎ **Step 3:** Reread Part III of this book.

✎ **Step 4:** Practice aloud the statements and responses you will use at the interview. If you can practice with someone who plays the part of the interviewer, that's even better. This will create a real interview atmosphere and increase your chances of success. Lacking a role-play partner, you can create that live answer by putting the anticipated objections and questions on a tape and responding to them.

✎ **Step 5:** Study all available information on the company.

✎ **Step 6:** Congratulate yourself continually for getting another interview after initial rejection. This is proof of your self-worth, ability, and tenacity. You have nothing to lose and everything to gain, having already risen phoenix-like from the ashes of defeat.

✎ **Step 7:** During the interview, ask for the job in a positive and enthusiastic manner. Your drive and staying power will impress the interviewer. All you must do to win the job is overcome the perceived negatives, and you have been given the time and information to prepare. Go for it.

✎ **Step 8:** Even when all has failed at the subsequent interview, do not leave without a final request for the job. Play your trump card: "Mr. Smith, I respect the fact that you allowed me the opportunity to prove myself here today. I am convinced I am the best person for the job. I want you to give me a trial, and I will prove on the job that I am the best hiring decision you have made this year. Will you give us both the opportunity?"

A reader once wrote to me as I was revising *Knock 'em Dead*, "I read the chapter entitled 'Snatching Victory from the Jaws of Defeat' and did everything you said to salvage what appeared to be a losing interview. My efforts did make a very good impression on the interviewer, but as it was finally explained to me, I really did not have equal qualifications for the job, and finally came in a close second. I really want to work for this growing company, and they say they have another position coming up in six months. What should I do?"

I know of someone who wanted a job working for a major airline. He had been recently laid off and had high hopes for a successful interview. As it happened, he came in second for the position. He was told that the firm would speak to him again in the near future. So he waited—for eight months. Finally, he realized that waiting for the job would only leave him unemployed. The moral of the story is that you must be brutally objective when you come out second-best, and, whatever the interviewer says, you must sometimes assume that you are getting the polite brush-off.

With that in mind, let's see what can be done on the positive side. First of all, send a thank-you note to the interviewer, acknowledging your understanding of the state of affairs and reaffirming your desire to work for the company. Conclude with a polite request to bear you in mind for the future.

Keep an eye out for any news item about the company in the press. Whenever you see something, cut it out and mail it to the interviewer with a very brief note that says something like: "I came across this in *Forbes* and thought you might find it interesting. I am still determined to be your next account manager, so please keep me in mind when the next opening occurs."

You can also call the interviewer once every couple of months, just to check in. Remember, of course, to keep the phone call brief and polite—you simply want to keep your name at the top of the interviewer's mind.

And maybe something will come of it. Ultimately, however, your only choice is to move on. There is nothing to gain waiting on an interviewer's word. Go out and keep looking, because chances are that you will come up with an even better job. Then, if you still want to work for that company that gave you the brush-off, you will have some leverage.

Most people fail in their endeavors by quitting just before the dawn of success. Follow these directions and you can win the job. You have proven yourself to be a fighter, and that is universally admired. The company representative will want you to succeed because you are made of stuff that is rarely seen today. You are a person of guts, drive, and endurance—the hallmarks of a winner. Job turn-downs are opportunities to exercise and build on your strengths, and, by persisting, you may well add to your growing number of job offers, now and in the future.

CHAPTER 19
Negotiating the Job Offer

THEY WANT YOU! Before you sign on the dotted line, however, you should be well schooled in the essentials of good salary and benefits negotiations. After all, you're never going to have this much leverage again unless you start over from square one, right?

The crucial period after you have received a formal offer and before you accept is probably the one point in your relationship with an employer at which you can say that you have the whip hand. The advantage, for now, is yours. They want you but don't have you; and their wanting something they don't have gives you a negotiating edge. An employer is also more inclined to respect and honor a person who has a clear understanding of his or her worth in the marketplace—they want a savvy and businesslike person.

You don't have to accept or reject the first offer, whatever it is. In most instances you can improve the initial offer in a number of ways, but you have to know something about the existing market conditions for those employed in your area of endeavor. If you are female, bear in mind that simply settling for a few points above your current rate of pay is bad advice for anyone and downright crazy for you.

The Women's Bureau of the U.S. Department of Labor tells us that men out-earn women in nearly every field. (For what it's worth, my research could not turn up a single industry in which this was not the case.) Even if a woman's responsibilities, background, and accomplishments are exactly the same as those of her male colleague, she is statistically unlikely to take home a paycheck equal to his. According to the Women's Bureau, male engineers make 14.3 percent more than their female counterparts. Male mathematicians make 16.3 percent more. Male advertising and public relations professionals make 28 percent more. Male lawyers and judges make 28 percent more. And male editors and reporters make a whopping 43 percent more than women performing the same or comparable work. My belief is that much of the gap can be attributed to a simple lack of knowledge of professional negotiating skills, and that women in the workplace are picking these skills up fast.

Man or woman, there is no guarantee you are being paid what you are worth. The simple facts are these: if you don't get it while they want you and don't have you, you sure can't count on getting it once they do have you. When a thirty-year-old under-negotiates his or her salary by just $4,000 on a new job, it will cost that person a minimum of $140,000 over the course of a career. Remember, every subsequent raise will come from a proportionately lower base; due to inflation real dollars lost over an entire career span could actually be double this figure.

KNOCK 'EM DEAD TIP

Check out the Bureau of Labor Statistics website at *www.bls.gov*. This website contains a wealth of job-related and economic information (though dated) from around the nation. You'll find information on state unemployment rates, salary information, anticipated job growth–rates for particular industries, growing fields, and publications and research papers on prices, living conditions, and technology. You will also find *www.salary.com*, a good resource for salary comparison; most websites have a salary calculator tool (often powered by Salary.com).

To get what you have coming at the negotiating table, take the time to understand what you have achieved, what you have to offer, and what you are worth to the employer. You should be able to get a better handle on that final item by doing good research, but remember that regional business conditions can affect pay levels.

Everything in this book has been written toward maximizing your professional worth, and salary negotiation is certainly no exception. There are no shortcuts. The ideas presented in this chapter will be helpful to you if they represent the culmination of your successful campaign to set yourself apart from the competition, but you cannot negotiate a terrific salary package if an employer is not convinced that you are in the top tier of applicants.

Follow this three-step procedure in planning your salary discussions with employers.

Step 1: Before getting into negotiation with any employer, work out your minimum cash requirements for any job. What is it going to take to keep a roof over your head and bread on the table? It's necessary to know this figure, but you need never discuss it with anyone—knowing it is the foundation of getting what you need, what you are worth, and what you want.

Step 2: Get a grip on what your skills are worth in the current market. There are a number of ways to do that. Consider the resources and methods outlined below:

- You can find salary surveys on online employment sites.
- You may be able to find out the salary range for the level above you and the level beneath you at the company in question.
- Ask headhunters—they know better than anyone what the market will bear. You should, as a matter of career prudence, establish an ongoing relationship with a reputable headhunter, because you never know when his or her services will come in handy.
- Many professional journals publish annual salary surveys that you can consult.

Step 3: This is the fun part. Come up with the figure that would make you smile, drop dead, and go to heaven on the spot. (But try to keep it somewhere within the bounds of reality—multimillion-dollar offers being in relatively short supply for most of us.)

You now have three figures: a minimum, a realistic midpoint desired salary, and a dream salary.

Your minimum is for personal consumption—never discuss it with anyone. Put it aside, and what do you have left? A salary range, just like the one every employer has for every interview you attend. Yours extends from your midpoint to your dream salary. Yes, that range represents the "top half" of what you want or, more accurately, could conceivably accept—but there's a reason for that. In the event, you will find it is far easier to negotiate down than to negotiate up, and you must find a starting point that gives you every possible advantage.

Negotiate When You Can

I have said throughout *Knock 'em Dead* that your sole aim at the interview is to get the job offer, because without it you have nothing to negotiate. Once the offer is extended, the time to negotiate has arrived, and there will never be a more opportune time.

Although questions of salary are usually brought up after you are under serious consideration, you must be careful to avoid painting yourself into a corner when you fill out the initial company application form that contains a request for expected salary. Usually you can get away with "open" as a response; sometimes the form will instruct you not to write "open," in which case you can write "negotiable" or "competitive."

KNOCK 'EM DEAD TIP

The crucial period after you have received a formal offer is when the issue of money is raised. While you have an advantage—they want you but don't have you—you want to get as much as possible, as competitively as possible. Getting what is best for you can require research into who gets paid what in your profession. Here are some resources for establishing salary norms:

www.wsj.com
www.homefair.com
www.jobs.com
www.salary.com

So much for basic considerations. Let's move on to the money questions that are likely to be flying around the room. The negotiation begins in earnest in two ways. The interviewer can bring up the topic with statements like:

- "How do you think you would like working here?"
- "People with your background always fit in well with us."
- "You could make a real contribution here."
- "Well, you certainly seem to have what it takes."

Or, if it is clearly appropriate to do so, you can bring on the negotiating stage. In that case, you can make mirror-image statements of the above that will make the interviewer face the fact that you certainly are able to do the job and that the time has therefore come to talk turkey:

- "How do you think I would fit in with the group?"
- "I feel my background and experience would definitely complement the work group, don't you?"

- "I think I could make a real contribution here. What do you think?"
- "I have what it takes to do this job. What questions are lingering in your mind?"

Now then. What do you do when the question of money is brought up before you have enough details about the job to negotiate from a position of knowledge and strength? Postpone money talk until you have the facts in hand. Do that by asking something like: "I still have one or two questions about my responsibilities, and it will be easier for me to talk about money when I have cleared them up. Could I first ask you a few questions about . . . ?"

Proceed to clarify duties and responsibilities, being careful to weigh the relative importance of the position and its individual duties to the success of the department you may join. The employer is duty-bound to get your services as reasonably as possible, while you have an equal responsibility to do the best you can for yourself. Your goal is not to settle for less than will enable you to be happy on the job—unhappiness at work can taint the rest of your life. The rest of the chapter is going to address the many questions that might be asked, or that you might ask, to bring matters to a successful conclusion.

"What is an adequate reward for your efforts?"

A glaring manageability question and money probe all in one. The interviewer probably already has a typist on staff who expects a Nobel Prize each time he or she gets out a faultless letter. Your answer should be honest and cover all bases. "My primary satisfaction and reward comes from a job well done and completed on time. The occasional good word from my boss is always welcome. Last but not least, I think everyone looks forward to a salary review."

"What is your salary history?" or "What was your salary progress on your last job?"

The interviewer is looking for a couple of things. First, he or she is looking for the frequency, percentage, and dollar value of your raises, which in turn tell him or her about your performance and the relative value of the offer that is about to be made. What you want to avoid is tying the potential offer to your salary history—the offer you negotiate should be based solely on the value of the job in hand. Again, this is even more important if you are a woman.

Your answer needs to be specifically vague. Perhaps: "My salary history has followed a steady upward path, and I have never failed to receive merit increases. I would be glad to give you the specific numbers if needed, but I shall have to sit down and give it some thought with a pencil and paper." The odds are that the interviewer will not ask you to do that; if he or she does, nod in agreement and say you'll get right to it when you get home. Don't begin the task until you are requested a second time, which is unlikely.

If for any reason you do get your back against the wall with this one, be sure to include in the specifics of your answer that "one of the reasons I am leaving my current job is that raises were standard for all levels of employees, so that despite my superior contributions, I got the same percentage raise as the tardy employee. I want to work in an environment where I will be recognized and rewarded for my contributions." Then end with a question: "Is this the sort of company where I can expect that?"

"What were you making on your last job?"

A similar but not identical question. It could also be phrased, "What are you making now?" or "What is your current salary?"

While I have said your current earnings should bear no relation to your starting salary on the new job, it can be difficult to make that statement clear to the interviewer without appearing objectionable. A short answer might include: "I am earning $X, although I do want you to know that a major reason for making a job change right now is to significantly increase my remuneration, as I currently am underpaid for my skills and experience."

It is important to understand the "areas of allowable fudge." For instance, if you are considerably underpaid, you may want to weigh the dollar value of such perks as medical and dental plans, pay in lieu of vacation, profit sharing and pension plans, bonuses, stock options, and other incentives. For many people, those can add between 20 to 35 percent to their base salary—you might honestly be able to mention a higher figure than you at first thought possible. Also, if you are due for a raise imminently, you are justified in adding it in.

It isn't common for current or previous salaries to be verified by employers, although certain industries, because of legal requirements, check more than others do (for instance, the stock market or the liquor business). Before your "current salary" disappears through the roof, however, you should know that the interviewer can ask to see a payroll stub or W-2 form at the time you start work or could make the offer dependent on verification of salary. After you are hired, the new employer may request verbal or written confirmation from previous employers, or might use an outside verification agency. In any instance where the employer contacts someone verbally or in writing, the employer must by law have your written permission to do so. That small print on the bottom of the job application form followed by a request for your signature usually authorizes the employer to do just that.

"Have you ever been refused a salary increase?"

This implies that you asked. An example of your justifiable request might parallel the following true story. An accountant in a tire distributorship made changes to an accounting system that saved $65,000 a year, plus thirty staff hours a week. Six months after the methods were obviously working smoothly, he requested a salary review; he was refused but was told he would receive a year-end bonus. He did: $75. If you can tell a story like that, by all means tell how you were turned down for a raise. If not, it is best to explain that your work and salary history showed a steady and marked improvement over the years.

"How much do you need to support your family?"

This question is sometimes asked of people who will be working in a sales job, where remuneration is based upon a draw against forthcoming commissions. If this scenario describes your income patterns, be sure you have a firm handle on your basic needs before you accept the position.

For salaried positions, this question is of dubious relevance. It implies the employer will try to get you at a subsistence salary, which is not why you are there. In this instance, give a range from your desired high-end salary down to your desired midpoint salary.

"How much will it take to get you?" "How much are you looking for?" "What are your salary expectations?" "What are your salary requirements?"

You are being asked to name a figure here. Give the wrong answer and you can get eliminated. It is always a temptation to ask for the moon, knowing you can come down later, but there are better approaches. It is wise to confirm your understanding of the job and its importance before you start throwing numbers around, because you will have to live with the consequences. You need the best possible offer without pricing yourself out of the market, so it's time to dance with one of the following responses.

"Well, let's see if I understand the responsibilities fully. . . ." You then proceed to itemize exactly what you will be doing on a daily basis and the parameters of your responsibilities and authority. Once that is done you will seek agreement: "Is this the job as you see it or have I missed anything?" Remember to describe the job in its most flattering and challenging light, paying special attention to the way you see it fitting into the overall picture and contributing to the success of the department, work group, and company. You can then finish your response with a question of your own: "What figure did you have in mind for someone with my track record?" or "What range has been authorized for this position?" Your answer will include, in part, something along the lines of, "I believe my skills and experience will warrant a starting salary between __________ and ___________."

You also could ask, "What would be the salary range for someone with my experience and skills?" or "I naturally want to make as much as my background and skills will allow. If I am right for the job, and I think my credentials demonstrate that I am, I am sure you will make me a fair offer. What figure do you have in mind?"

Another good response is: "I would expect a salary appropriate to my experience and ability to do the job successfully. What range do you have in mind?"

Such questions will get the interviewer to reveal the salary range and concentrate his or her attention on the challenges of the job and your ability to accept and work with those challenges.

When you are given a range, you can adjust your money requirements appropriately, latching on to the upper part of the range. For example, if the range is $40,000 to $50,000 a year, you can come back with a range of $45,000 to $55,000.

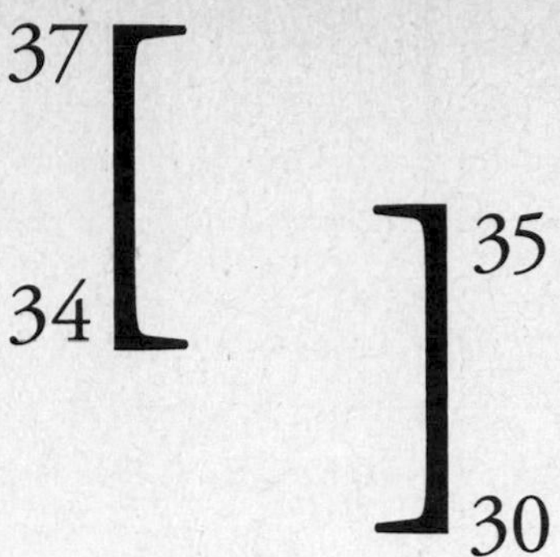

Consequently, your response will include: "That certainly means we have something to talk about. While your range is $40,000 to $50,000, I am looking for a minimum of $45,000 with an ideal of $55,000. Tell me, what flexibility is there at the top of your salary range?" You need to know this to put yourself in the strongest negotiating position, and this is the perfect time and opportunity to gain the information and the advantage.

All this fencing is aimed at getting the interviewer to show his or her hand first. Ask for too much, and it's "Oh dear, I'm afraid you're overqualified"—to which you can reply, "So overpay me." (Actually, that works when you can carry it off with an ingratiating smile.)

When you have tried to get the interviewer to name a range and failed, you must come up with specific dollars and cents. The key is to understand that all jobs have salary ranges attached to them. Consequently, the last thing you will ever do is come back with a specific dollar figure—that traps you. Instead, you will mention your own range, which will be from your midpoint to your maximum. Remember, you can always negotiate down but can rarely negotiate up.

"What do you hope to be earning two to five years from now?"

A difficult question. The interviewer is probing your desired career and earning path and is trying to see whether you have your sights set high enough—or too high. Perhaps a jocular tone doesn't hurt here: "I'd like to be earning just about as much as I can work out with my boss!" Then, throw the ball back with your own question: "How much is it possible to make here?"

If you give a specific figure, the interviewer is going to want justification. If you come up with a salary range, you are advised also to have a justified career path to go along with it.

You could also say, "In two years, I will have finished my CPA requirements, so with that plus my additional experience, industry norms say I should be earning between $X and $Y. I would hope to be earning at least within that range, but hopefully with a proven track record of contributions, I would be making above the norm." The trick is to use industry statistics as the backbone of your argument, express confidence in doing better than the norm, and, whenever possible, stay away from specific job titles unless pressed. Websites such as Salary.com allow you to identify salary norms for many jobs.

"Do you think people in your occupation should be paid more?"

This one can be used prior to serious salary negotiation to probe your awareness of how your job really contributes to the bottom line. Or it can occur in the middle of salary negotiations to throw you off balance. The safe and correct answer is to straddle the fence. "Most jobs have salary ranges that reflect the job's relative importance and contribution to a company. Those salary ranges reflect the norm for the great majority of people within that profession. That does not mean, however, that the extraordinary people in such a group are not recognized for their extra performance and skills. There are always exceptions to the rule."

Good Offers, Poor Offers

After a period of bantering back and forth like this, the interviewer names a figure, hopefully meant as a legitimate offer. If you aren't sure, qualify it: "Let me see if I understand you correctly: are you formally offering me the position at $X a year?"

The formal offer can fall into one of two categories.

✎**It sounds fair** and equitable: In that case, you still want to negotiate for a little more—employers almost expect it of you, so don't disappoint them. Mention a salary range again, the low end of which comes at about the level of their offer and the high end somewhat above it. You can say, "Well it certainly seems that we are close. I was hoping for something more in the range of $X to $Y. How much room do we have for negotiation here?"

No one will withdraw an offer because you say you feel you are worth more. After all, the interviewer thinks you are the best person for the job and has extended a formal offer, and the last thing he or she needs now is to start from square one again. The employer has a vested interest in bringing the negotiation to a satisfactory conclusion. At worst, the interviewer can stick to the original offer.

✎**It isn't quite** what you expected: Even if the offer isn't what you thought it would be, you still have options other than accepting or rejecting the offer as it stands. Your strategy for now is to run the money topic as far as you can in a calm and businesslike way. Once you have gone that far, you can back off and examine the other potential benefits of the job. That way you will leave yourself with an opening, if you need it, to hit the money topic once more at the close of negotiations.

If you feel the salary could do with a boost, say so. "I like the job, and I know I have what it takes to be successful in it. I would also be prepared to give you a start date of *[e.g.,]* March 1 to show my sincerity. But quite honestly, I couldn't justify it with your initial salary offer. I hope that we have some room for negotiation here." Or you can say, "I could start on March 1, and I do feel I could make a contribution here and become an integral part of the team. The only thing standing in the way is my inability to make ends meet based on your initial offer. I am very interested in the opportunity and flattered by your interest in me. If we could just solve this money problem, I'm sure we could come to terms. What do you think can be done about it?"

The interviewer will probably come back with a question asking how much you want. "What is the minimum you would be prepared to work for?" he or she might ask. You can reply, "I'd really like to make at least *[now respond with your midpoint]*. Is something in this range going to be a stumbling block?"

Depending on the interviewer's response, this is the time to be noncommittal but encouraging and to move on to the benefits included with the position: "Well, yes, that is a little better. Perhaps we should talk about the benefits."

Alternatively, the interviewer may come back with another question: "That's beyond our salary range for this job title. How far can you reduce your salary needs to fit our range?"

This question shows good faith and a desire to close the deal, but don't give in too easily—the interviewer is never going to want you as much as he or she does now. Your first response might be: "I appreciate that, but if it is the job title and its accompanying range that is causing the problem, couldn't we upgrade the title, thereby putting me near the bottom of the next range?" Try it—it often works. If it doesn't, it is probably time to move to other negotiable aspects of the job offer.

But not before one last try. You can take that final stab by asking, "Is that the best you can do?" With this question, you must look the interviewer directly in the eye, ask the question, and maintain eye contact. It works surprisingly well. Remember that the *tone* in which such a question is delivered is critically important: with the wrong intonation this can be interpreted as a statement of contempt.

Negotiating Your Future Salary

At this point, you have probably ridden present salary as hard as you reasonably can (for a while, anyway)—so the time has come to shift the conversation to future remuneration.

"Even though the offer isn't quite what I'd hoped for to start the job, I am still interested. Can we talk about the future for a while?" Then you move the conversation to an on-the-job focus. Here are a few arrangements corporate headhunters frequently negotiate for their recruits.

✎**A single, lump-sum** signing bonus—nice to have, but it is money here today and gone tomorrow: Don't make the mistake of adding it onto the base. If you get a $2,500 signing bonus, that money won't be figured in for your year-end review—your raise will be based on your actual salary, so the bonus is less meaningful than it appears.

✎**A 60-, 90-, or 120-day performance review** with raise attached: You can frequently negotiate a minimum percentage increase here if you have confidence in your abilities.

✎**A title promotion** and raise after two, three, or four months.

✎**A year-end bonus:** When you hear talk about a year-end bonus, don't rely on "what it's going to be this year" or "what it was last year," because the actual bonus will never bear any resemblance to either figure. Base your estimate of any bonus on a five-year performance history.

✎**Things other than cash:** Also in the realm of real disposable income are things like a company car, gas, maintenance, and insurance. They represent hard dollars you would not have to spend. It's not unusual to hear of employers paying car or insurance allowances, picking up servicing bills for your personal automobile, or paying gas up to a certain amount each month. But if you don't ask, you can never expect an employer to offer. What have you got to lose? The worst that can happen is that the employer declines. Remember to get any of those unusual goodies in writing—even respectable managers in respected companies can suffer amnesia.

Leverage and Evaluate the Offer

No two negotiations are alike, so there is no absolute model you can follow. Nevertheless, when you have addressed present and future remuneration, this might be the time to get some more information on the company and the job itself.

Even if you haven't agreed on a figure, you are probably beginning to get a feeling as to whether or not you can put the deal together; you know the employer wants to. Many of the following questions will be appropriate here, and some might even be appropriate at other times during the interview cycle.

Full knowledge of all the relevant facts is critical to your successful final negotiation of money and benefits. Your prudent selection of questions from the following list will help you negotiate the best offers and choose the right job for you. (At this point, asking some pertinent questions from this list also serves as a decompression device of sorts for both parties.) The questions come in these categories: nuts-and-bolts job clarification, job and department growth, corporate culture, and company growth and direction. The following section is also worth reading between first and second interviews.

Nuts and Bolts

First, if you have career aspirations, you want to land in an outfit that believes in promoting from within. To find out, ask a few of these questions: How long has the job been open? Why is it open? Who held the job last? What is he doing now? Promoted, fired, or quit? How long was he in that job? How many people have held this job in the last three years? Where are they now? How often have people been promoted from this position—and how many, and to where? Other questions that might follow include:

- "What is the timetable for filling the position?"
- The longer the job has been open and the tighter the time frame for filling it, the better your leverage. This can also be determined by asking: "When do you need me to start? Why on that date particularly?"
- "What are the first projects to be addressed?" or "What are the major problems to be tackled and conquered?"
- "What do you consider the five most important day-to-day responsibilities of this job?"
- "What personality traits do you consider critical to success in this job?"
- "How do you see me complementing the existing group?"
- "Will I be working with a team or on my own? What will be my responsibilities as a team member? What will be my leadership responsibilities?"
- "How much overtime is involved?"
- "How much travel is involved?" and "How much overnight travel?" With overnight travel you need to find out the number of days per week and month, and, more important, whether you will be paid for weekend days or given comp time. I have known companies that regularly expect you to get home from a long weekend trip at 1:00 A.M. and be at work at 8:30 A.M. on Monday—all without extra pay or comp time.

- "How frequent are performance and salary reviews? And what are they based on—standard raises for all, or are they weighted toward merit and performance?"
- "How does the performance appraisal and reward system work? Exactly how are outstanding employees recognized, judged, and rewarded?"
- "What is the complete financial package for someone at my level?"

Job and Department Growth

Gauging the potential for professional growth in a job is very important for some, while for others it comes slightly lower down the list. Even if you aren't striving to head the corporation in the next few years, you will still want to know what the promotional and growth expectations are.

- "To what extent are the functions of the department recognized as important and worthy of review by upper management?" If upper management takes an interest in the doings of your work group, rest assured you are in a visible position for recognition and reward.
- "Where and how does my department fit into the company pecking order?"
- "What does the department hope to achieve in the next two to three years? How will that help the company? How will it be recognized by the company?"
- "What do you see as the strengths of the department? What do you see as weaknesses that you are looking to turn into strengths?"
- "What role would you hope I would play in these goals?"
- "What informal and formal benchmarks will you use to measure my effectiveness and contributions?"
- "Based on my effectiveness, how long would you anticipate me holding this position? When my position and responsibilities change, what are the possible titles and responsibilities I might grow into?"
- "What is the official corporate policy on internal promotion? How many people in this department have been promoted from their original positions since joining the company?"
- "How do you determine when a person is ready for promotion?"
- "What training and professional development programs are available to help me grow professionally?"
- "Does the company encourage outside professional development training? Does the company sponsor all or part of any costs?"
- "What are my potential career paths within the company?"
- "To what jobs have people with my title risen in the company?"
- "Who in the company was in this position the shortest length of time? Why? Who has remained in this position the longest? Why?"

Corporate Culture

All companies have their own way of doing things—that's corporate culture. Not every corporate culture is for you.

- "What is the company's mission? What are the company's goals?"
- "What approach does this company take to its marketplace?"
- "What is unique about the way this company operates?"
- "What is the best thing you know about this company? What is the worst thing you know about this company?"
- "How does the reporting structure work? What are the accepted channels of communication and how do they work?"
- "What kinds of checks and balances, reports, or other work-measurement tools are used in the department and company?"
- "What advice would you give me about fitting into the corporate culture—about understanding the way you do things here?"
- "Will I be encouraged or discouraged from learning about the company beyond my own department?"

Company Growth and Direction

For those concerned about employment stability and career growth, a healthy company is mandatory.

- "What expansion is planned for this department, division, or facility?"
- "What markets does the company anticipate developing?"
- "Does the company have plans for mergers or acquisitions?"
- "Currently, what new endeavors is the company actively pursuing?"
- "How do market trends affect company growth and progress? What is being done about them?"
- "What production and employee layoffs and cutbacks have you experienced in the last three years?"
- "What production and employee layoffs and cutbacks do you anticipate? How are they likely to affect this department, division, or facility?"

- "When was the last corporate reorganization? How did it affect this department? When will the next corporate reorganization occur? How will it affect this department?"
- "Is this department a profit center? How does that affect remuneration?"

The Package

Take-home pay is the most important part of your package. That means you must carefully negotiate any possible benefits accruing to the job that have a monetary value but are nontaxable and add to your physical and mental happiness. Below is a list of commonly available benefits. Although many of these benefits are available to all employees at some companies, you should know that, as a rule of thumb, the higher up the ladder you climb, the more benefits you can expect. Because the corporate world and its methods of creating a motivated and committed workforce are constantly in flux, never assume that a particular benefit will not be available to you.

The basic rule is to ask—if you don't ask, there is no way you will get. A few years ago, it would have been unthinkable that anyone but an executive could expect something as glamorous as an athletic club membership in a benefits package. Today, however, more companies have a membership as a standard benefit, and an increasing number are even building their own health club facilities. What's this benefit worth in your area? Call a club and find out. Benefits in your package may include:

- 401(k) and other investment matching programs
- Accidental death insurance
- "Cafeteria" insurance plans—you pick the insurance benefits you want
- Car or car allowance
- Car insurance, maintenance, and/or gas
- Compensation days—for unpaid overtime/business travel time
- Country club or health club membership
- Deferred compensation
- Dental insurance—note deductibles and the percentage that is employer-paid
- Employment contract and/or termination contract
- Expense account
- Financial planning and tax assistance
- Life insurance
- Medical insurance—note deductibles and percentage that is employer-paid

- Optical insurance—note deductibles and percentage that is employer-paid
- Paid sick leave
- Pension plans
- Personal days off
- Profit sharing
- Short- or long-term disability compensation plans
- Stock options
- Vacation

Handling References When a Job Offer Arrives

A few words here on handling your references when an offer is imminent. When references get checked, employment dates and leaving salary are always verified; don't think of fudging, as it is cause for a dismissal that could dog your footsteps for years. Beyond that, your immediate past manager is the one most likely to be checked. Depending on the company and your level, coworkers and other past managers can also be contacted.

Call potential references, describe the job you have been (or are about to be) offered, explain why you think it is a good opportunity and why you believe you can be successful (omit these details when talking to exact peers unless the offer is already in the bag). Ask if he or she thinks it would be a good fit, and why.

You can then, if appropriate and time allows, tell the reference some of the questions he or she might be asked. These might include the length of time you have known each other; your relationship to each other; the title you worked under (be sure to remind your reference of promotions and title changes); your five or six most important duties; the key projects you worked on; your greatest strengths; your greatest weaknesses; your attitudes toward your job, your peers, and management; the timeliness, quality, and quantity of your work; your willingness to achieve above and beyond the call of duty (remind him of all those weekends you worked); whether he would rehire you (if company policy forbids rehiring, make sure your reference will mention this); your earnings; and any additional comments the reference would like to make. This whole list may be an overwhelming amount of information to unload on a colleague, so pass on questions tailored to your situation.

If you have any doubt about the quality of a pivotal reference, take the precaution of having a friend do a dummy check on all references just to confirm what they will say when the occasion arises. Of course, this only works if that friend is a consummate professional capable of carrying it off! This way you can distinguish the excellent references from the merely good.

Better yet, go to *www.allisontaylor.com*, the leader in the reference-checking business. For a modest fee (about $60 for a basic reference check), they verify references on your behalf. That way you'll know in advance just who will be your best spokespeople.

Offer Letters, Employment Agreements, Relocation, and Stock Options

Never resign an existing job until you have an acceptable written offer in hand. The rule is: if you don't have an offer in writing, you don't have an offer. When that offer letter or employment agreement does arrive, you are in the final stages of negotiation. This is the time when you'll see if the written offer reflects your understanding of previous conversations, and you'll see if there are some things still to negotiate.

An offer letter should include specifics about your compensation package, start date, benefits, policies and procedures, and relocation issues; an employee handbook detailing everything you are entitled to as an employee may well accompany the offer letter.

Employment agreements become more common the higher up the corporate ladder you climb and the more critical your work becomes to the success of the corporation. An employment agreement is a more restrictive document that goes into greater detail about what you can and cannot do as a result of employment with the company.

In the employment agreement, you'll find everything you would in an offer letter, plus issues such as assignment of inventions, nondisclosure, noncompete, severance, and relocation, all of which are likely to be addressed in detail. Any stock option agreement will probably be in a separate document but presented to you at the same time as the formal offer. As these contracts can be extremely limiting and even affect your employability after you leave the company, you may wish to consult with counsel. An employment lawyer can review and advise you on the specific implications of each clause and help you with revised and less restrictive wording. As you will have a solid understanding of the issues, you will be able to phrase your questions succinctly and control the costs of any such legal consultation.

Assignment of Inventions

If you design or create anything in your work that is eligible for copyright, trademark, or patent, you can expect an "assignment of inventions" clause in your agreement. It will request as a condition of employment that you turn over anything you create during your employment with the company. This is very likely to include work you do on your own time if it in any way relates to your duties with the company. Companies do pursue this particular issue with some persistence, so you will need to address any personal projects in advance to get appropriate waivers into the employment agreement.

Nondisclosure

A nondisclosure clause is intended to prevent your discussing company business with any outside source and blabbing the company's secrets to the competition. The wording is likely to be general and therefore more restrictive to you. The more specific the language about what you can and cannot say about your work, the better it is for you. You obviously don't object to protecting the integrity of your employer, but you would like to be able to talk intelligently about your responsibilities and achievements to a future potential employer.

Noncompete

The employer will likely present you with very general language restricting you from working for any competitor for a specific and probably extended period of time. Accepting this clause without careful analysis could restrict your employability when you leave the company, either by layoff or your own volition; after all, who is most likely to hire you? Someone in the same line of business, of course! By making this clause more specific, you will also make it less restrictive. Negotiate to specify by name which direct competitors you wouldn't be able to work for in that specified time frame. An employment lawyer's advice will help you.

Severance

Negotiate for as extensive a severance package as you can—say, a month's salary for every year of employment or every $10,000 of salary, with outplacement/job search assistance. Since outplacement is only as good as the person giving it, it is preferable to negotiate a dollar amount so that you can spend the money in the way you think most suitable to your needs and with the consultant of your choice.

If you sign a noncompete clause, request that your severance extend through the entire period of your noncompete restrictions. This is a perfectly reasonable request that should be accommodated without trouble.

Relocation

When job-related relocation comes around, we all find ourselves in an ocean of unexpected expenses. So once the overall offer is acceptable to you, key in on relocation issues. Many companies expect to pay all or part of your relocation costs unless you live within fifty miles of your new workplace, in which case you are usually on your own. Since the employer regularly addresses these issues, you should not be reticent about negotiating them.

Relocation packages vary enormously from person to person and company to company. However, if they want you badly enough, employers will usually try to accommodate reasonable requests.

The higher up the corporate ladder you climb, the more relocation services you are likely to receive. On the low end, you may get offered reimbursement for a moving truck and a few hundred dollars for incidental expenses. While the employer expects to bear the cost of your relocation, every dollar spent affects the bottom line of the HR department. So no matter where you stand on the corporate ladder, getting above and beyond the standard offer will require your asking for it.

For example, companies know your relocation costs will be treated as taxable income, but they won't say anything about it unless you do. Explain that the taxes you expect to pay can amount to 30 percent of the monies spent, and that this would place a heavy burden on you financially. With a typical executive relocation running around $50,000, the tax implications of relocating to accept a new job could come as a nasty shock. Ask that the company pick up the personal income tax burdens you incur as a result of your move.

Only some aspects of your relocation are tax deductible. For example, the costs of moving your personal belongings and one trip to the new location are deductible, but house hunting trips and the costs of temporary accommodation are not.

Other things you can ask the company to help or reimburse you for include:

- House hunting trips before you start. After all, it is in the best interests of the company to have you settled as quickly as possible.
- Temporary housing costs while you find a suitable permanent residence. Again, most companies will comply with at least 30 days, sometimes as many as 90 to 120 days.
- Shipping of autos, boats, and so on.
- Costs of a professional moving company packing, shipping, and delivering your household goods.
- Costs of selling and buying a house, if you are a homeowner.
- Job-search assistance for a working spouse. Try to get a dollar amount so that you can choose your service provider. Come to martinyate.com or knockemdead.com for more advice on coaching services.
- Help in finding schools for the kids.
- Orientation programs for the new community.

It will help your negotiating position to estimate these costs in advance. You can pick up the phone and request estimates, or you can visit websites like *www.homefair.com* and *www.homestore.com*, which have electronic calculation tools and cost-of-living comparisons. The latter will help you evaluate how far a dollar will go in the new town in comparison with where you live today.

When it comes to offer letters and employment agreements, the employer naturally hopes that you will accept them as they are presented, but you are under no obligation to do so. Every aspect of the offer is negotiable, and as these are largely issues that have not arisen in the interview cycle, the employer will expect a savvy professional to address them.

Negotiating Stock Options

Stock options, while typically handled in a separate document, will be offered at the same time as your other benefits. It is usually best to address the stock issue once all the others have been settled.

In good economic times, employers turn to stock options as an effective recruitment and retention incentive. Options give you the right to purchase a set amount of stock in the company at a predetermined price (usually attractive) and over a fixed period of time. In exercising your options (buying the stock), you need to remember that stocks can and do decrease in value, sometimes dramatically.

There are several types of stock options, each with its own specific tax ramifications. However, as an employee, you are most likely to be offered "incentive stock options." Fortunately, with this type of option, you only have to pay taxes on your gains when you sell the stock; if you keep the stock for at least a year after purchase, you will not have to pay capital gains tax.

When negotiating stock options, always bear in mind that they are a gamble. The employer is going to talk about the offered stock options as if they were money in the bank, but they are not. Don't get bamboozled by rosy descriptions of the company's future; stay focused instead on the current market value of the stock. This is especially important if you are being asked to accept options as part of your overall compensation package. In some instances, you can be asked to accept options in lieu of cash. If the options you are offered are in any way to replace salary, think carefully, as you can't eat stock options.

If you are accepting a job with a publicly traded company, learn the value and performance of that stock by obtaining public records. On the other hand, if the company is privately held, you'll have to rely on the information that is provided to you by the employer. In this instance, consider market segment, business strategy, operations, liquidity, and senior management track record. In effect, you are evaluating your faith in the company, the imminence of their going public, and whether or not the company is a start-up or a well-established entity.

Of course, if the stock options do not impact your take-home pay, it can't hurt to get as many as you can. There is a big difference between getting the options and actually exercising your right to buy and sell them. Your considerations will include: what the purchase price will be, when you can exercise your options, and the restrictions on when you can buy the stock and when you can sell it. These matters will all be laid out in the separate options agreement furnished by the employer at the same time as the employment agreement, so read it carefully before you start negotiations in this area.

Everything to do with stock is negotiable, so you don't have to accept whatever you are offered without question and negotiation. Naturally, you will ask for more options than you are initially offered. You may not exercise those options, but having them available is in your best interests.

Your stock options will have a vesting period—the length of time you must work for the company before you can exercise your options. The employer, who is using the options as a retention tool, wants the vesting period to be as long as possible, thus tying you to the company with the lure of the stock. You, on the other hand, want to shorten the vesting period and, if possible, get an "incremental vesting schedule."

An incremental vesting schedule allows you to buy a few shares every month or quarter, probably getting you fully vested in the same period of time, but in smaller, more frequent steps along the way. Another reasonable request is to ask for "accelerated vesting" in the event of the employer merging or being bought by another company. This way, you become fully vested at the time of the acquisition.

Your agreement will also limit the time period in which you can exercise your options—not only when you can first exercise them, but also the point at which your option ends. For your financial flexibility, you will want to negotiate to extend this period as far as you can, even after you leave the company. For example, if you have a noncompete clause, you are essentially still tied to the company for a specific period of time, so it is reasonable to ask if you can exercise your options through the same period of time covered by your noncompete and nondisclosure clauses.

If you are not offered a "cashless exercise provision" you should certainly negotiate for it. A cashless exercise provision allows you to buy stock without spending any of your hard-earned money. The way it works is that when you buy a block of stock, you are simultaneously allowed to sell as many shares as are required to cover the costs of buying the stock; hence it becomes a cashless exercise, leaving you with the stock but not out of pocket.

Getting the stock options is one thing. Exercising them is another step that you will not want to take without professional financial counsel.

Hopefully, you will be able to negotiate an agreement that is acceptable to both parties; you will then need to write both an acceptance and resignation letter. A career spans upward of half a century, so you don't want to burn bridges today that you may need to cross again tomorrow. Take the time to craft professional documents. One of the companion volumes to this work, *Knock 'em Dead Cover Letters*, will help you create powerful, professional letters for all occasions. The book is full of examples and has specific sections on acceptance, rejection, and resignation letters.

Evaluating the Offer

Once the offer has been negotiated to the best of your ability, you need to evaluate it—and that doesn't have to be done on the spot. Some of your requests and questions will take time to get answered, and very often the final parts of negotiation—"Yes, Mr. Jones, we can give you the extra $10,000 and six months of vacation you requested"—will take place over the telephone. Regardless of where the final negotiations are completed, never accept or reject the offer on the spot.

Be positive, say how excited you are about the prospect and that you would like a little time (overnight, a day, two days) to think it over, discuss it with your spouse, whatever. Not only is this delay standard practice, but it will also give you the opportunity to leverage other offers, as discussed in the next chapter.

Use the time you gain to speak to your mentors or advisers. First, a word of caution: In asking advice from those close to you, be sure you know exactly where that advice is coming from—you need clear-headed objectivity at this time.

Once the advice is in, and not before, weigh it along with your own observations—no one knows your needs and aspirations better than you do. While there are many ways of doing that, a simple line down the middle of a sheet of paper, with the reasons to take the job written on one side and the reasons to turn it down on the other, is about as straightforward and objective as you can get.

You will weigh salary, future earnings and career prospects, benefits, commute, lifestyle, and stability of the company, along with all those intangibles that are summed up in the term "gut feelings." Make sure you answer these questions for yourself:

- Do you like the work?
- Can you be trained in a reasonable period of time, thus having a realistic chance of success on the job?
- Are the title and responsibilities likely to provide you with challenges?
- Is the opportunity for growth in the job compatible with your needs and desires?
- Are the company's location, stability, and reputation in line with your needs?
- Is the atmosphere/culture of the company conducive to your enjoying working at the company?
- Can you get along with your new manager and immediate work group?
- Is the money offer and total compensation package the best you can get?

Notice that money is but one aspect of the evaluation process. There are many other factors to take into account as well. Even a high-paying job can be less advantageous than you think. For instance, you should be careful not to be foxed by the gross figure. It really is important that you get a firm handle on those actual, spendable, after-tax dollars—the ones with which you pay the rent. Always look at an offer in the light of how many more spendable dollars a week it will put in your pocket.

Accepting New Jobs, Resigning from Others

Once your decision is made, you should accept the job verbally. Spell out exactly what you are accepting: "Mr. Smith, I'd like to accept the position of engineer at a starting salary of $82,000. I will be able to start work on March 1. And I understand my package will include life, health, and dental insurance, a 401(k) plan, and a company car." Then you finish with: "I will be glad to start on the above date pending a written offer received in time to give my present employer adequate notice of my departure. I'm sure that's acceptable to you."

Notify your current employer in the same fashion. Quitting is difficult for almost everyone, so you can write a pleasant resignation letter, walk into your boss's office, hand it to him or her, then discuss things calmly and pleasantly once he or she has read it.

Notify any other companies that have been in negotiation with you that you are no longer on the market but that you were most impressed with meeting them and would like to keep communications open for the future. (Again, see the next chapter for details on how to handle—and encourage—multiple job offers.)

It bears repeating that your resignation is not the time to air your grievances; you have simply been presented with a great opportunity and are thankful for the skills this job gave you. This same person may be checked for a reference down the line, and you want the recollections to be positive.

CHAPTER 20
Multiple Job Interviews, Multiple Job Offers

RELYING ON ONE interview at a time can only lead to anxiety, so you must create and foster an ever-growing network of interviews and, consequently, job offers.

False optimism and laziness lead many job hunters to be content with only one interview in process at any given time. That severely reduces the odds of landing the best job in town within your chosen time frame. Complacency guarantees that you will continue to operate in a buyers' market.

The recommended approach is to generate as many interviews as possible in a two- to three-week period. Interviewing skills are learned and consequently improve with practice. With the improved skills comes a greater confidence, and those natural interview nerves disperse. Your confidence shows through to potential employers, and you are perceived in a positive light. Because other companies are interested in you, everyone will move more quickly to secure your services. This is especially important if you are unfortunate enough to be unemployed. Being out of work is when you need money the most and is the time when the salary you can command on the open market is substantially reduced. The interview activity you generate will help offset this.

By generating multiple interviews, you bring the time of the first job offer closer and closer. That one job offer can be quickly parlayed into a number of others. And with a single job offer, your unemployed status has, to all intents and purposes, passed.

Immediately, you can call every company with whom you've met, and explain the situation. "Mr. Johnson, I'm calling because while still under consideration with your company I have received a job offer from one of your competitors. I would hate to make a decision without the chance of speaking with you again. I was very impressed by my meeting with you. Can we get together in the next couple of days?" End, of course, with a question that carries the conversation forward.

If you were in the running at all, your call will usually generate another interview; Mr. Johnson does not want to miss out on a suddenly prized commodity. Remember: It is human nature to want the very things one is about to lose. Your simple offer can be multiplied almost by the number of interviews you have in process at the time.

A single job offer can also be used to generate interviews with new firms. It is as simple as making your usual telephone networking presentation, but it ends differently. You would be very interested in meeting with them because of your knowledge of the company/product/service, but also because you have just received a job offer—would it be possible to get together in the next couple of days?

Relying on one interview at a time can only lead to prolonged anxiety, disappointment, and, possibly, unemployment. That reliance is due to the combination of false optimism, laziness, and fear of rejection. Those are traits that cannot be tolerated except by confirmed defeatists, for defeat is the inevitable result of those traits. As Heraclitus said, "A man's character is his fate." Headhunters say, "The job offer that cannot fail will."

Self-esteem, on the other hand, is vital to your success, and happiness is found with it. With it you will awake each day with previously unknown vitality. Your vigor will increase, your enthusiasm will rise, and a desire to achieve will burn within. The more you do today, the better you will feel tomorrow.

Even when you follow this plan to the letter, not every interview will result in an offer. But with many irons in the fire, an occasional firm "no" should not affect your morale. It won't be the first or last time you face rejection. Be persistent and, above all, close your mind to all negative and discouraging influences. The success you experience from implementing this plan will increase your store of willpower and determination, affect the successful outcome of your job search, and enrich your whole life. Start today.

The key to your success is preparation. Failing is easy—it requires no effort. It is the achievement of success that requires effort, and that means effort today, not tomorrow, for tomorrow never comes. So start building that well-stocked briefcase today.

CHAPTER 21

How to Ace the Psychological Tests

CAREFUL! ANSWERING THESE questions casually can be hazardous to your professional health.

In late 1989, Congress banned most private-sector applications of the polygraph test, voice-stress analysis, and other electronic screening methods. While many government personnel (for instance, those involved in drug interdiction activities) are still subject to these tests, many private employers have had to change their ways, and are increasingly turning to psychological testing to weed out those they consider to be undesirable job applicants. These tests may be known as aptitude tests; personality profiles; personnel selection tests; or skills, aptitude, and integrity tests, but in the end they are all the same thing: an attempt to find out if you show signs of being a "risky" hire.

Although the 1989 legislation led to new popularity for psychological tests, they have been around for decades. Psychological exams come in two flavors. One is a face-to-face meeting with a psychologist, and the other (far more common) is a written test, often multiple choice.

In any discussion of this issue, we should bear in mind that psychology is, by the admission of its own practitioners, an inexact science, and that few of the tests used in employee selection were designed for that purpose. While these tests cannot be regarded as a definitive litmus test on your potential employability, many companies are grafting the imprecise discipline of psychological testing onto the equally imprecise one of employment selection. The result is cheap and easy to administer. Those seeking employment are often asked to answer "a few routine questions" that end up being anything but routine. The tests, which should not be used as the sole basis for a hiring decision, are nevertheless often used in a pass-or-fail way and have a huge effect on people's livelihoods. In your case, let's do everything we can to make sure they don't have a negative effect on your job prospects.

It isn't surprising that many of the companies using the tests are concerned about the honesty of prospective employees. Each year, American industry loses an estimated $40 billion from employee theft. While honesty is often one of the behavioral profiles examined, the tests can also examine aptitude and suitability for a position. Often, the exams are geared toward evaluating the amount of energy a person might bring to the job; how he or she would handle stress; and what his or her attitudes toward job, peers, and management would be.

Unfortunately, answering a psychological test with complete personal honesty may very well threaten your chance of being offered employment. That's the bad news. Here's the good news: you can ace the tests without having to compromise your personal integrity.

Not long ago, I did an in-house employee selection and motivation seminar for a large corporation. When asked for my opinion on the subject of psychological testing, I replied the tests were often used inappropriately as a pass-or-fail criterion for hiring, and anyone with half a brain could come up with the desired or correct answers. "The question is," I concluded, "how many people who could have served you well will you miss out on because of a test?"

The managers assured me they had a test that was "virtually infallible" in helping to identify strong hires and certainly not subject to the machinations of the average applicant. They asked if I would be prepared to take it. I not only agreed but also promised to prove my point. "Let me take the test twice," I said. "The first profile you get will tell you to hire me; the second will say I'm a bad risk."

I took the test twice that day. "Applicant #1" came back with a strong recommendation for hire. "Applicant #2" came back with a warning to exercise caution.

How was this possible? Well, none of us is the same person in the workplace as in our personal life. Over a period of time at work, we come to understand the need for different behavioral patterns and different ways of interacting with people.

Sometimes our more considered, analytical, and logical approaches pass over from our "professional self" into the personal realm. However, in the world of work, we are not expected to override the "corporate way" to do things according to our personal preferences. When this happens, and personal preferences take precedence over existing corporate theories of behavior, we get warnings and terminations. In other words, as professionals, we are inculcated with a set of behavioral patterns that enable us to be successful and productive for our employers.

Did I really "fool" the test? No. I was completely honest both times. The "winning" test was the one in which I viewed myself—and, thus, described myself—as a thoroughly professional white-collar worker in the job for which I was applying. The "losing" test was the one I used to describe myself as the kind of person I see myself as in my personal life.

This was not a hoax perpetrated by a smart aleck. I am that person they would have hired, and I possess a strong track record to back up my claim. I simply learned the behaviors necessary to succeed, adopted them, and made them my own—just as you have undoubtedly done, or are in the process of doing.

Many of the tests lack an awareness of the complexity of the human mind. They seem to miss the point when they ask us to speak honestly about our feelings and beliefs. They do not take into account that our learned behaviors in our professional lives are invariably distinct from the behaviors we display in our personal lives.

If you understand what you are likely to face, you can prepare and present yourself in the most effective way, and you can do it without compromising your integrity.

How to Prepare for, Read, and Answer the Tests

There are five different types of tests, designed to plumb different aspects of your doubtless troubled psyche:

- Personality
- Personnel selection
- Aptitude
- Skills
- Integrity

Let's take a look at each of these.

Personality Tests

Are you a people person? Do you get upset easily? Are you quick to anger? Employers are using tests of general personality more frequently these days to screen job candidates. They use these tests because they believe that certain personality traits are required for success in a particular position.

There are two basic kinds of personality tests: projective and objective.

Projective Personality Tests. The projective tests ask you to tell a story, finish a sentence, or describe what you see in a blob of ink. These tests, in some form or other, have been around for decades, and psychologists use them a great deal to help understand how we deal with tough issues.

One popular test shows you pictures of a scene and asks you to describe what's going on. The psychologist may ask you to "tell me more about it." These areas of your mind are also accessed through the use of incomplete sentences, where you are given the beginning of a sentence and have to fill in the rest of it on your own. So, for instance, you may be asked to complete a sentence such as "When I am at work, I . . . ."

In an employment-selection context, these tests are generally looking for leaders, achievers, and winners. They search for analytical and system thinking skills, and look at decision-making and consensus-building styles.

Objective Personality Tests. Objective personality tests ask dozens, sometimes hundreds, of questions using some sort of rating scale, like strongly agree to strongly disagree, true-or-false, or yes-or-no. These tests usually have good reliability and validity. They were not designed to be used for employee screening, although they often are.

Knowing the names of the most common tests can tip you off to the type of screening being done. Tests you might run into that screen personality include:

- NEO Personality Inventory: measures adjustment, extroversion, openness, agreeability, and conscientiousness.
- 16 PF: measures sixteen personality factors, including a lie scale.
- California Psychological Inventory: measures twenty personality scales such as empathy, tolerance, responsibility, and dominance. (This is a good personality test, but it can be expensive for an employer, so it isn't used as often as some others.)
- Minnesota Multiphasic Personality Inventory: a very long, heavy-duty test of major psychological problems, often (wrongly) used in employee selection.

Personnel Selection Tests

Personnel selection tests are personality tests designed specifically to screen job candidates. These tests measure psychological behaviors such as trustworthiness, reliability, and conscientiousness. Some of them also psychologically screen you for potential alcohol or substance abuse. Tests you might run into that examine these areas include:

- Hogan Personality Inventory
- Employee Reliability Inventory
- PDI Employment Inventory

Aptitude Tests

If you don't have the skills it takes to do the job, do you have the aptitude to learn? In a work world where the learning curve for new skill development becomes increasingly interesting to potential employers, we can expect to see the use of aptitude tests on the upswing. Judging your ability to develop skills in general or skills in a particular area is the premise behind these aptitude tests.

Some of the aptitude tests you might run into that examine these areas include:

- Wechsler Adult Intelligence Scale—Revised
- Raven's Progressive Matrices
- Comprehensive Ability Battery
- Differential Aptitude Tests

Skills Tests

If the job calls for typing seventy-five words per minute, you may be given a typing test. If you are a programmer, you may be asked to take an objective test of programming skills or asked to debug a program. There are tests to measure every possible skill: filing, bookkeeping, mechanical comprehension, specific computer programs, math, credit rating, and so on. Some of them are typical paper-and-pencil written tests. Newer tests present the information using a software program.

It's hard to argue against some of these tests. After all, if the job calls for you to type letters and reports all day, the employer wants to hire the best typist. If you're supposed to use Microsoft Word on the PC all day, the employer will look for the person with the best knowledge of that program. As long as the employer is measuring an important skill, testing skills makes sense.

Integrity Tests

Integrity tests are increasingly popular. Some companies are leery of personality tests, so they turn to integrity tests to screen out liars, cheats, and thieves. Some tests measure honesty, or integrity, whereas others measure other psychological traits.

The problem with these integrity tests is that they don't work. A psychologist wrote that in one case using an integrity test would eliminate 2,721 honest applicants so that 101 potentially dishonest applicants would be denied employment. I should point out that the integrity test itself actually is okay; it's just that so few people actually steal that the use of the test eliminates a heck of a lot of good applicants. Another major study found that 95.6 percent of people who take these tests and get a failing score are actually incorrectly classified!

Here are a couple of integrity tests in consistent use today:

- Personnel Selection Inventory
- Personnel Reaction Bank

So listen carefully and apply what you learn in this chapter so that you don't become an incorrectly classified statistic.

Getting to Know Yourself and Acing the Mind Readers

Born independently wealthy, very few of us would be doing the jobs we do. But we are doing them, and we have learned certain sets of skills and behavioral traits that are critical to our ability to survive and succeed professionally. The first thing you must do, then, is identify and separate the professional you from the personal you.

✎**Step 1:** Never answer a test question from the viewpoint of your innermost beliefs. Instead, use your learned and developed professional behavior traits and modus operandi. Ask yourself, "How has my experience as a professional taught me to think and respond to this?" To do this effectively (and to understand ourselves a little better in the process), we need some further insights into the three critical skill sets that every professional relies on to succeed:

- Professional/technical skills (whether you're a secretary or a senior vice president)
- Industry skills (such as—if you happen to be in banking—your overall knowledge of the world of banking: how things work, how things get done, what is accepted within the industry, and so on)
- Professional behavior traits (the traits, discussed in Chapter 10 of this book, that all employers look for and that will get you ahead once you are on the job)

✎**Step 2:** Look at yourself from the employer's point of view. (Review "The Five Secrets of the Hire" and "The Other Side of the Desk" for some helpful ideas.) Evaluate the traits that enable you to discharge your duties effectively. Examine the typical crises/emergencies likely to arise: What supportive behavioral traits are necessary to overcome them? As you do this, you will almost certainly relive some episodes that seemed to put you at a disadvantage for a time. When it was tough to do things the right way, you had to buckle down and see the problem through, even though doing so did not necessarily "come naturally." The fact is, though, you overcame the obstacle. Remember how you did so, and keep that in mind as you answer the questions.

Conversely, you will want to look at those instances where a crisis had a less-than-successful outcome. What traits did you swear you would develop and use for next time?

Highlighting such traits constitutes your acknowledgment of the supremacy of learned behavior in the workplace. It does *not* constitute lying. (Why do you think so many professionals strive to keep their business lives separate from their personal lives? What is the point of such a separation if the two lives are identical?)

✎**Step 3:** Think of people you've known who have failed on the job. Why did they fail? What have you learned from their mistakes and made a part of the "professional you"?

✎**Step 4:** Think of people you've known who have succeeded on the job. Why did they succeed? What have you learned from their success and made a part of the "professional you"?

Once you have completed this exercise in detail, you will have determined how a professional would react in a wide range of circumstances and identified the ways in which you have, over time, developed a "professional self" to match that profile.

Getting Ready for the Test

Any test can be nerve-wracking, but when it comes to these tests your livelihood is in the balance, so tip the odds in your favor with these tried and proven techniques:

- The tests instruct you to answer quickly, offering the first response that comes to mind. Don't. Following this path may cost you a job. Instead, look at the test in terms of the exercises outlined above; provide reasoned responses from the viewpoint of the "professional you."
- Time limits are usually not imposed. On the contrary, those administering the test will often begin the proceedings with a soothing "take your time, there's no pressure." (Except, of course, the minor pressure of knowing a job offer is on the line!)
- If there is a time limit, find out how much time you have. Figure out about how much time per question or section you have. Pacing yourself helps, because you won't panic

when you realize you've only got five minutes to complete the second half of a fifteen-minute test. Of course, you'll bring your watch.

- When in doubt, guess. Some of the really sophisticated tests you may have taken to get into college nailed you if you guessed wrong, but skill tests usually work differently. They add up all your right answers to get your test score. So, when in doubt, eliminate any of the obviously wrong answers, and take your best shot.
- With skill tests, ask for a warm-up or practice section. One computer-typing test has an optional practice session. Ask about it. If the test is on a computer, adjust your chair, keyboard, and monitor before the timer starts.
- For paper and pencil tests, make sure you have enough desk space and sharp pencils.
- If the test is going to be done with other applicants in a group situation, stay focused on what you are doing. If you have to sit in the front of the room so no one else distracts you, do it. If the test will be long and there's no break, make sure you won't get hungry (take a power bar) or have to use the bathroom.
- No matter what, use all your allotted time! Check your answers, and make sure they are written in the right places. Depending on your remaining time, review every other, or every fourth, question. Of course, if you can recall at the end which questions you were unsure about, review those first.
- You may not even realize you're taking an integrity test until the direction of the questions gives it away: "Have you ever stolen anything?" "Have you ever felt guilty?" "Have you ever told a lie?" Avoid the temptation to respond impulsively with something like "Lies? No, I prefer to chop down the damned cherry tree." The truth is, we have all done these things in our lives. When you are asked, for instance, whether there is anything you would ever change about yourself, or whether you think everyone is dishonest to some degree, the overwhelming likelihood is that your own honesty is being tested: the best answer is probably "yes."

In fact, if you never admit to these behaviors, you could be pegged as a faker. While fakers may be kept in the running, they've earned a question mark. Fakers are sometimes viewed as being eager to please or simply a bit out of touch with their true feelings.

Many of the better tests in use today also use lie scales that can detect when someone is faking. How do they do this? One way is to include questions like "I always tell the truth" or "I never have a negative thought about a coworker." When the test is developed, hundreds or thousands of people take it, and the researchers figure out what the typical response is to these questions. Anyone who deviates from the average response on enough of these faking questions is also flagged as a faker.

If you must answer questions about ethics in a face-to-face encounter, explain your answer, placing it far in the past where appropriate, and explain what you have learned from any negative experience. If such questions must be answered on paper, the best approach is to follow the dictates of your own conscience and try to bring the issue up after the test. You might say something like this:

"Gee, that question about lying was a tough one. I guess everyone has told a lie at some time in the past, and I wanted to be truthful, so I said 'yes.' But I'd be lying if I didn't tell you it made me nervous. You know, I saw a show on television recently about these tests. It told the story of someone who lost a job because of answering a question just like that; the profile came back with an untrustworthy rating."

This may reduce the odds of your being denied the job in the same way. If the test does come back with a question about your honesty, you will at least have sown seeds of doubt about the validity of such a rating in the interviewer's mind. That doubt, and your disarming honesty, might just turn the tables in your favor.

Be careful, and take a balanced approach as you answer integrity test questions. Honesty is the best policy:

- In a face-to-face meeting with a psychologist, use the same techniques we have discussed throughout *Knock 'em Dead* to qualify the questions before answering them; when you suspect a trap, employ the tricks that will help you clarify things and buy time.
- The written tests may contain "double blinds," where you are asked a question on page one, and then asked a virtually identical one thirty or forty questions later. The technique is based on the belief that most of us can tell a lie, but few of us can remember that lie under stress, and are therefore likely to answer differently later. This is held to show the potential for untruthfulness. The problem isn't that one answer is likely to deny you employment; the questions are asked in patterns to evaluate your behavior and attitudes on different topics.
- Read the test through before you start answering questions! (There's "plenty of time" and "no pressure," remember?) Review the material at least three times, mentally flagging the questions that seem similar. This way you will be able to answer consistently.
- Resist any temptation to project an image of yourself as an interesting person. These tests are not designed to reward eccentricity; think sliced white bread. You are happy at work and home. You enjoy being around people. You don't spend all your evenings watching movies. You don't spend your weekends with a computer or pursuing other solitary pastimes (unless you are a programmer or an aspiring Trappist monk). You have beliefs, but not too strong. You respect the beliefs of all others, regardless of their age, sex, race, or religion.
- Relax. One part of the Wechsler test (a developmental aptitude test) asks you to repeat back a string of numbers to the psychologist. If you're too hyped up, you'll get flustered and blow it. These tests measure intelligence plus your test-taking behavior. And you can certainly improve your test-taking behavior!

- Learn to visualize success in advance. Picture yourself at the test. Go through each step: you hear the instructions, the examiner says to begin. You read the test questions and realize you will do well. You get to a really tough part of the test. Visualize your success, and visualize your setbacks. Realize that you can and you will pull through okay because you have a clear vision of the professional you. When you finish the test, read through your answers a few times. If you don't like any answers, change them.
- Remember to use your professional, working mindset when you take these tests. Answer as you would if you were on the job and your boss were asking the questions.

Everything I have said here takes for granted that the overriding goal of the employer is to determine whether or not you are suitable for the job. If you can give an accurate, affirmative answer to that question, the approach you take in doing so is—to my way of thinking—of little consequence. If you have learned and applied what it takes to prosper in your profession, it is your right to provide an honest profile of your professional self, in whatever forum you are to be evaluated.

PART V
Where the Jobs Are

THIS SECTION TELLS you where today's top job markets are and gives you tips on how to break into them.

WHERE CAN I FIND A JOB? Today, when the headline writers are scaring us with the threat of unemployment remaining high, even in spite of an economic recovery, it's easy to fall under their spell and believe there are no jobs left out there. However, nothing could be further from the truth.

While job hunting in these troubled times is not easy, it's by no means impossible. The trick is to know in what fields there's a demand for skilled workers.

Effective job search today simply needs to be more efficient and organized than in the past, more focused and informed.

In this section, we'll look at the top fields for job growth and give you some important information on how to land employment and grow your career.

CHAPTER 22
Thirty Fast-Growing Occupations

EVEN IF YOU are currently employed, you should still pay attention to the changing job market and economic climate.

Now, as you are the one person who truly cares about your long-term economic survival, you are noting that one major result of a global economy, apart from cheap goods at Wally World and higher wages overseas, is the increasing instability of the professional workplace here at home. So the strategies for making informed career choices about professions, the credentials professions require for entry, and the industries in which you pursue employment are issues of importance to anyone who hopes to achieve stability and success in life.

The changing nature of our society impacts where the jobs are *now* and where they are likely to be in the *future*. You need to gain focus for and then keep an eye on the big picture—not only which jobs are more in demand, but also why they're growing and how they're changing. When you understand the trends that are changing the world of work, you have a foundation on which to base the career decisions that impact your life for years into the future.

With deeper knowledge, you will be more able to withstand the hysterics of the media news cycle. In mid-2010, while writing this new edition, I was doing countless radio appearances talking about the economy and where the jobs are and will be. I wanted to talk about the jobs that are out there for everyone, but all the media wanted to talk about was the "green" jobs that were going to change our world. Very topical, very newsworthy, but when it's your life you have to be practical about these things. Pursuing "green jobs" in the midst of a recession might not *always* be the smartest thing to do.

If you are looking for a job in your profession that carries a "green" tag, that's fair enough, but if you are changing careers on the basis of jobs you hope will come in this area, that's not so smart.

Here's a simple test I did, using the job aggregator *www.indeed.com*. I performed a national search of more than 4,000 job banks, looking for "green jobs." I got 31,000 hits for all job postings that had the word "green" somewhere in the job description. I then dropped the "green" designation and did a national search for just one title from this list, "pharmacist." I got 31,500 jobs.

That isn't to say you shouldn't pursue jobs and careers in the green sector of the economy. If you want to be true to your ideals and feel you're making a difference in your workplace, that's great—but do it with your eyes open.

By the same token, I haven't included some of the wildly touted high-growth jobs like "blogger," because although its growth percentage is phenomenal, the overall number of advertised jobs for this job title I could find on over 4,000 job sites was just 3,200. It is more prudent to anchor your search in jobs that are large in numbers now and projected for steady growth into the future. This leads to greater stability and more.

In this chapter, we'll focus on jobs whose history and growth projections are based on significant demographic changes in society, jobs that exist in lots of companies spread across every city in the country. Such positions mean more potential for job security, greater opportunity for professional growth, and more choice when you want to or must change jobs.

This list is meant as a starting point. There are many other jobs that have high growth potential in real numbers. Each job listing offers a brief overview of an occupation that the U.S. Bureau of Labor Statistics expects to grow at a minimum rate of 21 percent or more through the year 2018, and is categorized as "much faster than average." This growth will largely be fueled by our aging population and the globalization of the workplace. These "hot" occupations fall into the fields of health care (we live in an aging society), science and technologies (computers, information systems, and the environment), and business services (occupations in a variety of industries that reflect trends in our culture), as well as segments of education and social services (which are impacted by population changes and societal challenges). These are the growing sectors in America for the predictable future.

THE TOP THIRTY	
OCCUPATION	**ANTICIPATED GROWTH PERCENTAGE**
Sector: Health Care	
1. Veterinary Technician/Technologist	41%
2. Veterinarians	33%
3. Medical Assistant	34%
4. Pharmacy Technician	32%
5. Dental Hygienist	30%
6. Physical Therapist	27%
7. Physician Assistant	39%
8. Radiation Therapist	25%
9. Surgical Technician	24%
10. Athletic Trainer	37%
11. Registered Nurse	22.2%
12. Pharmacist	22%
Sector: Science and Technologies	
13. Computer Software Engineer	36%
14. Computer Scientist and Database Administrator	37%
15. Computer Systems Analyst	29%
16. Environmental Scientist and Hydrologist	25%
17. Environmental Engineer	25% to 30.6%
18. Biomedical Engineer	21% to 72%
Sector: Business Services	
19. Financial Analyst and Personal Financial Advisor	34; 41%
20. Gaming Surveillance Officer	34%
21. Court Reporter	25%
22. Actuary	24%
23. Interpreter and Translator	24%
24. Paralegal and Legal Assistant	22%
Sector: Education and Social Services	
25. Personal and Home Care Aide	50%
26. Social and Human Services Assistant	34%
27. Health Educator	26%
28. Postsecondary Teacher	23%
29. Instructional Coordinator	22%
30. Social Worker	22%

Source: **U.S. Bureau of Labor Statistics *(www.bls.gov).***

For each occupation listed, you'll find six key components explained in detail:

> **KNOCK 'EM DEAD TIP**
> If you are wondering what to do with that degree you already have or are thinking of pursuing, check out the new "What can do I do with this degree?" database at *www.knockemdead.com*.

- **Day-to-Day**: daily nature of the work; general job description.
- **The Big Picture**: the employment outlook through 2018 as projected by the U.S. Department of Labor.
- **Training Track:** the education or training needed to succeed.
- **The Bottom Line:** pros and cons about this career choice.
- **The Paycheck:** average earnings and the highs and lows for the category.
- **Web Links:** websites for national organizations and/or career opportunities in that field.

At the end of the chapter you will also find links to

- bls.gov reports that identify more high-growth jobs using different criteria; you will find some of the jobs mentioned here in each of those lists.
- Useful links to investigate the projected high-growth green jobs and the explosive growth jobs in new technology.

Health Care Professions

Employment in health care will continue to grow through 2016 for many reasons:

1. The number of people in older age groups, who have much-greater-than-average health care needs, will grow. As a result, the demand for health care will increase.
2. Employment in home health care and residential care should increase rapidly as life expectancies rise and as aging children rely more on long-term care facilities.
3. Advances in medical technology will increase the number of people who survive severe illness and injury. Those patients will then need extensive therapy and care.
4. New technology and medical breakthroughs will make it possible to identify and treat conditions that were previously unknown or untreatable.
5. Medical group practices and integrated health systems will become larger and more complex, increasing the need for administrative help.
6. Industry growth also will occur as a result of the shift from inpatient to less expensive outpatient and home health care because of improvements in diagnostic tests and surgical procedures. In addition, many patients would rather be treated and/or recover at home.

Jobs within the typical inpatient hospital scenario are expected to grow the least, while occupations outside that realm, such as pharmacy technicians and home care aides, are expected to grow rapidly. Hospitals will be the slowest growing segment within the health care industry because of efforts to control costs and the increasing popularity of outpatient clinics and other alternative care sites. Because of cost pressures, many health care facilities will lower staffing levels to reduce labor costs. Where patient care demands and regulations allow, health care facilities will substitute lower-paid providers instead and will cross-train their workforces.

Luckily, traditional inpatient hospital positions are no longer the only option for health care workers, so opportunities still abound. If you're seeking a career in the field, you must be willing to work in various settings.

Veterinary Technician/ Technologist

Day-to-Day

Veterinarians use the skills of veterinary technologists and technicians to provide state-of-the-art care to all kinds of animals. Vet technicians and technologists perform many of the same duties for a veterinarian that a nurse would for a physician, such as laboratory tests and clinical procedures. Although specific job duties vary by employer, technicians and technologists often perform the same tasks, despite some differences in formal education and training. Most workers in this occupation are called technicians.

Veterinary techs typically work in a private practice under the supervision of a licensed veterinarian. They conduct various tests and treat and diagnose medical conditions and diseases in animals. Veterinary technicians assisting small-animal practitioners usually care for companion animals, such as cats and dogs, but can also work with mice, sheep, cattle, monkeys, birds, fish, and frogs. Very few technicians work in mixed animal practices, where vets care for both small companion animals and larger, nondomestic animals.

Veterinary technicians may also work in research facilities, where they conduct experiments; record an animal's vital stats; analyze data; and attempt to make improvements in food safety, animal health, and comparative medicine (the field of study concentrating on similarities and differences between veterinary and human medicine).

The Big Picture

Expected to grow 41 percent through 2016.

Excellent job opportunities will likely stem from the limited output of qualified veterinary technicians from two-year programs. The current enrollment rates indicate that there will not be enough technicians to meet anticipated demand.

In addition, pet owners are more affluent and more willing to pay for advanced veterinary care because many consider their pet to be a family member. In addition, the number of pet owners who use veterinary services for their pets is expected to grow through 2016, substantially increasing employment opportunities.

Training Track

Most entry-level veterinary technicians have a two-year associate's degree from a community college accredited by the American Veterinary Medical Association (AVMA; *www.avma.org*). Courses are taught in both clinical and laboratory settings using live animals. About twenty colleges—including Purdue University, State University of New York (SUNY)–Canton, Michigan State University, and California Polytechnic University—offer four-year veterinary technology programs that culminate in a bachelor's degree in veterinary technology. (For a full list, visit *www.avma.org*.) These four-year colleges, in addition to some vocational schools, also offer two-year programs in laboratory animal science.

In 2009, 160 veterinary technology programs in forty-four states were accredited by the AVMA. Nine offered long-distance learning opportunities. Graduation from an AVMA-accredited veterinary technology program allows students to take the credentialing exam in any state in the country.

The Bottom Line

People who love animals find both career and personal satisfaction working with and helping them. However, the work can be physically and emotionally demanding. Vet techs must lift, hold, and restrain animals at times, and may be bitten or scratched as a result. In addition, the work setting can be noisy and cleaning cages can be unpleasant. Veterinary techs who work with abused animals or who euthanize animals may experience emotional stress.

THE PAYCHECK

Median annual earnings	$29,850
Highest 10 percent earned	>$41,490
Lowest 10 percent earned	<$19,770
Best-paying states	New York, Illinois, California, Connecticut, District of Columbia

A weak economy has not hurt the pet industry. According to the American Pet Products Association, Americans will spend approximately $45.4 billion on their pets in 2009. That's a $2.2 billion increase over 2008.

Web Links

www.avma.org
www.veterinarytechnicianschools.com
www.vet.com
www.veterinarytechjobs.com
www.wheretechsconnect.com

Veterinarians

Day-to-Day

Most veterinarians care for the health of pets, livestock, and animals in animal hospitals, zoos, racetracks, and laboratories. They diagnose animal medical conditions; vaccinate; prescribe medication to animals; treat and dress wounds; set fractures; perform surgery; and advise owners about proper feeding, behavior, and breeding.

Other veterinarians are researchers, studying all facets of human and animal health problems in both clinical and laboratory settings.

The Big Picture

Expected to grow 33 percent through 2016.

Pet owners are now more aware of the availability of veterinary care and are more willing to pay for extensive procedures than owners in the past. Veterinary science has caught up to human medicine, so procedures such as hip replacements, kidney transplants, and blood transfusions are now available for animals as well.

Furthermore, pet insurance is rising in popularity, which means that more money will be spent on care.

The majority of veterinarians practice in animal hospitals or clinics and care primarily for companion animals. Faster growth of pet cats is expected to increase the demand for feline veterinary services, while demand for veterinary care for dogs is projected to grow at a more modest pace.

The number of jobs for large-animal veterinarians will not grow as dramatically as jobs for companion-animal vets. Vets may find more job openings in rural areas, because many people do not want to work in isolated areas—however, they are likely to earn less money there. In addition, more pet owners are likely to take advantage of nontraditional veterinary services where a veterinarian may be on staff, such as "doggy day care centers," and pet spas and hotels.

Training Track

Veterinarians need a doctor of veterinary medicine (DVM or VMD) degree from a four-year program at an accredited college of veterinary medicine. There are currently twenty-eight colleges in twenty-six states that meet the accreditation standards set by the Council on Education of the American Veterinary Medical Association (AVMA; *www.avma.org*).

All states and the District of Columbia require that veterinarians be licensed before they can practice, and that they pass a national exam, the North American Veterinary Licensing Exam (*www.nbvme.org*). This eight-hour examination consists of multiple-choice questions and visual materials designed to test diagnostic skills. Beyond those requirements, specific licensing demands differ from state to state.

The Bottom Line

As with vet techs, many people find personal and career satisfaction in caring for animals. However, veterinarians in private or clinical practice often work long hours in a noisy, indoor environment. In addition, they sometimes have to interact with pet owners who are emotionally distressed or demanding. When working with animals that are frightened or in pain, veterinarians risk being bitten, kicked, or scratched. Solo practitioners may work extended and weekend hours, usually responding to emergencies.

There is currently a shortage of food supply veterinarians—those who protect the country's food supply from farm to table. These individuals treat local livestock populations. The supply of vets in this specialized area is expected to fall short by 4 to 5 percent annually through 2016, which makes this choice within the veterinary career category a hot prospect for people entering the field.

THE PAYCHECK

Median annual earnings	$71,990
Highest 10 percent earned	>$133,150
Lowest 10 percent earned	<$43,530
Best-paying states	District of Columbia, Connecticut, New Jersey, California, New York

Web Links

www.avma.org
www.thevetrecruiter.com
www.ihireveterinary.com
www.talktothevet.com
www.veterinarian-schools-report.com

Medical Assistant

Day-to-Day

Medical assistants are responsible for administrative and clinical tasks that help manage the offices of physicians and other health practitioners. (They are not the same as physician assistants, who examine, diagnose, and treat patients under the direct supervision of a physician.) The duties of medical assistants vary depending on the location, the size of the practice, and the practitioner's specialty. In small practices, medical assistants usually handle both administrative (e.g., answering phones, filing) and clinical duties (e.g., taking vital signs) and report to an office manager, physician, or other health practitioner. Those in large practices tend to specialize in a particular area, under the supervision of department administrators. Typical administrative tasks are updating and filing patients' medical records, filling out insurance paperwork, and arranging for hospital admissions and lab tests. They also perform general tasks such as answering phones, greeting patients, scheduling appointments, handling billing and bookkeeping, purchasing supplies and equipment, and keeping waiting and examining rooms neat and clean.

Medical assistants' simple medical responsibilities vary according to what is allowed by state law, but might include taking medical histories, recording vital signs, explaining procedures to patients, preparing patients for examinations, sterilizing medical instruments, and assisting physicians during examinations. Medical assistants may also collect and prepare laboratory specimens and sometimes even perform basic laboratory tests on the premises. They might instruct patients about medications and special diets, prepare and administer medications as directed by a physician, authorize drug refills as directed, send prescriptions to a pharmacy, draw blood, prepare patients for X-rays, take electrocardiograms, remove sutures, and change dressings.

The Big Picture

Expected to grow 34 percent through 2016.

Most medical assistants (62 percent) work in doctors' offices; 12 percent work in hospitals, including inpatient and outpatient facilities; and 11 percent work in offices of other health practitioners. As the health care industry expands because of medical advances and the aging of the baby boomer generation, there will be an increased need for all health care workers. Helping to drive job growth is the increasing number of group practices, clinics, and other health care facilities that need support personnel, particularly medical assistants who can handle both administrative and clinical duties. In addition, medical assistants work primarily in outpatient settings, a rapidly growing sector of the health care industry. Job opportunities should be excellent, particularly for those with formal training or experience and certification.

Training Track

Some medical assistants get on-the-job training, but they are expected to at least have a high school diploma or the equivalent. To be more employable, however, many complete one-year or two-year programs. Postsecondary medical assisting programs are offered in vocational-technical high schools, postsecondary vocational schools, and community and junior colleges. One-year programs yield a certificate or diploma, and two-year programs end in an associate's degree. Courses include anatomy, physiology, medical terminology, accounting, and insurance processing. Students also learn the hands-on medical skills: laboratory techniques, clinical and diagnostic procedures, pharmaceutical principles, the administration of medications, and first aid. Studying patient relations, medical law, and ethics is a plus.

Employers prefer to hire experienced workers or those who are certified. Although not required, certification indicates that a medical assistant meets certain standards of competence. There are various associations that award certification credentials to medical assistants, such as the American Association of Medical Assistants (*www.aama-ntl.org*). Some medical assistants become certified in a clinical specialty of interest to them.

The Bottom Line

Although medical assistants are dependent on practitioners and work under a physician who is responsible for their actions, they are still subject to individual liability for providing medical care. Medical assistants should consider obtaining an insurance rider (either through their employer or on their own) to protect them in the event of a lawsuit.

THE PAYCHECK

Median annual earnings	$26,290
Highest 10 percent earned	>$36,840
Lowest 10 percent earned	<$18,860
Best-paying states	District of Columbia, Alaska, Massachusetts, Connecticut, Washington

Web Links

www.medical-assistant-careers.com
www.aama-ntl.org
www.amtl.com
www.medicalassistant.net
www.medicalassistantjobsnow.com

Pharmacy Technician

Day-to-Day

Pharmacy technicians help licensed pharmacists provide medication and other health care products to patients. Technicians usually help by counting tablets and labeling bottles, as well as by answering phones, stocking shelves, and operating cash registers.

Pharmacy technicians who work in retail or mail-order pharmacies have varying responsibilities, depending on state rules and regulations. They usually receive written or electronic prescriptions from patients, or from a doctor's office. First, they verify that information on the prescription is complete and accurate. Next, they prepare the prescription by retrieving, counting, pouring/weighing, and sometimes mixing the medication.

In hospitals, nursing homes, and assisted-living facilities, technicians often have added responsibilities, including reading patients' charts and preparing the appropriate medication from the directions given. After the pharmacist checks the prescription for accuracy, the pharmacy technician may deliver it to the patient.

The Big Picture

Expected to grow 32 percent through 2016.

The increased number of middle-aged and elderly people—who use more prescription drugs than younger people due to health problems associating with aging—will spur demand for technicians in the near future. In addition, more and more drugs will appear on the market as doctors and scientists discover new treatments—and more pharmacy techs will be needed to administer those drugs. Many local pharmacies are doubling as patient-care centers, so pharmacy technicians will likely assume responsibility for some of the more routine tasks previously performed by pharmacists, including interacting with customers.

Training Track

Although most pharmacy technicians receive informal on-the-job training, employers prefer candidates who have completed formal training and certification. However, there are currently few state and no federal requirements for formal training or certification of pharmacy technicians. Two organizations, the Pharmacy Technician Certification Board (*www.ptcb.org*) and the Institute for the Certification of Pharmacy Technicians (*www.nationaltechexam.org*), administer national certification examinations. Certification is voluntary in most states, but is required by some states and employers. (Some technicians are hired without formal training, but under the condition that they will obtain certification by an agreed-upon deadline.) To be eligible for either exam, candidates must have a high school diploma or GED, no felony convictions of any kind within five years of applying, and no drug- or pharmacy-related felony convictions at any point.

Under both programs, technicians must be recertified every two years. Recertification requires twenty hours of continuing education (with at least one hour in pharmacy law) within the two-year certification period.

The Bottom Line

Drug dispensing machines may change the nature of the pharmacy tech's job. These machines increase productivity and attempt to ensure accuracy by counting pills and placing them into prescription containers. These machines currently are only used for the most common medications, however, and their effect on employment should be minimal.

Mathematics, spelling, and reading skills are important to this occupation. Pharmacy techs must be precise; details are sometimes a matter of life and death, and may result in job stress.

THE PAYCHECK

Median annual earnings	$28,500
Highest 10 percent earned	>$39,480
Lowest 10 percent earned	<$19,270
Best-paying states	Alaska, California, Washington, Hawaii, District of Columbia

Web Links

www.ptch.org
www.nationaltechexam.org
www.pharmacytechnician.org
www.pharmacytech.org
www.pharmacyjobs.rxcareercenter.com

Dental Hygienists

Day-to-Day

Dental hygienists clean teeth, examine gums, and record the possible presence of diseases or abnormalities for a dentist to investigate. They also teach patients how to practice good oral hygiene and provide other preventive dental care, possibly including taking X-rays.

In some states, hygienists are allowed to administer general anesthetics; in other states, they can only administer local anesthetics using syringes. Some states also allow hygienists to place and carve filling materials, temporary fillings, and periodontal dressings; remove sutures; and smooth and polish metal restorations.

The Big Picture

Expected to grow 30 percent through 2016.

Job prospects are expected to remain excellent in this field because of population growth, older people increasingly retaining more teeth, and the continued focus on preventative dental care. To meet this demand, facilities will employ more hygienists per office. In addition, as dentists' workloads increase, they are expected to have hygienists perform preventive dental care, such as cleaning, so that they may devote their own time to more complex procedures.

More than half of dental hygienists work part-time; flexible scheduling is an attractive feature of this job.

Training Track

Dental hygienists need a minimum of an associate's degree or certificate in dental hygiene in order to practice in a private dental office. A bachelor's or master's degree is usually required for research, teaching, or clinical practice in public or school health programs. In order to get into a degree program, candidates need a high school diploma and college entrance test scores. Some dental hygiene programs also require applicants to have completed at least one year of college courses. Specific entrance requirements vary from one school to another. Most dental hygiene programs grant an associate's degree, although some also offer a certificate, a bachelor's degree, or a master's degree.

Dental hygienists must be licensed by the state in which they practice. Nearly all states require candidates to graduate from an accredited dental hygiene school and pass both a written and clinical examination. The American Dental Association's Joint Commission on National Dental Examinations (*www.ada.org*) administers the written examination, which is accepted by all states and the District of Columbia, while state or regional testing agencies administer the clinical examination. In addition, most states require candidates to pass an examination on the legal aspects of dental hygiene practice.

The Bottom Line

Dental hygienists must have good manual dexterity because they need to move sharp dental instruments within a patient's mouth. In addition, hygienists can be exposed to infectious diseases, and may suffer backache from leaning forward to look inside patients' mouths.

THE PAYCHECK

Median annual earnings	$66,950
Highest 10 percent earned	$91,470
Lowest 10 percent earned	$44,180
Best-paying states	Alaska, Washington, California, Oregon, Nevada

Web Links

www.adha.org
www.dhed.net
www.dentalassistantjobs.com
www.dentalhygienistjobs.com
www.dentalhygienists.com

According to the American Dental Hygienists' Association's website (*www.adha.org*), two states—Colorado and Washington—have independent practice laws that allow registered dental hygienists to practice without the supervision of a dentist. These states acknowledge that dental hygienists, by virtue of their comprehensive education and clinical preparation, are capable of providing safe and effective preventive oral health care services to the public without dental supervision.

Physical Therapists

Day-to-Day

Physical therapists (PTs) help patients restore a variety of physical functions, improve their range of mobility, relieve pain, and prevent or limit permanent physical disabilities. They work with accident victims and individuals with disabling conditions such as lower-back pain, arthritis, heart disease, fractures, and head injuries.

When they begin working with a patient, PTs examine medical history and then measure range of motion, balance, posture, muscle strength, respiration, and motor function. When they have assessed the patient's condition, they develop a treatment plan and outline its projected result.

The treatment plan often includes daily exercises, especially for patients who have been immobilized or who lack flexibility, strength, or endurance. PTs encourage patients to use their muscles in various ways to improve their conditions. The goal is to improve how an individual functions at work and at home.

The Big Picture

Expected to grow 27 percent through 2016.

The increasing number of elderly people in the population will drive the demand for physical therapy services because older people are more vulnerable to chronic and debilitating conditions that require therapeutic services. Also, members of the baby boom generation are entering the prime age for heart attacks and strokes, which usually require cardiac and physical rehabilitation.

In addition, more children than ever will use physical therapy as scientific advances save the lives of newborns who have a variety of serious conditions. Job opportunities will be good, especially in acute hospital, rehabilitation, and orthopedic settings.

Training Track

In order to practice, a PT usually needs a master's degree from an accredited physical therapy program and a state license, which is awarded after the candidate passes national and state examinations. The Commission on Accreditation in Physical Therapy Education (*www.apta.org*) is the only agency that grants accreditation, and it only accredits master's degree and doctoral degree programs. In the future, a doctoral degree might be the required entry-level degree. Master's degree programs typically last two years, and doctoral degree programs last three years. Specific eligibility requirements for licensure vary by state.

The Bottom Line

PTs work in hospitals, clinics, and private offices that have special equipment. They also treat patients in hospital rooms, homes, or schools. Therapists often have to stoop, kneel, crouch, lift, and stand for long periods of time—making the job quite physically demanding. In addition, PTs often must manage heavy equipment and lift patients or help them move.

According to the U.S. Bureau of Labor Statistics, the number of physical therapy positions is greater than the number of practicing PTs because some of them work part-time for two or more jobs. For example, a therapist may work in a private practice and in another health care facility.

THE PAYCHECK

Median annual earnings	$66,200
Highest 10 percent earned	>$94,810
Lowest 10 percent earned	<$46,510
Best-paying states	Nevada, California, New Jersey, Rhode Island, Illinois

Confused about the difference between a physical therapist (PT) and an occupational therapist (OT)? A PT helps a patient rehabilitate his body from surgery or a specific injury, working to rebuild muscle groups. An OT focuses on helping a patient regain daily life skills, such as dressing, feeding, and living independently.

Web Links

www.apta.org
www.fsbpt.org
www.physical-therapy-jobs.net
www.ptjobs.com
www.physicaltherapy.com

Physician Assistants

Day-to-Day

Physician assistants (PAs) practice medicine under the supervision of physicians and surgeons. (They should not be confused with medical assistants, who perform routine clinical and clerical tasks; see earlier for more about that occupation.) Physicians delegate certain work to PAs, such as diagnostic, therapeutic, and preventive health care services. PAs conduct medical histories, examine and treat patients, order and analyze lab tests and X-rays, and make diagnoses. They also suture, splint, and cast patients' minor injuries. PAs also record progress notes, teach patients about conditions or behaviors, and answer patients' questions. PAs may prescribe some medications in all states, the District of Columbia, Guam, and the Commonwealth of the Northern Mariana Islands.

In some cases (such as in rural areas or inner city clinics, where the supervising physician may only be in the office one or two days a week), PAs may be the principal care providers in the practice. In those cases, the PA confers with the supervising physician and other medical professionals as needed and as required by law. Some PAs even make house calls or go to hospitals and nursing care facilities to check on patients, after which they report back to the physician about the patient's condition or progress. The supervising physician and state laws dictate exactly what a PA's duties will be at a certain practice.

The Big Picture

Expected to grow 39 percent through 2016.

Both private practice physicians and health care facilities are expected to employ more PAs to provide primary care and to assist with medical and surgical procedures because PAs are cost-effective. They earn less than full physicians, yet can effectively diagnose and treat a wide variety of common ailments and conditions. Job prospects are projected to be promising, especially in rural and inner-city clinics, because those settings have difficulty attracting physicians. Opportunities will be best in states that allow PAs a wider scope of practice. States' laws change frequently; visit *www.aapa.org/state-map* to view recent information by state.

Training Track

All states and the District of Columbia require PAs to complete an accredited, formal education program and pass a national licensure exam. PA programs usually last at least two years. Admission requirements vary by program, but many require at least two years of college and some health care experience. Most programs are in schools of allied health, academic health centers, medical schools, or four-year colleges; a few are offered by community colleges, the military, or large hospitals. Many accredited PA programs have clinical teaching affiliations with medical schools.

All states and the District of Columbia have legislation governing the qualifications or practice of PAs, who must pass the Physician Assistant National Certifying Examination. This test is administered by the National Commission on Certification of Physician Assistants (NCCPA; *www.nccpa.net*) and is open only to graduates of accredited PA programs. Only those who pass the examination may use the credential "Physician Assistant–Certified." To remain certified, PAs must complete 100 hours of continuing medical education every two years and pass a recertification exam every six years.

The Bottom Line

PAs can take on added responsibilities and earn higher paychecks as their knowledge base and experience grows. However, by the very nature of the profession, PAs always are supervised by physicians and while they often function as a fill-in to a physician, they will never have the same earning power or the prestige of the position.

Besides working in traditional doctors' offices, PAs should also find opportunities in institutional settings such as hospitals, academic medical centers, public clinics, and prisons. PAs may find open positions at inpatient teaching hospitals. This trend may take hold as facilities reduce the number of hours physician residents are permitted to work and instead use PAs to supply some of the medical services those residents would have offered.

THE PAYCHECK

Median annual earnings	$74,980
Highest 10 percent earned	>$102,230
Lowest 10 percent earned	<$43,000
Best-paying states	Alaska, Nevada, Connecticut, Washington, New Jersey

Web Links

www.aapa.org
www.nccpa.net
www.physicianassistantjobs.com
www.paworld.net
www.physicianassistant.com

Radiation Therapists

Day-to-Day

Radiation therapy is primarily used to treat cancer in the human body. Radiation therapists use machines called linear accelerators to administer radiation treatment to patients. These machines project intense X-rays at cancer cells. As the X-rays collide with human tissue, they produce highly energized ions that can shrink and sometimes eliminate cancerous tumors. This type of therapy is sometimes used as the sole treatment for cancer, but is usually used in conjunction with chemotherapy or surgery. For that reason, radiation therapists often work as part of a patient's oncology team.

As they administer the treatments, radiation therapists keep detailed patient records, which include the dose used per treatment, the total amount of radiation used to date, the area treated, and the patient's reactions. Radiation oncologists and dosimetrists (who calculate and manage radiation doses for each patient) review these records to measure the effectiveness of the treatment plan, to monitor the total amount of radiation exposure that the patient has received, and to minimize side effects.

The Big Picture

Expected to grow 25 percent through 2016.

Current statistics for the prevalence of cancer in the United States are striking. The American Cancer Society (ACS; *www.cancer.org*) estimates that men in the United States have approximately a 1 in 2 lifetime risk of developing cancer; women's lifetime risk is approximately 1 in 3. The ACS also notes that about 77 percent of all cancers are diagnosed in people aged fifty-five and older. Because an increasing percentage of the U.S. population is in this older age group, the number of people needing cancer treatment is expected to increase and thus spur demand for radiation therapists. In addition, as radiation technology advances and is able to treat more types of cancer, radiation therapy will be prescribed more often.

Training Track

Radiation therapists need a bachelor's degree, associate's degree, or certificate in radiation therapy. Many states also require radiation therapists to be licensed. Some states, as well as many employers, require that radiation therapists be certified by the American Registry of Radiologic Technologists (ARRT, *www.arrt.org*). To become ARRT-certified, an applicant must complete an accredited radiation therapy program, adhere to ARRT ethical standards, and pass the ARRT certification examination. The examination and accredited academic programs teach radiation protection and quality assurance, clinical concepts in radiation oncology, treatment planning and delivery, and patient care and education.

The Bottom Line

Though being a radiation therapist can be very rewarding when patients' health improves, it can also be stressful. Also, radiation therapists are obviously exposed to radioactive materials regularly; they must ensure that they are not exposed to dangerous levels of radiation. Following standard safety procedures can prevent overexposure.

THE PAYCHECK

Median annual earnings	$66,170
Highest 10 percent earned	>$92,110
Lowest 10 percent earned	<$44,840
Best-paying states	New Jersey, California, Montana, Washington, Oregon

Web Links

www.arrt.org
www.asrt.org
www.radworking.com
www.radiationtherapist.org
www.ihireradiology.com

Surgical Technician

Day-to-Day

Surgical technologists, who are also referred to as scrubs, surgical technicians, or operating room technicians, assist with surgeries under the supervision of surgeons, registered nurses, or other medical personnel. Surgical technologists are members of operating room teams, and work alongside surgeons, anesthesiologists, and nurses.

Before an operation, surgical techs prepare the operating room by compiling and arranging surgical instruments and equipment and sterile solutions. Techs also prep patients by cleaning and disinfecting incision sites. They also transport patients to the operating room, help position them on the operating table, and then cover them with sterile surgical drapes.

During surgeries, techs pass instruments and other supplies to surgeons and surgeon assistants, operate lights and suction machines, and observe patients' vital signs. They may hold retractors; cut sutures; and help count sponges, needles, supplies, and instruments. After the surgery, they arrange for specimens to be tested in labs and help apply dressings to the incision site.

The Big Picture

Expected to grow 24 percent through 2016.

The number of surgical procedures is expected to rise as the population grows and ages. In addition, technological advances, such as fiber optics and laser technology, will pave the way for new surgical procedures to be performed. More surgical techs will be needed to assist with this increase in volume.

Training Track

Surgical technologists must enroll in programs offered by community and junior colleges, vocational schools, universities, hospitals, and the military. Programs last from nine to twenty-four months and lead to a certificate, diploma, or associate's degree.

Most employers prefer to hire certified technologists. Technologists may obtain voluntary professional certification from the Liaison Council on Certification for the Surgical Technologist by graduating from a Commission on Accreditation of Allied Health Education Programs–accredited program (*www.caahep.org*) and passing a national certification examination. Once requirements are met, they can use the Certified Surgical Technologist (CST) designation. To maintain certification, surgical techs must participate in continuing education or re-examinations.

Certification also may be granted by the National Center for Competency Testing (NCCT; *www.ncctinc.com*). To qualify to take the exam, candidates must have completed an accredited training program; a two-year hospital on-the-job training program; or seven years of experience working in the field. After passing the exam, individuals may use the designation Tech in Surgery-Certified, TS-C (NCCT). This certification must be renewed every five years through either continuing education or re-examination.

The Bottom Line

Surgical techs must stand for long periods of time and remain alert during surgery. At times, they may be exposed to communicable diseases as well as unpleasant sights, odors, and materials.

Surgical technologists need manual dexterity to handle instruments quickly. They also must be conscientious, orderly, and emotionally stable in order to handle the demands of the stressful operating room environment.

"Scrubs" got their start in the military because nurses were not permitted on the battlefield or on combat ships during wartime. After the Korean War, the shortage of operating room nurses led army medics and navy corpsmen to careers as operating room technicians. In 1973, the official title of the position was changed to surgical technologist.

THE PAYCHECK

Median annual earnings	$36,080
Highest 10 percent earned	>$51,140
Lowest 10 percent earned	<$25,490
Best-paying states	District of Columbia, California, Maryland, Nevada, Minnesota

Web Links

www.nsaa.net
www.surgicaltechsuccess.com
www.getsurgicaljobs.com
www.ast.org

Athletic Trainer

Day-to-Day

Athletic trainers help people prevent, treat, and rehab musculoskeletal injuries. They work with everyone from professional athletes to industrial workers. Because these trainers are sometimes "first responders" when injuries occur (such as during a sports game), they must be able to recognize, evaluate, and assess injuries and provide immediate care when needed. Athletic trainers are not the same as fitness trainers or personal trainers, who are not health care workers, but rather train people to become physically fit.

Aside from treating injuries, athletic trainers often help people prevent injuries by advising the use of protective gear such as tape, bandages, and braces. They also educate people on what they should do to avoid putting themselves at risk for injuries, such as proper stretching routines.

Athletic trainers work under the supervision of a licensed physician and in a team with other health care providers. The level of medical supervision varies, depending on the setting.

The Big Picture

Expected to grow 37 percent through 2016.

Job growth will be concentrated in the health care industry, including hospitals and private practices. The demand for health care in general should grow dramatically because of medical breakthroughs, an increased emphasis on preventive care, and changes in population (a greater percentage of the population will be older). Athletic trainers will benefit because they are a cost-effective way to expand the services offered at a particular practice. Athletic trainers are now more widely accepted as health professionals thanks to more standardized licensing and regulation.

Fitness and recreational sports centers also will provide many new jobs, as these establishments become more popular and increase their client bases. The number of opportunities with sports teams—though perhaps the most famous of athletic trainer jobs—will not change much, however. Most professional sports teams and colleges and universities already have complete athletic training staffs.

Training Track

According to the National Athletic Trainers Association (*www.nata.org*), 68 percent of athletic trainers have a master's or doctoral degree. Athletic trainers may need a master's or higher degree to be eligible for some positions (especially those in colleges and universities), and to increase their advancement opportunities. Because some positions in schools involve teaching academic classes along with traditional athletic trainer duties, candidates may need a teaching certificate or license as well.

Nearly all states require athletic trainers to be certified by the Board of Certification, Inc. (BOC; *www.bocatc.org*). For certification, athletic trainers need a bachelor's degree from an accredited athletic training program and must pass a rigorous examination. To maintain their certification, trainers must participate in continuing education courses. In states where licensure is not required, certification is voluntary but will probably be helpful for job seekers and those in the field who want career advancement.

The Bottom Line

Athletic trainers in nonsport settings generally have an established schedule—usually about forty to fifty hours per week—with nights and weekends off. Athletic trainers who work for sports teams or facilities, however, have more varied schedules and work more hours per week. These athletic trainers must be present for team practices and games, which often take place on evenings and weekends, and their schedules can change on short notice when events have to be rescheduled due to bad weather. As a result, athletic trainers in sports settings may regularly work six or seven days per week, including late hours.

In high schools, athletic trainers who also teach may work sixty to seventy hours a week, or more. In National Collegiate Athletic Association Division I colleges and universities, athletic trainers generally work with one particular sports team; when that team's sport is in season, they work at least fifty to sixty hours a week.

Some athletic trainers may find the position stressful and be affected by the pressure to win that is associated with competitive sports.

THE PAYCHECK

Median annual earnings	$36,560
Highest 10 percent earned	>$57,580
Lowest 10 percent earned	<$21,940
Best-paying states	District of Columbia, Rhode Island, Illinois, Hawaii, Tennessee

Web Links

www.nata.org
www.bocatc.org
www.athletictrainer.com
www.collegeathletictrainer.org
www.nasm.org

Registered Nurses

Day-to-Day

Registered nurses (RNs) treat patients, educate them about medical conditions, and provide advice and emotional support to patients' family members. They work in all medical specialties and in a variety of settings (hospitals, clinics, nursing care facilities, private practices, and so on). RNs are responsible for a wide range of duties, including recording patients' medical histories and symptoms, helping perform diagnostic tests and analyzing the results, giving treatment and medications, and following up with patients' rehabilitation.

RNs can specialize in one or more areas of patient care or the medical field, including these four most common ways: work setting or type of treatment (such as operating room nurses), specific health conditions (such as oncology nurses), working with one or more organs or body system types (such as cardiac nurses), or working with a specific type of patient (such as geriatric nurses). Some RNs may combine specialties, such as pediatric oncology nurses, who deal with children and adolescents who have cancer.

The Big Picture

Expected to grow 22.2 percent through 2016.

Job opportunities for registered nurses are expected to be excellent through 2016, but may vary by type of employer and location. Still, registered nurses are projected to generate 587,000 new jobs, among the largest number of new jobs for any occupation. Additionally, hundreds of thousands of job openings will result from the need to replace experienced nurses who leave the occupation. Some experts predict that by 2025, there could be a vacancy rate of 40 percent or higher. Also, an aging baby boom population with longer life spans will require nursing care as they age.

Training Track

Registered nurses usually enter the field by obtaining a bachelor's degree, an associate's degree, or a diploma from an approved nursing program. Nurses most commonly complete an associate's degree or bachelor's degree program and then must complete a national licensing examination (the NCLEX-RN) in order to work in any state or territory or the District of Columbia. Nurses may be licensed in more than one state, either by taking that state's exam or by one state endorsing another state's license. Further training or education can qualify nurses to work in specialty areas and may improve career advancement.

The Bottom Line

Many nurses find the career immensely rewarding. However, the nursing field is rife with challenges. Nurses are likely to come into close contact with patients with infectious diseases and with toxic, harmful, or potentially hazardous materials and medications. They are also susceptible to back injury when moving patients, shocks from electrical equipment, and hazards posed by compressed gases and accidental needle pricks. RNs also may suffer emotional stress from caring for patients (and their families) who are suffering, the need to make critical decisions, and ethical dilemmas.

THE PAYCHECK

Median annual earnings	$57,280
Highest 10 percent earned	>$83,440
Lowest 10 percent earned	<$40,250
Best-paying states	California, Massachusetts, Hawaii, Maryland, New York

Web Links

www.nursingworld.com
www.nsna.org
www.aacn.nche.edu
www.nurse.com
www.nursingspectrum.com

The U.S. Bureau of Labor Statistics published in the November 2007 *Monthly Labor Review* that more than 1 million new and replacement nurses will be needed by 2016. Government analysts project that more than 587,000 new nursing positions will be created through 2016, making nursing the nation's top profession in terms of projected job growth.

Pharmacist

Day-to-Day

Pharmacists distribute prescription drugs to patients and advise their patients, as well as physicians and other health practitioners, on the selection, dosages, interactions, and side effects of medications. Compounding—the actual mixing of ingredients to form medications—is nowadays a small part of a pharmacist's practice, because most medicines are produced by pharmaceutical companies in a standard dosage and drug delivery form. The majority of pharmacists work in a retail drugstore or in a health care facility, such as a hospital, nursing home, mental health institution, or clinic.

Pharmacists in retail pharmacies dispense medications, give patients information about their prescriptions and about over-the-counter medications, and advise physicians about patients' treatments. They also provide information on durable medical equipment or home health care supplies. In addition, they may fill out insurance paperwork.

The Big Picture

Expected to grow 22 percent through 2016.

The increasing numbers of middle-aged and elderly people—who use more prescription drugs than younger people—will continue to spur demand for pharmacists. In addition, pharmaceutical companies are likely to bring more drug products to market, and insurance plans will begin covering more and more types of prescription drugs.

As the use of prescription drugs increases, demand for pharmacists will grow in most settings. Demand will also increase as cost-conscious insurers, in an attempt to improve preventative care, use pharmacists in areas such as patient education and vaccination.

Demand is also increasing in managed care organizations, where pharmacists analyze trends and patterns in medication use, and in pharmacoeconomics, which is the financial analysis of different drug therapies. New jobs also are being created in disease management—the development of new methods for curing and controlling diseases—and in sales and marketing. Rapid growth is also expected in pharmacy informatics—the use of information technology to improve patient care.

Training Track

Pharmacists need a Pharm.D. degree from an accredited college or school of pharmacy. The Pharm.D. degree has replaced the bachelor of pharmacy degree, which is no longer offered. To be admitted to a Pharm.D. program, an applicant must have completed at least two years of undergraduate study, although most have completed three or more years. About 70 percent of Pharm.D. programs require applicants to take the Pharmacy College Admissions Test (PCAT; *www.pcatweb.info*).

Besides graduating from an accredited school, a pharmacist also needs a license to practice pharmacy in all states and territories and the District of Columbia. All states, U.S. territories, and the District of Columbia require the North American Pharmacist Licensure Exam (NAPLEX; *www.nabp.net*), which tests pharmacy skills and knowledge.

The Bottom Line

The American Federation for Pharmaceutical Education reports that more than 8,000 vacancies exist in retail pharmacies, hospitals, and clinics. Demand is currently outpacing supply, which means that pharmacist job candidates should be well positioned for employment. The job can be stressful because of the detail orientation required.

THE PAYCHECK

Median annual earnings	$94,520
Highest 10 percent earned	>$119,480
Lowest 10 percent earned	<$67,860
Best-paying states	California, Maine, New Hampshire, Alaska, Minnesota

Web Links

www.aacp.org
www.ashp.org
www.aphanet.org
www.rxcareercenter.com
www.pharmacistjobs.com

Gallup's 2008 Annual Survey of the Honesty and Ethics of Professions ranked how the American public feels about the integrity of certain members of the workforce. For the seventh consecutive year, nurses earned the highest accolades. A full 84 percent of Americans feel their ethical standards are high or very high. In the number two spot were pharmacists/druggists, with 70 percent of the public ranking their ethical standards as high or very high.

Science and Technology Professions

Four types of technologies have invaded and impacted every corner of academia, industry, and commerce. They have ushered in a new era, and revolutionized the way we communicate and interact with each other.

- Biotechnology is changing the way we take care of our health and our food sources.
- Environmental technology is changing the way we take care of our environment and nurture our resources.
- Engineering technology is changing the way we build our manufacturing and supply systems.
- Information technology is changing the ways we increase our knowledge, communications, and competitiveness.

These technologies often work hand in hand with each other to achieve new breakthroughs, so it has become more and more difficult to define exactly where one technology stops and another begins. The same applies to job titles in these fields. Job titles such as engineer, scientist, and analyst are gradually becoming interchangeable, depending largely on the employer, context, and application of the work.

There's never been a better time to be a computer specialist. While computer technology continues to become increasingly sophisticated, so have the population's needs. Significant growth is still expected in this industry as organizations look for more efficient communications systems, improved Internet and wireless technologies, and tighter data security.

Almost 1 million new jobs are expected to be created over the next decade, making information technology the fastest growing profession of all career disciplines. In the corporate environment, the focus for the next decade will be on designing and adopting more sophisticated technologies, such as the expansion of client/server networking environments to facilitate the sharing of information; enhancement of communication systems, electronic commerce, and data storage systems to make them more efficient and secure; and "cybersecurity" to protect intellectual property and sensitive information, such as customer data.

The development of personal mobile devices and falling prices of computer hardware and software have made technology more accessible than ever before. These factors will drive a need for specialists and analysts who can integrate wireless/mobile technologies into existing networks.

Almost all industries will see an increase in employment of computer professionals over the next decade. Opportunities in the information sector will mainly be in computer systems design and related services, primarily software publishers and data processing and related industries. Self-employment opportunities for computer professionals have never been better. Entrepreneurial network systems and data communications analysts especially may find success in self-employment.

As was the case a decade ago, if you plan a career in information technology, you cannot be someone who likes the status quo; change and volatility are still very much a part of this industry. Your goal will probably not be to find a lifetime employer, but to maintain your employability. This will require constant upgrading of your skills on your own time and an awareness of industry trends. Interpersonal skills applied with nontechnical people will be paramount to your success, and, because of the increasing influence of overseas markets, languages and multicultural awareness will put anyone's career in good stead.

Computer Software Engineer

Day-to-Day

Computer software engineers apply the principles of computer science and mathematics to the design, development, testing, and evaluation of the software that make computers run. The exact job specifications of computer software engineers change rapidly due to constant improvements in technology.

Software engineers can be involved in the design and development of many types of software, including computer games; word processing and business programs; operating systems and network configuration; and compilers, which convert programs to machine language for execution on a computer.

Their job begins by analyzing users' needs, and then designing, testing, and developing software to meet those needs. In order to execute their plan, they create the detailed sets of instructions that tell the computer exactly what to do. They also may be responsible for converting these instructions into a computer language (coding), but programmers usually handle this task. Computer software engineers must be experts in operating systems to ensure that all facets of their plan will work and interact properly.

Computer *systems* software engineers coordinate the construction, maintenance, and expansion of an organization's computer systems. Based on the organization's needs, they coordinate each department's priorities—ordering, inventory, billing, and payroll for example—and make suggestions based on their expertise. They also might set up the organization's intranets—the networks that link computers within the organization and ease communication among various departments.

The Big Picture

Expected to grow 36 percent through 2016.

About 324,000 new computer software engineer jobs are expected to be generated by 2016, one of the largest employment increases of any occupation. Businesses will continue to compete against each other to boast the most advanced, secure, and user-friendly computer systems, so computer software engineers will be in demand. Demand will also increase as computer networking continues to grow, especially for Internet, intranet, and web applications. Likewise, electronic data-processing systems in business, telecommunications, and government will become more sophisticated and complex and will therefore need oversight by a computer software engineer.

Increased Internet usage, the proliferation of websites, and wireless technology also spawn new products and create worker demand. As individuals and businesses rely more on handheld computers and wireless networks, computer software engineers will need to integrate current computer systems with this new technology. Additionally, concerns over "cybersecurity" should result in businesses and government investing heavily in software that protects their networks and vital electronic infrastructure from attack. The expansion of cybersecurity will lead to an increased need for computer engineers to design and develop software and systems that will integrate with already existing older systems.

Training Track

Most employers prefer applicants who have at least a bachelor's degree (usually in computer science or software engineering) and experience with a variety of computer systems and technologies. Systems software engineers often study computer science or computer information systems. Those pursuing more complex or higher-level jobs will probably need a graduate degree. Some software vendors offer certification and training programs in their particular system, but most experts say that program certification alone is not sufficient for the majority of software engineering jobs.

The Bottom Line

Like other workers who spend long hours in front of a computer, software engineers are susceptible to eyestrain, back discomfort, and hand and wrist problems such as carpal tunnel syndrome.

Outsourcing is a concern in this industry. Firms may cut costs by shifting operations to foreign countries with lower wages and highly educated workers. However, jobs in software engineering are less prone to being off-shored than are jobs in other computer specialties, because software engineering requires constant communication, knowledge of the company's valuable intellectual property, and intense research and development.

THE PAYCHECK

Median annual earnings	$92,430
Highest 10 percent earned	>$135,780
Lowest 10 percent earned	<$57,810
Best-paying states	Massachusetts, California, Maryland, Virginia, Colorado

Web Links

www.softwarengineer.org
www.acm.org
www.computer.org
www.Dice.com

According to the Entertainment Software Association, computer and video game companies directly and indirectly employ more than 80,000 people in thirty-one states. Projected growth for 2009 is 250,000 jobs. The average salary is $92,300.

Computer Scientist and Database Administrator

Day-to-Day

Computer scientists are distinguished from other employees in computer technologies by the higher level of theoretical expertise and innovation they apply to complex problems and the creation or application of new technology. Computer scientists may research new theories, programming languages, or hardware. Some researchers work on multidisciplinary projects, such as virtual reality, human-computer interaction, or robots. They may work on a team with electrical engineers and other specialists.

Database administrators work with database software and determine ways to organize and store data. They may create new databases or update existing ones by integrating data from outdated systems into a new system. They also test and coordinate modifications to the system when needed and troubleshoot problems. Because many databases are connected to the Internet, database administrators also plan and coordinate security measures with network administrators. With the growing volume of sensitive data and the increasing interconnectedness of computer networks, data integrity, backup systems, and database security have become increasingly important aspects of the job.

The Big Picture

Expected to grow 37 percent through 2016.

Overall, job increases will be driven by very rapid growth in computer systems design and related services, which is projected to be one of the fastest-growing industries in the U.S. economy through 2016. Demand for database administrators will grow as companies' data becomes more complex and sophisticated, and as cybersecurity becomes increasingly important. Expansion of electronic commerce—doing business on the Internet—and the continuing need to build and maintain databases that store companies' critical proprietary information are fueling demand for database administrators.

Training Track

Jobs in these fields usually require at least a bachelor's degree; however, some jobs may require only a two-year degree. Relevant work experience also is very important. For more complex jobs, employers prefer candidates with graduate degrees. Most computer scientist positions require a PhD, as their main job function is research.

For database administrator positions, most employers seek applicants who have bachelor's degrees in computer science, information science, or management information systems (MIS).

Job seekers can better their chances by getting certified in relevant areas. Most certifications are offered through private companies, with many related to specific products. Many employers regard these certifications as the industry standard.

The Bottom Line

Due to spending long periods in front of a computer, computer scientists and database administrators are susceptible to eyestrain, back discomfort, and hand and wrist problems such as carpal tunnel syndrome or cumulative trauma disorder.

THE PAYCHECK

Median annual earnings of computer scientists	$93,950
Highest 10 percent earned	>$144,880
Lowest 10 percent earned	<$53,590
Median annual earnings of database administrators	$64,670
Highest 10 percent earned	>$103,010
Lowest 10 percent earned	<$37,350
Best-paying states for both positions	Maryland, California, New York, New Jersey, Virginia

Web Links

www.acm.org
www.computer.org
www.aitp.org
www.certdatabaseadministrator.com
www.itjobs.net
www.tech-centric.net

Computer Systems Analyst

Day-to-Day

Computer systems analysts help organizations use technology effectively and incorporate new aspects of technology into their existing systems. They may design and develop new computer systems to fill a company's needs by configuring new hardware and software, or they may upgrade an existing system. Computer systems analysts also fix problems with an organization's computers.

Most systems analysts work with a specific genre of computer systems—for example, business/accounting/financial systems or scientific/engineering systems—and become an expert in that particular system. Analysts who specialize in helping an organization select the proper system software and infrastructure are called "system architects." Analysts who specialize in developing and fine-tuning systems often are known as "systems designers."

When starting a project, systems analysts consult varied members of the organization to define the system's goals. Next, they devise a plan based on structured analysis, data modeling, information engineering, and mathematical model building to make sure their plans are efficient and complete. They also may prepare cost-benefit and return-on-investment analyses to help management decide whether the project would be cost-effective.

If a system is approved, systems analysts then narrow down what computer hardware and software is needed to set it up. Before the system goes "live," they coordinate tests and try out different aspects of the system to troubleshoot initial problems. Next, they prepare specifications, flow charts, and process diagrams for computer programmers to follow; then they work with programmers to "debug," or eliminate errors, from the system. Systems analysts who do more in-depth testing may be called "software quality assurance" analysts. In addition to running tests, these workers diagnose problems, suggest solutions, and determine whether program goals have been met.

The Big Picture

Expected to grow 29 percent through 2016.

Virtually every company needs to have some presence on the Internet—some merely have information available to consumers, but others have vast ordering systems. The explosion in technology in this area has helped fuel the need for computer systems analysts to develop and integrate these applications. In addition, the introduction of the wireless Internet and of handheld computers have created a need for experts who can integrate these technologies into existing networks. Analysts who are knowledgeable about systems integration and security should be in particularly high demand.

Most systems analysts work for companies who specialize in computer systems design. However, they are also employed by governments, insurance companies, financial institutions, hospitals, consulting firms, data processing services firms, universities, and managers of companies and enterprises.

Training Track

At the very least, a computer systems analyst must have a bachelor's degree in a technical field, such as computer science, information science, applied mathematics, engineering, or the physical sciences. Some employers seek applicants with at least a bachelor's degree in a business-related field such as management information systems (MIS). For higher level or more complex positions, companies will look for a candidate with a master's degree in business administration (MBA) with a concentration in information systems.

Employers generally look for people with expertise relevant to the job. For example, systems analysts who wish to work for a bank should have some expertise in finance, and systems analysts who wish to work for a hospital should have some knowledge of the health care industry.

The Bottom Line

Like other technology jobs, off-shoring will temper growth possibilities. Routine work may be sent to foreign countries to save money, although the Bureau of Labor Statistics anticipates 149,000 positions added to the workforce through 2016.

Many systems analysts work on a temporary or contract basis (approximately 29,000); usually on one specific project for a company or organization. Many of these analysts run their own contracting or consulting business. This arrangement is fine for some analysts, but others may prefer the stability of a full-time position.

THE PAYCHECK

Median annual earnings	$69,760
Highest 10 percent earned	>$106,820
Lowest 10 percent earned	<$42,780
Best-paying states	Virginia, New Jersey, Massachusetts, Rhode Island, Arizona

Web Links

www.acm.org
www.computer.org
www.iasahome.org
www.Dice.com
www.getcomputersystemsanalystjobs.com

Environmental Scientist and Hydrologist

Day-to-Day

In general, environmental scientists and hydrologists use their knowledge of the physical makeup and history of the Earth to protect the environment, study the properties of water (both above and below ground), locate water and energy resources, predict water-related hazards, and provide environmental site assessments and advice on air quality and hazardous-waste–site remediation.

More specifically, environmental scientists conduct research that helps them identify, lessen, and/or eliminate hazards that affect people, wildlife, and the environments. These workers measure and observe aspects of air, water, and soil to determine the way to clean and preserve the environment. Environmental scientists must understand the main ways that humans can protect the environment—conservation, recycling, and replenishment. They use this understanding to design and monitor waste disposal sites, preserve water supplies, and reclaim contaminated land and water to comply with federal regulations. They also write risk assessments, describing the likely effect of construction and other environmental changes; write technical proposals; and give presentations to necessary parties.

Hydrologists study the quantity, distribution, circulation, and physical properties of bodies of water. They usually focus their research on either underground water or surface water. They also examine precipitation, its rate of infiltration into the soil, its movement through the Earth, and its return to the ocean and atmosphere.

Consulting firms that help organizations comply with government regulations employ many environmental scientists and hydrologists. Environmental scientists who help create local, state, and federal governments' environmental policies may help identify ways that human behavior can be modified in the future to avoid such problems as groundwater contamination and depletion of the ozone layer. Some environmental scientists work in managerial positions, usually after spending some time performing field research or learning about environmental laws and regulations.

Some environmental scientists specialize in subfields such as environmental ecology and conservation, environmental chemistry, environmental biology, or fisheries science.

The Big Picture

Employment of environmental scientists and hydrologists is expected to grow 25 percent through 2016.

Engineers develop new technology, design software, and rebuild the infrastructure. They are the professionals who make new ideas come to life. The Bureau of Labor Statistics projects the addition of about 315,000 new engineering jobs through 2016, and considers this to be average growth based on the sheer number of people employed in these occupations. Out of the various engineering specialties, environmental engineers, hydrologists, and biomedical engineers are expected to grow the fastest.

A main reason for this growth is the increasing focus on compliance with environmental regulations and on cleaning up existing hazards. In addition, environmental scientists will be needed to help planners develop and construct eco-friendly buildings, transportation systems, and utilities that protect water resources and reflect efficient and beneficial land use.

Demand for hydrologists should also be strong, as the population increases and more people need to live in environmentally sensitive locations. As people increasingly migrate toward coastal regions, for example, hydrologists will assess building sites for potential hazards and to mitigate the effects of natural hazards such as floods, landslides, and hurricanes. Hydrologists also will be needed to study hazardous-waste sites and determine the effect of pollutants on soil and groundwater so that engineers can design remediation systems. Increased government regulations on water use and contamination, conservation, deteriorating coastal environments, and rising sea levels also will stimulate employment for these workers.

Consulting firms will likely continue to hire these scientists to help businesses and government address issues related to underground tanks, land disposal areas, and other hazardous-waste–management facilities. Currently, environmental consulting is focused on creating remediation and engineering solutions. New federal and state initiatives that integrate environmental activities into the business process itself will result in a greater focus on waste minimization, resource recovery, pollution prevention, and the consideration of environmental effects during product development. This shift in focus to preventive management will provide many new opportunities for environmental scientists and hydrologists.

Training Track

Entry-level positions may only require a bachelor's degree in an earth science, but environmental scientists increasingly need a master's degree in environmental science, hydrology, or a related natural science in order to practice at higher levels. A master's degree also is the minimum educational requirement for most applied research positions in private industry, in state and federal agencies, and at state geological surveys. Environmental scientists or hydrologists who plan to teach at the college level, or who want to do research, will need a doctoral degree.

The Bottom Line

Most entry-level environmental scientists and hydrologists spend the majority of their time in the field, while more experienced workers generally devote more time to office or laboratory work. Many beginning hydrologists and some environmental scientists, such as environmental ecologists and environmental chemists, often take trips that involve physical activity to examine sites and collect materials or data. When on these site visits, they will likely encounter warm or cold climates, and all kinds of weather. In their research, they may dig or chip with a hammer, scoop with a net, come in contact with water, and carry equipment. Travel is usually required to meet with prospective clients or investors or to visit sites. Researchers and consultants might face stress when looking for funding.

Demand for hydrologists who understand both the scientific and engineering aspects of waste remediation should be strong. Because few colleges and universities offer specific programs in hydrology, the number of qualified workers ready to work in that career will likely be small. Job prospects for environmental scientists also will be good, but less favorable than for hydrologists because of the larger number of people already poised to enter the field.

Funding for federal and state geological surveys depends largely on the political climate and budget situation. Thus, job security for environmental scientists and hydrologists may vary. During periods of economic recession, consulting firms may lay off environmental scientists and hydrologists; layoffs are much less likely in government.

THE PAYCHECK

Median annual earnings of environmental scientists	$56,100
Highest 10 percent earned	>$94,670
Lowest 10 percent earned	<$34,590
Best-paying states for environmental scientists	District of Columbia, Massachusetts, Colorado, Wisconsin, California
Median annual earnings of hydrologists	$66,260
Highest 10 percent earned	>$98,320
Lowest 10 percent earned	<$42,080
Best-paying states for hydrologists	Tennessee, New Hampshire, Massachusetts, Pennsylvania, Nevada

Web Links

www.agiweb.org
www.aihydro.org
www.hydroweb.com
www.earthworks-jobs.com
www.newscientistjobs.com
www.ecoemploy.com

Which American president first voiced his concern for the environment? It was Theodore Roosevelt. In a speech before the Colorado Live Stock Association in Denver, Colorado, on August 29, 1910, he said, "The nation behaves well if it treats the natural resources as assets which it must turn over to the next generation increased, and not impaired, in value."

Environmental Engineer

Day-to-Day

Environmental engineers use their knowledge of biology and chemistry to find solutions to environmental problems. They study water and air pollution, recycling, waste disposal, and public health issues. Many environmental engineers specialize in hazardous-waste management—they determine how serious and pervasive the hazard is, suggest how to contain and/or clean it up, and may develop regulations to prevent the same problem from happening again. Some are involved in planning major projects from the outset, for example, designing municipal water supply and industrial wastewater treatment systems.

Environmental engineers are concerned with local and worldwide environmental issues. They study and attempt to minimize the effects of acid rain, global warming, emissions, and ozone depletion. They may also be involved in the protection of wildlife. Many environmental engineers work as consultants, helping their clients comply with governmental or industry regulations, prevent damage to the environment, and clean up hazardous sites.

The Big Picture

Expected to grow between 25 percent and 30.6 percent through 2016.

Companies and organizations that must comply with environmental regulations will need the expertise of environmental engineers to do so. A shift in emphasis toward preventing new environmental harms in addition to controlling those that already exist, as well as increasing public health concerns about environmental hazards, also are expected to spur demand for environmental engineers. Job opportunities should be good even as more students earn degrees in this field.

Training Track

An advanced degree is a necessity for an environmental engineer. To stay current in their field, which is always evolving, engineers obtain a master's degree and take continuing education courses throughout their career. Online environmental engineering degrees, found primarily at the master's level, have become popular with working professionals who want to boost their careers but can't take the time off from work for a traditional degree.

The Bottom Line

A downturned economy will likely reduce the amount of money spent on environmental protection, thus reducing job opportunities. However, environmental engineers are less likely to be affected than other engineers due to the current emphasis on the importance of environmental responsibility.

THE PAYCHECK

Median annual earnings	$77,970
Highest 10 percent earned	>$115,430
Lowest 10 percent earned	<$45,310
Best-paying states	District of Columbia, New Mexico, Maryland, Hawaii, California

Web Links

www.aaee.net
www.environmentalengineer.com
www.environmentalcareer.com
www.greenjobs.com

Biomedical Engineers

Day-to-Day

Biomedical engineering is a specialized field that is responsible for developing devices and procedures that solve medical problems. For example, biomedical engineers are in large part the creators of artificial organs and prostheses, as well as certain instrumentation, medical information systems, and health management and care delivery systems. Biomedical engineers also design devices used in medical procedures, such as magnetic resonance imaging (MRI) machines and devices for automating insulin injections. Most engineers in this specialty need a solid educational background in another engineering specialty, such as mechanical or electronics engineering, in addition to specialized biomedical training. Some specialties within biomedical engineering include biomaterials, biomechanics, medical imaging, rehabilitation engineering, and orthopedic engineering.

The Big Picture

Expected to grow between 21 percent and 72 percent through 2016.

The BLS estimates that 3,000 new jobs will be created in the industry through 2016. The demand for increasingly sophisticated medical devices is propelling this increase. The fact that a higher percentage of the population will be older will also drive demand for better medical devices and equipment, much of which is designed by biomedical engineers. Pharmaceutical manufacturing and related industries will also use biomedical engineers to develop cost-effective equipment and procedures.

According to the Bureau of Labor Statistics, approximately 14,000 biomedical engineers are currently employed nationwide. The majority of them work for companies that make medical equipment and supplies. Other employers include pharmaceutical and drug companies, scientific and research development services, and health care facilities.

Training Track

Biomedical engineers need quite a bit of higher education—many entry-level people in this field have a master's degree. They often combine formal training in mechanical and electronics engineering with focused biomedical training. Some universities offer undergraduate degrees in biomedical engineering; courses may include neuroengineering; biofluid mechanics; engineering electrophysiology; diagnostic imaging physics; and drug design, development, and delivery.

All fifty states and the District of Columbia require licensure for engineers who offer their services directly to the public. Engineers who are licensed are called professional engineers (PE). This licensure generally requires a degree from a program accredited by the Accreditation Board for Engineering and Technology (*www.abet.org*), four years of relevant work experience, and successful completion of a state examination.

The Bottom Line

Because of the growing interest in this field, the number of students graduating with a degree in biomedical engineering has increased. So biomedical engineers, particularly those with only a bachelor's degree, may face competition for jobs.

THE PAYCHECK

Median annual earnings	$81,120
Highest 10 percent earned	>$121,970
Lowest 10 percent earned	<$47,640
Best-paying states	Massachusetts, Minnesota, California, Connecticut, Illinois

Web Links

www.biomedicalengineer.com
www.bmecareer.org
www.bmes.org
www.bmenet.org

The 1974 TV show, *The Six Million Dollar Man*, was about an ex-astronaut who was bionically rebuilt after a crash. Bionic implants were made to his right arm, both legs, and left eye, allowing him superior powers. The cost of his surgery in 2008 dollars would be $25,915,759, according to the inflation calculator at *www.westegg.com/inflation*.

Business Service Professions

The jobs profiled in this section are an amalgamation of finance, law, entertainment, and global services, with expected growth rates between 22 and 33 percent. This represents the long-term shift from goods-producing to service-providing employment, which is expected to continue. Service-providing industries are expected to account for approximately 15.7 million new jobs generated through 2016, while goods-producing industries will see overall job loss.

The jobs that will be added by 2016 will not necessarily be evenly distributed across major industrial and occupational groups. Changes in consumer demand, technology, and workforce demographics will contribute to the continually changing employment structure in the U.S. economy.

Financial Analysts and Personal Financial Advisors

Day-to-Day

Financial analysts and personal financial advisors provide both personal and organizational investment analysis and guidance. Both types of specialists gather financial information, analyze it, and make recommendations based on their clients' needs. However, their job duties differ because of the type of advice they give and their relationships with investors.

Financial analysts assess the economic performance of companies and industries for firms and institutions with money to invest. They work for investment banks, insurance companies, mutual and pension funds, securities firms, the business media, and other businesses. Financial analysts read company financial statements and analyze commodity prices, sales, costs, expenses, and tax rates in order to determine a company's value and to project its future earnings. They often meet with company officials to gain a better insight into the firm's prospects and to determine its managerial effectiveness. This information helps them advise the company they work for about whether or not to invest in a particular industry or company.

Financial analysts either work on the "buy" side or the "sell" side. Analysts on the buy side help companies that have a great deal of money to invest decide where to invest it. These companies, called institutional investors, include mutual funds; hedge funds; insurance companies; independent money managers; and charitable or nonprofit organizations, such as universities and hospitals, with large endowments. Conversely, analysts on the sell side help securities dealers such as investment banks and securities firms to sell their products. The business media also hire financial advisors to provide an impartial view of current economic events.

Financial analysts generally focus on a specific industry, region, or type of product. Within their areas of specialty, analysts assess trends in business practices, products, and competition. They must keep abreast of new regulations or policies that may affect the investments they are watching and monitor the economy to determine its effect on earnings.

Personal financial advisors help individuals with their financial needs. Advisors use their knowledge of investments, tax laws, and insurance to recommend short- and long-term financial plans. Planners help clients with financial goals such as retirement planning and funding college education. Many also provide tax advice or sell life insurance. Although most planners offer advice on most topics an individual or family would encounter, some specialize in areas such as retirement and estate planning or risk management.

Personal financial advisors usually work with many clients, and they often must find their own customers. Many personal financial advisors spend a great deal of their time making sales calls and marketing their services to get new clients. Many advisors also meet potential clients by giving seminars or lectures or through business and social contacts. Finding clients and building a customer base is one of the most important aspects of becoming successful as a financial advisor.

Financial advisors begin work with a client by setting up an in-person meeting where the advisor obtains as much information as possible about the client's current financial condition and future goals. The advisor then develops a comprehensive financial plan that identifies problem areas, makes recommendations for improvement, and selects appropriate investments compatible with the client's goals, attitude toward risk, and expectation or need for a return on the investment.

Financial advisors usually meet with established clients at least once a year to update them on potential investments and adjust their financial plan to any life changes—such as marriage, the birth of a child, or retirement. Financial advisors also answer clients' questions regarding how potential life changes, such as purchasing a house or taking a pay cut, would affect their financial state. Financial planners must give their clients realistic expectations about the outcomes of their suggestions.

Most personal financial advisors buy and sell financial products, such as securities and life insurance. Fees and commissions from the purchase and sale of securities and life insurance plans are major sources of income for most personal financial advisors.

The Big Picture

Employment of personal financial advisors is expected to grow 41 percent through 2016; over the same period, employment of financial analysts should grow 34 percent.

Personal financial advisors are projected to grow at a rate much faster than the average for all occupations through 2016. Growing numbers of advisors will be needed to assist the millions of workers expected to retire by 2016. As more members of the large baby boom generation reach their peak years of retirement savings, more people will seek the help of experts. Many companies also have replaced traditional pension plans with retirement savings programs, so more individuals are managing their own retirements than in the past, creating jobs for advisors. In addition, people are living longer and must plan to finance longer retirements, and the economic downturn has left some people insecure about managing their finances on their own. They may feel that the fees associated with using a personal financial advisor are worth it, given the challenges of investing and retiring during an economic crisis.

Employment of financial analysts is expected to grow by 34 percent through 2016, which is also much faster than the average for all occupations. Primary factors for this growth are increasing complexity of investments and overall growth in the industry. As the number and type of mutual funds increase, mutual fund companies will need more financial analysts to research and recommend investments.

Training Track

A bachelor's or graduate degree is required for financial analysts and is strongly preferred for personal financial advisors. Most companies require financial analysts to have at least a bachelor's degree in finance, business administration, accounting, statistics, or economics, and many require an advanced degree and certain licenses based on the type and responsibility level of the job.

The Financial Industry Regulatory Authority (FINRA; *www.finra.org*) is the main licensing organization for the securities industry. Depending on a financial analyst's work, many different licenses may be required, although buy-side analysts are less likely to need licenses. The majority of licenses require sponsorship of an employer, so companies do not expect individuals to have these licenses before starting a job. Licensed workers who change jobs need to have their licenses renewed with the new company.

Almost all personal financial advisors need the Series 7 and Series 63 or 66 licenses, which are issued by FINRA as well. These licenses grant the right to act as a registered representative of a securities firm and to give financial advice. Because the Series 7 license requires sponsorship, self-employed personal financial advisors must maintain a relationship with a large securities firm. This relationship allows them to act as representatives of that firm in the buying and selling of securities.

Financial analysts can earn the Chartered Financial Analyst (CFA) designation, sponsored by the CFA Institute (*www.cfainstitute.org*). To qualify for this designation, applicants need a bachelor's degree, four years of work experience in a related field, and a passing score on three examinations.

Personal financial advisors may obtain the Certified Financial Planner credential, often referred to as CFP. This certification, issued by the Certified Financial Planner Board of Standards (*www.cfp.net*), requires three years of relevant experience; the completion of education requirements, including a bachelor's degree; passing a comprehensive examination; and adherence to a code of ethics.

The Bottom Line

Continuing upheaval in the financial services industry is expected to spur demand for personal financial advisors in the banking industry. In recent years, banks and insurance companies have been allowed to expand into the securities industry. Although Congress is currently considering legislation to regulate the industry, we can foresee that financial services firms will continue to invest widely. Many firms are adding investment advice to their services and are expected to increase their hiring of personal financial advisors.

Despite overall employment growth, competition for financial analyst jobs will be intense because of the number of people who want to enter the occupation, given its high salary potential. A strong academic background is absolutely essential for those aspiring to financial analyst jobs. Good grades in courses such as finance, accounting, and economics are very important to employers. An MBA or certification is helpful in maintaining employment.

Personal financial advisors will also face competition, as many other services compete for customers. Many individuals enter the field by working for a bank or full-service brokerage. Most independent advisories fail within the first year of business, making self-employment challenging. Because the occupation requires sales, people who have strong selling skills will ultimately be most successful. A college degree and certification can lend credibility.

Both occupations must overcome a customers' fear of fraud and investment mismanagement—perceptions that have been outgrowths of recent Ponzi scheme stories (particularly Bernard Madoff) and the collapse of some of Wall Street's most well-known financial institutions.

THE PAYCHECK

Median annual earnings of financial analysts	$66,590*
Highest 10 percent earned	>$130,130
Lowest 10 percent earned	<$40,340
Best-paying states	New York, Connecticut, California, Illinois, Washington
Median annual earnings of personal finance advisors	$66,120**
Highest 10 percent earned	>$145,600
Lowest 10 percent earned	<$32,340
Best-paying states for both positions	New York, Massachusetts, Connecticut, Alaska, Colorado

*The bonuses that many financial analysts receive in addition to their salary can be a significant part of their total earnings. Usually, the bonus is based on how well their predictions compare to the actual performance of a benchmark investment.

**Personal financial advisors who work for financial services firms are generally paid a salary plus bonus. Advisors who work for financial investment or planning firms or who are self-employed either charge hourly fees for their services or opt to earn their money through fees on stock and insurance purchases. Advisors generally receive commissions for financial products they sell, in addition to charging a fee. Those who manage a client's assets may charge a percentage of those assets. Earnings of personal financial advisors who are self-employed have not been included in these figures.

Web Links

Financial Analysts

www.finra.org
www.wallstjobs.com
www.sifma.org
www.aafm.us
www.cfainstitute.org
www.efinancialcareers.com

Personal Financial Advisors

www.cfp.net
www.fpanet.org
www.imca.org
www.jobsinthemoney.com
www.efinancialcareers.com

Gaming Surveillance Officer

Day-to-Day

Gaming surveillance officers typically work at a casino or casino hotel. (Some state and federal agencies employ a limited number of surveillance agents or officers to observe whether casinos are following state and federal gaming laws, but these jobs are not plentiful.) The casino gaming surveillance officer's main priority is to prevent cheating and theft by casino employees and patrons. Gaming surveillance officers are also responsible for making sure that the company adheres to state gaming regulations.

Gaming surveillance officers may also be known as surveillance agents or gaming investigators. These individuals act as security agents for casino managers and patrons. Using primarily audio and video equipment in an observation room, they watch casino operations for irregular activities, such as cheating or theft, and monitor compliance to rules, regulations, and laws.

Some casinos use a catwalk over one-way mirrors located above the casino floor to augment electronic surveillance equipment. They are also responsible for keeping security recordings in order in case they need to be used as evidence in police investigations.

The Big Picture

Expected to grow 34 percent through 2016.

Casinos will continue to hire more surveillance officers as more states legalize gambling and as the number of casinos increases in states where gambling is already legal. Casino security forces will likely employ more technically trained personnel, as technology becomes increasingly important in thwarting cheating and theft.

Training Track

Gaming surveillance officers and investigators usually need some training beyond high school but do not necessarily need a bachelor's degree. Several educational institutes offer certification programs, which can make a candidate more attractive to an employer. Classroom training usually is conducted in a casino-like atmosphere and includes the use of surveillance equipment. Employers prefer either individuals with casino experience and significant knowledge of casino operations or those with law enforcement and investigation experience. Background checking and drug screening is typically part of the hiring process.

The Bottom Line

Gaming surveillance officers spend considerable time on their feet, either assigned to a specific post or patrolling buildings and grounds. They can develop eyestrain from constantly monitoring computer and television screens.

THE PAYCHECK

Median annual earnings	$27,130
Highest 10 percent earned	>$45,940
Lowest 10 percent earned	<$18,720
Best-paying states	Pennsylvania, Indiana, Connecticut, California, Nevada

Web Links

www.casinocareers.com
www.worldcasinojobs.com
www.americangaming.org
www.gamingfloor.com
www.casinosurveillancenews.com

According to the American Gaming Association, the casino workforce has increased nearly 80 percent over the last two decades. It has grown from 198,657 employees in 1990 to 357,314 in 2008.

Court Reporters

Day-to-Day

Court reporters prepare verbatim transcripts of speeches, conversations, legal proceedings, meetings, and other events. These jobs are important, as they record spoken words for correspondence, records, or legal confirmation. Though they are most well known for their role in the court system, they are also are essential wherever a spoken word needs to be translated into a written document. In addition, court reporters provide closed-captioning and real-time translating services to people who are deaf or hard-of-hearing.

There are several methods of court reporting. The most common is called stenographic, in which stenotypists document all statements made in official proceedings on a stenotype machine. The machine allows them to press multiple keys at once to record combinations of letters representing sounds, words, or phrases.

These symbols are electronically recorded, translated, and displayed as text. In real-time court reporting, the stenotype machine is linked to computers for simultaneous captioning, often for television programming.

Another method of court reporting is electronic reporting, in which the court reporter monitors an electronic recording (on either analog tapes or digital equipment), takes notes to identify speakers, and listens to the recording to ensure clarity and quality. Electronic reporters and transcribers often are responsible for producing a written transcript of the recorded proceeding as well.

The third method of court reporting is voice writing, in which a court reporter speaks directly into a voice silencer—a hand-held mask containing a microphone. As the reporter repeats the testimony into the recorder, the mask prevents the reporter from being heard by anyone else. Voice writers record everything that is said by judges, witnesses, attorneys, and other parties to a proceeding, including gestures and emotional reactions, and later prepare transcripts.

All reporters are responsible for accurate identification of proper names and places. Electronic reporters ensure that the record is discernible, and stenographic reports make sure the computer-generated translation reads properly.

Although the courtroom is the main workplace for court reporters, some also work in business, the media, and government agencies. Court reporters who specialize in captioning live television programming for people with hearing loss are commonly known as broadcast captioners. They work for television networks or cable stations, captioning news, emergency broadcasts, sporting events, and other programming.

The Big Picture

Expected to grow 25 percent through 2016.

Despite an anticipated growth in the number of court proceedings, the demand for court reporter services will be spurred largely by the growing need to create captions for live television and by the need to provide other real-time broadcast captioning and translating services for the deaf and hard-of-hearing. Federal legislation dictates that all new television programming and all Spanish-language programming be captioned for the deaf and hard-of-hearing. In addition, the Americans with Disabilities Act gives deaf and hard-of-hearing students in colleges and universities the right to request access to real-time translation in their classes. These factors are expected to continue to increase the demand for court reporters who provide "Communication Access Realtime Translation" services (captioning for deaf and hard-of-hearing people). Although these services differ from traditional court reporting, they require a similar skill set.

Court reporters with certification and those who choose to specialize in providing CART, broadcast captioning, or webcasting services should have the best job opportunities. The favorable job market also reflects the fact that fewer people are entering this profession, particularly as stenographic typists.

Further, because of the shortage of court reporters and in efforts to control costs, many courtrooms have installed tape recorders that are maintained by electronic court reporters and transcribers to record court proceedings. But these electronic reporters and transcribers are used in a limited capacity, so traditional stenographic court reporters will continue to be used in felony trials and other proceedings. Court reporters will continue to be needed to produce written legal transcripts and proceedings for publication.

Training Track

The amount of training required to become a court reporter depends on the type of reporting. It usually takes less than a year to become a novice voice writer, but it takes at least two years to become proficient at real-time voice writing. Electronic reporters and transcribers learn their skills on the job. The average length of time it takes to become a real-time stenotypist is approximately three years. Training is offered by about 130 postsecondary vocational and technical schools and colleges. The National Court Reporters Association (NCRA; *www.ncraonline.org*) has certified about seventy programs, all of which offer courses in both stenotype computer-aided transcription and real-time reporting.

Some states require voice writers to pass a test and to earn state licensure. As a substitute for state licensure, the National Verbatim Reporters Association (*www.nvra.org*) offers three national certifications to voice writers: Certified Verbatim Reporter (CVR), Certificate of Merit (CM), and Real-Time Verbatim Reporter (RVR). Earning these certifications is sufficient to be licensed in states that permit the voice method of court reporting.

Court reporters need both speed and accuracy, and must have excellent listening skills and hearing. They also need a command of English grammar, vocabulary, and punctuation in order to effectively produce the transcriptions. Those who work in courtrooms should have an expert knowledge of legal terminology and judicial procedure.

The Bottom Line

Work in this occupation presents few hazards, although sitting in the same position for long periods can be tiring, and workers can suffer wrist, back, neck, or eye strain. Court reporters also risk repetitive stress injuries such as carpal tunnel syndrome. In addition, the pressure to be accurate and fast can be stressful.

THE PAYCHECK

Median annual earnings	$45,610
Highest 10 percent earned	>$77,770
Lowest 10 percent earned	<$23,430
Best-paying states	Oregon, New York, California, Washington, Rhode Island

Web Links

www.aaert.org
www.ncraonline.org
www.nvra.org
www.usca.org
www.getcourtreporterjobs.com

Both the federal government and the National Court Reporters of America require prospective reporters to record a minimum of 225 words per minute. A champion court reporter has clocked in at 280 words per minute.

Actuaries

Day-to-Day

Through their knowledge of statistics, finance, and business, actuaries help businesses assess the risk of certain events occurring and then create policies that minimize the cost of that risk. For this reason, actuaries are essential to the insurance industry. In that field, actuaries estimate the probability and likely cost of an event such as death, sickness, injury, or loss of property. Actuaries also address specifically financial questions, such as advising how a company should invest its resources to maximize return on investments in light of potential risk.

The Big Picture

Expected to grow 24 percent through 2016.

Employment growth in the insurance industry—the largest employer of actuaries—is expected to continue at a stable pace, due largely to the rise in popularity of annuities, a financial product offered primarily by life insurance companies. In addition, the risk of terrorism and natural disasters has created a large demand for actuaries in property insurance.

More significant job growth for actuaries is likely in the health care and consulting industries, as health care issues and Medicare reform continue to receive attention. Increased regulation of managed health care companies and the desire to contain health care costs will continue to provide job opportunities for actuaries. In the health care field, actuaries will also be needed to evaluate the risks associated with new medical issues, such as genetic testing.

Training Track

Actuaries need a strong foundation in mathematics, statistics, and general business. They usually have a bachelor's degree and must pass a series of exams in order to become certified. About ten colleges and universities offer an actuarial science program, and most offer a degree in mathematics, statistics, economics, or finance.

Two professional societies sponsor programs that certify different paths within the actuarial field: the Society of Actuaries (SOA; *www.soa.org*) and the Casualty Actuarial Society (CAS; *www.casact.org*). The SOA certifies actuaries in the fields of life insurance, health benefits systems, retirement systems, and finance and investment. The CAS certifies actuaries in the property and casualty field, which includes car, homeowners', medical malpractice, workers' compensation, and personal injury liability.

The Bottom Line

Most actuaries work a traditional forty-hour week. Consulting actuaries, however, may experience more erratic employment, be expected to work more than forty hours per week, and may spend more time traveling to meet with clients. Actuaries should stay aware of national and global news; current economic and social trends and legislation; and developments in health, business, and finance in order to analyze how those events could affect insurance or investment practices. While many may be more comfortable working solo armed only with a calculator, good communication and interpersonal skills also are important, particularly for consulting actuaries.

THE PAYCHECK

Median annual earnings	$82,800
Highest 10 percent earned	>$145,600
Lowest 10 percent earned	<$46,470
Best-paying states	New Mexico, Pennsylvania, Indiana, Colorado, Delaware

Web Links

www.soa.org
www.actuary.com
www.actuary.org
www.beanactuary.org
www.actuarialgrads.com

Interpreters and Translators

Day-to-Day

Globalization has made the work of interpreters and translators integral across many industries, as they enable cross-cultural communication by converting one language into another. They must have a mastery of the subject matter in which they work in order to accurately convert information from one language (the source language) into another (the target language). In addition, they must be sensitive to the cultures they work with so as to understand nuances.

Interpreters and translators are often discussed together because they share some common traits. For example, both must be fluent in at least two languages—a native, or active, language and a secondary, or passive, language; a small number of interpreters and translators are fluent in two or more passive languages.

Interpreters convert one spoken language into another—or, in the case of sign-language interpreters, convert spoken communication into sign language. There are two types of interpretation: simultaneous and consecutive. Simultaneous interpretation requires interpreters to listen and speak (or sign) at the same time, meaning that the interpreter begins to convey a sentence while the speaker is still talking. Consecutive interpretation begins after the speaker has verbalized a group of words or sentences.

Translators, on the other hand, convert written materials from one language into another. They must have excellent writing, editing, and analytical abilities. Translators need to be sensitive to colloquialisms, slang, and other expressions that do not translate literally so they can be explained fully to the intended audience. Today, nearly all translation work is done on a computer, and most assignments are received and submitted electronically. A large percentage of them work from home, given this flexibility.

The Big Picture

Expected to grow 24 percent through 2016.

Strong demand for interpreters and translators is a result of the broadening of international relations and the increase in the number of foreign language speakers in the United States. Growth will be particularly strong in health care settings and in work related to homeland security. For example, Homeland Security will continue to need interpreters and translators of Middle Eastern and North African languages.

Current events and changing political environments, though often difficult to foresee, will increase the need for people who can work with other languages.

Demand will remain strong for translators of the languages referred to as "PFIGS" (Portuguese, French, Italian, German, and Spanish); Arabic and other Middle Eastern languages; and the principal Asian languages—Chinese, Japanese, and Korean. Demand for American Sign Language interpreters will also grow rapidly.

Training Track

The educational backgrounds of interpreters and translators vary, but they must have a thorough knowledge of at least two languages. Although it is not necessary to have been raised bilingual to succeed, many interpreters and translators grew up speaking two languages. Many interpreters and translators have a bachelor's degree in something other than a language, but then receive postgraduate certification. Most organizations seek candidates who have worked in the field for three to five years or who have a degree in translation studies or both.

There is currently no national certification required of interpreters and translators in the United States, but there are a variety of different tests that workers can take to demonstrate proficiency, including:

- The American Translators Association (*www.atanet.org*)
- The Translators and Interpreters Guild (*www.ttig.org*)
- The National Association of Judiciary Interpreters and Translators (*www.najit.org*)
- The U.S. Department of State (*www.state.gov*)
- The National Association of the Deaf (*www.nad.org*)
- Registry of Interpreters for the Deaf (RID; *www.rid.org*)

The Bottom Line

Because many interpreters and translators freelance, their schedules are often erratic, with extensive periods of no work interspersed with very busy periods. Freelancers are also likely to spend a lot of time looking for their next job.

The work can be stressful (due to tight deadlines) and exhausting, and translation can be lonesome. However, interpreters and translators may use their irregular schedules to pursue other interests, such as traveling or working a second job.

THE PAYCHECK

Median annual earnings	$43,130
Highest 10 percent earned	>$69,170*
Lowest 10 percent earned	<$22,170
Best-paying states	District of Columbia, Virginia, New York, New Jersey, Michigan

*Note: Limited information suggests that some highly skilled interpreters and translators—for example, high-level conference interpreters—working full-time can earn more than $100,000 annually. Individuals classified as language specialists for the federal government earned an average of $76,287 annually in 2007.

Web Links

www.atanet.org
www.bilingualcareer.com
www.linguistservices.com
www.languagejobs.com
www.multilingualjobs.org
www.proz.com

What language is the world's most popular? English ranks number two with just over 500 million speakers, but Mandarin Chinese comes in first with more than 1 billion speakers.

Paralegals and Legal Assistants

Day-to-Day

Paralegals play a key supporting role to many types of lawyers. In fact, paralegals—who are also called legal assistants—have been assuming more significant responsibilities in legal offices, although they must work under a lawyer. They are explicitly prohibited from carrying out duties considered to be the practice of law, such as setting legal fees, giving legal advice, and presenting cases in court, but they can contribute in a number of other ways.

The paralegal is particularly vital when helping lawyers prepare for closings, hearings, trials, and meetings. They might investigate the facts of cases and ensure that all relevant information is considered. They also identify laws, research past judicial decisions, find legal articles (using the Internet and special computer software), and locate other materials that could come into play during a case. After they analyze and organize that information, paralegals may prepare written reports that attorneys use in determining how cases should be handled. If a client files a lawsuit, paralegals may help prepare the legal arguments, draft pleadings and motions to be filed with the court, obtain affidavits, and assist attorneys during trials. Paralegals also file all-important case documents so attorneys can access them quickly and accurately.

In addition to this preparatory work, paralegals help draft contracts, mortgages, and separation agreements. They also may assist in preparing tax returns, establishing trust funds, and planning estates. In smaller practices, paralegals may also maintain financial office records.

Paralegals are found in all types of organizations, but most are employed by law firms, corporate legal departments, and government offices. They support lawyers who practice many different facets of law, including litigation, personal injury, corporate law, criminal law, employee benefits, intellectual property, labor law, bankruptcy, immigration, family law, and real estate. As the law becomes more complex, paralegals become more specialized. For example, paralegals specializing in labor law may concentrate exclusively on employee benefits.

The Big Picture

Expected to grow 22 percent through 2016.

Private law firms employed seven out of ten paralegals and legal assistants; most of the remainder worked for corporate legal departments and various levels of government. Within the federal government, the U.S. Department of Justice is the largest employer, followed by the Social Security Administration and the U.S. Department of the Treasury. Some paralegals freelance, contracting their services to attorneys, corporate legal departments, or legal staffing services.

Demand for paralegals is expected to grow as the expanding population uses more legal services, especially in areas such as intellectual property, health care, international law, elder issues, criminal law, and environmental law. The growth of prepaid legal plans should also contribute to the demand for legal assistance.

Private law firms will continue to be the largest employers of paralegals, but a growing array of other organizations, such as corporate legal departments, insurance companies, real estate and title insurance firms, and banks also hire paralegals. Corporations in particular are expected to increase their in-house legal departments to cut freelancing costs.

Training Track

People entering this career either have an associate's degree in paralegal studies or a bachelor's degree coupled with a certificate in paralegal studies. (Only a small number of schools offer a bachelor's and master's degree in paralegal studies.) Some employers will train paralegals on the job. The most common method of training, however, is through a community college paralegal program that leads to an associate's degree.

Although most employers do not require certification, earning a voluntary certification from a professional society may offer job seekers advantages in the labor market. Certification is offered by the National Association of Legal Assistants (*www.nala.org*), the American Alliance of Paralegals (*www.aapipara.org*), and the National Federation of Paralegals Association (*www.paralegals.org*).

The Bottom Line

During recessions, demand declines for some discretionary legal services, such as planning estates, drafting wills, and handling real estate transactions. Corporations are less inclined to initiate certain types of litigation when plagued by falling sales and profits. As a result, certain companies affected by the downturn may actually lay off or reduce the hours of their full-time paralegals.

However, during recessions, corporations and individuals are more likely to face problems that require legal assistance, such as bankruptcies, foreclosures, and divorces. Paralegals, who provide many of the same legal services as lawyers at a lower cost, tend to stay busy for that reason.

THE PAYCHECK

Median annual earnings	$43,040
Highest 10 percent earned	>$67,540
Lowest 10 percent earned	<$27,450
Best-paying states	District of Columbia, New York, California, Alaska, Illinois

Web Links

www.abanet.org
www.nala.org
www.paralegals.org
www.aafpe.org
www.aapipara.org
www.nals.org
www.paralegaljobs.com
www.lawcrossing.com
www.lawjobs.com

Educational and Social Services Professions

In the next ten years, more than three out of every ten new jobs created in the U.S. economy will be in either the health care and social assistance or public and private educational services sectors. Employment growth will be driven by increasing demand for health care and social assistance because of an aging population and longer life expectancies. Also, as more and more women enter and remain in the labor force, demand for childcare services is expected to grow. Public and private educational services will grow by 10.7 percent and add 1.4 million new jobs through 2016. Rising student enrollments at all levels of education will create demand for educational services.

The six professions highlighted expect growth rates between 22 percent and 51 percent—again, these are all considered much faster than average by the Bureau of Labor Statistics.

Personal and Home Care Aides

Day-to-Day

Personal and home care aides help people who are elderly, ill, and/or have a physical or mental disability. They may make it possible for those people to live in their own homes or to live comfortably in residential care facilities instead of in health facilities or institutions. Most personal and home care aides work with patients who need more extensive personal and home care than family or friends are able to provide. Some aides work with families in which a parent is incapacitated and small children need care. Others help discharged hospital patients who have relatively short-term needs while they recover from an illness or injury. Personal and home care aides—who may also be called homemakers, caregivers, companions, and personal attendants—sometimes also provide housekeeping and routine personal care services.

The Big Picture

Expected to grow 50 percent through 2016.

This field is expected to grow by about 389,000 jobs, due, in large part, to the rise in the number of elderly people. Elderly people face mounting health problems and some will need assistance with daily activities.

This trend is caused by several developments. First, the high cost of inpatient care in hospitals and nursing homes forces patients to return to their homes from these facilities as quickly as possible. (Patients who simply need assistance with everyday tasks and household chores rather than observational medical care can reduce medical expenses by returning to their homes.) Second, most patients—particularly the elderly—increasingly prefer care in the familiar environment of their homes rather than in nursing homes or other in-patient facilities. Third, better and more portable medical technologies have helped home care become easier and more feasible.

In addition to private home settings, personal and home care aides also work in residential facilities for the disabled, elderly, or mentally challenged.

Training Track

Most personal and home care aides receive short-term on-the-job training specific to the job they'll be doing, such as learning information on nutrition and special diets in order to properly cook for a client. They may be trained in basic housekeeping tasks and how to respond to an emergency situation. In some states, the only requirement for employment is on-the-job training, which generally is provided by employers. Other states may require formal training, which is available from community colleges, vocational schools, elder care programs, and home health care agencies.

The National Association for Home Care and Hospice (NAHC; *www.nahc.org*) offers national certification for personal and home care aides. Certification is voluntary, but shows an employer that the individual has met industry standards. Certification requires the completion of a seventy-five-hour course, observation and documentation of seventeen skills for competency assessed by a registered nurse, and passing a written exam developed by NAHC.

Personal and home care aides must have a desire to help people and not mind hard work. They should be healthy, responsible, compassionate, patient, emotionally stable, cheerful, and discreet (because they work in private homes). Some employers may require a physical exam, criminal background check, credit check, and good driving record for employment. Additionally, personal and home care aides are responsible for their own transportation to reach patients' homes.

The Bottom Line

A home health aide's work setting and environment differs from case to case. Some homes are neat and pleasant, whereas others are messy and depressing. Some clients are pleasant and cooperative; others are angry, depressed, or difficult. Some aides form close attachments to their patients and must deal with the emotional difficulties of a patient's deteriorating health and even death.

Aides may spend a large portion of each day traveling between clients' homes. About 33 percent of aides work part-time, and some work weekends or evenings to suit the needs of their clients.

THE PAYCHECK

Median annual earnings	$19,690
Highest 10 percent earned	>$25,650
Lowest 10 percent earned	<$14,230
Best-paying states	Alaska, New Jersey, Massachusetts, Minnesota, District of Columbia.

Web Links

www.hahc.org
www.caregiver-employment.com
www.carepathways.com

The U.S. Census Bureau estimates there will be 57.8 million baby boomers living in 2030. That year, boomers will be between the ages of sixty-six and eighty-four years old.

Social and Human Services Assistants

Day-to-Day

Social and human services assistants help social workers, health care workers, and other professionals provide services to people. "Social and human services assistant" is a generic term for workers with a wide array of job titles, including human service worker, case management aide, social work assistant, community support worker, mental health aide, community outreach worker, life skills counselor, or gerontology aide. They are usually supervised by nurses, psychiatrists, psychologists, physical therapists, or social workers. This career encompasses a wide variety of job titles, including: case worker, youth worker, social services liaison, child advocate, residential counselor, eligibility counselor, gerontology aide, juvenile court liaison, intake interviewer, community outreach worker, group home worker, and rehabilitation case worker.

The amount of responsibility and supervision they are given varies a great deal. Some have little direct supervision—they may run a group home, for example—while others work side by side with their manager. Social and human services assistants assess clients' needs; determine their eligibility for benefits and services such as food stamps, Medicaid, or welfare; and help them to obtain those benefits. They also arrange for transportation; provide emotional support; and report progress to supervisors and case managers.

In a community setting, social and human services assistants may organize and lead group activities, assist clients in need of counseling or crisis intervention, or administer food banks or emergency fuel programs. In halfway houses, group homes, and government-supported housing programs, they assist adults who need supervision with personal hygiene and daily living skills. They ensure that clients take their medication, educate their family members, and confer with medical personnel and other caregivers to provide insight into clients' needs.

In psychiatric hospitals, rehabilitation programs, and outpatient clinics, social and human services assistants work with psychiatrists, psychologists, social workers, and others to help clients master everyday living skills, communicate more effectively, and maintain healthy relationships. They support the client's participation in a treatment plan, such as individual or group counseling or occupational therapy.

The Big Picture

Expected to grow 34 percent through 2016.

Job prospects in this career are expected to be excellent, particularly for applicants with relevant education. Demand for social services will expand with the growing elderly population, who are more likely to need adult day care, meal delivery programs, support during medical crises, and other services. In addition, more social and human services assistants will be needed to provide services to other people in need, such as pregnant teenagers, people who are homeless, people who have a mental or developmental disability, and people who are substance abusers.

As social welfare policies shift focus from benefit-based to work-based programs, there will be more demand for people to teach job skills to the people who are new to, or returning to, the workforce.

The number of people who have a disability is increasing, and many need help to care for themselves. More community-based programs and supportive independent-living sites are expected to be established to house and assist the homeless and those with mental or physical disabilities. Furthermore, as substance abusers are increasingly being sent to treatment programs instead of prison, employment of social and human services assistants in substance abuse treatment programs also will grow.

Opportunities are expected to be good in private social-service agencies. Employment in private agencies will grow as state and local governments continue to contract out services in an effort to cut in-house costs. Also, some private agencies have begun hiring more social and human services assistants in place of social workers, who are more educated and more highly paid.

Training Track

Many employers prefer to hire people with certificates or associate's degrees in subjects such as human services, gerontology, or one of the social or behavioral sciences. Depending on the particular job, an employer may require a bachelor's or master's degree in human services or a related field, such as counseling, rehabilitation, or social work.

Human services degree programs train students to observe patients, record information, conduct patient interviews, implement treatment plans, employ problem-solving techniques, handle crisis intervention matters, and use proper case management and referral procedures. Many programs also offer internships to give students hands-on experience, and most also teach specialized courses related to addictions, gerontology, and child protection.

The kind of work social and human services assistants are assigned and the degree of responsibility that is given to them depends largely on their level of education. For example, workers with no more than a high school education are likely to receive extensive on-the-job training to work in direct-care services—helping clients to fill out paperwork, for example. Workers with a college degree, however, might conduct supportive counseling, coordinate program activities, or manage a group home. Social and human services assistants with proven leadership ability, especially from paid or volunteer experience, often have less direct supervision. Regardless of the academic or work background of employees, most employers provide some form of in-service training to their employees such as seminars and workshops. It is becoming more common for employers to require a criminal background check, and in some settings, workers may be required to have a valid driver's license.

The Bottom Line

The work, though satisfying, can be emotionally draining. Understaffing and relatively low pay may add to the pressure. Working conditions vary as well—some work in offices, clinics, and hospitals, while others work in group homes, shelters, sheltered workshops, and day programs. Some traveling may be involved to see clients. Some clients can be potentially dangerous, though most agencies do everything they can to ensure their workers' safety. Most assistants work forty hours a week; some work in the evening and on weekends depending on clients' needs.

Many human services jobs involve direct contact with people who are vulnerable to exploitation or mistreatment. Social and human services assistants must have a strong desire to help others, effective communication and time-management skills, and a sense of responsibility; employers value patience and understanding.

THE PAYCHECK

Median annual earnings	$25,580
Highest 10 percent earned	>$40,780
Lowest 10 percent earned	<$16,180
Best-paying states	Connecticut, Maryland, California, District of Columbia, Alaska

Web Links

www.cshse.org
www.nationalhumanservices.org
www.socialservice.com
www.hscareers.com
www.getsocialhumanserviceassistantjobs.com

Health Educators

Day-to-Day

Health educators teach individuals and communities about behaviors that promote healthy living and prevent health problems. They attempt to prevent illnesses by informing and educating people about topics such as proper nutrition, the importance of exercise, how to avoid sexually transmitted diseases, and healthy habits and lifestyles. Although programming is a large part of their job, health educators also serve as a resource on health topics.

Before starting a training session, they assess the needs of their audience, which helps them determine which topics to cover and how to best present the information. For example, they may hold programs on breast self-examinations for women who are at higher risk for breast cancer or teach classes on the effects of binge drinking to college students. Health educators must take age and cultural norms of their audience into account—they cannot run a program targeted at the elderly in the same way they would run one for a college-aged population. Also, health educators must plan programs that are consistent with the goals and objectives of their employers. For example, many nonprofit organizations educate the public about just one disease or health issue and, therefore, limit their programs.

After assessing their audiences' needs, health educators must decide how to meet those needs. They may organize a lecture, class, demonstration or health screening, or create a video, pamphlet, or website. Often, planning a program requires working with other people in a team or with their coworkers.

Next, health educators need to implement their proposed plan. This may require finding funding by applying for grants, writing curriculums for classes, or creating written materials that will be made available to the public. Also, they must solve basic logistics problems, such as finding speakers or locations for an event.

Generally, after a program is presented, health educators evaluate its success. This could include tracking the absentee rate of employees from work and students from school, surveying participants on their opinions about the program, or other methods of collecting evidence that suggests whether the programs were effective. These evaluations help them and the organization they work for improve plans for the future by learning from mistakes and capitalizing on strengths.

The basic goals and duties of health educators are the same, but their jobs vary greatly depending on the type of organization in which they work. Most health educators work in medical care settings, colleges and universities, schools, public health departments, nonprofit organizations, and private business.

The Big Picture

Expected to grow 26 percent through 2016.

The rising cost of health care has increased the need for health educators. As health care costs continue to rise, insurance companies, employers, and governments are trying to curb the cost by teaching people how to live healthy lives and avoid costly treatments for illnesses. They often emphasize awareness of a number of illnesses—such as lung cancer, HIV, heart disease, and skin cancer—that may be avoided with lifestyle changes. In addition, many illnesses, such as certain types of cancer, are best treated with early detection, so it is important for people to understand how to detect possible problems on their own.

This emphasis on health education has led to a growing demand for qualified health educators. In the past, it was thought that anyone could do the job of a health educator and the duties were often given to nurses or other health care professionals. However, in recent years, employers have recognized that those trained specifically in health education are better qualified and more successful.

Training Track

Entry-level health educator positions generally require a bachelor's degree in health education. More than 250 colleges and universities offer bachelor's programs in health education or a similarly titled major. These programs teach students the theories behind health education and the skills necessary to implement programs. Courses typically include psychology, human development, and a foreign language, and many programs offer internship or other volunteer opportunities.

Graduate health education programs are available, often under titles such as community health education, school health education, or health promotion. These degrees can lead to a master of arts, master of science, master of education, or a master of public health degree. Many students pursue their master's in health education after majoring or working in another related field, such as nursing or psychology. A master's degree is required for most health educator positions in public health. Once hired, on-the-job training for health educators varies greatly depending on the type and size of employer.

Health educators can also become a Certified Health Education Specialist, a credential offered by the National Commission of Health Education Credentialing, Inc. (*www.nchec.org*). The certification is awarded after passing an examination on the basic areas of responsibility for a health educator.

The Bottom Line

Health educators work primarily in two industries, with 20 percent working in state and local government and 53 percent working in health care and social assistance. In addition, a small percentage of health educators work in grant-making services and social advocacy organizations.

Demand for health educators will increase in most industries, but their employment may decrease in schools, which are facing budget cuts. Many schools are instead asking teachers trained in other fields, such as biology or physical education, to teach the subject of health education.

The work environment of a health educator is based on the industry, but is usually an office or a classroom. Many spend a lot of time away from the office implementing and attending programs, meeting with community organizers, speaking with patients, or teaching classes.

THE PAYCHECK

Median annual earnings	$41,330
Highest 10 percent earned	>$72,500
Lowest 10 percent earned	<$24,750
Best-paying states	Maryland, District of Columbia, Georgia, Rhode Island, Nevada

Web Links

www.aahperd.org/aahe
www.sophe.org
www.publichealtheducation.com

Postsecondary Teachers

Day-to-Day

Postsecondary teachers instruct students in a wide variety of academic and vocational subjects beyond the high school level. Most of these students are working toward a degree, but many others are studying for some kind of certification to improve their knowledge or career skills. Teachers at this level include college and university faculty, career and technical education teachers, and graduate teaching assistants. Professors at this level working at four-year colleges and universities typically perform a significant amount of research in the subject they teach.

Nowadays, postsecondary teachers use computer technology, including the Internet, e-mail, and software programs, to broaden and expand upon their classroom learning sessions. They may use computers as teaching aids during lectures and may post course content, notes, syllabi, and other information on the Internet. The use of e-mail, chat rooms, social media sites, and other technology is now critical to student-teacher communication.

The use of computers in postsecondary schools even extends to what is known as distance learning, where instructors use the Internet to teach courses to students at remote sites. Faculty who teach these courses must be able to adapt existing lectures or material to make them successful online or design a new course that takes advantage of the format.

Most full-time faculty members serve on one or more academic or administrative committees, which could deal with the policies of their institution, departmental matters, academic issues, curricula, budgets, equipment purchases, and hiring. Some work with student and community organizations. Department chairpersons are faculty members who teach fewer courses because they have heavier administrative responsibilities.

The Big Picture

Expected to grow 23 percent through 2016.

Because of the size of this occupation and its much-faster-than-average growth rate, postsecondary teachers will account for 382,000 new jobs through 2016, which is among the largest number of new jobs for an occupation. Projected increases in college and university enrollment over the next decade will be the main source of the growth.

Higher enrollments and the need to replace the large numbers of postsecondary teachers who are likely to retire over the next decade will create job openings across the nation. Many postsecondary teachers were hired in the late 1960s and the 1970s to teach members of the baby boom generation; they are expected to retire soon and will need to be replaced.

Training Track

Four-year colleges and universities usually require candidates for full-time, tenure-track positions to hold a doctoral degree. However, they may hire candidates with a master's degree or doctoral candidates for certain disciplines. Doctoral programs take an average of six years of full-time study beyond the bachelor's degree; this includes time spent completing a master's degree and a dissertation.

Training requirements for postsecondary career and technical education teachers vary by state and subject. In general, career and technical education teachers need a bachelor's or graduate degree, plus at least three years of work experience in their field. In some fields, a license or certificate may be required.

Most postsecondary school faculty strive to achieve tenure, which protects the ability to teach and conduct research without fear of being fired for advocating controversial or unpopular ideas. The process of attaining tenure can take approximately seven years, with faculty moving up the ranks in tenure-track positions—instructor, assistant professor, associate professor, and professor—as they meet specific criteria. Tenure may be also granted if the individual maintains an exemplary teaching record, contributes outstanding research to the field, and plays an active role on the campus.

The Bottom Line

Postsecondary professors often face the time-management challenge of teaching students while conducting research and publishing their findings. They have also found their workloads increasing due to recent cutbacks in support workers, the hiring of more part-time faculty, and the fact that many now have to teach online classes. Many find that developing the courses to put online is very time-consuming, especially when learning how to operate the technology and answering large amounts of e-mail.

THE PAYCHECK

Median annual earnings	$56,120
Highest 10 percent earned	>$113,450
Lowest 10 percent earned	<$27,590
Best-paying states	Massachusetts, New York, New Hampshire, Virginia, Illinois

Web Links

www.collegenet.com
www.acteonline.org
www.preparing-faculty.org
www.hired.net
www.hireedjobs.com

In 2007, the five colleges with the highest enrollment were: Community College of the

Air Force (332,095), City University of New York [CUNY] (261,602), University of Phoenix/Online (239,912), Miami-Dade College (86,292), and Florida Community College at Jacksonville (80,000).

Instructional Coordinators

Day-to-Day

Instructional coordinators—who are also known as curriculum specialists, personnel development specialists, instructional coaches, or directors of instructional material—try to improve the quality of education in the classroom. They develop curricula, select textbooks and other materials, train teachers, and assess educational programs for quality and adherence to state and federal regulations and standards. They also help implement new technology into classrooms.

At the primary and secondary school level, instructional coordinators usually specialize in specific subjects, such as reading, mathematics, or science. At the postsecondary level, coordinators usually branch out and may work with employers to develop training programs that produce qualified workers.

Instructional coordinators begin a project by evaluating how well a school or training program's curriculum meets students' needs. Based on their research and observations of current operations, they recommend improvements. To aid in their evaluation, they may meet with teachers to learn about certain subjects and explore how curriculum materials meet students' needs and relate to occupations. Coordinators also may develop questionnaires and interview school staff about the curriculum. Then they research teaching methods and develop procedures to ensure that instructors are implementing the curriculum successfully and meeting program goals.

Some instructional coordinators also review textbooks, software, and other educational materials and make recommendations on which to purchase. They monitor the ways in which teachers use materials in the classroom, and they supervise workers who catalogue, distribute, and maintain a school's educational materials and equipment.

Some instructional coordinators find ways to use technology to improve or expand the current curriculum. For example, they might recommend installing educational software, such as interactive books or fun math exercises. Instructional coordinators may invite experts—such as computer hardware, software, and library or media specialists—to offer their insight into programs.

In addition to developing curriculum and instructional materials, many instructional coordinators also plan and provide education for teachers and administrators. They may also mentor new teachers and train experienced ones in the newest instructional methods. This role becomes especially important when a school district introduces a new curriculum or testing policy. For example, when a state or school district introduces standards or tests that students must pass, instructional coordinators often explain the standards to teachers then show them how best to teach their students the necessary information.

The Big Picture

Expected to grow 22 percent through 2016.

Job growth for instructional coordinators will stem from the increasing emphasis on continuing education for teachers and on programs for students with special needs, including those for whom English is a second language. These students often require more thorough educational resources. Those with experience in math and reading curriculum development will be the most in demand.

Although budget constraints may limit employment growth to some extent, a continuing emphasis on improving the quality of education will mean that these workers should maintain a steady level of employability. In addition, the emphasis on accountability should cause more schools to focus on improving standards of educational quality and student performance. Growing numbers of coordinators will be needed to incorporate the new standards into existing curricula and inform teachers and administrators of the changes.

Training Track

A master's or higher degree—usually in education—plus a state teacher or administrator license is the educational standard for instructional coordinators. Certain employers may require a master's degree, depending on the setting and program particulars.

Instructional coordinators should also have specific training in the specific field for which they are responsible, such as mathematics or history. Courses in research design teach how to create and implement research studies to determine the effectiveness of a given method of instruction or curriculum and how to measure and improve student performance.

Instructional coordinators usually must take continuing education courses to keep their skills current, as they are responsible for making sure others know of the latest trends. Topics that are perennially popular for continuing ed classes include teacher evaluation techniques, curriculum training, new teacher induction, teacher support, and observation and analysis of teaching.

The Bottom Line

Instructional coordinators who specialize in subjects targeted for improvement by the No Child Left Behind Act—namely, reading, math, and science—will be preferred by employers.

Many instructional coordinators find their work rewarding because they are able to specialize in areas that interest them and contribute to educational improvement, yet not be subjected to the typical daily classroom stress.

THE PAYCHECK

Median annual earnings	$52,790
Highest 10 percent earned	>$87,510
Lowest 10 percent earned	<$29,040
Best-paying states	Connecticut, California, District of Columbia, New Jersey, Virginia

Web Links

www.astd.org
www.ascd.org
www.academiccareers.com
www.chronicle.com/jobs
www.jobsineducation.com

Social Workers

Day-to-Day

Social workers help people cope with issues in their everyday lives, maintain healthy relationships, and solve personal and family problems. Some social workers work with clients who face a disability or a life-threatening disease or a social problem, such as inadequate housing, unemployment, or substance abuse. Some assist families that have serious domestic conflicts, sometimes involving child or spousal abuse. Other social workers conduct research, advocate for improved services, or go into planning or policy development. Many social workers specialize in serving a particular population or working in a certain setting.

Child and family social workers provide social services to improve the social and psychological functioning of children and their families and to maximize the well-being of families and improve the child's academic experience. They may assist single parents; arrange adoptions; or help find foster homes for children who have been neglected, abandoned, or abused. Some work with senior citizens by running support groups for them; advising them and their family members about housing, transportation, long-term care, and other services; and coordinating and monitoring these services. Through employee-assistance programs, social workers may help people cope with job-related pressures or with personal problems that affect the quality of their work.

In schools, social workers serve as the link between students' families and the school, working with parents, guardians, teachers, and other school officials to ensure students reach and maintain their academic and personal potential. In addition, they address problems such as misbehavior, truancy, and teenage pregnancy and advise teachers on how to cope with these situations.

Child, family, and school social workers may also be known as child welfare social workers, family services social workers, child protective services social workers, occupational social workers, or gerontology social workers. They often work for individual and family services agencies, schools, or state or local governments.

Medical and public health social workers provide psychosocial support to people, families, or vulnerable populations so they can cope with chronic, acute, or terminal illnesses, such as Alzheimer's disease, cancer, or AIDS. They also help plan for patients' needs after discharge from hospitals, such as arranging for at-home services, such as meals-on-wheels or home care. Some work on interdisciplinary teams that evaluate certain kinds of patients—geriatric or organ transplant patients, for example. Medical and public health social workers may work for hospitals, nursing and personal care facilities, individual and family services agencies, or local governments.

Mental health and substance abuse social workers help individuals with mental illness or substance abuse problems, including abuse of alcohol, tobacco, or drugs. They may set up individual and group therapy, crisis intervention, social rehabilitation, and sessions to teach skills needed for everyday living. They also may help plan for supportive services to ease clients' return to the community. Mental health and substance abuse social workers usually work in hospitals, substance abuse treatment centers, individual and family services agencies, or local governments.

Other types of social workers include social work administrators, planners, and policymakers, who develop and implement programs to address issues such as child abuse, homelessness, substance abuse, poverty, and violence. These workers research and analyze policies, programs, and regulations, then suggest legislative and other solutions. They may help raise funds or write grants to support these programs.

The Big Picture

Expected to grow 22 percent through 2016.

Social workers who specialize in the aging population or work in rural areas will see the largest potential for growth. The increasing elderly population and the aging baby boom generation will create greater demand for health and social services, resulting in rapid job growth among gerontology social workers. Employment of social workers in private social service agencies may increase, but agencies may also restructure services and hire more social and human services assistants, who are paid less, instead of social workers. Employment in state and local government agencies may grow somewhat in response to growing needs for public welfare, family services, and child protective services, but many of these services will be contracted out to private agencies. The number of social workers hired for public social services agencies may fluctuate, depending on the economy and government funding levels.

Opportunities for social workers in private practice will probably expand, but growth may be somewhat hindered by restrictions that managed care organizations put on mental health services. The growing popularity of employee-assistance programs is expected to spur demand for private practitioners, some of whom provide social work services to corporations on a contractual basis. However, companies may not fund employee-assistance programs well or at all during recessions.

Among the areas of social work that will see the biggest percentage increase is mental health and substance abuse, which is expected to increase 30 percent through 2016. In particular, social workers specializing in substance abuse will experience strong demand because substance abusers are increasingly being placed into treatment programs instead of being sentenced to prison. Also, growing numbers of the substance abusers who *are* sentenced to prison or probation are also being required by correctional systems to have substance abuse treatment added as a condition to their sentence or probation. As this trend grows, demand for social workers will strengthen, as they will be needed to help these people fulfill the terms of their sentencing.

Additionally, growth of medical and public health social workers is expected to be 24 percent. Hospitals continue to limit the length of patient stays, so the demand for social workers in hospitals will grow more slowly than in other areas. But hospitals are releasing patients earlier than in the past, so social worker employment in home health care services is growing.

Training Track

A bachelor's degree in social work (BSW) is the most common minimum requirement to qualify for a job as a social worker; however, majors in psychology, sociology, and related fields may qualify for some entry-level jobs, especially in small agencies. A master's degree in social work (MSW) is typically required for positions in health settings and is required for clinical work as well. Some higher-level jobs in public and private agencies (supervisors, administrators, and staff training positions) may require an advanced degree, such as a master's degree in social services policy or administration. College and university teaching positions normally require a doctorate in social work (DSW or PhD).

The National Association of Social Workers (*www.socialworkers.org*) offers voluntary credentials that may help prospective job seekers. Social workers with a master's degree in social work may be eligible for the Academy of Certified Social Workers (ACSW), the Qualified Clinical Social Worker (QCSW), or the Diplomate in Clinical Social Work (DCSW) credentials, based on their professional experience.

The Bottom Line

A social worker's hours can be long and they often witness social injustices such as abuse, rape, incest, and more. It requires a balance between empathy and some level of detachment. Social workers must resign themselves to not winning every battle and taking heart in those that do get won. It is a career that requires tenacity and patience. Problems cannot be righted at once; often it takes time and tremendous effort. People typically go into social work for the reward of helping people rather than the money. They must also be able to tolerate the administrative frustrations of the system.

THE PAYCHECK

Median annual earnings	$43,580
Highest 10 percent earned	>$68,500
Lowest 10 percent earned	<$25,540
Best-paying states	South Dakota, Mississippi, West Virginia, New Jersey, Rhode Island

Web Links

www.socialworkers.org
www.cswe.org
www.aswb.org
www.socialworkjobs.com
www.socialworker.com

According to the National Association of Social Workers, the Department of Veterans Affairs is the largest employer of social workers in the country. It employs more than 6,000 social workers to assist veterans and their families with individual and family counseling, client education, substance abuse treatment, crisis intervention, and other services.

The Current Employment Scene and the American Recovery and Reinvestment Act (ARRA)

The goal of ARRA is to bring relief to America's unemployed through the creation of approximately 3.5 million jobs. President Obama's economic stimulus plan in 2009 targeted four strategic sectors to receive funds for direct or indirect job revitalization: energy (459,000 anticipated jobs), infrastructure (377,000 anticipated jobs), education (250,000 anticipated jobs), and health care (244,000 anticipated jobs).

Revitalization has been slow in coming, but that doesn't mean that those people who are out of work, or others who are thinking about beginning a career or changing professions, should discount the stimulus plan as they make their current or future employment choices. Two websites will help you stay current of where the spending is being allocated and which projects are moving forward: *www.recovery.gov* and *www.stimuluswatch.org*. For example, Recovery.gov reports that the five largest proposed stimulus projects according to number of jobs to be created are as follows:

1. Solar LA Program, Los Angeles, California (energy): 32,243 anticipated jobs
2. Newark Elizabeth Light Rail, Newark, New Jersey (transit): 20,000 anticipated jobs
3. North Corridor Light Rail System, Columbus, Ohio (transit): 11,000 anticipated jobs
4. North Corridor Rail Line, Charlotte, North Carolina (transit): 9,380 anticipated jobs
5. South Florida East Coast Corridor Transit Extension, Miami, Florida—(transit): 6,000 anticipated jobs

Stimuluswatch.org will tell you the status of each project.

Relocating

Are you thinking about relocating to a city with a promise of better job opportunities? The website *www.NewGeography.com* has published a list of cities that are well positioned to receive stimulus funding and therefore are likely to have good employment outlooks. The top ten cities are:

1. Atlanta, Georgia
2. Austin, Texas
3. Boston, Massachusetts
4. Columbus, Ohio
5. Denver, Colorado
6. Des Moines, Iowa
7. Indianapolis, Indiana
8. Madison, Wisconsin
9. Minneapolis/St. Paul, Minnesota
10. Nashville, Tennessee

Tomorrow's Careers

Anyone new to the job market and anyone already in it but seeking a career change should make plans for the future with an informed outlook. Do your homework regarding employment prospects for the next decade and what you need to succeed in a particular profession. Keep pace with those areas gaining momentum and attention because of technological innovation and/or cultural attitudes. For example, here are some new and emerging occupations that are expected to take a firmer hold over the next decade:

- Cancer registrar
- Distance learning specialist
- Ergonomics engineer
- Genetics counselor
- Resettlement coordinator for disaster recovery
- Search engine optimization analyst
- Transplant coordinator
- Victim advocate

Then there is also the clean energy boom, which is expected to produce more than 4.2 million new green jobs through 2038, according to a study by the U.S. Conference of Mayors released in October 2008. Under assumed scenarios and with government commitment and investment, the report projects green jobs could contribute 10 percent of new jobs through the next three decades, representing the fastest-growing segment of the U.S. economy.

Green jobs have yet to be measured by the Bureau of Labor Statistics, but are expected to be analyzed before the end of 2010. These positions will fall into two core categories: jobs that directly impact the environment and interact with our natural resources, and those that are at eco-friendly employers that want to be good corporate citizens through sustainability initiatives.

U.S. Secretary of Labor Hilda L. Solis reported before the U.S. Senate Committee on Health, Education, Labor and Pensions regarding green job skills training for workers. She said, "Green jobs play an important role in our economic recovery. The promise of green jobs is not only to help restart the economy and put Americans back to work, but also to help make America more energy independent. Investment in our nation's clean energy future will not only secure America's energy supply but will do so in ways that promote economic stability and the advancement of our communities." Here are some new and emerging occupations that are expected to be outcomes of the green workforce.

- Aquatic ecologist
- Conservation biologist
- Corporate waste compliance coordinator
- Energy efficiency builder
- Solar power installer
- Storm water technician
- Sustainability officer
- Wind turbine fabricator

Here are some web resources for green jobs:

www.greeneconomypost.com
www.greenjobs.com
www.sustainablebusiness.com
www.ecobusinesslinks.com/environmental_jobs.htm
www.greenbiz.com

Believe it or not, saving the planet isn't new. On April 22, 1970, Earth Day was launched and celebrated by nearly 20 million people who made their voices heard by demanding a healthy, sustainable environment.

Links to More Lists

The following links provide lists of other high-growth jobs defined by different criteria than I've used in the section above. Consult them for other possible options.

www.bls.gov/news.release/ecopro.t03.htm
www.bls.gov/news.release/ecopro.t07.htm
www.bls.gov/news.release/ecopro.t06.htm
www.bls.gov/news.release/ecopro.t04.htm
www.bls.gov/news.release/ecopro.t10.htm
www.bls.gov/news.release/ecopro.t08.htm
www.hubpages.com/hub/Green_Collar_Jobs
www.emagazine.com/view/?3945
www.sustainlane.com/green-jobs/jobs
www.greencareersguide.com/
www.indeed.com/q-Green-jobs.html

APPENDIX

How to Make Contact and Recognize a Buy Signal

EVERY ACTIVITY IN your job search should focus on getting you into conversations with the people who can hire you. The frequency of these conversations will determine the length of your job search.

E-Mail and Letters

How many e-mails to send out every week is a difficult question to answer. You want to approach and establish communication with every possible employer because this will create the maximum opportunity for you.

Two contacts a week is the behavior of the long-term unemployed. On the other hand, mass e-mailing 700 employers with one resume isn't the smartest answer either. Your campaign needs strategy. Every job search campaign is unique; nevertheless, you should maintain a balance between the *number* of written pitches you send out on a weekly basis and the *types of people to whom they are sent*. Start off with a balanced e-mail and mailing campaign, and your phone follow-ups can maintain equilibrium, too.

The key is to organize and balance your job search activities so that you send as many resumes as possible directly to people by name in a volume that will allow you to make follow-up calls to those people. Start out with modest goals: try to send at least five to ten e-mails each day addressed to someone by name and spread across each of the following areas:

- In response to Internet job postings
- To contacts in any of your professional networks
- To contacts in any of your personal networks
- To the contacts you identify within target companies
- To headhunters
- To miscellaneous contacts

Will you need to create and use more than one type of letter in your search? Of course you will, because you will be approaching many different types of people for different reasons. However, you don't have to craft every written communication entirely from scratch. You can create great letters quickly from the templates in *Knock 'em Dead Cover Letters*, where you will find letters for just about every job search scenario, plus more information on creating and managing effective e-mail campaigns.

The key is to do each variation once and do it right, then save copies of these letters in folders within your career management database so you can access them at any time.

KNOCK 'EM DEAD TIP

Every name and contact you develop should go into a career management database with all relevant information. These contacts can be nurtured and developed over the years.

Multiple Submissions

You will sometimes find it valuable to make a number of contacts within a given company, especially the larger ones, to assure all the important players know of your existence. Let's say you are a young engineer who wants to work for Last Chance Electronics. It is reasonable to e-mail cover letters and accompanying resumes to any, or all, of the following people by name (and also to send hard copies through traditional mail): the company president, the vice president of engineering, the chief engineer, the engineering manager, the vice president for human resources, the technical recruitment manager, and the technical recruiter.

You wouldn't necessarily send all these communications out at once but might rather spread them over a few weeks. Keep a log of your e-mail (and mail) contacts so you will know when to follow up with a phone call—usually about two days after an e-mail and five days after a traditional letter; exclude Monday mornings from this count, as everyone is busy getting up to speed for the week.

Keep track of these contacts beyond the initial follow-up period. Resumes do get misplaced, and employment needs change. You can comfortably resend e-mails to everyone on your list every couple of months; when you do this, it isn't necessary to remind them of earlier submissions. Most recipients won't register that they heard from you two months ago, and of those who do, most won't take offense. Any who might are people who have no need for your professional skill set and whom you are therefore unlikely to run into anytime soon.

A professionally organized and conducted campaign will proceed on two fronts:

Front One: A carpet-bombing approach to every possible employer in your target area.

Front Two: A carefully targeted approach to a select group of companies. You will continue to add to this primary target list as you unearth fresh opportunities in your day-to-day research efforts. While this may be your primary target list, at the beginning of the job search you are building both the list and contacts within the companies, so you may not be e-mailing to these companies initially; you may choose to wait until comfortable with your developing job search skills—no point in getting into a conversation with a dream employer until you know how to handle that conversation.

In both these approaches you respond to job postings and upload your resume to their corporate databases in the standard way. Then as your direct research and networking identifies specific individuals within these companies, begin e-mailing/mailing to one or two contacts within the company. Repeat the e-mails/traditional letters to other contacts when your follow-up calls to these people result in referrals or dead ends. Remember, just because Harry in engineering says there are no openings in the company doesn't make it so. Any one of the additional contacts you make within that company could be the person *who is the person or who knows the person* with the perfect job for you. Even when a company states it has a hiring freeze there are always, always exceptions.

Once your campaign starts to gain traction and you begin to schedule interviews from your calls, your emphasis will change. Those interviews will require preparation before and follow-up after.

This is the point at which most job searches stall. We get so excited about an interview and convince ourselves, "This will be the offer." In anticipation our job search activities slow to a halt.

Here's an unsettling fact of life: The offer that can't fail usually does fail, and you are left depressed and without anything happening in your job search.

You *must* commit to keep that job search pump primed with ongoing activity to generate interviews and to keep your psychological pump primed too.

The more direct contacts you make through e-mail, the more follow-up calls you can make to pitch your candidacy, schedule interviews and get leads for more openings.

Internet Resume Distribution Services

I am not a big fan of resume blasters (these sites will blast your resume to thousands of companies for a fee, but the response odds often aren't that good).

You can achieve much the same thing with a little investment of time by doing Google searches with terms relevant to your profession ("Health care recruiter" "C-level recruiter," and so on). Once you've compiled a list of e-mail addresses for companies that have these positions, open or not, you can send a mass mailing of your resume. Respond directly to any recruiters you find through this mass mailing.

The advantage of doing this kind of Google search yourself is that you can compile more company information while preparing your mailing.

Making Contact

At the same time you are uploading to resume databases and e-mailing and mailing your resume, you should pick up the phone and call the people you have already approached in one of these ways.

It is easier to wait patiently, but if you really want a job offer sooner rather than later, everything in your job search needs to be geared to getting into conversations with the people who can hire you. And that means you initiating some conversations.

The more often these conversations happen, the quicker your search will end in success, and *this is never more important than during an economic downturn*. At such times your competition is fierce, and employers recognize initiative and motivation as a differentiating factor in your candidacy.

What's the best way to proceed? Make as many of these follow-up or marketing phone calls as you send e-mails and traditional letters pitching your resume. This means you've got to have a prepared, powerful pitch. You'll need this in any case. If you're networking effectively, you'll constantly run into people who are in a position to hire you. That kind of encounter requires you to switch from a standard networking presentation into a full marketing pitch. The sooner you learn the ins and outs of these conversations, the quicker they will turn into legitimate in-person interviews.

Many people deceive themselves into thinking this part of the search is not possible because they are terrified of picking up the phone to call strangers. But it is something you can and must learn to do successfully.

Our discussions on making networking presentations in person over the telephone focused on talking to peers about getting leads on possible job openings and referrals or introductions to hiring managers. There is a difference between a networking call to a peer and an intentional marketing call presenting the professional you—Me Inc.—to a potential employer.

In a past professional incarnation as a headhunter, I spent every day on the telephone talking to strangers. Even though I developed a global reputation as a trainer in the headhunting community I was also always terrified making calls, which of course no one at the time ever knew. ;-) This isn't unusual for anyone engaged in a critical performance. In fact it is a very natural reaction. Success comes from harnessing the adrenaline rush you feel in such circumstances in productive ways.

I'd be surprised if you, too, weren't terrified at the prospect of actually calling prospective employers. Three pieces of advice helped me in my hour of abject terror:

- That I would never meet these people unless they were interested in what I had to offer, in which case they'd be happy I called.

- Because I was on the phone, no one would know who I was or how scared I felt and looked.
- The third thing that helped was learning how to make almost every call successful, and as outrageous as that sounds, it can be done.

Most job hunters have but a single goal when they pick up the phone: "Get an interview." This approach offers only one chance of success, but many more for failure, which will be accompanied by feelings of inadequacy and depression. You will multiply your marketing-call success rate when you have a multiple-goal strategy. When headhunters make marketing calls, they need to maximize the impact of every call, so they always have these five goals in mind:

- I will arrange an interview date and time.
- If my contact is busy, I will arrange another time to talk.
- I will develop leads on promising job openings elsewhere in this and other companies.
- I will leave the door open to talk with this person again in the future.
- I will send a resume for subsequent follow-up.

These commonsense goals will work for you too. Keep them in mind every time you talk with someone during your job search, because every conversation holds the potential for turning into an interview or leading you toward another conversation that will generate first a phone interview then a face-to-face meeting. You are now going to learn how to:

- Develop a concise word picture of your professional strengths.
- Be prepared for a telephone interview every time you pick up the phone.
- Recognize "buy signals" and objections as they crop up in your conversations, and learn how to turn them into interviews.
- Turn apparent dead-end conversations into live leads for interviews.

You might worry about calling people directly because you are concerned they will be annoyed by the perceived intrusion. This is a misconception: the first job of any manager is to get work done through others, so every smart manager is always on the lookout for talent, and if not for today, for tomorrow. If that isn't enough to allay your fears, keep in mind that the person on the other end of the line has more than likely been in your position and is sensitive to how you feel.

Paint a Word Picture

The secret is being succinct. With a presentation that comes in at well under a minute, you can't be construed as wasting anybody's time.

The technique is to paint a convincing word picture of yourself. Your presentation should be short, to the point, and "specifically vague"—specific enough to make the listener prick up his or her ears with interest, and at the same time vague enough to encourage questions that kick-start the conversation. Your aim is to paint a representation of your skills with the widest appeal while keeping it brief out of courtesy and to avoid giving information that might rule you out. Your presentation needs to GAIA:

- **G**et the listener's **A**ttention.
- Generate **I**nterest so they will **A**sk questions

The types of questions you are asked also enable you to identify the company's specific needs. Then you can customize any ongoing conversation toward those needs. Here are the steps.

Step 1

Your first step is to give the employer a snapshot of who you are and what you do. The intent is to give that person a reason to stay on the phone. You may sometimes have an introduction from a colleague, in which case you will build a bridge with that.

Or you may have gotten the name and contact information from, for example, a professional association database, in which case you will use that as a bridge.

Otherwise your introduction will cut right to the chase with a generalized job title (this increases the opportunity for positive response) and a brief description of your capabilities. You will outline your most desirable skills as you determined them with the Target Job Deconstruction exercises and illustrate with a couple of achievements, if this is appropriate.

Say enough about yourself to whet the listener's appetite and ignite a desire to know more. For example, you might initially describe yourself as experienced, rather than identifying a specific number of years in your field. This encourages the listener to qualify your statement with a question: "How much experience do you have?"

Step 2

This is where you color in your word picture. Pull out a couple of items from the resume-building exercises in Chapter 2 and follow your introductory sentence with a small selection. Keep them brief and to the point, without embellishments.

Step 3

You have introduced yourself professionally and succinctly. Now get to the reason for your call and move the conversation forward.

The entire presentation can be spoken aloud in a conversational tone in well under a minute and is constructed to finish with a question that encourages a positive response. At this point the right question is not, "Can you hire me?" You're just looking for agreement about the desirability of your skills.

You should never make these calls without taking the time to construct a written presentation. Doing so makes you capture the essence of the "professional you." Read your pitch word for word the first few times, until you have the meat of it by heart, then keep it to hand as a safety net.

Once you make your presentation over the telephone for real, there will likely be a silence on the other end of the line. Be patient, as the employer may need a few seconds to digest your words. When the employer does respond, it will either be with a question, denoting interest (a "buy signal"), or with an objection.

Questions and Buy Signals

When the silence is broken by a question, you breathe a sigh of relief because any question denotes interest and, in the terminology of the sales process, is a buy signal. The employer can ask questions that show interest: "Do you have a degree?" "Have you done this kind of work?" "Have you done that kind of work?"

Conversation is a two-way street, and you are most likely to win an interview when you take responsibility for your half. Just as the employer's questions show interest in you, your questions should show your interest in the work done at the company. By asking questions of your own in the normal course of conversation—questions usually tagged on to the end of one of your answers—you will forward the conversation. Also, the questions you ask help define what skills and qualities are important to the employer. This will increase your knowledge and help you customize your answers. If you leave all the interrogation to the employer, it will place you on the defensive, and at the end of the talk, you will be as ignorant of the real parameters of the job as you were at the start.

Try to give short reasonable answers and finish your reply, whenever possible, with a question. In answer to your questions, the interviewer will explain the job's specifics, and as that happens, you will be able to present your most relevant skills and experiences.

Because we come from different backgrounds, you and I will never talk alike, so don't think you have to learn the sample responses that follow parrot-fashion. Just capture the essence and put them in your own words.

Joan Jones: "Good morning, Mr. Grant. My name is Joan Jones. I am an office equipment salesperson experienced in selling to corporations, institutions, and small business. As the number-three salesperson in my company, I increased sales in my territory 15 percent, to over $1 million. In the last six months, I won three major accounts from my competitors.

"The reason I'm calling, Mr. Grant, is that I'm looking for a new challenge, and as I know and respect your product line, I felt we might have areas for discussion. Are these the types of skills and accomplishments you look for in your staff?"

[Pause]

Mr. Grant: "Yes, they are. What type of equipment have you been selling?" *[Buy signal!]*

Joan Jones: "A comprehensive range from furniture through office machines and supplies; I sell according to my customers' needs. I have been noticing a considerable interest in _____ recently. Has that been your experience?"

Grant: "Yes, I have actually." *[Useful information for you.]* "Do you have a degree?" *[Buy signal!]*

Joan Jones: "Yes, I do." *[Just enough information to keep the company representative chasing you.]* "I understand your company prefers degreed salespeople to deal with its more sophisticated clients." *[Your research is paying off.]*

Grant: "Our customer base is very sophisticated, and they expect a certain professionalism and competence from us." *[An inkling of the kind of person the company wants to hire.]* "How much experience do you have?" *[Buy signal!]*

Joan Jones: "Well, I've worked in both operations and sales, so I understand both the sales and fulfillment processes." *[General but thorough.]* "How many years of experience are you looking for?" *[Turning it around, but furthering the conversation.]*

Grant: "Ideally, four or five for the position I have in mind." *[More good information.]* "How many do you have?" *[Buy signal!]*

Joan Jones: "I have two with this company, and one and a half before that, so I fit right in with your needs, don't you agree?" *[How can Mr. Grant say "no" to Ms. Jones?]*

Grant: "Uh-huh. . . . What's your territory?" *[Buy signal!]*

Joan Jones: "I cover the metropolitan area. Mr. Grant, it sounds as if we might have something to talk about." *[Remember, your first goal is the face-to-face interview.]* "I am planning to take personal time off next Thursday or Friday. Can we meet then?" *[Make Mr. Grant decide which day he can see you, rather than whether he will see you at all.]* "Which would be best for you?"

Grant: "How about Friday morning? Can you bring a resume?"

Your questions show interest, carry the conversation forward, and teach you more about the company's needs. By the end of the conversation you have an interview arranged and several key areas to promote when you arrive:

- The company sees growth in a particular area, so be sure you research where they stand in this area.
- They want both professional and personal sophistication.

- They ideally want four or five years' experience.
- They are interested in your metropolitan contacts.

Occasionally your calls will go this smoothly, but not always. This example doesn't show you any number of other tricky questions that, inadequately handled, can rule you out of consideration. These include questions that appear to be simple buy signals, yet are in reality a part of every interviewer's arsenal of "knockout" questions—so called because they can save time by quickly ruling out certain types of candidates. Let's look at some questions in more depth.

Buy Signal: "How much experience do you have?"

Too much or too little experience could easily rule you out. Be careful how you answer this question and try to gain time. It is a vague question, and you have a right to ask for qualifications. Employers typically define jobs by years' experience. At the same time there is a major move away from simple chronological experience toward the more important concern about what you can deliver on the job. Managers and HR pros are now more open to thinking in terms of "performance requirements" and "deliverables" than ever before.

Here are a couple of ways to handle it:

"Could you help me with that question? If you give me a brief outline of the performance requirements, I can give you a more accurate answer." Or, "I have _____ years' experience, but they aren't necessarily typical. If you'd give me a few details on the performance requirements I'd be able to give you a more accurate answer."

The employer's response, while gaining you time, tells you what it takes to do the job and therefore what aspects of your experience are most relevant. Take mental notes as the employer talks—you can even write them down if you have time. Then give an appropriate response.

You can move the conversation forward by asking a follow-up question of your own. For example: "The areas of expertise you require sound like a match to my experience, and it sounds as if you have some exciting projects at hand. What projects would I be involved with in the first few months?"

Buy Signal: "Do you have a degree?"

If your degree matches the stated requirements of the position, by all means go ahead and state it. If you don't have any degree and the position requires one, all is not lost. As Calvin Coolidge said, "The world is full of educated derelicts." You may want to use the "life university" answer. For example: "My education was cut short by the necessity of earning a living at an early age. My past managers have discovered that this in no way speaks of a lack of processing power. However, I am currently enrolled in classes to complete my degree."

It would cost you about $100 to enroll in degree-relevant classes and make this an honest answer, and in the process you'd be doing the right thing by your career. Ongoing education is important for your long-term career survival and economic success and dramatically improves your earning and promotional potential, so enrollment in any and all career-relevant classes is to your benefit.

In a security-conscious world, an increasing percentage of employers are verifying educational credentials and references. Do not lie about this during the interviews or on your resume. If you are found out, you could be terminated with cause—which can lead to further employment problems down the line.

Buy Signal: "How much are you making/do you want?"

This is a direct question looking for a direct answer, yet it is a knockout question, so you should proceed warily. Earning either too little or too much could ruin your chances before you're given the opportunity to shine in person. There are a number of options that could serve you better than a direct answer. First, you must understand that questions about money at this point in the conversation are being used to screen you in or screen you out. The answers you give now should be geared toward getting you in the door and into a face-to-face meeting. For now, your main options are as follows:

- **Direct answer:** If you know the salary range for the position and there is a fit, give a straightforward answer.
- **Indirect answer:** "In the fifties." Or "in the 120s."
- **Put yourself above the money:** "I'm looking for an opportunity that will give me the opportunity to make a difference with my efforts. If I am the right person for the job, I'm sure you'll make me a fair offer. By the way, what is the salary range for this position?"
- **Give a range:** Come up with two figures: a fair offer considering your experience and job location, and a great offer considering your experience and job location, "Hopefully between $X and $Y. What's most important is an opportunity to make a difference. If I am the right person for the job, I'm sure you'll make me a fair offer. By the way, what is the salary range for this position?"

When you give a salary range rather than a single figure, you have more flexibility and have greater chance of "clicking" with the employer's approved range for the position.

When you are pressed a second time for an exact dollar figure, be as honest and forthright as circumstances permit. If you have the skills for the job and you are concerned that your current low salary will eliminate you before you have the chance to show your worth, you might add, "I realize this is well below industry norms, but it does not reflect on my expertise or experience in any way. It speaks of the need for me to make a strategic career move to where I can be compensated competitively and based on my skills."

If your current earnings are higher than the approved range, you could say, "Mr. Smith, my current employers feel I am well worth the money I earn due to my skills, dedication, and honesty. When we meet, I'm sure I can convince you of my ability to contribute to your department. A meeting would provide an opportunity to make that evaluation, wouldn't it?"

After you have answered one or two buy-signal questions, ask for a meeting. If you simply ask, "Would you like to meet me?" there are only two possible responses—"yes" or "no"—and your chances of success are about fifty-fifty. When you suggest, however, that you will be in the area on a particular date or dates ("It seems we might have something to talk about, and if you agree, I'm going to be in town on Thursday and Friday, Mr. Grant. Which would be better for you?"), you have asked a question that moves the conversation along dramatically. Your question gives the company representative the choice of meeting you on Thursday or Friday, rather than meeting you or not meeting you. By presuming the "yes," you reduce the chances of hearing a negative, and increase the possibility of a face-to-face meeting.

How to Deal with Objections

By no means will every presentation call you make be met with a few simple questions and then an invitation to interview. Sometimes the silence will be broken with an objection. This usually comes in the form of a statement, not a question: "Send me a resume," or "I don't have time to see you," or "You are earning too much," or "You'll have to talk to personnel," or "I don't need anyone like you right now." These seem like brush-off lines, but they can sometimes be turned into interviews, and when that isn't possible, they can almost always be parlayed into leads elsewhere.

Notice that all the following suggested response models have a commonality with buy-signal responses. They all end with a question, one that helps you learn more about the reason for the objection, perhaps to overcome it and lead the conversation toward a meeting.

In dealing with objections, nothing is gained by confrontation, while much can be gained by an appreciation of the other's viewpoint. Consequently, most objections you hear are best handled by first demonstrating your understanding of the other's viewpoint. Start your responses with phrases like "I understand," or "I can appreciate your position," or "I see your point," or "Of course." Follow up with statements like "However," or "Also consider," or a similar line that allows the opportunity for rebuttal and to gather further information.

It's not necessary to memorize these responses verbatim, only to understand the underlying concept and then to put together a response in words that are sympathetic to your character and style of speech.

Objection: "Why don't you send me a resume?"

The employer may be genuinely interested in seeing your resume as a first step in the interview cycle, or it may be a polite way of getting you off the phone. You should identify the real reason without causing antagonism, and at the same time open up the conversation. A good reply would be, "Of course, Mr. Grant. Would you give me your exact title and your e-mail address? Thank you. So that I can be sure that my qualifications fit your needs, what skills are you looking for in this position?" or "What specific job title and opening should I refer to when I send it?"

Notice the steps:

- Agreement with the prospective employer
- A demonstration of understanding
- A question to further the conversation (in this instance to confirm that an opening actually exists)

Answering in this fashion will open up the conversation. Mr. Grant will relay the aspects of the job that are important to him, and you can use the additional information to move the conversation forward again or to draw attention to relevant skills in:

- Your executive briefing or cover letter
- A customized resume
- Your face-to-face meeting

Following Mr. Grant's response, you can recap the match between his needs and your skills:

"Assuming my resume matches your needs, as I think we are both confident that it will, could we pencil in a date and time for an interview next week? I am available next Thursday and Friday; which would be preferable to you?"

A penciled-in date and time very rarely gets canceled.

Objection: "I don't have time to see you."

If the employer is too busy to see you, it indicates that he or she has work pressures, and by recognizing that, you can show yourself as the one to alleviate some of those pressures through your problem-solving skills. You should avoid confrontation, however; it is important that you demonstrate empathy for the person with whom you are speaking. Agree, empathize, and ask a question that moves the conversation forward:

"I understand how busy you must be; it sounds like a competent, dedicated, and efficient professional *[whatever your title is]* could be of some assistance. Perhaps I could call you back at a better time to discuss how I might make a contribution in easing the pressure at peak times. When are you least busy, in the morning or afternoon?"

The company representative will either make time to talk now or will arrange a better time for the two of you to talk further.

You could also try, "Since you are so busy, what is the best time of day for you? First thing in the morning, or is the afternoon a quieter time?" Or you could suggest, "If you would like to see my resume you could study my background at your leisure. What's your e-mail address? Thanks, what would be a good time of day to follow up on this?"

Objection: "You are earning too much."

Don't give up immediately; follow the process through: "Oh, I'm sorry to hear that—what is the range for that position?" Depending on the degree of salary discrepancy, you might reiterate your interest. If the job really doesn't pay enough—and there will be openings for which you are earning too much—you've gotten "close, but no cigar!" Just a bit further on, I'll tell you how to make a success of this seeming dead end.

Objection: "We only promote from within."

Your response could be, "(smiling)Your development of employees is a major reason I want to get in! I am bright, conscientious, and motivated. When you do hire from the outside, and it must happen on occasion, what do you look for?" or "How do I get into consideration for such opportunities?"

The response finishes with a question designed to carry the conversation forward and to give you a new opportunity to sell yourself. Notice that the response logically presupposes that the company does hire from the outside, as all companies obviously do, despite your being told otherwise.

Objection: "You'll have to talk to Human Resources."

In this case, you reply, "Of course, Mr. Grant. Whom should I speak to in HR, and what specific position should I mention?"

You cover a good deal of ground with that response. You establish whether there is a job there or whether you are being fobbed off on HR to waste their time and your own. Also, you move the conversation forward again while modifying it to your advantage. Develop a specific job-related question to ask while the employer is answering the first question. It can open a fruitful line for you to pursue. If you receive a nonspecific reply, probe a little deeper. A simple phrase like, "That's interesting. Please tell me more," or "Why's that?" will usually do the trick.

Or you can ask, "When I speak to HR, will it be about a specific job you have, or is it to see whether I might fill a position elsewhere in the company?"

Armed with the resulting information, you can talk to HR about your conversation with Mr. Grant. Remember to get the name of a specific person in HR with whom to speak, and quote this prior contact by name in any e-mail or verbal contact:

"Good morning, Ms. Johnson. Cary Grant, over in marketing, suggested we should speak to arrange an interview for the open sales associate requisition."

This way you show HR that you are not a time waster, because you have already spoken to the person for whom the requisition is open.

Don't look at the HR department as a roadblock. It may contain a host of opportunities for you. In many companies different departments could use your talents, and HR is probably the only department that knows all the openings. With larger companies you might be able to arrange interviews for two or three different positions!

Objection: "I really wanted someone with a degree."

You should have learned the proper response to "Do you have a degree?" But in case you were abducted by aliens a few pages ago, you could respond by saying, "Mr. Smith, I appreciate your viewpoint. It was necessary that I start earning a living early in life. If we meet, I am certain you would recognize the value of my additional practical experience." If you have been smart enough to enroll in a course or two in order to pursue that always-important degree, you should add, "I am currently enrolled in courses to complete my degree, which should demonstrate my professional commitment, and perhaps that makes a difference?"

You might then ask what the company policy is for support and encouragement of employees continuing their education. Your response will end with, "If we were to meet, I am certain you would recognize the value of my practical experience, in addition to my ongoing professional commitment. I am going to be interviewing at the end of next week, and I know you will find the time to meet well spent. Is there a day and time that would be best for you?"

Objection: "I don't need anyone like you now."

Short of suggesting that the employer fire someone to make room for you (which, incidentally, has been done successfully on a few occasions), the chances of getting an interview with this company are slim. With the right questions, however, your contact will give you a personal introduction to someone else who could use your talents.

Live Leads from Dead Ends

Not every company has the right job for you, nor are you right for every job. But you can still turn this rejection into a successful call. You can ask, "When do you anticipate new needs in your area?" or "May I send you my resume and keep in touch for when the situation changes?" or "Who else in the company might have a need for someone with my background and skills?" or "Can you think of peers at other companies who might have a need for someone with my background?"

Remember, your calls have multiple goals: to arrange an interview, to arrange another time for a telephone interview, to send a resume for future follow-up, and to develop leads on job openings elsewhere.

So now we come to job lead development questions. By adding these questions, you will achieve a measure of success, leaving you energized and with a feeling of achievement after every conversation.

The person on the other end of the line is a professional who naturally knows people in other departments, subsidiaries, and other companies, any of whom may have an interesting opportunity for you. If you ask the right questions you'll find that most people, realizing they could well find themselves in your position one day, will be glad to advise you on who might have openings. While nearly everyone you call will be pleased to point you in the right direction, they can only be expected to do so if you *ask*, so don't be shy about asking for leads.

These are the seven categories of questions that you need to absorb so that you can move through them smoothly in person and over the telephone:

1. Leads in department
2. Leads in company
3. Leads in other divisions of company
4. Leads to other companies
5. Contacts in other companies
6. Contact info exchange
7. Open door to keep in touch

You will find the entire series of questions to ask in these categories in the section in Chapter 3 on questions to ask your contacts. In fact, if you are paying attention to the *Knock 'em Dead* method, you will already have a list of prioritized job development questions prepared from this advice. If not, reread that section and develop a personalized list. You can have one on your desktop and one taped by your telephone.

When you follow the *Knock 'em Dead* plan of attack, you are going to have plenty of calls to make, and once you have made twenty or thirty calls, what was once a nightmare will have become another professional survival skill.

A good strategy is to develop a list of ten or twenty calls where your presentation will be the same in each instance (for example, following up on a resume you sent last week). Then write out a script for yourself, listing the points you want to make on each call and including a list of questions you will ask to get leads if the call doesn't generate an interview. Then screw up your courage, and make those twenty calls one after the other without stopping to do a jig when the call goes well or to dwell on rejection. Remember that any rejection is because of a lack of need rather than a rejection of you personally. When you do this, you will make more calls, get more results, and get acclimated to using the telephone as a powerful job search tool.

Follow up on all leads. Too many people become elated at securing an interview for themselves and cease all efforts to generate additional interviews in the belief that a job offer is definitely on its way. Your goal is to have a choice of the best jobs in town, and without multiple interviews, there is no way you'll have that choice. Asking interview development questions ensures that you are tapping all the secret recesses of the hidden job market.

Remember: Networking and marketing are continuous activities, as shown below.

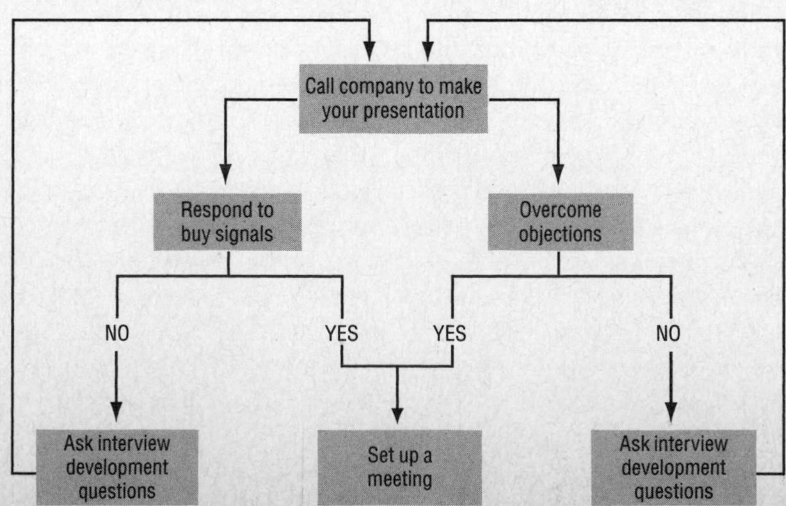

Corporate Gatekeepers

When you are making marketing and networking calls, an overly officious clerical assistant will sometimes try to thwart you in your efforts to present your credentials directly to a potential employer—at least it might appear that way.

In fact, it is very rare that these "corporate gatekeepers," as they are known, are directed to screen calls from professionals seeking employment, as to do so only increases employment costs to the company. What they are there to do is to screen nuisance calls from salespeople and the like.

However, to arm you for the occasional objectionable gatekeeper standing between you and making a living, you might try the following techniques used by investigative reporters, private eyes, and headhunters.

Pre-empting Questions

Most gatekeepers are trained at most to find out your name and the nature of your business. But when they are asking the questions, they control the conversation. You can remain in control by pre-empting their standard script: "Good morning. I'm Mr. Yate. I need to speak to Nikki Jones about an accounting matter. Is she there?" Should a truly obnoxious gatekeeper ask snidely, "Perhaps I can help you?" you can effectively use any of the following options: "Thank you, but I'd rather discuss it with Ms. Jones." "It's personal." "It's a professional matter." Or you can blind them with science: "Yes, if you can talk to me about the finer points of *[some esoteric aspect of your profession]* 10K reporting." They invariably can't, so you're in like Flynn.

Diction, tone of voice, confidence, and clarity are all-important when dealing with clerical staff. They are trained to respect and respond to polite authority, so always demonstrate self-confidence in your manner. When you are clear about whom you want to speak to and can predict possible screening devices, you usually get through. With such gatekeepers you should also avoid using your first name in your introduction, as in "Martin Carlucci"; instead, try "Mr. Carlucci" or "Ms. Carlucci," which is always more authoritative.

When you have been given a name by a networking contact, you can use that introduction to get past corporate gatekeepers: "Tell him Bill Edwards asked me to call."

Go Up the Ladder

If you can't get through to the person you want to speak to—say, the accounting manager—instead of wasting the call you can go up the ladder to the controller or the vice president of finance. Interestingly, the higher you go, the more accessible people are. In this instance, the senior manager may well not schedule an interview with you but instead refer you back down to the appropriate level. Sometimes that VP will switch you directly to the person with whom you want to speak; even if that doesn't happen, the next time you call you have a nice, hefty name to drop when dealing with the pesky gatekeeper: "Your divisional vice president of finance, Mr. Craig Wilde, asked me to call Mr. Jones. Is he there?" Even if you didn't speak directly to that VP up the corporate ladder, and VP Bigshot's secretary referred you back down the ladder, you can now say with all honesty, "Mr. Bigshot's office recommended . . . ." Then the conversation with your target can begin with your standard introduction, but be sure to mention first the name of the person who referred you.

If you haven't yet gleaned any names from a particular company through your networking activities and are being thwarted by a gatekeeper, try these approaches:

- Over time you will develop a list of companies where you have no contacts. You can refer to this list when you run into a brick wall on a marketing call. "Jack, I was planning to contact _____, Inc. Would you happen to know anyone there who could give me a heads-up?" Or "Jack, do you know anyone at _____ or _____ that I could speak to? Any lead would be most appreciated."
- Check your association membership databases and your online networks and look for members who work or have worked at a target company. Regardless of their titles, these people can bring you one step closer to the right hiring authority contact.
- Visit the company's website and look for names there. Don't forget to read the media clippings that always get posted, since they invariably contain a quote or two from company representatives. You should also do "Google news" searches for media coverage of the company and its executives.
- For especially desirable companies, check back with those people who know you well and respect your work: your references. They might know or be able to find out the names of people working within your target.

When none of your research, networking, or marketing activities has presented you with a name, try these techniques:

- There is usually more than one person worth speaking to at any company, so whoever you speak to, ask for more than one name and title. For example, in the finance area (depending on your level), any or all of the following could provide useful contacts: accounting supervisor, accounting manager, assistant controller, controller, vice president of finance, chief financial officer, executive vice president, president, chief operating officer, chief executive officer, and chairman. The last eight of these can usually be found on the company website or in reference databases and directories. Anyone who gives you one name will invariably give you more than one. Some years ago in Colorado I sat with a job searcher who used these techniques to gather 142 names from receptionists in one hour!
- In some companies where security is at a premium, gatekeepers are expressly forbidden to give out names and titles. In this case, you can use some side-door techniques: There are certain people in every company who by the very nature of their jobs have contact with people at all levels of the company and who are not given the responsibility to screen calls. These include people in the mailroom; maintenance; shipping and receiving; second-, third-, and fourth-shift employees; new or temporary employees; advertising and public relations people; sales and marketing people; travel center; Q/A; and customer service employees.

Another approach for getting by pesky gatekeepers is to vary the times when you call a target company. Try before 9 A.M., immediately after 5 P.M., and during lunch hours. Managers often pick up their own lines at these times.

Voice Mail

Voice mail is on the increase. Rather than treating it as a dead end, turn it into a useful means of getting through to your target contact.

When you have an introduction, you can use it to navigate voice mail systems and to leave as a teaser on your voice mail message: "Good morning, my name is William Powell. Ms. Loy suggested I give you a call. She thought we might have something to talk about. I'll try you later."

Don't leave long messages; be brief and get on with your job search and make another call. In cases where you don't get a response and need to call back again, do so, but if the person doesn't pick up and you get routed to the voice mail again, hang up and move on to your next call. If you leave countless voice mail messages, it will make you look needy.

When you lack a name, check to see if the system has a directory, and if it does, take note of as many names and extensions as you can. If there is no directory, and the voice mail system tells you to enter an extension key, keep keying until you hit one that results in a human voice. It doesn't matter who answers as long as someone does. The conversation goes something like this:

"Jack speaking."

"Jack, this is Martin Yate. I'm calling from outside and I'm lost on this darned telephone system." This usually gets a smile. "I'm trying to get hold of *[whatever the title is]*. Could you check who that would be for me?"

Stay the Course

No matter how many interviews your calls and e-mail campaigns are generating, you must continue to research potential job openings. While you have to maintain contact with interested companies, you must also make yourself carry out a daily marketing schedule, which includes making calls and sending e-mails and resumes to both nurture your existing contact base and expand it in each of the following areas:

- Internet job postings and the company websites you discover from them
- Members of all your professional and personal networks
- Leads developed from job fairs and other research efforts
- Headhunters
- Follow-up letters to phone calls and from meetings

The balance you maintain is important because most job hunters are tempted to send the easy e-mails and make the easy calls (networking with old friends) and ignore the more challenging but more productive marketing calls. Don't stop searching even when an offer for a dream job is pending and your potential boss says, "Robin, you've got the job, and we're glad you can start on Monday. The offer letter is in the mail." *Never accept any "yes" as an absolute until you have it in writing, you have started work, and the first paycheck has cleared at the bank!* Until then, keep your momentum building. As someone who has worked in HR on the corporate side, I can tell you that job offers do get withdrawn with not a whit of concern for the poor hunter.

The Last Man Standing Wins

It is trite but true that you have never failed until you quit trying. Job searches will always take longer during economic downturns and will take longer the less professionally you approach them. Nevertheless, we have a huge economy, and even in the worst times people are landing new jobs. It's just that they're the ones who are working smarter and harder than everyone else.

If you are in the midst of a long job search, try to keep things in perspective. Although your 224th contact may not have an opening for you, ask questions and you may well discover that he or she has the good lead you need. Don't ask the questions and you'll never know.

In the job search there are only two "yeses": The employer's "we want you to work for us" and your "I can start on Monday." Every other conversation is, in reality, a "no" that brings you closer to the big "yes." Never take rejections of your resume or your phone call as rejections of you. There is a great opportunity right around the corner, so long as you keep turning that corner to maintain your forward momentum.

Stacking the Odds in Your Favor

We all have 168 hours a week to become bagmen or billionaires and to make our lives as fulfilling as they can be. For some of us this means a better job; for others it means getting back to work to keep a roof over our heads. How we manage these hours will determine our success. These job search commandments will see you successfully through the job change and career transition process:

Start conversations: It has been said that in order to gain that next job it takes on average twenty-five conversations with men or women who have the authority to hire you. What do we learn from this? Make every effort to get into conversations with decision makers with hiring authority and sooner or later you will get that job offer. It doesn't matter if it takes 25 or 125 such conversations, the essential truth still holds: get into conversations with enough hiring authorities and you will get that desired job offer. To get into those critical conversations isn't easy; it might take you hundreds of contacts, but if you make the commitment every day of your job search, you will succeed, and you will succeed more quickly than your peers.

Work at getting a new job: Work forty hours per week at it. Divide your time equally between all the intelligent job search approaches. No one knows which tactic is the one that will work for you, but this integrated approach gives you the shortest odds.

Research the companies you contact: In a tightly run job race, the candidate who is most knowledgeable and intelligently enthusiastic about the employer has a distinct advantage.

Follow up on the resumes you send out with phone calls: Resubmit your resume to identified openings after six or seven weeks. Change the format of your resume and submit it again. (See *Knock 'em Dead Resumes* for specific ideas on how to do this.)

Stay in telephone contact with your job leads: Call them back on a regular basis to maintain top-of-the-mind awareness. If you find yourself needing to call existing contacts more than once every couple of months, you should be putting more emphasis on building your networks and doing direct research.

Develop examples of your professional profile that make you special—and rehearse building these examples into your interview responses. You will learn all about developing a desirable professional profile in Chapter 10.

Send follow-up notes with relevant news clippings, cartoons, and so on to those in your networks. It's a light touch that helps people keep you in mind, you'll find lots of ideas for follow-up in Chapter 17.

Work on your self-image: Use this time to get physically fit. Studies show that unfit, overweight people take longer to find suitable work.

Maintain a professional demeanor during the work week (clothing, posture, personal hygiene).

Use regular business hours for making contacts: Use the early morning, lunchtime, after 5 P.M., and Saturday for doing the ongoing research and writing projects that maintain momentum.

Take off the blinders: We all have two specific skills: our professional/technical skills—for example, computer programming; and our industry skills—for example, banking. Professional/technical skills can be transferable to other industries, and industry skills can open other opportunities in your industry. For example, that programmer, given decent communication skills, could become a technical trainer and/or writer for programmers or technophobes.

Don't feel guilty about taking time off from your job search: Just do it responsibly. If you regularly spend Saturday morning in the library doing research, you can take Wednesday afternoon off to go to the driving range once in a while.

Maintain records of your contacts in the career management database. They will benefit not only this job search but also those in the future.

Never stop the research and job search process until you have a written job offer in hand and you have accepted that job in writing with an agreed-upon start date. Even then, continue with any ongoing interview cycles.

Remember: It's all up to you. There are many excuses not to make calls or send resumes on any given day. There are many excuses to get up later or knock off earlier. There are many excuses to back off because this one's in the bag. But there are no real *reasons*. There are no jobs out there for those who won't look, while there are plenty of opportunities for those who work at it.

The more you do today, the better you will feel about yourself.

Using a Contact Tracker

As you get your job search up to speed, the number of baited hooks you have in the water will grow dramatically. The resumes you send out will require follow-up calls, and the networking and research calls you make to potential employers will create the need to mail out resumes, which in return will generate more follow-up calls.

Without tracking mechanisms in place this can quickly get out of hand. It would be crazy to make this effort to get your job search and career management plan functioning, and then let important opportunities fall through the cracks for lack of attention to detail.

You can create a contact tracker on a spreadsheet program, with columns for company name, telephone number, contact name, e-mail address, the date you sent a resume and the date you should follow up with a call (or vice versa), and room for comments on the substance of conversations.

Follow-Up: The Key Ingredient

In theory, the perfect e-mails you send cold or as a result of phone calls will receive a response rate of 100 percent. Unfortunately, there is no perfect letter, e-mail, or call in this less-than-perfect world. If you sit waiting for the world to beat a path to your door, you may wait a long time.

An IT executive of my acquaintance once advertised for an analyst. By Wednesday of the following week he had over 100 responses. Ten days later he was still plowing through them when he received a follow-up call (the only one he received) from one of the respondents. The job hunter was in the office that afternoon, returned the following morning, and was hired before lunchtime.

What's the take-away? The candidate's paperwork was languishing in the pile, waiting to be discovered. The follow-up phone call got it discovered. The IT executive just wanted to get on with his work, and the job hunter in question made it possible by making himself visible on the employer's radar. Follow-up calls, and follow-up calls on the follow-up calls, really do work.

Make phone calls to initiate contact, and you'll get requests for resumes and requests to come right on over for an interview. Make follow-up calls on mailed and e-mailed resumes and you will generate further interviews.

Index

A
ABC prioritizing, 15
Accelerated vesting, 269
Accepting job offers, 271
Actuary, 291, 323–24
Age, questions about, 213
Alcohol (at meal meetings), 222
Alumni associations, 56, 65–66
American Recovery and Investment Act (ARRA), 339
Americans with Disabilities Act, 212
Aptitude tests, 281
ASCII format, 87
Associations
  alumni, 56, 65–66
  professional, 34, 57–58, 95
Athletic trainer, 291, 304–5
Auden, W. H., 129

B
Bailey, F. Lee, 140
Behavioral profiles, 31–32
Benefits, negotiating, 263–64
Biomedical engineer, 291, 316–17
Blogging, professional, 290
Body language, 11, 125–34
  barricades, 132–33
  eyes, 130–31
  facial signals, 130–32
  feet, 132
  glasses, 131–32
  the greeting, 127
  hands, 127–28
  head, 131
  legs, 129–30
  mouth, 131
  seating, 129–30
  walking, 132–33
  web sites, 12
Bonuses, 259
Breathing techniques, 134, 137, 192
Briefcases, 118, 122
Bureau of Labor Statistics, 250, 290, 340
Business cards, 72, 98, 99
Business service professions, 290, 291, 317–27
Buy signals, 347–50

C
Campus recruiters, 98
CareerBuilder.com, 53
Career change, 6, 76
Career counselors/job search counselors, 94
Cashless exercise provision, 269
Children, questions about, 214
Chronological resumes, 39
Citizenship, questions about, 212
CLAMPS, 206
Coffee-machine syndrome, 161
College career services, 97–98
Combination resumes, 39
Commitment, 18
Communication skills, 10–11, 16, 17, 147–48
Competitive differentiation, 19–23
Computer scientist and database administrator, 291, 310–11

Computer software engineer, 291, 309–10
Computer systems analyst, 291, 311–12
Conference of Mayors, U.S., 340
Confidence, 149
Contact, making, 342–60
  buy signals, 347–50
  corporate gatekeepers and, 355–57
  dealing with objections, 351–53
  dealing with rejection, 353–54
  multiple submissions, 343–45
  painting a word picture, 346–47
Contact trackers, 359
Contingency recruiters, 94, 95
Coolidge, Calvin, 349
Core competencies, 41, 85, 86
Corporate culture, 262
Corporate gatekeepers, 355–57
Court reporter, 291, 321–23
Cover letters, 47–49, 147, 343–45
Creativity, 16–17
Credit history, 204–5
Critical thinking, 13–14, 16, 17, 31

D

Daily Plan/Do/Review cycle, 15, 156
Databases, 26–27, 41, 59–60, 65–66, 82–83
Dedication, 148
Degree, requirements for, 349, 353
Deliverables, 29, 30, 187–88
Dental hygienist, 291, 298–99
Department of Labor, Women's Bureau, 250
Determination, 18, 148
Dictionary of Occupational Titles, 169
Directories, 59–60
Disabilities, 212
Dress and grooming, 11, 98, 111–23, 137
  general guidelines, 114
  the look, 113
  for men, 113, 115–19
  personal hygiene, 123
  web sites, 12
  for women, 113, 119–23
Dunhill, 95

E

Economy (financial), 6, 28, 52, 89, 290, 345
Economy (professional), 19, 149
Edison, Thomas, 190
Educational and social services professions, 290, 291, 328–29
Educational credentials, 349, 353
Efficiency, 149
Einstein, Albert, 14
E-mail
  interview follow-up, 240–42
  to multiple contacts, 343–45
  professional address, 81
Emotional IQ, 11, 12
Employers, prior
  interview questions about, 158–59, 174, 177–78, 207
  networking with, 66–68
Employment agencies, 93–97
Employment agreements, 265, 268, 269. *See also* Offer letters
Encyclopedia of Associations, 58
Energy, 18, 148, 156
Environmental engineer, 291, 315–16
Environmental scientist and hydrologist, 291, 313–15
Executive briefing, 48–49
Executive search firms, 94
Experience, 28, 156–57, 226–27, 347, 349

F

Facebook, 61, 62
Fair Credit and Reporting Act, 204
Financial analyst and personal financial advisor, 291, 317–20
Firings/terminations, 166–68

Follow-up, 239–44, 357, 358, 360
Functional resumes, 39

G
GAIA, 346
Gaming and surveillance officer, 291, 320–21
GAP analysis, 44, 83
Goal-oriented people, 14–15, 148, 168
Green jobs, 290, 340–41
Grumman, 226

H
Handshake, 118, 127, 138, 234
Headhunters, 94
Health care professions, 290, 291, 292–307
Health educator, 291, 331–33
Heraclitus, 274
Hidden job market, 87–88
Hobbies, 57, 68, 70
HotJobs, 53
How to Get Control of Your Time and Your Life (Lakein), 166, 217
Human resources, 352–53

I
In-basket exercise, 216–17
Incremental vesting schedule, 269
Instructional coordinator, 291, 335–36
Integrity tests, 281–82, 284, 285
Interim management sector, 97
Internet. *See also* Web sites
  digital dirt on, 61–62
  for the direct approach, 91–92
  for finding names, 90–91
  job search basics, 80–82
  networking on, 60–61, 62–63
  percentage of jobs found on, 53, 54, 55
  portfolios on, 101
  resume distribution services, 344–45
  resumes on, 26–27, 81–82, 84–85, 101
  security and confidentiality concerns, 81–82
Internships, 98
Interpreter and translator, 291, 324–26
Interview questions, 140–42
  closed-ended, 162, 193, 197, 198
  illegal, 190, 212–14
  interviewee, 107, 109–10, 136–37, 171–72, 234
  open-ended, 198
  probing, 173–84
  for recent graduates, 225–32
  in stress interviews, 196–212
  in telephone interviews, 107, 108–10
  tough, 154, 155–72
Interviews, 7, 105–248. *See also* Body language; Dress and grooming; Interview questions; Stress interviews
  arrival time, 137
  closing, 233–35
  extended cycle, 242–43
  first impressions, 126, 194
  follow-up, 239–44
  in hotel lobbies, 220–21
  identifying negative aspects, 240
  meal meetings, 221–23
  multiple, 273–75
  personal zone in, 129
  preparations for, 135–38
  professional behavior in, 146–50, 154–55
  rejection and, 245–48
  secrets of the hire, 143–51
  skilled interviewers, 186–91
  strange venues for, 219–23
  telephone, 105–10
  traps to avoid, 141
  unconscious incompetent interviewers, 191–94
Inventions, assignment of, 265–66

J

Job fairs, 98–100, 106
Job interviews. *See* Interviews
Job offers
accepting, 271
multiple, 273–75
negotiating (*see* Negotiation)
Job postings, 26, 29–30, 52–53, 88–89, 357
Job search. *See also* Competitive differentiation; Contact, making; Networking; Network integrated job search; Resumes; Transferable skills; Values
commandments of, 358–59
perseverance in, 357–58
realities of, 5–23
Job sites, 83–88

K

Keywords, 26–27, 60, 61, 85, 87, 90, 91, 243
Knockemdead.com, 6, 9, 10, 11, 19, 32, 33, 62, 83, 84, 96, 100, 243, 267, 292
Knock 'em Dead Cover Letters (Yate), 47, 52, 77, 110, 243, 269, 343
Knock 'em Dead Professional Communication (Yate), 100
Knock 'em Dead Resumes (Yate), 44, 68, 87, 358
Knockout questions, 349, 350

L

Lakein, Alan, 166, 216, 217
Language abilities, foreign, 40, 211, 213
Leadership, 16, 17, 180–81
Learned behaviors, 8–9
Letters
contact follow-up, 357, 358
cover, 47–49, 147, 343–45
interview follow-up, 110, 240–42
to networking contacts, 77
offer, 265, 268, 357, 359
reference, 136
Linkedin.com, 60, 61, 62
Listening skills, 11, 12, 147–48

M

Magazines, job leads in, 100–101
Manageability, 146
Management Recruiters, 95
Marital status, questions about, 213–14
Medical assistant, 291, 295–97
Merrill Lynch, 226
Mirroring techniques, 133
Mirror statements, 198, 252
Mock meetings, 215–16
Monster.com, 53
Motivation, 18, 145, 148

N

Names
correct spelling and pronunciation, 110, 234
finding, 88–89, 90–91
proper address, 107, 138
National Association of Colleges and Employers (NACE), 10
Negotiation, 249–71
assignment of inventions, 265–66
benefits, 263–64
company growth/direction and, 262–63
corporate culture and, 262
evaluation and, 259–60, 270–71
leverage in, 259–60
noncompete agreements, 265, 266, 269
nondisclosure agreements, 265, 266, 269
professional growth and, 261–62
relocation, 266–68
salary (*see* Salary)
severance package, 265, 266
stock options, 265, 268–69

Networking, 51–77, 99, 345
  community, 57
  concluding, 77
  handling referrals, 76–77
  personal, 68–71
  professional, 56
  questions, 74–76
  social, 55–57, 60–65, 88
  strategies and tactics, 57–60
  support groups, 71
  through conversations, 71–74
  trading information, 82, 84
Network integrated job search, 79–101
  the direct approach, 88–92
  for hidden jobs, 87–88
  resources, 93–101
Newsletters, 60
Newspapers, job leads in, 53, 100–101
Nizer, Louis, 140
Noncompete agreements, 265, 266, 269
Nondisclosure agreements, 265, 266, 269
Note taking, 108, 136

O

Obama, Barack, 339
Objective personality tests, 280
O'Brien, Dan, 226–27
Occupational Outlook Handbook, 31
Offer letters, 265, 268, 357, 359. *See also* Employment agreements

P

Paralegal and legal assistant, 291, 326–27
Passive marketing, 101
Performance/professional profiles, 40–41, 81, 84–85, 358
Performance reviews, 259, 261
Personal and home care aide, 291, 328–29
Personality tests, 279–80
Personnel selection tests, 280–81
Pharmacist, 291, 306–7
Pharmacy technician, 291, 297–98
Physical therapist, 291, 299–300
Physician assistant, 291, 300–301
Piercings, 115
Portfolios, web, 101
Postsecondary teacher, 291, 333–35
Pride and integrity, 18–19, 149
Private employment agencies, 93
Privately held companies, 268
Problem identification and solution, 38–39, 144, 150–51, 177
Procedures, 19, 149, 190–91
Productivity, 19
Professional associations, 34, 57–58, 95
Professional brand, 9, 146–47. *See also* Learned behaviors; Transferable skills; Values
  benefits of, 23
  components of, 7
  in resumes, 44–47
Profiles
  behavioral, 31–32
  performance/professional, 40–41, 81, 84–85, 358
Projective personality tests, 280
Promotions, 44, 52, 83, 352
  interview questions about, 183, 201
  negotiating, 259, 260, 261
PSRV process, 38–39, 170
Psychological tests, 277–86
  acing, 282–83
  aptitude, 281
  getting ready for, 283–86
  integrity, 281–82, 284, 285
  lie scales, 284
  personality, 279–80
  personnel selection, 280–81
  preparing for, reading, answering, 279–82
  skills, 281, 284
  types of, 279–82
Publicly traded companies, 268

Q
Questionnaires
  Competitive Differentiation, 20–23
  Resume, 32–33
Questions
  interview (*see* Interview questions)
  knockout, 349, 350
  networking, 74–76
  in telephone conversations, 346, 347–50

R
Radiation therapist, 291, 301–2
Recruitment process, 26–27, 52–54
References, 136
  checking, 164–65, 264–65, 349
  networking and, 66–68
Registered nurse, 291, 305–6
Rejection, 205, 245–48, 353–54
Reliability, 18, 148
Religious beliefs/affiliations, 118, 146, 190, 212, 213
Religious groups, 68, 70
Relocation, 86, 158, 265, 266–68, 340
Resigning from a job, 265, 271
Resume banks, 26–27, 47, 80, 83, 84, 87
Resume blasters, 344
Resumes, 6–7, 25–47, 60, 77, 98–99
  building, 32–37
  chronological, 39
  combination, 39
  customized/targeted, 29, 243
  feedback on, 67–68
  follow-up on, 358, 360
  functional, 39
  Internet, 26–27, 81–82, 84–85, 101
  Internet distribution services, 344–45
  in interviews, 136
  mistakes on, 147
  multiple, 84–85
  multiple submissions, 343–45
  passive marketing with, 101
  professional brand integration in, 44–47
  requests to send, 351
  rules for, 39–42
  sanitized, 81–82
  steps for preparing, 28–32
  template, 43
Robert Half, 95
Robespierre, Maximilien, 16
Role playing, 217
Roosevelt, Theodore, 315
Ryze, 62

S
Salary
  buy signals and, 350
  dealing with objections, 352
  gender discrepancies in, 250
  negotiating, 250–60, 261, 270–71
  premature mention of, avoiding, 41–42, 109, 136–37, 235
  range, 85, 255–56, 257, 258, 350
  stress interview questions on, 201, 203
  verification of, 254, 264
  web sites, 250, 252, 257
Science and technology professions, 290, 291, 308–17
Self-image, 358
Severance packages, 265, 266
Sexually suggestive behavior, 128, 130
Shaw, George Bernard, 10
Skills
  communication, 10–11, 16, 17, 147–48
  listening, 11, 12, 147–48
  technical, 10, 16, 17
  technology communication, 11
  transferable, 7, 8–17
  verbal, 11
  writing, 11, 12
Skills tests, 281, 284
Smoke-tacking, 55
Smoking, 107–8, 138, 222

Social and human services assistant, 291, 329–31
Social graces, 11, 12
Social networking, 55–57, 60–65, 88
Social worker, 291, 336–39
Solis, Hilda L., 341
Spiders, jobsite, 29, 83
Spoke, 62
Sports, interest in, 178–79
Standard and Poors, 92
State employment agencies, 93
Stock options, 265, 268–69
Stress interviews, 195–218
  assessment center techniques, 214–17
  examples of questions/answers, 198–212
  questioning tactics, 196–98
Surgical technician, 291, 302–4

T

Target Job Deconstruction (TJD), 28–32, 40, 44, 68, 83, 84, 85, 145, 168, 175, 347
Target Job Title (TJT), 28–29, 39–40, 44, 45, 85
Task-oriented people, 14, 168
Tattoos, 115
Taxes, 267, 268, 270
Teamwork, 12–13, 16, 17, 146, 148, 178–79
Technical skills, 10, 16, 17
Technology communication skills, 11
Telephone
  cell, turning off, 138
  interview contact numbers, 137
  interviews via, 105–10
  making contact via, 344, 345–57, 358, 360
  separate, 81
  voice mail and, 356–57
Temporary service companies, 96–97
Tests. *See* Psychological tests
Theft, employee, 278
Time management and organization (TM&O), 14–15, 16, 17, 216–17
Title VII, 212
To Do lists, 15
Transferable skills, 7, 8–17
Travel, 158, 260

U

University of Chicago, 126

V

Values, 8–9
  business, 19
  professional, 18–19
Verbal skills, 11
Vesting period, 269
Veterinarian, 291, 294–95
Veterinary technician/technologist, 291, 293–94
Voice mail, 356–57
Volunteer work, 58–59, 70–71

W

Web sites. *See also* Internet
  company, 53, 137, 231, 356, 357
  dress and grooming, 12
  for green jobs, 341
  for high-growth jobs, 341
  job, 83–88
  salary, 250, 252, 257
Wikipedia, 58, 61
Writing skills, 11, 12